"A book to stretch the mind"

Comment by a leading authority on books:

A potpourri of American writers made wholly his own by some elusive alchemy of personal acceptance and translation — this book reinstates Lin Yutang as the urbane philosopher and commentator on "the importance of living." The two books can safely be linked in presenting this new volume. . . . Here we have his own honest findings drawn from his adventures in reading. Here are the writers important to American thought. Here, through Chinese eyes, is a selectivity that is as diverse and catholic as conceivable, bringing into focus under one guise David Grayson, Santayana; the Holmes, father and son; Thoreau and Emerson; E. B. White and Clarence Day and James Thurber; Lincoln, Jefferson, Franklin; Will Rogers; Einstein, and many more. Through his mind and imagination, through their words — and those of others — he has given us his summation of our way of life and love and work and play; of religion and democracy; of the arts of living; of laughter; of our hopes and fears and aspirations for a world at peace. Epigrams — his own and others — inextricably intertwined; philosophy — again his own and others; interpretation — often remote from our American thought. All in all, a stimulating and provocative book, well worth the difficulty in getting at the kernel, a book to stretch the mind.—*Virginia Kirkus Bookshop Service.*

ON
The Wisdom of America

By LIN YUTANG

Once more in the lively vein of *The Importance of Living*, the Oriental philosopher turns his searching eye on American writing, from pre-revolutionary times to now. Everyone knows that Chinese values often differ from our own. This is particularly true with regard to ways of living, to what is good and true and beautiful. Hence it is not surprising to learn that what Lin Yutang likes in American writings is not always what our critics and public have traditionally approved. The line or passage that he picks for quotation may be one that we never noticed. Equally, it is pleasant to see that here and there the Chinese choice is one of our own favorites. And some of the authors whom we think of as most typically American come off badly when put to the Oriental test. This lends spice and challenge to the book.

Nearly half of the text is by Lin Yutang himself. The rest is what he chose on his excited journey through American books. The arrangement is topical. Themes that we remember fondly from *The Importance of Living* recur here in good American garb, which seems to fit them well — the pursuit of happiness, loafing versus hustling, the enjoyment of the senses, hobbies. By contrast, some of our cherished criteria may seem a little battered when Lin Yutang is through with them.

Thus we have a book worthy of reading for itself — both the American content and the Chinese commentary — and also a guide of a new sort to treasures of our own literature that may have escaped us.

ON THE WISDOM
OF AMERICA

BOOKS BY LIN YUTANG

Published by The John Day Company

MY COUNTRY AND MY PEOPLE

THE IMPORTANCE OF LIVING

MOMENT IN PEKING

WITH LOVE AND IRONY

A LEAF IN THE STORM

BETWEEN TEARS AND LAUGHTER

THE VIGIL OF A NATION

THE GAY GENIUS: THE LIFE
AND TIMES OF SU TUNGPO

CHINATOWN FAMILY

ON THE WISDOM OF AMERICA

LIN YUTANG

On

THE WISDOM
OF AMERICA

THE JOHN DAY COMPANY · NEW YORK

To HONG

who taught me insight and wisdom

CONTENTS

PREFACE ON A
SUNDAY MORNING

I LIVED for over ten years in the United States without daring to write a book about the country. For that matter, even with my almost ten years in Manhattan, I wouldn't dare to write a book about New York, that dark, fathomless, mysterious city. I wouldn't dare to write even about Eighty-fourth Street. I don't know enough about it. It seems a much easier task to write about the spiritual journey through American writing from which I have just returned. I daresay I have never given myself such a wild holiday, with time so liberally and wholeheartedly spent on visiting all the inspiring sights of America's spiritual topography, without a thought of the morrow. I had taken many excursions before and the landscape is not unfamiliar. But I did enjoy visiting more leisurely and at close hand the broad pastures of Oliver Wendell Holmes, the snow-capped peaks of Emerson, the granite monolith of Thoreau, the dark cavern of Edgar Allan Poe, the seven-thousand-foot-high plateau city of Mount Santayana, the laughing valley of Ben Franklin, the awe-inspiring sculptured rocky dome of Lincoln, the Greek edifice of Jefferson.

Returning from such a grand tour, I have put down these notes of a journey, of what I as a Chinese observed, what I think, what I love and what have been my disappointments. I have soliloquized along the way. The point of view is individualistic, and limited, I know, as every personal viewpoint must be. What interests me is to see the American approach to life, noting how some of the great American minds have grappled with the problems of God and life and immortality, and the toils and struggles and joys of human life, those things which mean so much to me. As William James says, "The most interesting and valuable things about a man are his ideals and over-beliefs," the over-beliefs and basic assumptions about God, and religion, and the home, and marriage, and life, and death, and about what constitutes happiness. Thus my quest is a quest for American wisdom about living. There can never be a synthesis of the American philosophy of life; America is so diverse. Yet a general sketch of these vistas of American wisdom may be made, however inadequate and however limited it may be by a personal vision.

A society without a philosophy of life is a frightening thing. Such beliefs, so far as I can see, are in complete rout and confusion today. If we cannot obtain a general agreement as to what the American nation as a whole thinks about such problems, we can at least obtain a view of what some of her best and most perceptive minds thought about them, what their perplexities were, and of what they were assured, convinced. Every nation has its clear visions, its moments of clairvoyance, its honest grapplings with the things real but unseen that lie at the bottom of all the motive forces for our conduct and being. To be spiritually reinstated in some of those beliefs and over-beliefs, one must go back to those who have gone before us and who were able to see life without sentimentality and without illusion. To seek the calm and balanced quality of the thinking of American sages, who present the inner and the outer life of man in some pattern of order and harmony—that must be the aim of this quest. In a way, all the important thoughts of any nation should be considered as efforts toward such clarity of relationships.

God save us from the absolutist attitude that we shall know all the truths! Truth we shall never know; it is only clarity we are striving for. A wise man is content if he makes one good guess at truth in three, or if through hard thinking and striving for some general principle, as Justice Holmes did, he finally arrives at an imperfect but tolerably workable formula for living. Perhaps even more important than knowing the truth is the general unsettling of our complacent beliefs and gilt-edged assumptions that must ever mark the beginning of any kind of thinking life. No one begins to think until he has some of that brute complacency thoroughly thrashed out of him with the rawhide of the wiser minds. Humanity constantly drowses, is thrashed, wakes up, and falls to drowsing again. Each generation begins its own thinking this way. We all make a bet on life, not because we like to gamble but because we are already born and have to live through this span of sixty or seventy years and so perforce must bet on some faith or other.

Yet some have made better guesses than others, and great thinkers like Emerson, Franklin, and Santayana are merely those who seem to the majority of us to be the better guessers. The voyage of life is long, and we are all in it, and the passengers all try to guess at the final destination—the so-called "end of living." On the horizon stretches an impenetrable mist, and at different ports we put off a few passengers, urging them to come back and tell us what is the port so as to help us in our calculations, and a few promise; but they never return. And so, like the ship *Saint Christopher* that Santayana tells us about, captained by St. Peter and heading for Mechanopolis and trying to find the blue heaven, we continue to ride the waves, and all the philosophers can tell us is to keep up our pluck. The best of them, however, tell us that the important thing is not to worry about the port of destination but to enjoy the voyage on which we are likely to be a long time and where we are now at any rate, that we make the voyage livable while we go along. "Let us sail for the sake of sailing," cry some of the true sailors. As for seeking the blue heaven, why, it is over our heads all the time (so says Santayana).

I remind myself that there has been some pretty vigorous thinking and writing in the last hundred and seventy years of American national life. American thinking minds have traversed the journey before, have undertaken the quest and explored life's beauties and possibilities again and again. No matter how great they were, in their personal lives they faced the same problems of living as ourselves. The lively correspondence between John Adams and Thomas Jefferson on religion and philosophy and old age and death seems as fresh today as ever. The Americans have some good ancestors; too bad they don't have ancestor worship. *Do* they worship their ancestors? I often wonder. It is good to know one has good ancestors; it's a kind of subconscious feeling that makes for strength and pride. None of them is very old, but their past (we can stretch it to three hundred years) still can be admired. I do not mean the killing of the Indians and fighting the Mexicans; I mean that there have been some redoubtable men, hardy, strong, and cheerful, like Jefferson and Franklin, who make some of the moderns, bent on analyzing the foibles of their insides and presenting them as worthy of respect, seem by comparison rather ridiculous.

Who are the great American ancestors? And what is the American

spirit? Who knows? A man has a number of ancestors, some credit-
able and some otherwise. A person who has a pirate sea captain for
one of his great-grandfathers and a bluestocking grandmother and a
Scotch great-grandmother can have quite a mix-up in his blood. The
combination of the sea captain's love of adventure and Scotch prudence
can be a terrific thing. Even Jefferson admitted that "as to commerce,
indeed, we have strong sensations." Emerson talked about finding "the
sources of the Nile" and discovering the "infinitude of the private
man." Mark Twain thought of money, Herman Melville laughed at
fame, Hawthorne brooded, and Walt Whitman proposed to plant the
"brotherly kiss" on everybody, thus establishing a democracy of am-
biguous sexuality. But Franklin talked like an American Confucius,
with good hard sense yet with wit and imagination, and Oliver Wendell Holmes rambled in his talk like an American Montaigne.

Our task is not so much discovery as re-discovery. What one needs
is not so much thinking as remembering. Sometimes it suffices to sit
quietly and listen well, when venerable men have thought before us.
Constant forgettings of truths once perceived are the very charm of
the human mind; the history of human thought is nothing more than
the story of these forgettings and rememberings and forgettings again.
Before the cock crows thrice we deny Truth again and again.

It will be seen that in writing this book of American wisdom I
have relied as much on letters and journals as upon the learned men's
published essays. I have definitely shut out formal philosophy. I rather
think it should consist of thoughts, intimate rather than formal, presented rather than argued, thoughts somewhat unshaped and plastic,
but spontaneous and tender, suggesting tolerance, waywardness, individuality, and a highly personal tone. It should consist of thoughts
kodaked, as it were, at the moments of their birth, when the universe
or life tickled these writers and produced a tintinnabulation in their
brains, no more than that. Such thoughts are sometimes likely to be
clairvoyant and lucid, as these same authors' thoughts are not when they
set out to present an idea to the public and get so involved. It seems
that in collecting these spontaneous thoughts I am like a listener at a
lecture who watches, not principally for the development of the speaker's scheme, but for the escaped smiles and half-suppressed emotions,
and particularly for the moments when the speaker forgets his notes

and is carried away into a sudden burst of spontaneous eloquence. I love to see a speaker lose his notes and to overhear, when I can, what he whispers to the chairman.

For my part, I can only promise to be serious, but not solemn, and intimate as far as I dare. Emerson says nobly that the maker of a sentence "launches into the infinite and builds a road into Chaos and the old Night, and is followed by those who hear him with something of wild, creative delight." I wish I could feel that way, but very rarely have I that comfort. More often I am like Mrs. Emerson, who gives a new order to her maid in the kitchen and feels like a child who throws a stone and runs away.

One word more. In looking at American as well as at Chinese thought, I have always felt myself a modern, sharing the modern man's problems and pleasures of discovery. Wherever I say "we," I mean "we moderns." I have kept my Oriental background as far as I can, but I have leaned backward not to make comparisons with Chinese analogies since this book is to be about American wisdom. What there is in my whole point of view, in what I have read and absorbed into my being from my Chinese reading, will, I am sure, be reflected in its emphases and preferences and enthusiasms. The Chinese are always enthusiastic (I may say excited) about something, particularly the problems of daily living. You cannot tell them not to be. But I suppose that is all to the good. When Christopher Morley talks about "The Last Pipe" or when David Grayson talks about the binding power of doughnuts, rich, brown, with just a bit of white sugar to set them off, or of a deep, thick, golden-yellow pumpkin pie, baked in a brown crockery plate, and exclaims, "A wonderful pie!" we understand each other. Not faith, hope, and charity, but doughnuts, hot muffins, and pumpkin pies will make the nations united, which is a unity considerably more real than that of the United Nations at present.

Lastly I must thank Mr. Richard J. Walsh, Sr., for valuable advice and criticism before the book went to press, and Miss Anne J. Smith, who has been so helpful in securing the books I wanted, from across the Atlantic.

                                                              L.Y.T.

Cannes, France
March 26, 1950

ON THE WISDOM
OF AMERICA

Chapter I

THE WISDOM OF LIVING

I. THE SCOPE OF WISDOM

THE only important problem of philosophy, the only problem which concerns us and our fellow men, is the problem of the wisdom of living. Wisdom is not wisdom unless it knows its own subject and scope. That scope cannot be, must not be, may not be other than the field of living for living men. I would reduce it to this utter simplicity and not tolerate the intrusion of that most unfortunate branch of knowledge, metaphysics. The problem of the living man is a vast field enough, of which we know so little, vastly alive with human sentiments, hopes, and longings; with our animal heritage, of which we now and then try to be ashamed; with our primordial, dark, subterranean urges, known in Christian theology as the demon in us, and with our inexplicable nobility, inexplicable considering our background, known in Christian theology as the God within us; with our fantastic cleverness and what to do with our cleverness; with our noble patriotism and love of the national flag and the excitement of brass bands and the not so noble slaughter of international warfare. The world, the living world, is a subject much to be thought about, sometimes too much. Can we not leave alone the problem of immortality, which is the proper subject and precinct of the dead? They are dead in our sense, and if they are not dead, they will be in a better position to discuss what they know; we know necessarily so little about it until we cross the frontier. I hope they have better luck with their subject than we do with ours. Emerson noted in his *Journals,* "The blazing evidence of immortality is our dissatisfaction with any other solution"—a much quoted line. It may well stand; the evidence is of a negative character and appeals to a kind of subjective compulsion within our minds. But its chief merit is literary, consisting in the use of the adjective "blazing";

I

otherwise it would not be so much quoted. But a Chinese may, with just as much felicity, say, "The blazing evidence of mortality is that we all turn up our toes." The scope of wisdom, whether American or otherwise, is therefore a simple proposition; we all die, but in this short span what can we do best with life?

"Knowledge of the possible is the beginning of happiness," says George Santayana. This seems to sum up in a line for me the best that Americans have said or thought about the proper field of wisdom. I am aware that Santayana is a continental Latin in his intellectual make-up and an American in that he was born of an American mother and grew up and taught in Boston and Cambridge, but he is a cosmopolite and I want to include him because American wisdom would be immeasurably poorer without this titan of human and naturalistic wisdom. His thoughts have the character of a city built high on the top of a mountain plateau; the air is rarefied, but the atmosphere is still intensely human.

But knowledge of the possible in human life has not been the characteristic of Western philosophy. Idle speculations, with few concessions to the realities of living, seem to me to occupy the content of Western formal philosophy—speculations about immortality, about free will, about absolute truth and essence and substance, and the possibility or impossibility of knowledge. John Dewey once dryly remarked, "There is something ironical in the very statement of the problem of the possibility of knowledge. At the time when science was advancing at an unprecedented rate, philosophers were asking whether knowledge was possible." [1] Dewey might have added correctly, "and denying that it was." How the question of free will was even posed is itself indicative of the idle speculative temper. Any man asked by a waitress whether he will have tea or coffee, with or without cream, cold or hot or iced, Ceylon tea or China tea, with lemon or milk, and one, two, or three lumps of sugar, knows that he is free. Any murderer, after perfecting his plans, knows that at the last moment the decision to do it or not to do it is dependent upon himself; even an abnormal temporary paralysis of the will through hatred or jealousy or fear only proves that a normal will functions. Yet the ink that has been wasted

[1] From *Whither Mankind,* edited by Charles A. Beard. Copyright, 1928, Longmans, Green & Company. Reprinted by permission.

in the discussion of free will and determinism is enough for a hippo-
potamus to swim in comfortably.

There is a complete separation of the intellect and the senses in such
Western philosophers; in fact, there have been a feud and a distrust
and mutual suspicion for the last three centuries. The Western philosopher is a man who, by the evidence of all his speculations, is
stamped as one who distrusts his senses. He cannot even observe his
own mental process in ordering tea or coffee; probably only William
James ever said quite plainly that after a lecture in Cambridge he was
free to go down Divinity Avenue or Oxford Street as he chose. Perhaps
it would be simpler to describe a Western philosopher merely as a man
who doubts he exists; perhaps we may even say it is the business of
Western philosophy not to know. How the robust American sense of
fact staged a persistent revolt against this sort of idle futility we shall
soon see. But I may quote here one of the wisest of modern Americans,
Clarence Day, who had the humor and the perception to remark, "Too
many moralists begin with a dislike of reality; a dislike of men as they
are. They are free to dislike them, but not at the same time to be moralists. Their feeling leads them to ignore the obligation which should
rest with teachers—'to discover the best that man can do, not to set
impossibilities before him and tell him that if he does not perform
them he is damned.'"[2]

Wisdom is principally a sense of proportion, more often a sense of
our human limitations. Let those who will rack their brains about
whether the ultimate absolute is spirit, or essence, or matter; they will
rack their brains only for the pleasure of it but will not wreck the universe. The universe will go on, and life will go on in spite of them.
Some one has wittily remarked that Bertrand Russell is angry with God
for not existing, for he would like to have the pleasure of smashing him
if he did. Wisdom for me, therefore, consists in a keen sense of what we
are not—that we are not gods, for instance—coupled with a willingness
to face life as it is; in other words, it consists of two things, a wistfulness about living and common sense. John Dewey, a typical American spirit, is only trying, by the heavy and ponderous road of abstract
philosophy couched in sentences of sustained dilution, to tell us to rely

[2] Reprinted from *This Simian World*, by Clarence Day, by permission of Alfred A.
Knopf, Inc. Copyright, 1920, 1948, Katherine B. Day and Clarence Day.

4 ON THE WISDOM OF AMERICA

on experience and have faith in experience, which he once identified
with common sense.[3]

Long ago there was an American who did not have to recover his
common sense but had it with him all the time. He was a man singularly gifted by God and perfectly born of his mother, who looked at
the world, enjoyed it and was content. *He* was not distracted. Benjamin Franklin, that charmer of lightning and ladies, was wistful. He
knew what he was about, what the world was about, and what America was about. How few of us can say that of ourselves!

It is, therefore, with that wisest of Americans (perhaps also the
greatest) that I wish to begin my selections of American wisdom,
awakening a sense of wistfulness about living. All philosophy, all depth
of human thought, must begin with a facing of the short span of man's
life on this earth and its vanity, and once that is faced honestly, common sense goes with it.

One day in 1778, while living in Passy, then a suburb of Paris, Franklin went out in the company of Madame Brillon to Moulin Joli, an
island in the Seine about two leagues away, where a society of cultivated men and women spent a pleasurable day together. Franklin
observed there a kind of insect, the ephemera, whose life span was less
than a day, and wrote the following piece, which was rapidly passed
round and became well known among his friends in Paris society.
He composed this for Madame Brillon, whom he was courting gallantly and whose husband was still living. The result of the courtship
was that Franklin did not get what he wanted, the favors of the French
lady—what he called "Christian charity"—but he did compose a number of bagatelles, often under her direct inspiration, which must rank
among the best of his writings and show him as a gifted writer.

"What will fame be to an ephemera who no longer exists?"
BY BENJAMIN FRANKLIN

You may remember, my dear friend, that when we lately spent that
happy day in the delightful garden and sweet society of the Moulin

---

[3] "For such a faith (in experience) is not at present either articulate or widely held.
If it were, it would be not so much philosophy as a part of common sense"—*Living
Philosophies*. Simon and Schuster. I still maintain it is common sense, though a part of
"philosophy."

Joli, I stopped a little in one of our walks, and stayed some time behind the company. We had been shown numberless skeletons of a kind of little fly, called an ephemera, whose successive generations, we were told, were bred and expired within the day. I happened to see a living company of them on a leaf, who appeared to be engaged in conversation. You know I understand all the inferior animal tongues. My too great application to the study of them is the best excuse I can give for the little progress I have made in your charming language. I listened through curiosity to the discourse of these little creatures; but as they, in their national vivacity, spoke three or four together, I could make but little of their conversation. I found, however, by some broken expressions that I heard now and then, they were disputing warmly on the merit of two foreign musicians, one a *cousin,* the other a *moscheto;* in which dispute they spent their time, seemingly as regardless of the shortness of life as if they had been sure of living a month. Happy people! thought I; you are certainly under a wise, just, and mild government, since you have no public grievances to complain of, nor any subject of contention but the perfections and imperfections of foreign music. I turned my head from them to an old gray-headed one, who was single on another leaf, and talking to himself. Being amused with his soliloquy, I put it down in writing, in hopes it will likewise amuse her to whom I am so much indebted for the most pleasing of all amusements, her delicious company and heavenly harmony.

"It was," said he, "the opinion of learned philosophers of our race, who lived and flourished long before my time, that this vast world, the Moulin Joli, could not itself subsist more than eighteen hours; and I think there was some foundation for that opinion, since, by the apparent motion of the great luminary that gives life to all nature, and which in my time has evidently declined considerably towards the ocean at the end of our earth, it must then finish its course, be extinguished in the waters that surround us, and leave the world in cold and darkness, necessarily producing universal death and destruction. I have lived seven of those hours, a great age, being no less than four hundred and twenty minutes of time. How very few of us continue so long! I have seen generations born, flourish, and expire. My present friends are the children and grandchildren of the friends of my youth, who are now, alas, no more! And I must soon follow them; for, by the course of nature, though still in health, I cannot expect to live above seven or eight minutes longer. What now avails all my toil and labour in amassing honey-dew on this leaf, which I cannot live to enjoy! What the political struggles I have been engaged in for the good of my compatriot inhabitants of this bush, or my philosophical studies for the benefit of our race in general! for in politics what can laws do without morals? Our present race of ephemeræ will in a course of minutes become corrupt, like those of other and older bushes, and consequently as wretched. And in philosophy how small our progress! Alas! art is long, and life is short! My friends would comfort me with the idea of a name they say I shall leave behind me; and they tell me I have lived long enough to nature and to glory. But what will fame be to an ephemera who no longer exists? And what will become of all history in the eighteenth hour, when the world itself, even the whole Moulin Joli, shall come to its end and be buried in universal ruin?"

To me, after all my eager pursuits, no solid pleasures now remain but the reflection of a long life spent in meaning well, the sensible conversation of a few good lady ephemeræ, and now and then a kind smile and a tune from the ever amiable *Brillante*. . . .

—"The Ephemera" (addressed to Madame Brillon)

It may be appropriate to mention here that the insect *fuyu,* whose life span was less than twenty-four hours, was mentioned by the Chinese philosopher Chuangtse, who often used the monstrously big and the absurdly small in birds and animals to illustrate the relativity of the phenomena of life. Once he tried to drive home the sense of futility of wars by his story of the "Battle of the Microbes." The King of Wei, like many modern rulers, was caught in the dilemma of war and peace. The enemy had broken a peace treaty, and he desired revenge. One general suggested assassination of the treaty breaker, another suggested a punitive expedition, and yet another regretted the destruction of cities that were built with so much human labor. Both preparedness and unpreparedness for war seemed reckless, and the King was puzzled as to what to do. I permit myself for once the telling of a Chinese story here because modern man finds himself in the same dilemma. A Taoist philosopher went up to the King and told him that the solution lay in Tao. On being asked to explain, the Taoist asked the King, "Have you heard of a thing called the snail?"

"Yes."

"There is a kingdom at the tip of the left feeler of a snail, and its people are called the Ch'us. And there is a kingdom at the tip of its right feeler whose people are called the Mans. The Ch'us and the Mans have constant wars with one another fighting about their territories. When a battle takes place, the dead lie about the field in tens of thousands and the defeated army runs for fifteen days before it reaches its own territory."

"Indeed!" said the King. "Are you telling me a tall tale?"

"It's not a tall tale at all. Let me ask you, do you think there is a limit to space in the universe?"

"No limit," replied the King.

"And if you could roam about in the infinity of space and arrive at the Country of Understanding, would not your country seem to exist and yet not to exist?"

"It seems so," replied the King.

"Now," said the philosopher, "in the center of the Country of Understanding there is your country, Wei, and in the country of Wei there is the capital of Liang, and in the center of the city of Liang there is Your Majesty. Do you think there is any difference between that King and the King of the Mans?"

"No difference," said the King. The philosopher withdrew, and the King of Wei felt lost.[4]

2. THE PHILOSOPHERS' BLINDMAN'S BUFF

"Suppose I arrange the works of the essential philosophers—leaving out the secondary and transitional systems—in a bookcase of four shelves; on the top shelf (out of reach, since I can't read the language) I will place the Indians; on the next the Greek naturalists; and to remedy the unfortunate paucity of their remains, I will add here those free inquirers of the renaissance, leading to Spinoza, who after two thousand years picked up the thread of scientific speculation, and

[4] *The Wisdom of Laotse*, Modern Library.

besides, all modern science: so that this shelf will run over into a whole library of what is not ordinarily called philosophy. On the third shelf I will put Platonism, including Aristotle, the Fathers, the Scholastics, and all honestly Christian theology; and on the last, modern or subjective philosophy in its entirety. I will leave lying on the table, as of doubtful destination, the works of my contemporaries. There is much life in some of them. I like their watercolor sketches of self-consciousness, their rebellious egotisms, their fervid reforms of phraseology, their peep-holes through which some very small part of things may be seen very clearly: they have lively wits, but they seem to me like children playing blindman's buff; they are keenly excited at not knowing where they are. They are really here, in the common natural world, where there is nothing in particular to threaten or allure them; and they have only to remove their philosophical bandages in order to perceive it." [5]

That was George Santayana soliloquizing in Europe on the progress of philosophy, after he had retired from Harvard. We are grateful for such confidences on the part of a professor of philosophy and only wish more of them had the same charm of candor and the same wit to know what they are about. "Seem like children playing blindman's buff . . . keenly excited at not knowing where they are"—what an apt characterization of the joys of philosophizing in the last three hundred years of modern subjective philosophy! "Fichte and Nietzsche, in their fervid arrogance, could hardly outdo the mental impoverishment of Berkeley and Hume in their levity: it really had been a sight for the gods to see one of these undergraduates driving matter out of the universe, while the other drove out the spirit." That Santayana's summing up of the burden of modern philosophy is both fair and accurate, in regard to its general preoccupation with laboratory examination of self-consciousness with a self-conscious mind, all students of philosophy today must admit.[6]

<hr/>

[5] George Santayana, *Soliloquies in England.*
[6] Speaking about this exclusive preoccupation with self-analysis of human consciousness, to the complete neglect of moral life and of the natural world, Santayana very aptly and picturesquely says, "This thoughtful dog has dropped the substance he held in his mouth, to snatch at the reflection of it which his own mind gave him. It is wonderful with what a light heart, with what self-satisfaction and even boasts, the youngest children of the philosophical family jettison all their heirlooms."—*Soliloquies in England.*

Almost exclusively, the problem attacked by modern philosophy is the problem of knowledge, of how we can know reality. The net outcome of three centuries of such inquiry is that we know nothing and can know nothing of reality, of the thing-in-itself. Through the long gray corridors of modern learning, one hears the frightened cries of these philosophers—"Where am I?" "Do I exist?" "Am I real?" "How do I know that I exist?"—cries that reverberate with increasing exasperation and are echoed by the gray-plastered hallways until it seems the only thing which remains real is the fear of the unknowable.

Two men in the present generation seemed dissatisfied with this state of affairs; while admitting the excitement of the game of blindman's buff, they also had the wit to tire of it and call it slightly unfair, unfair to themselves, unfair to the world of reality, and unfair to the business of living. One, William James, completely an American, with Irish wit under his red head, and the other, George Santayana, as good as American but with a European and generally Catholic background, were seen constantly cheating their playmates by stealthily lifting their philosophical bandages to have a peep at the sun and the trees and the birds outside. This habit of lifting their bandages was generally deplored; unless all played at the game of pretending not to know where they were, the illusion would be destroyed. William James was always regarded with some suspicion; he was described as "making raids into philosophy," by which it was meant that philosophy was not his mansion. I would admit that; to me, William James was a man who happened to drift into teaching philosophy as a means of making a living, of which means in his later years he rather tired, and who, locked up in a room with his hundreds of books on continental philosophy and psychology, was all the time pacing the floor and peeping through a keyhole at the outside world of sunlight, who heard the still inner voice, "The world is real for me, real enough for my purposes." The two men were not too close together; it was not James's fault, and yet when Santayana wrote in 1918, we "are really here, in the common natural world, where there is nothing in particular to threaten or allure us," the ghost of James must have been gratified.

The situation, I think, may be summed up in a paragraph. Since Descartes, the father of modern philosophy, began to question his own existence and fell back on his consciousness to prove that he existed, this branch of human knowledge has been occupying itself, very principally, with the problem, whether reality is real and whether we can know it at all. There grew then a paradox: how can matter, which is not mind, produce consciousness, and how can mind, which is not matter, reach out to establish connections with the external world? Having artificially separated mind and matter, which were nothing but the philosophers' own concepts, they were confronted with an unbridgeable chasm, across which no flight of speculative fancies enabled them to fly, until quite lately, thanks to the progress of modern physics, Whitehead pointed out the falseness of their basic assumptions that mind and matter were independent substances and declared somewhat triumphantly that consciousness is but a function of an event and therefore necessarily an integral part of reality.[7] This is just another of those "fervid reforms of phraseology" that, played strictly according to the rules of the game, seem to save the situation and rescue the world of reality for us. To be sure, it is playing with words again, but as it is played according to Hoyle, the evidence is admitted, and the layman watchers of the game like myself heave a sigh of relief. It had been a game of concepts and words and definitions all along. More recently, Northrop of Yale marked an important advance in thought by readmitting the value and validity of immediate, intuitive perceptions,[8] which are the only approach God has given us for knowing the outside world, and which the willful men in their intellectual arrogance have chosen to ignore.

To be sure, these impressive structures of thought, from Kant and Hegel down, were a mirage; yet they held men's speculative thought for ages. Many inquiring minds studying the nature and validity of thought and reality and spirit have derived great pleasure in their contemplation, for they fairly scintillate with the multicolored cobwebs these magicians wove around them. The students of thought were for the most part so desirous of emulating their fellows and anxious not to be thought stupid that each was ready, individually, to try to see what he could see and discover what he could discover in the filaments of light and color in their intricate schemes. They never stopped to ask, If the sum total of philosophy was the impossibility of knowledge,

---

[7] See Alfred North Whitehead, *Science and the Modern World,* especially Chapter IX.
[8] F. S. C. Northrop, *The Meeting of East and West,* especially pp. 304-306, 443-454.

was not something fundamentally wrong? If the material world was perceptually, morally, socially, and aesthetically real, but logically unreal, was not something wrong with the tool of thought itself? Clearly something was not right in our definition of truth itself. The nature of truth as philosophers argue about it is one thing. The nature of truth as a hillbilly says to himself, "The skies are dark on the northwest; I must finish planting the potato patch tonight, before supper," is clearly another. How to bridge that gap is no mean task for a philosopher who wants to satisfy both his sense of fact and his intellectual pride.

Since we have decided not to occupy ourselves with formal philosophy, we may enlist the help of William James and George Santayana to polish off the systems in a few paragraphs and then escape with them to the fullness of living. Both James and Santayana betrayed professional secrets of the philosophers. What James said amounted to a confession of total ignorance of the philosophers, that they were all subjective guessers—without their pretended objectivity, according to James, and without love of truth, according to Santayana. William James was an American phenomenon, crude, free, forever curious and undisciplinable. When he applied his American sense of fact and robust sense of life to the academic disciplines of European structures, something was bound to happen.

"But practically one's conviction that the evidence one goes by is of the real objective brand, is only one more subjective opinion added to the lot. For what a contradictory array of opinions have objective evidence and absolute certitude been claimed! The world is rational through and through,—its existence is an ultimate brute fact; there is a personal God,—a personal God is inconceivable; there is an extramental physical world immediately known,—the mind can only know its own ideas; a moral imperative exists,—obligation is only the resultant of ideas; a permanent spiritual principle is in everyone,—there are only shifting states of mind; there is an endless chain of causes,—there is an absolute first cause; an eternal necessity,—a freedom; a purpose,—no purpose; a primal One,—a primal Many; a universal continuity,—an essential discontinuity in things; an infinity,—no infinity. There is this,—there is that; there is indeed nothing which some one has not thought absolutely true, while his neighbor deemed it absolutely false; and not an absolutist among them seems ever to have considered that the trouble may all the time be essential, and that the intellect, even with truth directly in his grasp, may have no infallible signal for knowing whether it be truth or no." [9]

The final stab at philosophic systems is given by George Santayana, who wields his weapon of irony with as much finesse as the matadors of his race wield theirs, plunges it straight into the heart of the matter, which in this case is the heart of a European bull, and draws blood from it.

"To covet truth is a very distinguished passion. Every philosopher says he is pursuing the truth, but this is seldom the case. As a philosopher has observed, one reason why philosophers often fail to reach the truth is that often they do not desire to reach it. Those who are genuinely concerned in discovering what happens to be true are rather the men of science, the naturalists, the historians. . . . But professional philosophers are usually only apologists: that is, they are absorbed in defending some vested illusion or some eloquent idea. Like lawyers or detectives, they study the case for which they are retained, to see how much evidence or semblance of evidence they can gather for the defence, and how much prejudice they can raise against the witnesses for the prosecution; for they know they are defending prisoners suspected by the world, and perhaps by their own good sense, of falsification. They do not covet truth, but victory and the dispelling of their own doubts. What they defend is some system, that is, some view about the totality of things, of which men are actually ignorant. No system would have ever been framed if people had been simply interested in knowing what is true, whatever it may be. What produces systems is the interest in maintaining against all comers that some favourite or inherited idea of ours is sufficient and right. A system may contain an account of many things which, in detail, are true enough; but as a system, covering infinite possibilities that neither our experience nor our logic can prejudge, it must be a work of imagination and a piece of human soliloquy. It may be expressive of human experience, it may

[9] William James, "The Will to Believe." The best summing up of man's various attempts to break the universe of objects and make it over into some sort of order by his "theorizing faculty" is to be found in his essay, "Reflex Action and Theism." The review is quite complete. Both essays are found in *Essays on Faith and Morals*, Longmans, Green & Company, 1947.

be poetical; but how should any one who really coveted truth suppose that it was true?" [10]

Elsewhere, in the essay on "Masks," Santayana continues his pin-pricking of professional philosophers. "No one," he says, "would be angry with a man for unintentionally making a mistake about a matter of fact; but if he perversely insists on spoiling your story in the telling of it, you want to kick him; and this is the reason why every philosopher and theologian is justly vexed with every other." I am informed that at the UNESCO Conference at Mexico City, some one made an attempt to call a conference of theologians and philosophers in the foolish hope that they might come to agree upon some common denominator of beliefs, unaware that it would be easier for the president of Palmolive to concede the virtue of Ivory soap than for an Episcopalian bishop to concede merits in Baptist theology.

In viewing man's attempts at philosophy, there is really only one important distinction, pertinent thinking and impertinent thinking. That thinking which concerns itself with life is pertinent, that which forgets or abandons it is impertinent. Man's instinct, even in the field of thought, is a quest for life, even though philosophers frequently forget this. Is not barrenness in itself a sufficient condemnation of a philosophy? In the Middle Ages, the ecclesiastics enjoyed the "benefit of clergy." Isn't there in modern society also a demoralizing, corrupting benefit of the university professor which exempts him from the trial of everyday living for pompous untruths? Would that the benefit of the savants were abolished and that a general conviction be established that writers on philosophy should not be exempt from trial at the secular court of common human life! Certainly, modern philosophy has the gift of missing the obvious. At the same time, its lack of adaptability is immense; it shows an inability to shift its pastures and move away from barren grounds to more fertile valleys, at which primitive cattle and sheep seem superior.

[10] George Santayana, "Emerson," *Little Essays.*

better his impatience, his distractions, his refusal to yield final ground
and become solidified! The adjectives Santayana applied to William
James may well fit Emerson; he was "restless, spasmodic, and self-inter-
rupted," lest the real life escape and we become encased in a dead carcass of a system where rigor mortis has set in. Perpetually dissatisfied,
perpetually afraid of not having the whole truth and suspicious that
the facets of truth served up by classificatory systems were only slices
of reality, Emerson was famous for interrupting himself. He was forever distracted, though by nothing except real life itself. What troubled him was the sight of a girl passing in the street, and being a
Yankee, he felt he had to square his thought with such a reality, such
a piece of life. He speaks his mind most clearly on this subject in his
essay "Nominalist and Realist," where at the end he makes a confession
of his mental processes. "There is nothing we cherish and strive to
draw to us but in some hour we turn and rend it. We keep a running
fire of sarcasm at ignorance and the life of the senses; then goes by,
perchance, a fair girl, a piece of life, gay and happy, and making the
commonest offices beautiful by the energy and heart with which she
does them; and seeing this we admire and love her and them, and say,
'Lo! a genuine creature of the fair earth, not dissipated or too early
ripened by books, philosophy, religion, society, or care!' insinuating a
treachery and contempt for all we had so long loved and wrought in
ourselves and others." [13] That was why when Emerson came out of the
conventicle or the reform meeting, or out of the rapturous atmosphere
of the lecture room, he heard nature whispering to him, "Why so hot,
little sir?" That little whisper, "Why so hot, little sir?" was the salvation of Emerson, as it was of William James later.

4. THE DEMAND FOR FAITH

On the whole, one must plead not guilty for American thinking
against the charge of showing any predilection toward idle, abstract
speculation, such as Hegelian philosophy shows. Americans have a
kind of innate love for facts rather than for Ideas with a capital *I*.
I am aware that German influence has been strong in academic circles,

[13] See also Emerson's "Illusion," which is devoted entirely to developing the idea of the
illusoriness of our moods. It is incidentally one of the best that Emerson wrote.

that many American professors have tried very hard to be unintelligible and refined and abstract and unconcerned about life—and have succeeded. They often indulge in academic jargon as much as European professors do. Grammarians, doctors, scientists, sociologists, and now even educationalists, all have the language of their professions, and there is a certain pride, a certain comfort, in being able to luxuriate in long words of Latin origin when talking to fellow practitioners of the trade. (There is even a feeling of familiar ease and generous rhythm in the professorial language of Parrington.) In a philosopher, however, whose proper field of study is life, the effect of talking in the abstract can be debilitating and disastrous. With all allowance for John Jay Chapman's facetious over-effectiveness of expression, there is something essentially true and representative of typically American feeling in what he says to William James about Josiah Royce. "I am concerned about Royce. I never heard a man talk so much nonsense in one evening. . . . I know you would say that it's mere philosophy and not to be taken seriously; but these things do have some influence sometimes. That man—mind you I love and revere him—but he's not as interesting as he was ten years ago. His mind has less of life in it. His constant strain and endeavor to evacuate his mind and have nothing but destruction in it is beginning to tell. . . . Let him come to grinding contact with life. . . . Let his mind get full of images and impressions, pains, hungers, contrasts—life, life, life." In another letter, he says, "If he [Royce] could only get rid of the notion that there is such a thing as philosophy, what a fellow he would be." [14]

On the whole, I say, Americans are fortunate in this respect. There has been a succession of philosophers who could write; Emerson, William James and George Santayana all wrote beautifully, which simply means that their contact with life had not been destroyed, that their English had not been dehydrated. In our day, Irwin Edman is a good example of a professional philosopher who prefers to write unprofessionally—and beautifully. The outstanding exception is John Dewey, the most unquotable of American authors. The laborious elaboration of a sentence, the careful and long qualifications, the mind groping to express itself precisely, correctly, never stating an imperative without

[14] *John Jay Chapman and His Letters,* edited by M. A. Howe. Houghton Mifflin Company. Copyright, 1937, M. A. DeWolfe Howe. Reprinted by permission.

being aware of all its ramifications—what is this? Irwin Edman gave the best explanation. Dewey's students were often bored at his lectures, finding it difficult to follow the intricate monotony of his thoughts. Edman realized one day that he was listening to a professor who, looking out of the window, was actually thinking aloud to himself—surely it was a privilege to watch the process of thinking of a great mind! His writing is like his lectures, yet what is this careful, searching process, groping for the exact expression? Is it not the experimental style of an experimentalist philosopher?

In fact, the exception proves the rule. The sustained dilution of Dewey's language, quite abstract, was merely a means to give America an adequate national philosophy, worthy of the American respect for present-day experience. His hostility to metaphysical speculation, his impatience with the supernatural in human beliefs, his tremendous faith in experience, his common sense definition of knowledge, his opening of men's minds to the immense possibilities of testing and experimenting in every field of knowledge by action—are these not the final expression of the American sense of fact in a broad and all-encompassing philosophy? The question of philosophic knowledge ceases to be metaphysical and becomes one with scientific knowledge; it becomes a question of the best procedure of experimenting, learning and testing by results. With good common sense Dewey asks, as we "know" certain things in science and technology by testing them, why should we not do the same in all branches of knowledge and conduct? The answer to the question in philosophy "What do we know?" is "Let's find out by experience." There is something so close to life and so matter-of-fact in such an answer as to drive an abstract thinker mad, but few Americans will be driven mad by it. In the end, I know, as America looks to its future, it will be the American attitude toward life.

John Dewey has not only expressed the despair of any constructive philosophy of the speculative type; he has offered a solution in his demand for faith and an organized outlook on life and his definition of faith as a "tendency to action." His, I think, is one of the most applicable ideas that ever shot across the mind of man. Just as Jefferson gave birth to the most fruitful idea of political action, so Dewey has given us the broadest and most fruitful ideas for social action.

"A faith, being a tendency to action . . ."

BY JOHN DEWEY

The chief intellectual characteristic of the present age is its despair of any constructive philosophy—not just in its technical meaning, but in the sense of any integrated outlook and attitude. The developments of the last century have gone so far that we are now aware of the shock and overturn in older beliefs. But the formation of a new, coherent view of nature and man based upon facts consonant with science and actual social conditions is still to be had. What we call the Victorian Age seemed to have such a philosophy. It was a philosophy of hope, of progress, of all that is called liberalism. The growing sense of unsolved social problems, accentuated by the war, has shaken that faith. It is impossible to recover its mood.

The result is disillusionment about all comprehensive and positive ideas. The possession of constructive ideals is taken to be an admission that one is living in a realm of fantasy. We have lost confidence in reason because we have learned that man is chiefly a creature of habit and emotion. The notion that habit and impulse can themselves be rendered intelligent on any large and social scale is felt to be only another illusion. Because the hopes and expectations of the past have been discredited, there is cynicism as to all far-reaching plans and policies. That the very knowledge which enables us to detect the illusory character of past hopes and aspirations—a knowledge denied those who held them—may enable us to form purposes and expectations that are better grounded, is overlooked.

In fact, the contrast with the optimism of the Victorian Age is significant of the need and possibility of a radically different type of philosophy. For that era did not question the essential validity of older ideas. It recognized that the new science demanded a certain purification of traditional beliefs—such, for example, as the elimination of the supernatural. But in the main, Victorian thought conceived of new conditions as if they merely put in our hands effective instruments for realizing old ideals. The shock and uncertainty so characteristic of the

From *Living Philosophies*. Simon and Schuster. Copyright, 1930, Forum Publishing Company. Copyright, 1931, Simon and Schuster. Reprinted by permission.

present marks the discovery that the older ideals themselves are un-determined. Instead of science and technology giving us better means for bringing them to pass, they are shaking our confidence in all large and comprehensive beliefs and purposes.

Such a phenomenon is, however, transitory. The impact of the new forces is for the time being negative. Faith in the divine author and authority in which Western civilization confided, inherited ideas of the soul and its destiny, of fixed revelation, of completely stable insti-tutions, of automatic progress, have been made impossible for the culti-vated mind of the Western world. It is psychologically natural that the outcome should be a collapse of faith in all fundamental organizing and directive ideas. Skepticism becomes the mark and even the pose of the educated mind. It is the more influential because it is no longer directed against this and that article of the older creeds but is rather a bias against any kind of far-reaching ideas, and a denial of systematic participation on the part of such ideas in the intelligent direction of affairs.

It is in such a context that a thoroughgoing philosophy of experience, framed in the light of science and technique, has its significance. For it, the breakdown of traditional ideas is an opportunity. The possibility of producing the kind of experience in which science and the arts are brought unitedly to bear upon industry, politics, religion, domestic life, and human relations in general, is itself something novel. We are not accustomed to it even as an idea. But faith in it is neither a dream nor a demonstrated failure. It is a faith. Realization of the faith, so that we may work in larger measure by sight of things achieved, is in the future. But the conception of it as a possibility when it is worked out in a coherent body of ideas, critical and constructive, forms a philosophy, an organized attitude of outlook, interpretation, and con-struction. A philosophic faith, being a tendency to action, can be tried and tested only in action. I know of no viable alternative in the present day to such a philosophy as has been indicated.

Chapter II

COUNSEL FOR LIVING

I. ALL IS RIDDLE

IF life is vanity, ephemeral and transient, what can one do about
it? There is a narrow margin between wisdom and folly by which
some philosophical but wholesome minds escape from darkness and
confusion into the region of light and faith in living, into an intimate
enjoyment and appreciation of common life. It could be a life rich to
overflowing; the universe is entertainment enough if we do not try
to read or anticipate its plot. In fact, there are more plots than one,
and they always thicken at the sound of the first inquisitive whisper.
The eternal mystery! Who would not like to rend the curtain hiding
it? Who would not like to know the hand of God, to see with
all-comprehending wisdom the careful, cunning workmanship of the
Great Author of this greatest mystery story and cease from guessing
or suspecting everyone present of having committed countless murders
in the universe since existence began? This tremendous, monstrous
whodunit has never been solved. We have no absolute certainty—one
guess is as good as another—apart from the clarity of Christian faith,
but how few are the Christians! Meanwhile, the universe is miraculous
still, and too much study is a weariness of the flesh. "Canst thou by
searching find God? Canst thou find out the Almighty by perfection?
It is as high as heaven: what canst thou do? deeper than hell, what
canst thou do?" My answer is that you cannot find God by philosophy,
and even if you do, God will be a syllogism of subzero temperature.
You cannot find God by mathematical physics, and even if you do,
God will be only a terribly long algebraic equation. What indeed can
one do? What does Emerson, the wisest of the Americans, say? "The
noblest theory of life sat on the noblest figures of young men and
maidens, quite powerless and melancholy. It would not rake or pitch

21

a ton of hay; it would not rub down a horse; and the men and maidens it left pale and hungry."[1] "Life is a succession of lessons which must be lived to be understood. All is riddle, and the key to a riddle is another riddle." Emerson never wrote finer or wiser words than in the following passage: "Life itself is a bubble and a skepticism, and a sleep within a sleep. Grant it, and as much more as they will.—but thou, God's darling! heed thy private dream; thou wilt not be missed in the scorning and skepticism; there are enough of them; stay there in thy closet and toil until the rest [the philosophers] are agreed what to do about it. Thy sickness, they say, and thy puny habit require that thou do this and avoid that, but know that thy life is a flitting state, a tent for a night, and do thou, sick or well, finish that stint."

The veil that cannot be lifted, the door to which there is no key, the curtain that hides the eternal verities from us and which cannot be rent asunder, the riddle of Berkeley that has never been solved, and meanwhile the passage from life to death like a bright meteor in a summer night shot into darkness—this has always been humiliating to the human intellect. The pathos of life lies in the fact that we are given a short span under the sun and that nothing we accomplish lasts very long, but the further pathos is that we cannot know, and thus life becomes a double tragedy. What shall I do in order to be saved? Shall one go on all fours or on all eights and imitate the octopus like Dreiser's titan, or see life as a struggle where the lobster with the strongest claws wins? But that evidently is nonsense, for such is vanity and chasing after the wind. The Preacher's answer is that, in spite of its vanity, "Life is sweet and it is pleasant for the eyes to see the sun." See by what a narrow margin wisdom is divided from folly! "At all times be thy garment white, and let oil not be lacking for thy head. Enjoy life with the woman of thy love, all the days of thy vain life, which God has given thee under the sun, for that is thy portion in life, and the compensation for thy toil under the sun."

There is much confusion on the subject of pleasure; all philosophies

---

[1] Essay on "Experience." The passage was inspired, I think, by the sight of Bronson Alcott pitching hay or Hawthorne trying to milk a cow at Brook Farm. Margaret Fuller's transcendental cow hooked the other cows. The place must have been a pandemonium. Hawthorne wrote to Sophia Peabody, his fiancée: "April 14th, 10 a.m. Sweetest, I did not milk the cows last night because Mr. Ripley was afraid to trust them to my hands, or me to their horns—I know not which." Letter April 13, 1841.

agree that happiness is the end of living, for to teach that the contrary, pain, is the *summum bonum* would be insane and would be rejected at once by man's instinct for life, but the methods of reaching and securing happiness vary. Justice Holmes's answer is the following: "That the universe has in it more than we understand, that the private soldiers have not been told the plan of the campaign, or even that there is one, rather than some vaster unthinkable to which every predicate is an impertinence, has no bearing upon our conduct. We still shall fight—all of us, because we want to live, some at least because we want to realize our spontaneity and prove our powers, for the joy of it, and we may leave to the unknown the supposed final valuation of that which in any event has value to us. It is enough for us that the universe has produced us and has within it, as less than it, all that we believe and love. If we think of our existence not as that of a little god outside, but as that of a ganglion within, we have the infinite behind us. It gives us our only but our adequate significance." [2]

Yes, real or not, we have to take the world as it is and man as he is without demanding perfection and then damning him for what the theologians think he should be but is not. Santayana's answer is the same. Granted that all life is an illusion, "the only evil in illusion is that it deceives, there is beauty in its being. . . . True insight is not deceived by the prattle of the child, but is not offended by it." "Life is an illusion if we trust it, but it is a truth if we do not trust it; and this discovery is perhaps better symbolized by the Cross than by the Indian doctrine of illusion. It is while we exist, not after we are dead to existence, that we need counsel." [3] And so Paris would embrace Helen, which was Doxa or Epiphaneia, or Seeming or Phantom. "As all desperate lovers, in the absence of their true love, embrace what best they can find, though a false object, so spirit, which, if not entangled in circumstance and heavy with dreams would embrace the truth, must embrace appearance instead." The rape of Helen, representing the immediate, was thus "adulterous substitution, dazzling but criminal." But we may well ask, what else can man do?

[2] From *Collected Legal Papers,* by Oliver Wendell Holmes. Copyright, 1920, Harcourt, Brace & Company, Inc. Reprinted by permission.
[3] Essay on "War Shrines," *Soliloquies in England.*

2. HEED THY PRIVATE DREAM

Emerson, the sage of Concord, is truly the sage of America. Not only has he been a perpetual inspiration to the young, but people in old age go to him, as Justice Holmes did, for a reappreciation of truths they perhaps did not fully understand in their youth. John Jay Chapman said, "He let loose something within me which made me in my own eyes as good as any one else," [4] an experience shared by many a young man. Later in life, of course, Chapman ran out on him; Emerson, with Goethe, had become his two favorite "rag dolls"—"I keep them in a convenient drawer, and when the mood returns, pull out one of them and study him—ask him questions and talk to him—and always end by mussing his hair, batting his head against the wall, and consigning him to the guard-room." [5] But that was just like the temperamental Chapman. A more serene spirit, Justice Holmes, said at the age of eighty-nine, "The only fire-brand of my youth that burns to me as brightly as ever is Emerson." [6]

How account for his perpetual freshness? To be sure, he wrote principally on eternal topics, but the key to his greatness is to be found in a short sentence in his *Journals*, "I like a man who likes to see a fine barn as well as a good tragedy"—the statement of a thinker who refused to be tricked by his thoughts into forgetting the world of life. He was a man who said, "If you do not quit the high chair, lie quite down and roll on the ground a good deal, you become nervous and heavy-hearted. . . . I shall talk of Chenangoes and my new garden sprout; have you heard of my pig? . . . And never a word more of Goethe or Tennyson." (*Journals,* May 24, 1838.) He read as much as any man ever read, he would grind an author or a book into an epithet, but he also wrote, "What could we in Concord do without Bigelow's and Wesson's bar-rooms and their dependencies?" (*Journals,* June 22, 1843.) Out of his reading, his ventures into nature, his cogita-

[4] See Chapman, preface to revised edition, *Emerson and Other Essays,* 1909.

[5] *John Jay Chapman and His Letters,* edited by M. A. Howe. Houghton Mifflin Company. Copyright, 1937, M. A. DeWolfe Howe. Reprinted by permission.

[6] Letter to Sir Frederick Pollock, May 20, 1930. Reprinted by permission of the publishers from Mark DeWolfe Howe, Editor, *Holmes-Pollock Letters: Correspondence of Mr. Justice Holmes and Sir Frederick Pollock, 1874-1932.* Cambridge, Mass.: Harvard University Press, 1941.

tions, and his persistent looking at common life, he had a full balance of deep perceptions into the illusoriness of life and a firm common-sense foothold on living. So his optimism was not shallow or facile, and his deeper, finer perceptions never ended in an irresponsible, intellectual pose. That is why he is the "clear-eyed Olympian," and the "Buddha of the West." [7]

Two of his best essays, "Illusion" and "Experience," show that Emerson's wisdom had these ingredients of wistfulness and common sense complete. Because he saw life's illusoriness, he saw all the more reason to have "respect for the present hour." "The fine young people despise life, but in me and in such as with me are free from dyspepsia, and to whom a day is a sound and solid good, it is a great excess of politeness to look scornful and to cry for company." This is the kind of meat in Emerson that strengthens life and stimulates the appetite for living. I give here some excerpts from "Experience," which show the quality of his "spermatic, man-making words" and the intense brilliance of his short, sharp lines.

"Set up the strong present tense against all the rumors of wrath, past or to come."

BY RALPH WALDO EMERSON

But what help from these fineries or pedantries? What help from thought? Life is not dialectics. We, I think, in these times, have had lessons enough of the futility of criticism. Our young people have thought and written much on labor and reform, and for all that they have written, neither the world nor themselves have got on a step. Intellectual tasting of life will not supersede muscular activity. If a man should consider the nicety of the passage of a piece of bread down

[7] Oliver Wendell Holmes's poem "At the Saturday Club":
"Where in the realm of thought, whose air is song,
Does he, the Buddha of the West, belong?
He seems a wingèd Franklin, sweetly wise,
Born to unlock the secrets of the skies."
And James Russell Lowell's "Fable for Critics":
"A Greek head on right Yankee shoulders, whose range
Has Olympus for one pole, for t'other the Exchange;
. . .
C.'s [Carlyle's] the Titan, as shaggy of mind as of limb,—
E. [Emerson] the clear-eyed Olympian, rapid and slim."

his throat, he would starve. At Education-Farm the noblest theory of life sat on the noblest figures of young men and maidens, quite power-less and melancholy. It would not rake or pitch a ton of hay; it would not rub down a horse; and the men and maidens it left pale and hungry. . . . Do not craze yourself with thinking, but go about your business anywhere. Life is not intellectual or critical, but sturdy. Its chief good is for well-mixed people who can enjoy what they find, without question. Nature hates peeping, and our mothers speak her very sense when they say, "Children, eat your victuals, and say no more of it." To fill the hour,—that is happiness; to fill the hour and leave no crevice for a repentance or an approval.

We live amid surfaces, and the true art of life is to skate well on them. Under the oldest mouldiest conventions a man of native force prospers just as well as in the newest world, and that by skill of han-dling and treatment. He can take hold anywhere. . . . To finish the mo-ment, to find the journey's end in every step of the road, to live the greatest number of good hours, is wisdom. It is not the part of men, but of fanatics, or of mathematicians if you will, to say that the short-ness of life considered, it is not worth caring whether for so short a duration we were sprawling in want or sitting high. Since our office is with moments, let us husband them. Five minutes of today are worth as much to me as five minutes in the next millennium. Let us be poised, and wise, and our own, today. Let us treat the men and women well; treat them as if they were real; perhaps they are. Men live in their fancy, like drunkards whose hands are too soft and tremulous for successful labor. It is a tempest of fancies, and the only ballast I know is a respect to the present hour. Without any shadow of doubt, amidst this vertigo of shows and politics, I settle myself ever the firmer in the creed that we should not postpone and refer and wish, but do broad justice where we are, by whomsoever we deal with, accepting our actual companions and circumstances, however humble or odious, as the mystic officials to whom the universe has delegated its whole pleasure for us. . . .

The fine young people despise life, but in me and in such as with me are free from dyspepsia, and to whom a day is a sound and solid good, it is a great excess of politeness to look scornful and to cry for company. I am grown by sympathy a little eager and sentimental, but leave me alone and I should relish every hour and what it brought me, the potluck of the day, as heartily as the oldest gossip in the bar-room. I am thankful for small mercies. I compared notes with one of my friends who expects everything of the universe and is disap-pointed when anything is less than the best, and I found that I begin at the other extreme, expecting nothing, and am always full of thanks for moderate goods. I accept the clangor and jangle of contrary tend-encies. I find my account in sots and bores also. They give a reality to the circumjacent picture which such a vanishing meteorous appear-ance can ill spare. In the morning I awake and find the old world, wife, babes, and mother, Concord and Boston, the dear old spiritual world and even the dear old devil not far off. If we will take the good we find, asking no questions, we shall have heaping measures.

The great gifts are not got by analysis. Everything good is on the highway. The middle region of our being is the temperate zone. We may climb into the thin and cold realm of pure geometry and lifeless science, or sink into that of sensation. Between these extremes is the equator of life, of thought, of spirit, of poetry,—a narrow belt. . . .

The mid-world is best. Nature, as we know her, is no saint. The lights of the church, the ascetics, Gentoos, and corn-eaters, she does not distinguish by any favor. She comes eating and drinking and sinning. Her darlings, the great, the strong, the beautiful, are not children of our law; do not come out of the Sunday School, nor weigh their food, nor punctually keep the commandments. If we will be strong with her strength we must not harbor such disconsolate consciences, borrowed too from the consciences of other nations. We must set up the strong present tense against all the rumors of wrath, past or to come.

So many things are unsettled which it is of the first importance to settle;—and, pending their settlement, we will do as we do. Whilst the debate goes forward on the equity of commerce, and will not be closed for a century or two, New and Old England may keep shop. Law of copyright and international copyright is to be discussed, and in the interim we will sell our books for the most we can. Expediency of literature, reason of literature, lawfulness of writing down a thought, is questioned; much is to say on both sides, and, while the fight waxes hot, thou, dearest scholar, stick to thy foolish task, add a line every hour, and between whiles add a line. Right to hold land, right of property, is disputed, and the conventions convene, and before the vote is taken, dig away in your garden, and spend your earnings as a waif or godsend to all serene and beautiful purposes.

—"Experience," *Essays: Second Series*

3. WHO IS THE DREAMER?

What Emerson says in pithy, epigrammatic lines, David Grayson communicates in a more vivid concrete manner in his *Adventures,* books which are a mixture of sketches and philosophical musings and comments on life, written in a prose as lucid and easy and friendly and mature as the spirit which inspires them. David Grayson (friend of Woodrow Wilson) is an enviably serene spirit in American literature.

Were he a Chinese, Chinese readers would probably fall on his neck; they would admire in him exactly those qualities which they admire in Tao Yuanming, that farmer poet, a man whose good cheer and inner content come from the fact that he has completely made peace with himself and with this good earth. Both have recovered their equilibrium from living very close to nature. Grayson's overflowing sense of gratitude for the gift of living often reminds me of the line of Tao Yuanming where he sings "and the evening dew wets my gown" with rapturous content as he comes home from the field with a hoe on his shoulder. How few are the poets who can write such simple lines, instinct with a sweet serenity of spirit! The greatest Chinese poets have tried to imitate him, but have not succeeded, because the delight of finding one's gown wet from brushing the evening grass on the wayside can be felt only by very great and simple souls. Holmes of the "Breakfast Table" says, "The great end of being is to harmonize man with the order of things." Tao Yuanming did it, and the American Grayson has done it. Those who think it is easy should try and see, but lucky are the men who have succeeded.

What did this man have that his spirit could be so serene? Here is one who somehow found his handles to get hold of life. He left the vexatious problems of philosophy a million miles behind him; instead he found his way to what Thoreau called the "kernel" of living; he found the world good, his neighbors friendly, and God in high heaven as well as in the flower at his feet. Any time, in any age or country, when I find a man with such serenity of spirit, he compels my respect, for I know he has achieved something that the world in general and the modern world in particular sadly lack. David Grayson's serenity is almost Greek, as we shall have occasion to see later, but his background and personality and accent are distinctly twentieth-century American. So are the gray bag he carries, and his garden sage and his lilac bush and his tall elms. Such serenity is always enviable; besides, it makes the modern vexed and distracted spirits ashamed of themselves. It is easy to discover that he does not know evil and has not plumbed the depths of criminology and sin like Dostoevski. Simplicity and sweet serenity have not been literary fashions during the last decades. David Grayson's *Adventures* and *More Adventures*[8] held their ground for three decades and continued to be read, to the author's own pleasant surprise, but so far as I can learn, he has as yet found no place in the literary history of America. I think the critics are wrong. Perhaps the consummate simplicity of his style, which is the despair of more learned writers, has deceived them into ignoring him. But David Grayson will be enjoyed and appreciated by the public long after his *Woodrow Wilson: Life and Letters,* the product of his less real literary self, Ray Stannard Baker, is confined to the library shelves of research historians. He will be enjoyed and appreciated as long as the American friendly spirit and wistfulness of living endure.

His serenity is so unique in contemporary America that I must call it almost a phenomenon. If that lamp perhaps does not shine with much power and intensity, yet how clear is its light, and how comforting it is to sit under it and share its warmth and glow! Grayson is mature, if any American thinker is mature. As for his philosophy of life, it is a native American one. Grayson has digested Emerson well, and he glorifies the present hour. He reads and reads, the *Meditations of Marcus Aurelius,* Epictetus, and Montaigne, Thoreau, Matthew Arnold, and the *Leaves of Grass,* too, but these are inwardly assimilated, homogenized, and *lived;* and out of these cogitations come his

---

[8] The *David Grayson Omnibus* contains *Adventures in Contentment, Adventures in Friendship,* and *The Open Road. More Adventures* contains *Adventures in Understanding, Adventures in Solitude,* and *Great Possessions.* Published by the Garden City Publishing Company.

own perceptions, fresh as morning daisies and tripping across his pages in the native garb of true American sentiments. The lucidity of his thought has strength behind it, like the smiling surface of a broad and deep river. Born in Michigan, he is not exactly a Yankee, yet I like to think of him as a philosophical super-Yankee. I do not mean taciturnity and shrewdness at a bargain, but a supershrewdness in guessing at what life is all about. Let us see him confront a true Yankee, his neighbor Horace, about life's dreams. He had just "followed his nose" and gone up the hills in early morning to track the scent of a certain clump of pine trees, and he came down feeling like Moses after seeing the burning bush.

"A life uncommanded now is uncommanded; a life unenjoyed now is unenjoyed . . . for the past is gone and no one knows the future."

BY DAVID GRAYSON

"Takin' the air, David?"

I amuse Horace. Horace is an important man in this community. He has big, solid barns, and money in the bank, and a reputation for hardheadedness. He is also known as a "driver"; and has had sore trouble with a favorite son. He believes in "goin' it slow" and "playin' safe," and he is convinced that "ye can't change human nature."

His question came to me with a kind of shock. I imagined with a vividness impossible to describe what Horace would think if I answered him squarely and honestly, if I were to say:

"I've been down in the marshes following my nose—enjoying the thorn apples and the wild geraniums, talking with a woodpecker and reporting the morning news of the woods for an imaginary newspaper."

I was hungry, and in a mood to smile at myself anyway (good-humoredly and forgivingly as we always smile at ourselves!) before I met Horace, and the flashing vision I had of Horace's dry, superior smile finished me. Was there really anything in this world but cows and calves, and great solid barns, and oatcrops, and cash in the bank?

"Been in the brook?" asked Horace, observing my wet legs.

Talk about the courage to face cannon and Cossacks! It is nothing to the courage required to speak aloud in broad daylight of the finest things we have in us! I was not equal to it.

"Oh, I've been down for a tramp in the marsh," I said, trying to put him off.

But Horace is a Yankee of the Yankees and loves nothing better than to chase his friends into corners with questions, and leave them ultimately with the impression that they are somehow less sound, sensible, practical, than he is—and he usually proves it, not because he is right, but because he is sure, and in a world of shadowy half-beliefs and half-believers he is without doubts.

"What ye find down there?" asked Horace.

"Oh, I was just looking around to see how the spring was coming on."

"Hm-m," said Horace, eloquently, and when I did not reply, he continued, "Often git out in the morning as early as this?"

"Yes," I said, "often."

"And do you find things any different now from what they would be later in the day?"

At this the humor of the whole situation dawned on me and I began to revive. When things grow hopelessly complicated, and we can't laugh, we do either one of two things: we lie or we die. But if we can laugh, we can fight! And be honest!

"Horace," I said, "I know what you are thinking about."

Horace's face remained perfectly impassive, but there was a glint of curiosity in his eye.

"You've been thinking I've been wasting my time beating around down there in the swamp just to look at things and smell of things—which you wouldn't do. You think I'm a kind of impractical dreamer, now, don't you, Horace? I'll warrant you've told your wife just that more than once. Come, now!"

I think I made a rather shrewd hit, for Horace looked uncomfortable and a little foolish.

"Come now, honest!" I laughed and looked him in the eye.

"Waal, now, ye see——"

"Of course you do, and I don't mind it in the least."

A little dry gleam of humor came in his eye.

"Ain't ye?"

It's a fine thing to have it straight out with a friend.

"No," I said, "I'm the practical man and you're the dreamer. I've rarely known in all my life, Horace, such a confirmed dreamer as you are, nor a more impractical one."

Horace laughed.

"How do ye make that out?"

With this my spirit returned to me and I countered with a question as good as his. It is as valuable in argument as in war to secure the offensive.

"Horace, what are you working for, anyhow?"

This is always a devastating shot. Ninety-nine out of every hundred human beings are desperately at work grubbing, sweating, worrying, thinking, sorrowing, enjoying, without in the least knowing why.

"Why, to make a living—same as you," said Horace.

"Oh, come now, if I were to spread the report in town that a poor neighbor of mine—that's you, Horace—was just making his living, that he himself had told me so, what would you say? Horace, what are you working for? It's something more than a mere living."

"Waal, now, I'll tell ye, if ye want it straight, I'm layin' aside a little something for a rainy day."

"A little something!" this in the exact inflection of irony by which here in the country we express our opinion that a friend has really a good deal more laid aside than anybody knows about. Horace smiled also in the exact manner of one so complimented.

"Horace, what are you going to do with that thirty thousand dollars?"

"Thirty thousand!" Horace looks at me and smiles, and I look at Horace and smile.

"Honest now!"

"Waal, I'll tell ye—a little peace and comfort for me and Josie in our old age, and a little something to make the children remember us when we're gone. Isn't that worth working for?"

He said this with downright seriousness. I did not press him further, but if I had tried I could probably have got the even deeper admission of that faith that lies, like bed rock, in the thought of most men—that honesty and decency here will not be without its reward there, however they may define the "there." Some "prophet's paradise to come!"

"I knew it!" I said. "Horace, you're a dreamer, too. You are dreaming of peace and comfort in your old age, a little quiet house in town where you won't have to labor as hard as you do now, where you won't be worried by crops and weather, and where Mrs. Horace will be able to rest after so many years of care and work and sorrow—a kind of earthly heaven! And you are dreaming of leaving a bit to your children and grandchildren, and dreaming of the gratitude they will express. All dreams, Horace!"

"Oh, waal——"

"The fact is, you are working for a dream, and living on dreams—isn't that true?"

"Waal, now, if you mean it that way——"

"I see I haven't got you beaten yet, Horace!"

He smiled broadly.

"We are all amiable enough with our own dreams. You think that what you are working for—your dream—is somehow sounder and more practical than what I am working for."

Horace started to reply, but had scarcely debouched from his trenches when I opened on him with one of my twenty-fours.

"How do you know that you are ever going to be old?"

It hit.

"And if you do grow old, how do you know that thirty thousand dollars—oh, we'll call it that—is really enough, provided you don't lose it before, to buy peace and comfort for you, or that what you leave your children will make either you or them any happier? Peace and comfort and happiness are terribly expensive, Horace—and prices have been going up fast since this war began!"

Horace looked at me uncomfortably, as men do in the world when you shake the foundations of the tabernacle. I have thought since that I probably pressed him too far; but these things go deep with me.

"No, Horace," I said, "you are the dreamer—and the impractical dreamer at that!"

For a moment Horace answered nothing; and we both stood still there in the soft morning sunshine with the peaceful fields and woods all about us, two human atoms struggling hotly with questions too large for us. The cow and the new calf were long out of sight. Horace made a motion as if to follow them up the lane, but I held him with my glittering eye—as I think of it since, not without a kind of amusement at my own seriousness.

"I'm the practical man, Horace, for I want my peace now, and my happiness now, and my God now. I can't wait. My barns may burn or my cattle die, or the solid bank where I keep my deferred joy may fail, or I myself by tomorrow be no longer here."

So powerfully and vividly did this thought take possession of me that I cannot now remember to have said a decent good-bye to Horace (never mind, he knows me!). At least when I was halfway up the hill I found myself gesticulating with one clenched fist and saying to myself with a kind of passion: "Why wait to be peaceful? Why not be peaceful now? Why not be happy now? Why not be rich now?"

For I think it truth that a life uncommanded now is uncommanded; a life unenjoyed now is unenjoyed; a life not lived wisely now is not lived wisely: for the past is gone and no one knows the future.

As for Horace, is he convinced that he is an impractical dreamer? Not a bit of it! He was merely flurried for a moment in his mind, and probably thinks me now, more than ever before, just what I think him. Absurd place, isn't it, this world?

—Great Possessions, III

4. WHEN LAUGHTER IS WISER THAN TEARS

Santayana's philosophy of animal faith may be described as a disillusioned, but sweet, acceptance of our finite existence. Seeing the transience of the temporal world and at the same time its ephemeral beauty, and accepting the finitude of existence, a man may nevertheless find the way clear for life and happiness. "This once acknowledged and inwardly digested, life and happiness can honestly begin," says Santayana. There is some profound reflection and extraordinarily beautiful writing on the subject by this gifted philosopher. For not often is a philosopher also a poet and a born writer.

"There is no cure for birth and death save to enjoy the interval."

BY GEORGE SANTAYANA

If to be saved were merely to cease, we should all be saved by a little waiting . . . What can save the world, without destroying it, is self-knowledge on the part of the world, not of course reflective self-knowledge (for the world is not an animal that can think) but such a regimen and such a philosophy established in society as shall recognize truly what the world is, and what happiness is possible in it. The force that has launched me into this dream of life does not care what turns my dream takes nor how long it troubles me. Nature denies at every moment, not indeed that I am troubled and dreaming, but that there are any natural units like my visions, or anything anomalous in what I hate, or final in what I love. Under these circumstances, what is the part of wisdom? To dream with one eye open; to be detached from the world without hostility to it; to welcome fugitive beauties and pity fugitive sufferings without forgetting for a moment how fugitive they are; and not to lay up treasures, except in heaven.

How charming is divine philosophy, when it is really divine, when it descends to earth from a higher sphere, and loves the things of earth without needing or collecting them! What the gay Aristippus said of his mistress: I possess, I am not possessed, every spirit should say of an experience that ruffles it like a breeze playing on the summer sea. A thousand ships sail over it in vain, and the worst of tempests is in a teapot. This once acknowledged and inwardly digested, life and happiness can honestly begin. Nature is innocently fond of puffing herself out, spreading her peacock feathers, and saying, What a fine bird am I! And so she is; to rave against this vanity would be to imitate it. On the contrary, the secret of a merry carnival is that Lent is at hand. Having virtually renounced our follies, we are for the first time able to enjoy them with a free heart in their ephemeral purity. When laughter is humble, when it is not based on self-esteem, it is wiser than tears. Conformity is wiser than hot denials, tolerance wiser than priggishness and puritanism. It is not what earnest people renounce that makes me pity them, it is what they work for. No possible reform will make existence adorable or fundamentally just . . . So much tension is hysterical and degrading; nothing is ever gained by it worth half what it spoils. Wealth is dismal and poverty cruel unless both are festive. There is no cure for birth and death save to enjoy the interval.

The easier attitudes which seem more frivolous are at bottom infinitely more spiritual and profound than the tense attitudes; they are nearer to understanding and to renunciation; they are nearer to the cross. Perhaps if England had remained Catholic it might have remained merry; it might still dare, as Shakespeare dared, to be utterly tragic and also frankly and humbly gay. The world has been too much with it; Hebraic religion and German philosophy have confirmed it in a deliberate and agonized worldliness. They have sanctioned, in the hard-working and reforming part of the middle classes, an unqualified respect for prosperity and success; life is judged with all the blindness of life itself. There is no moral freedom. In so far as minds are absorbed in business or in science they all inevitably circle about the same objects, and take part in the same events, combining their thoughts and efforts in the same "world's work." The world, therefore, invades and dominates them; they lose their independence and almost their distinction from one another. Their philosophy accordingly only exaggerates a little when it maintains that their individual souls are all manifestation of a single spirit, the Earth-spirit. They hardly have any souls they can call their own, that may be saved out of the world, or that may see and judge the world from above.

—"War Shrines," *Soliloquies in England*

What if the material world as we know it is an illusion? "The only evil in illusion is that it deceives; there is beauty in its being." "The world which torments us is truly beautiful; indeed, that is one of its ways of tormenting us; and we are not wrong in loving, but only in appropriating it." "It is certainly not an illusion that I have now the experience of being alive and of finding myself surrounded, at least in appearance, by a tolerably tractable world, material and social. It is not an illusion that this experience is now filling me with mixed and trooping feelings. . . . I would not say that not to exist would not be better; but, so long as we exist, however precariously and 'unreally,' I think it the part of wisdom to find a way of living well rather than to deprecate living."

Chapter III

OUR ANIMAL HERITAGE

I. MODERN MAN PSYCHOANALYZED

NO civilization can exist without some fairly stable ideas of man, his history, God, the soul, the universe, and the purpose of man's existence. These ideas, as far as I can make out, are in a state of rather disgraceful confusion, disgraceful for a twentieth-century man who boasts of his great progress. Of all these subjects, nothing interests me more than that of man, unless it is woman. So we will first take up man, that most curious, and even at this late date I may still say most hopeful, of animals. We will examine him a little, turn him about and see why at times he is so ignoble and, at others, so noble. We have made quite a mess of the idea of man, as well as of all other ideas pertinent to human life, and I hate any kind of a mess, disorderliness, fuzziness, and confusion. It is really extraordinary how we can all present a perfectly neat appearance at a friend's party, with shoes shined and tie to match (and the lady's handbag matching her shoes, too), and yet be disgracefully disorderly inside our heads.

It is not a pretty picture. Professor William Ernest Hocking has written a penetrating analysis of the plight of modern man's beliefs in *What Man Can Make of Man*. He has traced how we have lost our ground, how certain ideas dominated man for centuries and there was a constant revision of ideas according to which man was trying to reshape his life by reshaping ideals; how the beliefs in liberty, progress, and the inalienable rights of man were generally undermined; how science, which was once a noble vision and a passion, overshot its mark in dismissing values from the universe; how from the scientific attitude, "We have no place for the purposes and values of things in our laboratories," the professor imperceptibly shifted to the position, "We have now dismissed purposes and values from the universe." Once

Professor Hocking lost his patience and said some words that sting: "Or shall we say, without wishing to startle our scientific friend, that this desiccated picture of the world is a damnable lie—for values are *there;* values are among the inescapable facts of the world, and whoever disseminates this death's head world-view in the schools and colleges of this or any other land is disseminating falsehood, with the browbeaten connivance of a whole herd of intellectual sheep, and of culpable guardians of the young."[1]

In the absence of values and purposes, the modern man is inwardly, vaguely, but truly uncomfortable. Somewhere in the back of our psyche, there is an emotional emptiness, an irritating feeling of discomfort that the world is not all well. There is an emptiness that leaves us a prey to any cheat or *Gauleiter* who offers us a sop to stop this emotional hunger, because man is a spiritual, emotional animal and he wants to be emotionally played on, to have something to believe in, to have a leader, a mission, and his own individual part in the mission, to share the sense of a great brotherhood, and to know that he is helping the world to go somewhere. And so a brand of fanaticism comes into the vacuum, takes the place of what in better times should be a sense of repose and content, and the external disorder starts from a disintegration of the beliefs of the man within. Not until that private anarchy be remedied can external public order be restored. Behind international anarchy there is a private anarchy, and we would be idiots if we didn't see that the former stemmed from the latter, for public order comes from the private beliefs of man. It would be insane to look for public order where private anarchy exists.

I think it is not the particular tenets or political conflicts alone that cause this restlessness of the modern spirit. It is the broad bases of belief and the over-all assumptions of human purpose that man spiritually needs and now lacks, because they have been put to rout by three centuries of furious and erratic and, in many cases, unjust thinking. Previous ages and centuries all had a faith of some sort; St. Augustine had his City of God, and though there were Caesar Borgias, murders, plagues, and wars and quite as much misery, they didn't shake a man's beliefs. In the eighteenth century, the physiocrats and the encyclopedists

---

[1] From *What Man Can Make of Man*. Harper & Brothers. Copyright, 1942, by William Ernest Hocking. Reprinted by permission.

were all men of hope, of belief that the world was about to come into a better order; in the nineteenth, there was John Stuart Mill with his gospel of social welfare, and there were Carlyle and Cardinal Manning with their Victorian faith in the conjunction of the moral laws of man and the laws of God. Matthew Arnold was often skeptical and sad, but he believed. Yes, the world was a good one still and getting better.

In the United States, the generation of Washington and Franklin and Jefferson were men fitted out with a tolerable balance of faith. Jefferson comfortably believed that man's rights were "unalienable" and "self-evident." The generation of Emerson and Thoreau was bold, extremely bold; their spirits roamed the earth to Germany, to England, to Persia, India, and China for spiritual truths they were eager to discover, and their contemporaries like William Ellery Channing and Theodore Parker were busy trying to reshape old beliefs and fight new evils, while Lincoln and Holmes were at least stable and "got along." In the post-Civil War period, the nation was too busy expanding; Mark Twain couldn't think, but men born and growing up to maturity in the Gilded Age still could write essays, and when they could write essays, casual, intimate, savoring life's flavors slowly and leisurely, one may infer also that society was contented and stable. It was the generation that gave us Agnes Repplier, John Jay Chapman, Frank Moore Colby, David Grayson, Logan Pearsall Smith, Paul Elmer More, Clarence Day, John Livingston Lowes, James Branch Cabell, and Christopher Morley.[2] These had leisure and culture; their voice was generally low and their tone conversational and soothing; their essays attested to such qualities, and they wrote them because men and women had the leisure and contentment to read them. When the Gilded Age broke with the turn of the century, a new voice was heard, often sensational and strident; it turned to wit, satire, and parody when it wasn't muckraking, because the meanness of it all had become apparent, and the best weapon was wit and satire. The young girl of

[2] Many of these wrote, of course, in the nineteen thirties even and are our contemporaries, but I am talking of the generation as a generation. Agnes Repplier was born in 1855, Chapman in '62, Santayana in '63, More in '64, Smith and Colby in '65, Lowes in '67, Grayson in '70, and Day in '74. Of this class of learned essayists, Christopher Morley, born in 1890, seems to be the last. This leads me to think that one's literary style is formed between the ages of twenty and thirty, and with this the prevalent temper of the decade when one is in his twenties has much to do.

twenty of the Lost Generation had to mumble her words through a
cigarette between her lips with a hoarse and tired voice suggesting
that she had not gone to bed before four o'clock that morning. Somehow the world had become less jolly. No one pretended that he read
Mencken or Dorothy Parker for the reward of contentment and repose, but rather to be delightfully and gleefully ruffled. Instead of
soothing table talk, we need and love the salty wit, the neat turn of
phrase, and the whole "schimpflexikon." The world, we say, needs to
be saved, and everyone was trying to save it by rousing something or
other in our breast. The Victorian era had passed, and discussions about
beauty and serenity seemed baby talk and jejune.

"The liberty to live well," what an irony that phrase has in such
times as these! [3] On the whole, we may say that the medieval ages had
faith—in God; the eighteenth century had a glorious faith—in man's
reason, which was going to set right everything after vanquishing the
iniquitous tyranny of the church; the nineteenth century had faith—
in progress, in the concept of an ascending evolution and in mechanistic
physics which was going to explain everything to us, very satisfactorily.
Above all, it had faith in substance; substance of mind and substance
of matter, which underlay all motion and all progress. Millions of people in previous centuries lived and labored and died, and although
many were not able to read, or did not read the books of the learned,
they were spiritually comfortable because they were psychologically
integrated; somewhere, in feelings they could not express, there existed
certain basic beliefs and assumptions that were not questioned. It was
these beliefs and assumptions that gave the individual the feeling of
inner security. The Insecurity Council of the United Nations reflects
but the spiritual insecurity of the inner man today, and Austin and
Vishinsky, confronting each other with words and words, knew at
lunch or an evening soiree that they were essentially attorneys and
had acted that morning brilliantly or not so well as attorneys only, and
beyond that nothing more. But it is these beliefs now in the shadow
that make life livable and that make the world go.

We moderns have none of that benefit of inner conviction that the
world is going somewhere, is in progress and not headed for the abyss.

---

[3] The phrase is George Santayana's—essay on "Classical Liberty," *Soliloquies in England*.

Today those big, broad assumptions are cast in doubt or gone. We cannot find our approach to God; we are not sure of the progress of the future; some people are quite ready to exchange liberty and equality for a mess of pottage, especially when it concerns the liberty of other peoples. Democracy itself has so many counterfeits that the average man is justifiably confused. We have cut adrift from the past and we are not sure of the future; all we have is the present and the will to fight, if we know what to fight for. This is wasteful of energy and suggests a kind of *malaise*.

Perhaps psychoanalysts can answer the question, or perhaps they cannot unless they are also philosophers and can help men and women back toward their beliefs. Hocking, in the before-mentioned book, which is really only an essay and should be read at one sitting, has skillfully shown how often the individual problems of the psychoanalytic patient must be tied up with the general problems of the world.

The Psychiatrist and the Soul

BY WILLIAM ERNEST HOCKING

For it is one of the clear signs of modern progress that we have forgotten what the "soul" is, and put in no claims to its possession. Thumbing over the texts of psychology will yield little information and no comfort; by one of the queerest inversions of scientific history, the loss of the *psyche* is one of the chief points of pride of the science of the *psyche*. Some of the enthusiasts in this field abandon scientific caution: they say, "There is no such thing as a soul"—an unscientific mode of assertion—instead of saying, "We do not find any soul," an assertion not open to doubt, and leaving always open the hopeful question, "Do you know where to look for it?"

In this important matter the psychiatrists have done better, for being practical people they have had to recognize facts. Like many another normal function, the soul announces itself as a fact when it becomes disordered. It gets out of order partly because the spirit of the times has encouraged it to identify its desires with its rights, and partly because of that scientific conscience which has deprived it of all value in its own eyes. For both reasons it becomes incapable of ascertaining any meaning in its existence. Now the soul is simply the human self in its dealings with its total horizon, trying to hold its bearings in the infinite universe of fact and meaning. When it loses its bearings it is a matter of life or death for the soul to recover them. Hence, greatly trusting, it today consults the psychiatrist.

The psychiatrist mutters something about the need for "integration."

The soul replies, "I realize the need; but I cannot integrate myself. I am trying to be modern, and modernity seems to me inwardly contradictory and adrift. How can a broken pot mend its own break?"

The psychiatrist responds, "Take refuge in Society. You are introverted, self-concerned and secretive. Hence you are a divided person. Confess what you are hiding; confess to me, for I represent Society. This act will restore your objectivity toward yourself. Then socialize your impulses."

The soul: "I am not sure that Society is so worthy of respect. It seems the source of the difficulty, not the cure for it. It does not know where it is going."

The psychiatrist: "If you feel this doubt, you must take refuge not in yourself, nor in Society, but in your ideal aims. Everyone has some such aims. Use your imagination to fuse these into a unity. Give yourself to the service of this unity, and you will be integrated: you will again be a soul."

The soul: "I have been taught that ideal aims are but myths."

The psychiatrist: "I cannot assure you that they are not. But even fictions have a healing power. Everyone is helped by having some sort of myth. Give yourself to the healing fiction."

The soul: "I see your difficulty. You believe nothing, and cannot heal me without a belief. The fiction might heal me if I did not know it to be a fiction. Knowing this, I cannot give myself to it. But I see that you have done your best. Farewell."

The sick soul and the psychiatrist are twin features, peculiar features of this end of the modern era. The psychiatrist is the embodiment of applied science, attempting to deal with the ravages of the mistakes of science. What he finds is, that more science is not enough.

—What Man Can Make of Man

2. ADAM AND EVE

It would be unfair and untrue to say that the intellectual labors of man in the last three hundred years have been in vain in bringing a better knowledge of himself, on pretty solid grounds. The only point is that this knowledge should be wisely interpreted and applied for his own good; one must concede that generally the interpretation is less happy and successful than the discovery of the information. Our failure to bring all this historical, biological, and psychological knowledge into a meaningful belief appears to be colossal. Monkeys that we are phylogenetically, we are always much better in catching and turning about bits of information than in tying them up together for our own use. What is man, anyhow? Do we know the answer to that question better than man did a hundred years ago? I would not bet yes and I would not bet no.

The medieval theologians gave us, on rather dogmatic grounds, two things, a "soul" and "original sin." (Actually the invention of the soul went back much further; our savage ancestors discovered it long ago when one of them waked up from a dream and thought that his soul had walked out and gone on a private holiday without taking his body along and had just returned to its abode; but it was the theologians who made it a sin not to believe in the soul, besides taking it rather arbitrarily away from the animals.) These two things were asserted firmly and clearly for us to believe, for without a soul there would be nothing to save and without original sin there would be no need of saving it. But their perceptions were better than their presentation. They could not quite make their ideas clear, so that the modern man, requiring clearer ideas on the subject, is confused and holds back his belief, or frankly calls them medieval myths. The overwise think that they know and say to the theologians, "My dear sir, you can't put that kind of stuff over on us. We are living in a scientific world." But the truly wise know that myths represent certain broad human generalizations of the early perceptions of man and that these perceptions are as good as our own. The theologians were only bad, and very bad, on one point; they separated the soul from the body, not only as a way of talking but by conceiving them as independent substances. Our refusal to separate them constitutes an initial gain of modern philosophy and knowledge.[4]

I have been bothered since my Presbyterian childhood by the questions of the soul and original sin. All people grant that the story of the fall of man arising from the eating of an apple is a myth with sociological meaning. The apple was not necessarily an apple, but could be any fruit, perhaps a fig or a mango, or just a luscious pear. The important points are that it was luscious and tempting, that it was forbidden and man ate it, signifying disobedience. That Eve first ate it and gave it to the perfectly innocent Adam, who was compelled to do so against his better judgment, is, of course, a man's story. Adam would have eaten the apple first if a woman had written the story. Genesis, we could almost swear by such internal evidence, was written by a man. But this is neither here nor there. The point is, there was clearly a psychological discord between suppressed desire and duty or reason. The apple looked good, it smelled good, and Adam was hungry. The plain truth is, if the couple in the Garden of Eden had suppressed their desire and gone on passing that apple tree and merely looking at it and smelling it, something would have happened that night.

Modern psychology would have written that story of the original sin differently, somewhat as follows:

"I can't sleep," said Adam or Eve—let us say it was Eve.

"What's the matter? Did you eat anything wrong?" answered Eve, or Adam.

"No, that's the whole trouble!" said Eve.

"What do you mean?" said Adam.

"*That* apple! I *didn't* eat it," said Eve, as she tossed about among her leaves.

"Curious, isn't it? I have been thinking about it, too."

This dialogue was repeated night after night until both were developing neuroses. Abdominal symptoms began to appear in Eve.

[4] Quite a lot of unnecessary nonsense was brought about by this confusion: is the soul an essence, a substance, an independent entity or a being? Once they started that sort of thing, the next question debated by the philosophers was: what is an entity? Is it a being or substance, etc? And some philosophers got very angry and sneered at their colleagues for confusing entity with being, or substance with essence. May God help them!

Adam, good spouse that he was, brought her figs and watermelons and bananas, but they didn't do her any good. Adam called it her imagination, Eve felt insulted, and the first quarrel began. One night Adam heard his spouse muttering in her sleep, "Ap, Ap, Ap!" He didn't consult a psychoanalyst, but he thought it curious.

Another morning, to Adam's surprise, Eve appeared quite cheerful.

"Oh, it was so good!" she said when she rolled over and touched Adam's shoulder.

"What was so good?"

"That apple. I ate it. The taste of it still lingers on my tongue and my jaws."

"Fiddlesticks!" cried her husband. "You didn't sleep-walk, did you?"

"But I swear to you I ate it," said Eve, vehemently. And she described to him vividly how she had gone to the tree and plucked the apple and sunk her teeth into the juicy pulp.

It was no use arguing with a woman. They agreed to go and see. To Eve's great surprise, the apple was still there. But she persisted in her story against all evidence. Adam began to reflect. He remembered that the same thing had occurred to him two or three times, that he thought he did things in his sleep while his body was lying with his beloved. What was it? Something had left his body, and it did things, sometimes quite crazy, which he evidently did not do.

Adam had discovered the soul. Eve liked the word immensely. But the symptoms continued. Eve's stomach refused to take anything, and she grew visibly emaciated and Adam was alarmed. He could not live without her, of course.

"Darling," he said to her one day. "We must do something. I know the trouble."

"Yes?" said Eve, looking up adoringly.

"This life we are leading is not right. You can see. We have nothing to do all day, and you are suffering from ennui."

"Ennui! It sounds so—so foreign. God speaks only English, you know."

"He is very intelligent that way. Anyway, I like the word, and when I say it, it is, of course, good English. Say it, and you'll feel better." Adam was of course an Englishman.

Eve said the word many times, and it delighted her and increased her respect for her husband. He was so good at inventing names for things.

"I have thought long about it," continued her husband. "I feel jumpy, and my muscles are getting flabby. Let's get out of here. I can't stand this damned perfection of a paradise. Yes, let's go and pluck that apple and eat it, you half and me the other half, and then get out of here! I'll be glad when I can do something, digging things, breaking things, throwing things. I'll throw stones, hundreds of them a day. And I want to tear and break a thousand branches. What did God give me these hands for? I may not dig, I may not break; I may not throw things and smash things in here. Eve, you know me, you believe in me, don't you? I am clever. I can make things grow. These things aren't mine. They will never be mine unless I make them grow myself."

Eve was no longer listening. Her eyes had dilated when she first heard her husband say that they were going to pluck that apple.

"Will you? Will you, really?" she asked, impetuously.

"I don't know. Do you think we should—really? I was only chattering. You know I love to chatter."

Suddenly an uncontrollable urge took possession of her, as if she was no longer herself. "Let's go and pluck *that thing* and quit the place. I must eat that apple or die!"

So Adam and Eve walked hand in hand silently and felt as if something greater than themselves was guiding their steps toward a certain destination. Several times Adam paused and got lost.

"Where is that tree?" he cried.

"You silly! Next turn to the right."

"How do you know?"

"My soul. Oh, I love that beautiful word. I feel it down here," she said, as she pointed to her belly.

"Oh, no, it can't be down there. I feel my soul is up here." Adam pointed to his head.

"Of course, it is down here. Oh, you man, don't you feel it?"

Eve was quite cheerful now. She found her way to the tree readily by letting her abdominal soul guide her.

They went to the tree, they plucked the apple and ate it, and they ran. There was thick undergrowth near the border, and Eve's toe struck a sharp flint. But they were unaccountably happy; a feeling went up and down their spines several times, which Eve, this time, invented a word for—thrill. They had done something wrong, but they had done the first thing on their own initiative. Eve panted a great deal, and Adam lifted his hand and wiped away something on his brow.

"What is that?" she asked.

"Sweat," said Adam, as readily as if he had known the word since his eyes first saw the light of the sun; for he was so expert at coining names now that he just let his lips and tongue form any new sound and the sound fitted. "Sweat," he said. "It is a fine feeling. I never felt so fine before."

Their excitement was great, and it was not only because of what they had done, but because of what they were going to see once they got outside.

"Do you feel better now, after eating that apple?" he asked. "Are you no longer sick?"

"I'm feeling fine, I'm sick no more, hang it all."

"What do you mean, hang it all?"

"I mean what I mean. It's a feeling that—well, it's just hang it all. Adam mine, of all the words your clever head has invented, I do not like the word 'sick.'"

"And why not?"

"It's too simple, it's sort of unrefined."

"There you go again! Say refined or unrefined, but not sort of."

"Adam dear, you are very clever, but you miss all the fine points. Perhaps I don't think as clearly as you do, or as you say you do, but sometimes things are not just refined or unrefined, but only sort of, not quite, as we have agreed to say. You know, my stomach has cleared up a lot since eating that apple. I can think so much better now. Your word 'sick' does not strike me as right. I want something better, something more—" she hesitated a little to form her ideas—"something more complicated—yes, complicated."

"Oh! you woman! Sick is a good word. It is forceful."

"No, I want something else. Give me another."

"It depends," said Adam knowingly. "It depends on where you are sick. In your case I should say you've got gastritis."

"Oh, you darling! Oh, wonderful, wonderful! I've got gastritis! Or, I've had it. It's all gone now! Adam my love, what are we going to do when we get outside?"

Adam thought a long time. He groped for some word big and strong. Slowly the sound formed in his ears, and he said briefly,

"I want to *conquer*."

By this time they had reached the outside and their eyes saw the landscape. It was not too good and it was not too bad. It wasn't as if no trees had grown outside the Garden. There were dense forests and prowling tigers and jackals and sheep. Holding his hand, Eve felt her heart palpitate a little as she said, "Now we are on our own. You will go and *kongker*, and I will be with you always."

"Yes, I will conquer all these," said Adam, as he stretched his arms and pointed to the forests and tigers.

That is the story of the escape from Eden, as modern man would have written it. The psychological discord was there. There was a soul there right enough; Adam thought it was in his head and Eve thought it was in her abdomen, but the soul was an indisputable fact and it caused the conflict of desires and duties and had within it the original sin. Eve had it within her, and so had Adam, and sometimes this subliminal consciousness was stronger than the conscious self and over-ruled the latter's decisions. As long as this conflict of suppressed desire and duty remained, they were unhappy, and desire was eventually the stronger of the two. In escaping from Paradise, Adam and Eve did the only psychologically sound thing they could have done, by not being idle, by seeking peace through work and exercise of their bodies, by achieving the feeling of recovered individuality and independence, by being on their own. On discovering the escape, the all wise God was pleased and said to Himself, "I am glad they have gone away. I was merely trying them. I knew they would have a nervous breakdown in this garden, and I wanted to see if they had the guts to go on their own, if they were worth my trouble in creating them. I intend now merely to watch and see how that young Adam is going to conquer the world, as he says to his wife. He is going to have trouble, that creature of mine. He is not perfect or wise like me, but I love him and

I won't damn him for being confused. I can forgive a few things. He has got to work out his own happiness."

The theological original sin is better understood now. The serpent becomes extraneous and superfluous in the story, and the bad habit of punishing children for their ancestors' crimes need not be repeated. Original sin is the entirety of our animal heritage from the days of our creation, all the genes, good, bad, and indifferent, that we carry in ourselves since the day at birth. The sin lies in the conflicts and discords. This sin, this lack of perfection, this fumbling and forgetting and aimless searching for good but never quite attaining it, this vast discord of man resulting in wars and slaughter, the stamp of greed and folly, pettiness, selfishness, shortsightedness, exhibited by statesmen and diplomats who, for all their learning, cannot bring us the peace and security the world wants—all this muddle of noble aspirations and sad failures comes from the very nature of our soul. The human soul, we have learned, is nine-tenths subliminal urges representing the animal heritage of millions of years, and considerably less than one-tenth conscious reason, which has had great development only since ten thousand years ago. This sin which we carry within ourselves from our birth is strictly original in the sense that it is hereditary, and that is all that the medieval theologians perceived and meant by that word. They perceived well enough that men had these wicked impulses prompting them from within and that was the way they were born. Modern psychology has thrown considerable light on the nature of these dark, primordial forces. Myths, are they? They are nine tenths of our minds, your mind and my mind.

To speak quite simply, man's original sin is no more than the sum total of all the instincts of the race for survival with which every individual is endowed in genes the moment he is conceived in his mother's womb. They are the instincts of sex, and hunger and fighting, which necessitate anger, fear, jealousy, cunning, and hatred, all contributing toward, and necessary for, the perpetuation of the race and the preservation of the individual's life. What a collection of different and difficult things the word "instinct" is made to do duty for, only the biologist fully appreciates it; it includes the beaver's cunning in building a dam, the squirrel's instinctive wile in hiding his food underground for winter, the capacity for social co-operation and organization in ants and bees, the migration of birds, and the urge of an Atlantic eel to go on a five-hundred-mile voyage to the fiords of Norway and lay his spawn, all enormously complicated processes carried by a kind of race memory, without even a word of reminder from the individual's mother on her deathbed.

As all animals obey their instincts for survival, they are all satisfied. What distinguishes men from animals is the rise of self-consciousness and reason. This rise of reason comes very late in history, but it produces two important results, one intellectual and one moral. First, reason, or the conscious self, begins to exercise criticism on the functions of man's subconscious instincts and to reshape his own life according to its notion of goodness, fitness, and beauty; second, it sometimes exercises a veto on the instinctive self for what seems to be lacking in those desirable qualities, thus assuming moral responsibility for its actions. All birds are satisfied with their lives; only man is an exception; reason's dissatisfaction, its criticism and its desire to reshape man's life never end.

Man had no idea, until modern biology and psychology showed him, how complicated, how deep and irresistible and tyrannous, and at the same time how difficult even to grasp and comprehend, those instincts of the collective unconscious can be. It seems to me that Santayana's "vegetative dream" of man and C. G. Jung's "collective unconscious" are virtually the same thing. We now have merely to take it for granted that such complicated and tyrannical race instincts and race memories do exist. Man went on comfortably assuming that he acted in the light of reason, and until modern psychology probed his soul's depths, he had no idea that the subconscious self is still our ruler, whose forces are described as dark, cavernous, despotic, and practically "autonomous." The soul or psyche, then, would comprise this conscious and this unconscious self, and a continual war is going on between the life of reason and the life of instinct, from which the notion of sin is seen as apparent. St. Paul, without the help of Freud, could have meant by the "spiritual man" and the "natural man" only this distinction of conscious reason and the animal impulses and instincts of the old Adam. But so extraordinary are the operations of the subconscious, racial instincts that psychoanalysis has to create almost a mythology to explain them, personifying Eros, Libido, Logos, Animus and Anima because they act as such mysterious forces.[5]

Perhaps one ought to add, before leaving the subject of psychology, that there is a great deal of loose talk and triviality and trumpery in this field, which passes out of the realm of science into popular quackery. The immense fraud in the name of Freud is unbelievable. I have read a newspaper report of an American professor of psychology who analyzes the different ways of putting out cigarette butts and deduces the most uncomfortable conclusions for all of us smokers. By any of the half-dozen ways we may crush a cigarette butt we are caught either with a sadistic instinct, a repression or frustrated ego, or just a bland antisocial, selfish, irresponsible complex, so that the only way out of it is not to smoke at all. Is it too much to say that such fraud is not Freud? I want to be kind and sociable, but I want so much to say that a lot of modern psychology is often a study of the moron, for the moron, and by the moron that I might as well say it outright. This is a book on American wisdom, and wisdom is often merely the refusal to swallow humbug. It is refreshing to read James Thurber's book, *Let Your Mind Alone,* especially the chapters, "Sex ex Machina," and "The Conscious vs. the Unconscious." He is somewhat hard on Louis E. Bisch, M.D., Ph.D., there, but we will repress our laughter, think straight, and be strictly impersonal. A certain man forgot such things as winding the alarm clock or banking the furnace at night, with the result that there was no heat the next day (he was living in the

[5] Chinese understanding of the human soul divided it into *hun* and *p'o,* translated by Richard Wilhelm as *animus* and *anima.* According to the Chinese interpretation the *animus* is the male principle; it dwells in the eyes and is bright and active: the *anima* is the female principle; it dwells in the abdomen and is dark and earthbound. In other words, *anima* or *p'o* is no more than the race instincts binding us to this mortal life and eventually to death. Redemption lies in releasing the *hun* from the bondage of *p'o* of which there are seven, thus achieving its own immortality. C. G. Jung accepts this, but prefers to translate *hun* as corresponding to his *logos,* reserving *animus* exclusively for the conscious system of woman's mind. "The *animus,* on a lower level, is an inferior *logos,* a caricature of the differentiated masculine mind, just as the *anima,* on a lower level, is a caricature of the feminine *eros.*" See the important discussion of "Animus and Anima" in Jung's long commentary on Richard Wilhelm's *Secret of the Golden Flower,* Harcourt, Brace & Company, 1938, pp. 114–120.

But before the advent of modern psychology, it was the Hindus who had probed most into the regions of the urges of animal life, and the whole yoga doctrine is but an experiment to place under yoke or control these lower subconscious animal urges. Salvation lies in freeing the mind, *purusha,* from the baser gross mind-stuff, resulting in a feeling of joy and ecstasy.

country). Dr. Bisch concluded that in this case the unconscious was trying to tell him that he did not like living in the country although he consciously maintained that he did, for the good of the children. Thurber's Empirical Law No. 1, if I am not mistaken, tells us that any man can forget to fix the clock and the furnace, especially the furnace, because the clock is usually right there where it can be seen, whereas the furnace isn't.

There is that unfortunate Mr. C. who ran right into an automobile because he dashed forward, hesitated, and leaped back, and who was analyzed by Dr. Bisch as follows: "Sex hunger . . . Always keyed up and irritable because of it. Undoubtedly suffers from insomnia and when he does sleep his dream life must be productive, distorted and possibly frightening. Automobile, unquestionably, has sex significance for him. . . ." Now my first instinct is to distrust that scientific jargon, the *"possibly* frightening" and *"unquestionably* has sex significance"— words that remind me of magic formulas. Thurber contends that an automobile bearing down upon you is probably not a sex symbol, but an automobile bearing down upon you. Hurray for American wisdom! [6]

The tragedy of the American spirit is that, when a fad does come about, so many applaud because they do not understand and so few laugh at them for telling them what they already know. There is already a tendency to talk of "the coefficient of happiness," and "secondary factors of social response in the tertiary stage of pattern-stimuli reaction in a general conformity drift in any highly industrialized social organization." God bless these idiots! These psychologists and sociologists are making life too complicated for us, as if modern life were not complicated enough already! Everybody is telling me that I may have within my being either an inflated or a deflated ego, a couple of reflex actions, three or four fixations, a perhaps not altogether too singular mother-love complex, a dozen inhibitions concealed somewhere in my psyche, in addition to some mild manifestation of sadistic impulse on some totally and apparently irrelevant lines. I have the

---

[6] Thurber is equally felicitous in exposing self-help and success books in the same volume. A companion spirit is Irwin Edman, who treats of the same fads with the same candid humor in the chapter "We Superstitious Moderns" in *Adam, the Baby, and the Man from Mars.*

libido, the eros, the id, which are all like squids as far as I am concerned, and now I may have a peculiarly high stimuli response and perhaps am in the category of all great business executives who by all intelligence tests show an alarmingly low I.Q.—lower than the average Columbia freshmen. I must never say don't to my child for fear that I may establish an inhibition and be responsible for her persistent headaches forty years from now, and the child will grow up without inhibitions until he or she enters a business office and then at the age of twenty-two or twenty-three first learns that there are certain don'ts in life, the transgression of which neither life, nor God, nor society will condone.

3. WE SIMIANS

The foregoing parable of why Adam and Eve ate the apple is a preliminary to our understanding of Clarence Day's *This Simian World,* which must ever be considered a little classic essay on man, one of the most delectable the twentieth century has produced. It cannot be imitated and it cannot be repeated, and it could have been written only in the twentieth century. Clarence Day is one of the most perceptive of American writers (and to a less extent, perhaps James Thurber also), a kind of reassuring proof that the qualities of wisdom and gaiety have not departed from contemporary America. Bless their souls! Their spirit is still free, though Day was chained to bed by arthritis and Thurber suffers from acute eye trouble. No matter, their inner vision is thereby improved. Day saw what Henry Adams, with his nose glued to the grindstone of a materialistic theory of history, could never see at the end of three quarters of a century of learning and culture and impassioned quest for truth. No, not your bank presidents or your builders of empires or your laborious scholars can see the truth, but your arthritic patients, your crippled, blind, and semi-invalids, your Robert Louis Stevensons and Parkmans and Prescotts and Gamaliel Bradfords, see life with a clearer and better vision. William James said, "Yet so blind and dead does the clamor of our own practical interests make us to all other things, that it seems almost as if it were necessary to become worthless as a practical being, if one is to hope to attain to any breadth of insight into the impersonal worths as such, to have any perception of life's meaning on a large objective scale. Only your mystic, your dreamer, or your insolvent tramp or loafer can afford so sympathetic an occupation, an occupation which will change the usual standards of human value in the twinkling of an eye, giving to foolishness a place ahead of power, and laying low in a minute the distinctions which it takes a hard-working conventional man a lifetime to build up." [7]

Clarence Day's *This Simian World* is a formidable though delectable criticism of man's foibles, such as his disorderly and easily distracted mind, his incapacity for reflection, his health habits, and his polygamous habits. The longish essay should be read as a whole, and I have included a sizable amount on the theory that in any selection from that unique pen, the longer the selection, the longer will be the sustained delight for the reader. I have supplied the numbered headings; the reader will know what I mean—that these are the seven cardinal sins of mankind under attack. Such sins are not quite so damnable as to require the fire of purgatory; they include our laziness in just going out and looking at nature, instead of learning from her how to live, and our desire to stuff our minds with newspaper stories of murder and some of our amatory habits. But at least, they have this merit; they are all understandable by reason of our simian heritage. This piece is American irony at its best.

This Simian World

BY CLARENCE DAY

Imagine a prehistoric prophet observing these beings, and forecasting what kind of civilizations their descendants would build. Anyone could have foreseen certain parts of the simians' history: could have guessed that their curiosity would unlock for them, one by one, nature's doors, and—idly—bestow on them stray bits of valuable knowledge: could have pictured them spreading inquiringly all over the globe, stumbling on their inventions—and idly passing on and forgetting them.

(1) Disorderliness. To have to learn the same thing over and over

---

[7] William James, "On a Certain Blindness in Human Beings," *Talks to Teachers on Psychology.* Copyright, 1939, Henry James. Permission of Paul R. Reynolds & Son.

again wastes the time of a race. But this is continually necessary, with simians, because of their disorder. "Disorder," a prophet would have sighed: "that is one of their handicaps; one that they will never get rid of, whatever it costs. Having so much curiosity makes a race scatter-brained.

"Yes," he would have dismally continued, "it will be a queer mixture: these simians will attain to vast stores of knowledge, in time, that is plain. But after spending centuries groping to discover some art, in after-centuries they will now and then find it's forgotten. How incredible it would seem on other planets to hear of lost arts.

"There is a strong streak of triviality in them, which you don't see in cats. They won't have fine enough characters to concentrate on the things of most weight. They will talk and think far more of trifles than of what is important. Even when they are reasonably civilized, this will be so. Great discoveries sometimes will fail to be heard of, because too much else is; and many will thus disappear, and these men will not know it." *

Let me interrupt this lament to say a word for myself and my ancestors. It is easy to blame us as undiscriminating, but we are at least full of zest. And it's well to be interested, eagerly and intensely, in so many things, because there is often no knowing which may turn out important. We don't go around being interested on purpose, hoping to profit by it, but a profit may come. And anyway it is generous of us not to be too self-absorbed. Other creatures go to the other extreme to an amazing extent. They are ridiculously oblivious to what is going on. The smallest ant in the garden will ignore the largest woman who visits it. She is a huge and most dangerous super-mammoth in relation to him, and her tread shakes the earth; but he has no time to be bothered, investigating such-like phenomena. He won't even get out of her way. He has his work to do, hang it. . . .

We of course observe everything, or try to. We could spend our lives looking on. Consider our museums for instance: they are a sign of our breed. It makes us smile to see birds, like the magpie, with a mania for this collecting—but only monkeyish beings could reverence museums as we do, and pile such heterogeneous trifles and quantities in them. Old furniture, egg-shells, watches, bits of stone. . . . And next

---

* We did rescue Mendel's from the dust heap; but perhaps it was an exception. *Note by C. D.*

door, a "menagerie." Though our victory over all other animals is now aeons old, we still bring home captives and exhibit them caged in our cities. And when a species dies out—or is crowded (by us) off the planet—we even collect the bones of the vanquished and show them like trophies.

Curiosity is a valuable trait. It will make the simians learn many things. But the curiosity of a simian is as excessive as the toil of an ant. Each simian will wish to know more than his head can hold, let alone ever deal with; and those whose minds are active will wish to know everything going. It would stretch a god's skull to accomplish such an ambition, yet simians won't like to think it's beyond their powers. Even small tradesmen and clerks, no matter how thrifty, will be eager to buy costly encyclopedias, or books of all knowledge. Almost every simian family, even the dullest, will think it is due to themselves to keep all knowledge handy.

Their idea of a liberal education will therefore be a great hodge-podge; and he who narrows his field and digs deep will be viewed as an alien. . . .

(2) *Love of chatter.* One of their curious educational ideas—but a natural one—will be shown in the efforts they will make to learn more than one "language." They will set their young to spending a decade or more of their lives in studying duplicate systems—whole systems—of chatter. Those who thus learn several different ways to say the same things, will command much respect, and those who learn many will be looked on with awe—by true simians. And persons without this accomplishment will be looked down on a little, and will actually feel quite apologetic about it themselves.

. . . Heavens, what a genius for tongues these simians have! Where another race, after the most frightful discord and pains, might have slowly constructed *one* language before this earth grew cold, this race will create literally hundreds, each complete in itself, and many of them with quaint little systems of writing attached. And the owners of this linguistic gift are so humble about it, they will marvel at bees, for their hives, and at beavers' mere dams.

(3) *Love of purposeless reading.* To return, however, to their fear of being too narrow, in going to the other extreme they will run to in-

credible lengths. Every civilized simian, every day of his life, in addition to whatever older facts he has picked up, will wish to know all the news of all the world. If he felt any true concern to know it, this would be rather fine of him: it would imply such a close solidarity on the part of this genius. (Such a close solidarity would seem crushing, to others; but that is another matter.) It won't be true concern, however, it will be merely a blind inherited instinct. He'll forget what he's read, the very next hour, or moment. Yet there he will faithfully sit, the ridiculous creature, reading of bombs in Spain or floods in Thibet, and especially insisting on all the news he can get of the kind our race loved when they scampered and fought in the forest, news that will stir his most primitive simian feelings,—wars, accidents, love affairs, and family quarrels.

To feed himself with this largely purposeless provender, he will pay thousands of simians to be reporters of such events day and night; and they will report them on such a voluminous scale as to smother or obscure more significant news altogether. Great printed sheets will be read by every one every day; and even the laziest of this lazy race will not think it labor to perform this toil. They won't like to eat in the morning without their papers, such slaves they will be to this droll greed for knowing. They won't even think it is droll, it is so in their blood.

Their swollen desire for investigating everything about them, including especially other people's affairs, will be quenchless. Few will feel that they really are "fully informed"; and all will give much of each day all their lives to the news.

Books too will be used to slake this unappeasable thirst. They will actually hold books in deep reverence. Books! Bottled chatter! things that some other simian has formerly said. They will dress them in costly bindings, keep them under glass, and take an affecting pride in the number they read. Libraries,—store-houses of books,—will dot their world. The destruction of one will be a crime against civilization. (Meaning, again, a simian civilization.) Well, it is an offense to be sure—a barbaric offense. But so is defacing forever a beautiful landscape; and they won't even notice that sometimes; they won't shudder anyway, the way they instinctively do at the loss of a "library.". . .

Those who know many facts will feel wise! They will despise those who don't. They will even believe, many of them, that knowledge is power. Unfortunate dupes of this saying will keep on reading, ambitiously, till they have stunned their native initiative, and made their thoughts weak; and will then wonder dazedly what in the world is the matter, and why the great power they were expecting to gain fails to appear. Again, if they ever forget what they read, they'll be worried. Those who *can* forget—those with fresh eyes who have swept from their minds such facts as the exact month and day that their children were born, or the numbers on houses, or the names (the mere meaningless labels) of the people they meet,—will be urged to go live in sanitariums or see memory doctors!

(4) Aversion to deep thinking. By nature their itch is rather for knowing, than for understanding or thinking. Some of them will learn to think, doubtless, and even to concentrate, but their eagerness to acquire those accomplishments will not be strong or insistent. Creatures whose mainspring is curiosity will enjoy the accumulating of facts, far more than the pausing at times to reflect on those facts. If they do not reflect on them, of course they'll be slow to find out about the ideas and relationships lying behind them; and they will be curious about those ideas; so you would suppose they'd reflect. But deep thinking is painful. It means they must channel the spready rivers of their attention. That cannot be done without discipline and drills for the mind; and they will abhor doing that; their minds will work better when they are left free to run off at tangents.

Compare them in this with other species. Each has its own kind of strength. To be compelled to be so quick-minded as the simians would be torture, to cows. Cows could dwell on one idea, week by week, without trying at all; but they'd all have brain-fever in an hour at a simian tea. A super-cow people would revel in long thoughtful books on abstruse philosophical subjects, and would sit up late reading them. Most of the ambitious simians who try it—out of pride—go to sleep. The typical simian brain is supremely distractable, and it's really too jumpy by nature to endure much reflection.

Therefore many more of them will be well-informed than sagacious.

This will result in their knowing most things far too soon, at too early a stage of civilization to use them aright. They will learn to make valuable explosives at a stage in their growth, when they will use them not only in industries, but for killing brave men. They will devise ways to mine coal efficiently, in enormous amounts, at a stage when they won't know enough to conserve it, and will waste their few stores. They will use up a lot of it in a simian habit called travel. This will consist in queer little hurried runs over the globe, to see ten thousand things in the hope of thus filling their minds.

Their minds will be full enough. Their intelligence will be active and keen. It will have a constant tendency however to outstrip their wisdom. Their intelligence will enable them to build great industrial systems before they have the wisdom and goodness to run them aright. They will form greater political empires than they will have strength to guide. They will endlessly quarrel about which is the best scheme of government, without stopping to realize that learning to govern comes first. (The average simian will imagine he knows without learning.)

The natural result will be industrial and political wars. In a world of unmanageable structures, wild smashes must come.

(5) *Love of gadgets, especially talking gadgets.* Inventions will come so easily to simians (in comparison with all other creatures) and they will take such childish pleasure in monkeying around, making inventions, that their many devices will be more of a care than a comfort. In their homes a large part of their time will have to be spent keeping their numerous ingenuities in good working order—their elaborate bell-ringing arrangements, their locks and their clocks. In the field of science to be sure, this fertility in invention will lead to a long list of important and beautiful discoveries: telescopes and the calculus, radiographs, and the spectrum. Discoveries great enough, almost, to make angels of them. But here again their simian-ness will cheat them of half of their dues, for they will neglect great discoveries of the truest importance, and honor extravagantly those of less value and splendor if only they cater especially to simian traits.

To consider examples: A discovery that helps them to talk, just to talk, more and more, will be hailed by these beings as one of the highest of triumphs. Talking to each other over wires will come in this class. The lightning when harnessed and tamed will be made to trot round, conveying the most trivial cacklings all day and night.

Huge seas of talk of every sort and kind, in print, speech, and writing, will roll unceasingly over their civilized realms, involving an unbelievable waste in labor and time, and sapping the intelligence talk is supposed to upbuild. In a simian civilization, great halls will be erected for lectures, and great throngs will actually pay to go inside at night to hear some self-satisfied talk-maker chatter for hours. Almost any subject will do for a lecture, or talk; yet very few subjects will be counted important enough for the average man to do any *thinking* on them, off by himself. . . .

(6) *No respect for their bodies.* Discoveries in surgery and medicine will also be over-praised. The reason will be that the race will so need these discoveries. Unlike the great cats, simians tend to undervalue the body. Having less self-respect, less proper regard for their egos, they care less than the cats do for the casing of the ego,—the body. The more civilized they grow the more they will let their bodies deteriorate. They will let their shoulders stoop, their lungs shrink, and their stomachs grow fat. No other species will be quite so deformed and distorted. Athletics they will watch, yes, but on the whole sparingly practice. Their snuffy old scholars will even be proud to decry them. Where once the simians swung high through forests, or scampered like deer, their descendants will plod around farms, or mince along city streets, moving constrictedly, slowly, their litheness half gone.

They will think of Nature as "something to go out and look at." They will try to live wholly apart from her and forget they're her sons. Forget? They will even deny it, and declare themselves sons of God. In spite of her wonders they will regard Nature as somehow too humble to be the true parent of such prominent people as simians. They will lose all respect for the dignity of fair Mother Earth, and whisper to each other she is an evil and indecent old person. They will snatch at her gifts, pry irreverently into her mysteries, and ignore half the warnings they get from her about how to live.

Ailments of every kind will abound among such folk, inevitably, and they will resort to extraordinary expedients in their search for relief. Although squeamish as a race about inflicting much pain in cold blood, they will systematically infect other animals with their own rank diseases, or cut out other animals' organs, or kill and dissect them, hoping thus to learn how to offset their neglect of themselves.

Conditions among them will be such that this will really be necessary. Few besides impractical sentimentalists will therefore oppose it. But the idea will be to gain health by legerdemain, by a trick, instead of by taking the trouble to live healthy lives.

Strange barrack-like buildings called hospitals will stand in their cities, where their trick-men, the surgeons, will slice them right open when ill; and thousands of zealous young pharmacists will mix little drugs, which thousands of wise-looking simians will firmly prescribe. Each generation will change its mind as to these drugs, and laugh at all former opinions; but each will use some of them, and each will feel assured that in this respect they know the last word.

And, in obstinate blindness, this people will wag their poor heads, and attribute their diseases not to simian-ness but to civilization.

(7) *Sexuality.* The simians are always being stirred by desire and passion. It constantly excites them, constantly runs through their minds. Wild or tame, primitive or cultured, this is a brand of the breed. Other species have times and seasons for sexual matters, but the simian-folk are thus preoccupied all the year round.

This super-abundance of desire is not necessarily good or bad, of itself. But to shape it for the best it will have to be studied—and faced. This they will not do. Some of them won't like to study it, deeming it bad—deeming it bad yet yielding constantly to it. Others will hesitate because they will deem it so sacred, or will secretly fear that study might show them it ought to be curbed. . . .

A doctor, who was making a study of monkeys, once told me that he was trying experiments that bore on the polygamy question. He had a young monkey named Jack who had mated with a female named Jill; and in another cage another newly-wedded pair, Arabella and Archer. Each pair seemed absorbed in each other, and devoted and happy. They even hugged each other at mealtime and exchanged bits of food.

After a time their transports grew less fiery, and their affections less fixed. Archer got a bit bored. He was decent about it, though, and when Arabella cuddled beside him he would more or less perfunctorily embrace her. But when he forgot, she grew cross.

The same thing occurred a little later in the Jack and Jill cage, only there it was Jill who became a little tired of Jack.

Soon each pair was quarreling. They usually made up, pretty soon, and started loving again. But it petered out; each time more quickly.

Meanwhile the two families had become interested in watching each other. When Jill had repulsed Jack, and he had moped about it awhile, he would begin staring at Arabella, over opposite, and trying to attract her attention. This got Jack in trouble all around. Arabella indignantly made faces at him and then turned her back; and as for Jill, she grew furious, and tore out his fur.

But in the next stage, they even stopped hating each other. Each pair grew indifferent.

Then the doctor put Jack in with Arabella, and Archer with Jill. Arabella promptly yielded to Jack. New devotion. More transports. Jill and Archer were shocked. Jill clung to the bars of her cage, quivering, and screaming remonstrance; and even blasé Archer chattered angrily at some of the scenes. Then the doctor hung curtains between the cages to shut out the view. Jill and Archer, left to each other, grew interested. They soon were inseparable.

The four monkeys, thus re-distributed, were now happy once more, and full of new liveliness and spirit. But before very long, each pair quarreled—and made up—and quarreled—and then grew indifferent, and had cynical thoughts about life.

At this point, the doctor put them back with their original mates.

And—they met with a rush! Gave cries of recognition and joy, like faithful souls reunited. And when they were tired, they affectionately curled up together; and hugged each other even at mealtime, and exchanged bits of food. . . .

To be sure, these particular monkeys were living in idleness. This corresponds to living in high social circles with us, where men do not have to work, and lack some of the common incentives to home-building. The experiment was not conclusive.

Still, even in low social circles—

—*This Simian World* (IX-XII)

4. WHAT ARE WE MAKING OF OURSELVES?

All this is very illuminating; it is good to know oneself. But Clarence Day does not for one moment suggest that we should go down on all fours, since to be down on all fours in a *quadrumana* is hardly a more dignified position than being on four legs. We are caught somewhere on the road of evolution between the ape and the angel, the "angel stage" being the stage where man has got full control of his substrata of racial instincts or eliminated them and does not use his reason merely to give reason for what his subliminal self wants him to do. Any student of biology knows that the angel stage is very distant; I myself doubt that it is desirable, with reason operating in a sort of vacuum of instincts, but anyway eons must pass before the strong instincts for race and individual survival can be eliminated or become atrophied. We shall have ghosts of philosophers walking the earth, then, but the strong probability is that before men cease to hate and to become angry and to fence off their enemies, mankind will have perished, and some of the better equipped brutes will have stepped into our place. All this is therefore idle speculation. Meanwhile, the important question is, what are we making of ourselves?

The world of James Thurber is perhaps somewhat kaleidoscopic, but his dogs are so human and his men and women can be so canine or feline at times. Sometimes he talks of bowerbirds, sometimes he talks of husbands and wives, and in many unexpected places he becomes illuminating and important. His intelligence is of a different order from that of dutiful writers; his perceptions are quicker, his imagination bolder, and the burden of his spirit is lighter because he carries it easily. As a Chinese I am all for naturalism, provided it is naturalism of the Thurber-Day variety, that is, a frank recognition of the brotherhood of animalkind, mankind included, or of the Santayana variety of skepticism and animal faith, with its sweet irony and also its courage and open-eyed wisdom. Both varieties have a down-to-earth quality that high-flown theories and dogmatic theology lack. When Thurber's mind rubs against that of some dutiful, hard-working, unimaginative statistical mind, which is occupied only with its zeros and percentages, the friction usually provides some beautiful sparks.

Can mankind improve itself?

BY JAMES THURBER

Now that Man, in spite of his sins, stands a fair chance of lasting another twelve thousand million years, other things being equal, it might be interesting to speculate on what he is going to be like at the end of that time, or even in one twelve-thousandth of that time. There is always, of course, the chance, sun or no sun, that the insects may get him within the next two or three hundred years, but after worrying about this since 1907, I have come to the conclusion that Man will finally master the tiny creatures, in spite of their greater agility and superior cleverness. My confidence in Man's ultimate supremacy over the weevil and the slug has been greatly strengthened by the findings of the late Dr. Frederick Tilney, the eminent brain specialist. After many years of research, Dr. Tilney came to the conclusion that Man is using only one-fourth of his stock of fourteen billion brain cells. In short, he is using only 3,500,000,000 brain cells. Offhand, to the layman, to you and me, this might seem like a great many brain cells to be using, since it runs into ten figures and we Americans are impressed by anything that runs into more than four. We must, however, fight against the kind of complacency which would lead us to sit back and be satisfied with the use of only three and a half billion brain cells. When we wake up in the morning we should not say to ourselves, gleefully, "I am using more than three billion brain cells. Good Lord, think of it!" We should, on the contrary, say, "I am using only one-fourth of the brain cells with which a generous Providence has provided me. Is that any way to live, for God's sake?"

It was Dr. Tilney's belief that when Man begins to use all his brain cells—in a thousand years, say, or ten million—he will become wise enough to put an end to wars, depressions, recessions, and allied evils. Dr. Tilney seemed to believe that a man four times as mentally powerful as we are today would, if handed a rifle by some throwback major who was still using only 3,500,000,000 brain cells, exclaim, "Don't be a fourth-wit, my man," and refuse to go to war. I am sorry that I cannot go the whole way with Dr. Tilney in his sanguine prophecies.

What, I keep saying to myself, is to keep Man from becoming four times as ornery, four times as sly and crafty, four times as full of devilishly ingenious devices for the extinction of his species? In the history of mankind the increase of no kind of power has, so far as I can find out, ever moved naturally and inevitably in the direction of the benign. It has, as a matter of fact, almost always tended in the direction of the malignant; don't ask me why, it just has. This tendency, it seems to me, would be especially true of the power of the mind, since it is that very power which is behind all the deviltry Man is now up to and always has been up to.

Let us turn our attention for a moment to those prehistoric Americans, Sandia man, Folsom man, and the Minnesota Maid, whose fossilized remains have been dug up from the substrata of this ancient continent. I have no way of knowing for sure, but I venture to say that the cells which were actually functioning in the brains of Sandia, Folsom, and the Maid did not number more than 875,000,000, or about one-fourth as many as are working today in your brain or mine or Mussolini's. Now, it should follow, if Dr. Tilney was on sound ground, that the man of today is four times as pacific and four times as economically sound as Sandia and Folsom. Anybody who has more than eleven hundred cells working in his cortex knows that this is not true. Man, as pacifist and economist, has gone steadily from bad to worse with the development of his brain power through the ages. I view with alarm, therefore, any future increase of his cortical activity.

Let us proceed to another dolorous conclusion. *Time,* the weekly scientific journal, reported some time ago that the Minnesota Maid "apparently fell or was thrown into a Glacial Period lake." How *Time,* always infallible, knew that the Maid either fell or was thrown into the lake I don't know. I should have thought there was also the possibility that, driven to distraction by people who were using only 875,000,000 brain cells, she may have swum quietly out into the lake to drown, of her own accord. However, let us assume that she was thrown. Now, you would think, if Dr. Tilney was right, that the increase of Man's functioning brain cells in the millions of years which have elapsed since the Maid's death would have prompted Man to refrain from throwing Woman into lakes. This is, unhappily, not the case. I estimate, after sitting for half an hour thinking, that more than four times as many women are thrown into lakes in America nowadays as were thrown into them during the era in which the Minnesota Maid lived. How many, at this rate of increase, will be thrown into American lakes twelve thousand million years from now, I leave to your imagination.

The only note of cheer I can strike, in conclusion, is to point out the possibility that, in spite of Dr. Tilney's beliefs, Man may never be able to use more than one-fourth of his brain cells. In that case he is not likely to become much more troublesome than he is now. He is certain, at any rate, not to become four times as troublesome. This is, I know, not much in the way of hope for the future, but it is, after all, something. At any rate, it is all I have to offer.

—My World—and Welcome to It

Chapter IV

THE RHYTHM OF LIFE

I. WHERE IS WOMAN?

ANY realistic philosophy of life must deal with certain given biological facts of human existence—the facts of birth and death, youth and old age and the difference between man and woman. Philosophy cannot alter these given facts; the wisest thing philosophy can do is to recognize them. It can, by seeing human life as a rhythm or a natural cycle, like all other phenomena of the universe, enable man to reconcile himself to that rhythm as something both natural and good. The day has its dawn and sunset, and is infinitely the richer for them. The year has its spring and autumn, and is infinitely the more enjoyable for them. Why should not man's life, too, have its spring of youth, its summer of manhood, its autumn of maturity, and its winter of old age and repose?

"A son," says Tselai in a parable by Chuangtse, "must go whithersoever his parents bid him, East, West, North or South. *Yin* and *Yang* are no other than a man's parents. If *Yin* and *Yang* bid me die quickly, and I demur, then the fault is mine, not theirs. The Great (God or Universe) gives me this form, this toil in manhood, this repose in old age, this rest in death. Surely that which is such a kind arbiter of my life is the best arbiter of my death." By falling in step with nature's universal rhythm, one can accept these given facts of life not only with calm resignation, but even with a naturalistic comfort and satisfaction.

Men think a great deal about women, but the writers seem to say very little of it, or very little of it that is not inane. That is to be expected, because when a man speaks about woman, he is no longer a poor mortal but becomes a representative of half of humanity and judge of the other half. It would seem that both these roles are rather difficult for any man to fill with distinction. The only certainty he has

67

is that man is always right. He immediately takes the position of an outside critic and judge, similar to a traveler's book about a foreign country and not without his faults of supercilious criticism and patronizing (and misplaced) praise. A mild sort of sex prejudice is there, too, similar to race prejudice, a sort of covert war between the sexes as to which is superior, without ever agreeing upon a standard of superiority. When a magazine runs an article "What Is Wrong with Man?" or "What Is Wrong with Woman?" we know the subject is controversial, surcharged with immense possibilities. It seldom occurs to the writers that women are extraordinarily like the male human beings. They love flummery; they get out of engagements for parties, get excited about nothing, don't know the meaning of the words they use, tell secrets, yes, and sometimes betray their friends—exactly like men. When I read such criticisms, I say to myself, "Why, wonderful; they are just like ourselves!" And so we come to the paradox that the only correct way to write about women is to regard them as men, that sisters are seldom better than their brothers, but the brothers are also seldom superior to their sisters, that apart from a plus and a minus here and there, women are extraordinarily like the good, glorious, cocksure, and vain male animal.

Both men and women love to exaggerate the differences. Women are as much sinners in this respect as the men. I share Heywood Broun's resentment against the women's facile assumption that fathers can never hold babies, that there is a great deal to it which a father can never learn. As for the sixth sense, I see as many women lose at the roulette table as men, the sixth sense being the inability to tell clearly why you want to do a thing when you do it. I believe women think and feel on the whole very much as men do, that mentally there is much less sex difference than physically, although some women like to encourage the men to think otherwise. So if the question is asked, "Where is woman in this book?" the answer is that she is everywhere, sharing all men's problems of politics and religion and love. James Branch Cabell was for "domnei," or woman worship, for putting woman on a pedestal—a dangerous attitude, but then he was also for hero worship of men, for showing man in knight's armor riding on a high horse. He was speaking about romance, about women in art and literature. In real life, any woman would be grateful for being accepted as an ordinary human being, like any man, perhaps at most slightly raised on a two-inch heel, not much higher, and certainly not on a pedestal. It just won't work. Woman shares all man's foibles, all man's pettiness and vanity, as she shares all his hopes and ambitions. Woman is venal; woman is vain; woman is realistic. What do we take her for? An angel? The falsehood lies in the implication that man isn't all these things.

E. B. White, angered by the patronizing inanities of a man writing in *Harper's* on "Getting Along with Women," wrote a reply in which he succeeded in the rare accomplishment of treating woman as man, to the point where the question of getting along with women does not even come up. My impression is that he merely likes them a lot. Such a point of view, I believe, is really civilized. In addition, E. B. White is natural here; he just pours himself out, and the result is delightful.

Getting Along with Women
BY E. B. WHITE

Who is this wonder man in *Harper's Magazine,* this prince of good fellows who gets along with women? Did any of you read that article? It was in the October issue. I mean the article called "Getting Along with Women," written by a man who shows right off the bat what women think of him by signing the piece "Anonymous." He gets along so well with women he dassn't even sign his name. Well, *I* dast. My name is White, and I *don't* get along with women, and I think anybody who got along with women the way this man Anonymous tells you to would be a smack. I would rather be at continual odds with women, and am.

One thing that struck me right away about Anonymous's article was that he apparently has no real taste for women anyway, and of course it's easy enough to get along with women if you don't care for them. It simply isn't a problem. Anonymous says some very fine things about women, but they don't ring true. They haven't got what I call "glow." According to Anonymous, women don't even belong to the same race as men. He says that what you've got to have to get along is the ability to "see in every woman something of the woman eternal." Well, that's just what I can't do. I see in every woman the woman temporary, or the woman dishevelled, or the woman terribly attractive, or the woman beloved. The reason I can't see the woman eternal is that I don't think woman is a day more eternal than I am.

Another thing he says about women is that they are the "keepers of the life-tides." I think that is silly, too. I've never seen a woman with a life-tide, and if a woman did have a life-tide, she probably couldn't keep it, because if she's anything like my Gloria, she can't keep anything. I can just see Gloria trying to keep a life-tide when she doesn't even know where she put the key to the front door except she thinks it was in her purse. It is as keeper of the life-tides, according to Old Know-it-all, that woman has a truly great kinship with Nature, far greater than man's. "Once let a man understand this relationship between woman and Nature, and he will bow before her outbursts and condone them." Oh, is that so? Well, sir, I have found out that when a woman has burst out at me, it wasn't because of any kinship with Nature, it was usually because I damn well had it coming to me. Furthermore, if anybody around my house is going to have kinship with Nature, *I'll* handle it. That's understood. I am just as "natural" as any woman, and I'm far naturaler than a lot. I know enough about Nature not to call her Mother, for one thing. I call her Father. Old Father Nature. Good old Pop! I have been out messing around with old Pop Nature when a lot of my fine women friends were safe indoors with their lares, penates, bridge lamps, and old copies of *Harper's*. No, woman isn't the keeper of any tides. Woman is, on the whole, scared to death of tides, particularly the strong tides which characterize the eastern section of the coast of Maine around Mount Desert Island.

But I'll let that go. Let's see how a man should behave to get along with women, according to old Daddy Anonymous, the king of Get Alongers.

"If you really are intent on getting along well with your woman," he says, "anything you do to help things along is justifiable." Now isn't that just fine? For the sake of getting along, anything goes. Anonymous, even if I were intent on getting along with my (as you call her) woman, I could think of a dozen things which I would not consider justifiable. And so could she. In fact, she could probably think of

more things than I could, which is another reason we don't get along—
she's always got the edge on me, that way. You want to know some of
the things I would not consider justifiable? Lying is one. Acting different from the way I feel is two. Giving in by so much as an inch in
a matter of principle is three. Offering her a handkerchief is four. And
if you want the other eight, you know my name.

"Keep your head," says Anonymous, "and you'll be able to manage
her all right." Manage her, eh? That gives you a pretty good idea of
what the author of "Getting Along with Women" means by getting
along with women. He means managing women. He is talking not
about marital harmony or sexual rapport or general amicability, he is
talking about managerial prowess. I am not quibbling here, or turning
a chance phrase to my advantage: Anonymous mentions "managing"
over and over again. In the very first paragraph he introduces a poor,
inept male who couldn't get along with women. "The man," he says,
"has not managed her." And again: "Most women can be managed
with praise." Manage, manage, manage. The picture I got of Anonymous's woman, after reading his article, was of a little girl whom
he kept out in the kitchen and fed on Ken-L Ration. Once in a while
he gave her a couple of life-tides to play with, and some praise to keep
her from screaming and annoying the neighbors, and all the time he
kept murmuring to himself what a wonderful creature she was (for
him to manage), and seeing in her "something of the woman eternal,"
a kin of Nature, warmly human, wanting to be possessed and "en-
wrapped in the strong mantle of maleness." Not just wrapped, mind
you, but *en*wrapped. But does he ever go out there and enwrap her?
Not that I can make out.

I just don't understand this man. He says men are imaginative,
women are realistic. "For confirmation of this truism," he says, "I give
you Hans Christian Andersen, the Brothers Grimm, Andrew Lang,
Homer, Virgil, and the nameless spinner of Scheherazade's adventures." O.K., Anonymous, two can play at gift-giving. I give you Marie
de France, the Sisters Brontë, Beatrix Potter, Selma Lagerlöf, Lady
Murasaki, Laura E. Richards, Helen Bannerman, Lily F. Wesselhoeft,
and Beatrice Lillie. No, on second thought I think I'll *keep* Beatrice
Lillie. You don't deserve her, and I doubt if you could manage her.

This fellow Anonymous not only claims to know all about women, he seems to know all about us men, too. All about me, I don't doubt. Listen to this one: "One chief reason for the failure of a man in love to get along with his woman seems to him of course to be a tendency on her part to ask too much. . . . He grows resentful, they quarrel, and then what? He turns to some other woman for comfort." I do, eh? All right, Smarty, what's the other woman's name? Come on, what's her name? You're pretty sure of yourself, aren't you? I bet you'd be surprised to know what I *do* turn to, when I grow resentful and quarrel. It's not another woman, either. It's a pineapple maraschino nut sundae with a whiskey base. Ha!

He seems to know all about my carnal side, too. He speaks of certain men (and I can only assume he means me) who "think of women primarily as bodies sent for man's gratification. . . . Given a pretty woman and a drink, and they become clumsily chivalrous." Well, Sir Galahad, it might interest you to learn that given a pretty woman and a drink, I do *not* become clumsily chivalrous, I become grace itself. I have friends who keep the finest liquors and the prettiest women always on hand, just so they can give them to me and see how beautifully I carry on. How d'ya like that, Anonymous? And whether I think of a woman as "primarily" or "secondarily" a body sent for man's gratification is quite possibly a point too fine for an old Get Alonger like you to get mixed up with, you old Amicable Relations Establisher, you. Don't start me off about the body of woman, please, or this will grow too esoteric for anything.

After he has explained how to get along with women you love, Anonymous plunges on into new fields: he explains how to get along with women you *don't* love—as though anybody cared. For heaven's sake, who wants to get along with a woman in whom he's not interested? I say chuck her and get one you *do* love, one who fascinates you so completely that getting along with her is practically out of the question. But not Anonymous. No, he says: "The clever man lets the same qualities in him be apparent to all women, whether sweetheart, friend, or business associate—his maleness, his consideration, his understanding. And toward all women alike, if he be wise, he exhibits a genuine appreciation, just as in their various relationships he displays a sense of humor." Anonymous apparently got his idea about the necessity of having a sense of humor from a friend of his named Charley

Calder, whom he quotes. Charley says that a man "has got to be dip-lomatic, and he's got to have a sense of humor." I think Charley Calder is just as odd a character, in his own way, as Anonymous. Diplomacy and a sense of humor, to my mind, are mutually exclusive qualities. They do not coexist. Sense of humor is just another name for sense of directness; diplomacy means sense of indirectness, or mild chicanery. I don't see how a man can have both, or, if he had them, how he could use 'em against a woman.

But enough of this tedious theme! I will leave Anonymous to his amicability, his sense of humor, his little hypocrisies and artifices. It's five o'clock. Twilight is settling down on the city, and with it comes the infinitely alluring prospect of going forth to meet a pretty woman, and of not making the slightest effort to get along with her, and of succeeding.

—*Quo Vadimus*

2. THE RACE OF LIFE

"Our brains are seventy-year clocks," says Oliver Wendell Holmes, Sr. "The Angel of Life winds them up once for all, then closes the case, and gives the key into the hand of the Angel of the Resurrection. Tic-tac! tic-tac! go the wheels of thought; our will cannot stop them; they cannot stop themselves; sleep cannot still them; madness only makes them go faster; death alone can break into the case, and, seizing the ever-swinging pendulum, which we call the heart, silence at last the clicking of the terrible escapement we have carried so long beneath our wrinkled foreheads."

What Dr. Holmes expresses graphically by the image of a clock Chuangtse expresses in a more poetic language. "For whether the soul is locked up in sleep or whether in waking hours the body moves, we are striving and struggling with the immediate circumstances. Some are easy-going and leisurely, some are deep and cunning, and some are secretive. Now we are frightened over petty fears, now disheartened and dismayed over some great terror. Now the mind flies forth like an arrow from a crossbow, to be the arbiter of right and wrong. Now it stays behind as if sworn to an oath, to hold on to what it has secured. Then, as under autumn and winter's blight, comes gradual decay, and submerged in its own occupations, it keeps running its course, never to return. Finally, worn out and imprisoned, it is choked up like an old drain, and the failing mind shall not see light again."[1]

So we are in this race of life, from childhood, manhood, to old age and death, colored by friendships, achievements, failures, and relative successes, followed by the imperceptible stealthy footsteps of time. It would be good to be able to say, "The years draw to a close and I am content." There is pathos and humor in it. Perhaps somewhere after forty, a wrinkle creeps up here and a straggling white hair puts in its appearance there, marking the approach of life's early autumn. Perhaps the symphony of autumn's colors is richer, more desperate, more flambuoyant than that of summer, and we catch a little breath but know that this is the universal rhythm of life. How to fall in step with life's rhythms is perhaps the very center of a good philosophy of life, which can bring the peace of content. The hoop that we used to trundle as a boy has lost its charm, and certain marks of value, like the college diploma or some ribbon or insignificant prize for which we fought with all our energies as if life itself depended on it, seem of as little worth as the pair of shoes we discarded long ago. We can even think with a little touch of irony and laughter of some of the foolish ambitions, the impossible ventures, the laudable fancies with which youth colored its own life. In middle age, streets seem narrower, great men seem commoner, and titles of office less impressive, while our opinions seem ever more and more assured, and we are apt to imagine ourselves fast approaching the infallibility of the Pope, at least in our own homes. "Tut! Tut!" we say to every youth's young dream. "If you had lived as long as I have and seen as much . . ." That is about the time to draw ourselves up and see the image of old age suddenly visible walking by our side as a companion. That is the time to flex our intellectual muscles, draw a deep breath, and change directions.

Once in a while youth speaks with a powerful voice to middle age. Randolph S. Bourne wrote at twenty-seven a book, *Youth and Life* (1913), that shows striking qualities of a keen and searching mind, with a strange mixture of the fire of youth and the mature insight of older age.[1a] Moral passion is a characteristic of youth, and Bourne was

[1] *The Wisdom of Laotse,* Modern Library, p. 234.
[1a] The best thing he wrote in that book, I believe, is the chapter on "The Life of Irony." It is among the best ever written on irony, and it is rewarding reading.

apt to be moralistic, yet his reflections are not without some deep observations of the age-old problems of human life. Again here was an example of a vital intellect overcoming the handicaps of a deformed body, and his early death from influenza in 1918 was greatly lamented by those who expected so much of him. In a way, his pacifism recalls to mind the Garry Davis of our own days—somebody who believes something very much—as only youth can.

Youth Speaks to Middle Age

BY RANDOLPH S. BOURNE

Middle age steals upon a youth almost before he is aware. He will recognize it at first, perhaps, by a slight paling of his enthusiasms, or by sudden consciousness that his early interests have been submerged in the flood of routine work and family cares. The later years of youth and the early years of middle life are in truth the dangerous age, for then may be lost the virtues that were acquired in youth. Or, if not lost, many will be felt to be superfluous. There is danger that the peculiar bias of the relish of right and wrong that the virtues of youth have given one may be weakened, and the soul spread itself too thin over life. Now one of the chief virtues of middle life is to conserve the values of youth, to practice in sober earnest the virtues that came so naturally in the enthusiasm of youth, but which take on a different hue when exposed to what seem to be the crass facts of the workaday world. But there is no reason why work, ambition, the raising of a family, should dull the essential spirit of youthful idealism. It may not be so irrepressible, so freakish, so intolerant, but it should not be different in quality and significance. The burdens of middle life are not a warrant for the releasing of the spiritual obligations of youth. They do not give one the right to look back with amused regret to the dear follies of the past. For as soon as the spirit of youth begins to leave the soul, that soul begins to die. Middle-aged people are too much inclined to speak of youth as a sort of spiritual play. They forget that youth feels that it itself has the serious business of life, the real crises to meet. To youth it is middle age that seems trivial and playful. It is after the serious work of love-making and establishing one's self in economic independence is over that one can rest and play. Youth has little time for that sort of recreation. In middle age, most of the problems have been solved, the obstacles overcome. There is a slackening of the lines, a satisfied taking of one's reward. And to youth this must always seem a tragedy, that the season of life when the powers are at their highest should be the season when they are oftener turned to material than to spiritual ends. Youth has the energy and ideals, but not the vantage-ground of prestige from which to fight for them. Middle age has the prestige and the power, but too seldom the will to use it for the furtherance of its ideals. Youth has the isolation, the independence, the disinterestedness so that it may attack any foe, but it has not the reserve force to carry that attack through. Middle age has all the reserve power necessary, but is handicapped by family obligations, by business and political ties, so that its power is rarely effective for social or individual progress.

—Youth and Life (III)

Oliver Wendell Holmes, Sr., once wrote of the race of life so picturesquely and with such gusto and human warmth that I do not think the following piece will ever grow old.

"The Filly is not to be despised, my boy."
BY OLIVER WENDELL HOLMES

I find the great thing in this world is not so much where we stand, as in what direction we are moving: To reach the port of heaven, we must sail sometimes with the wind and sometimes against it,—but we must sail, and not drift, nor lie at anchor. There is one very sad thing in old friendships, to every mind which is really moving onward. It is this: that one cannot help using his early friends as the seaman uses the log, to mark his progress. Every now and then we throw an old schoolmate over the stern with a string of thought tied to him, and look,—I am afraid with a kind of luxurious and sanctimonious compassion,—to see the rate at which the string reels off, while he lies there bobbing up and down, poor fellow! and we are dashing along with the white foam and bright sparkle at our bows;—the ruffled bosom of prosperity and progress, with a sprig of diamonds stuck in it! But this is only the sentimental side of the matter; for grow we must, if we outgrow all that we love.

Don't misunderstand that metaphor of heaving the log, I beg you. It is merely a smart way of saying that we cannot avoid measuring our rate of movement by those with whom we have long been in the habit of comparing ourselves; and when they once become stationary, we can get our reckoning from them with painful accuracy. We see just what we were when they were our peers, and can strike the balance between that and whatever we may feel ourselves to be now. No doubt we may sometimes be mistaken. If we change our last simile to that very old and familiar one of a fleet leaving the harbor and sailing in company for some distant region, we can get what we want out of it. There is one of our companions;—her streamers were torn into rags before she had got into the open sea, then by and by her sails blew out of the ropes one after another, the waves swept her deck, and as night came on we left her a seeming wreck, as we flew under our pyramid of canvas. But lo! at dawn she is still in sight,—it may be in advance of us. Some deep ocean-current has been moving her on, strong, but silent,—yes, stronger than these noisy winds that puff our sails until they are swollen as the cheeks of jubilant cherubim. And when at last the black steam-tug with the skeleton arms, which comes out of the mist sooner or later and takes us all in tow, grapples her and goes off panting and groaning with her, it is to that harbor where all wrecks are refitted, and where, alas! we, towering in our pride, may never come.

So you will not think I mean to speak lightly of old friendships, because we cannot help instituting comparisons between our present and former selves by the aid of those who were what we were, but are not what we are. Nothing strikes one more, in the race of life, than to see how many give out in the first half of the course. "Commencement day" always reminds me of the start for the "Derby," when the beautiful high-bred three-year-olds of the season are brought up for trial. That day is the start, and life is the race. Here we are at Cambridge, and a class is just "graduating." Poor Harry! he was to have been there too, but he has paid forfeit; step out here into the grass behind the church; ah! there it is:—

"Hunc lapidem posuerunt
Socii mœrentes."

But this is the start, and here they are,—coats bright as silk, and manes as smooth as *eau lustrale* can make them. Some of the best of the colts are pranced round, a few minutes each, to show their paces. What is that old gentleman crying about? and the old lady by him, and the three girls, what are they all covering their eyes for? Oh, that is *their* colt which has just been trotted up on the stage. Do they really think those little thin legs can do anything in such a slashing sweepstakes as is coming off in these next forty years? Oh, this terrible gift of second-sight that comes to some of us when we begin to look through the silvered rings of the *arcus senilis!*

Ten years gone. First turn in the race. A few broken down; two or three bolted. Several show in advance of the ruck. *Cassock,* a black colt, seems to be ahead of the rest; those black colts commonly get the start, I have noticed, of the others, in the first quarter. *Meteor* has pulled up.

Twenty years. Second corner turned. *Cassock* has dropped from the front, and *Judex,* an iron-gray, has the lead. But look! how they have thinned out! Down flat,—five,—six,—how many? They lie still enough! they will not get up again in this race, be very sure! And the rest of them, what a "tailing off"! Anybody can see who is going to win,—perhaps.

Thirty years. Third corner turned. *Dives,* bright sorrel, ridden by the fellow in a yellow jacket, begins to make play fast; is getting to be the favorite with many. But who is that other one that has been length-ening his stride from the first, and now shows close up to the front? Don't you remember the quiet brown colt *Asteroid,* with the star in his forehead? That is he; he is one of the sort that lasts; look out for him! The black "colt," as we used to call him, is in the background, taking it easily in a gentle trot. There is one they used to call *the Filly,* on account of a certain feminine air he had; well up, you see; the Filly is not to be despised, my boy!

Forty years. More dropping off,—but places much as before.

Fifty years. Race over. All that are on the course are coming in at a walk; no more running. Who is ahead? Ahead? What! and the winning-post a slab of white or gray stone standing out from that turf where there is no more jockeying or straining for victory! Well, the world marks their places in its betting-book; but be sure that these matter very little, if they have run as well as they knew how! . . .

—*The Autocrat of the Breakfast Table* (IV)

3. OLD AGE

There seems to be a conspiracy of silence about old age in American literature, even among writers who discourse on almost anything on earth. The Americans live it, but they would rather not talk about it. There may be no reticence about sex, but there is certainly a general reticence about old age, except as something to be laughed at. Yet some great Americans have certainly enjoyed it. Jefferson, for instance, was one. At sixty-nine, surrounded by a family of adoring grandchildren and great-grandchildren, he gave up reading newspapers "in exchange for Tacitus and Thucydides, for Newton and Euclid," and found himself "much happier." Blessed with a strong constitution and with "organs of digestion which accept and concoct, without ever murmuring, whatever the palate chooses to consign to them," he had not yet lost a tooth by age at seventy-six, as he told Doctor Vine Utley in a letter (March 21, 1819). He had not had a fever for more than twenty-four hours above two or three times in his life. This he ascribed to his habit of bathing his feet in cold water every morning for sixty years past. "I enjoy good health, too feeble, indeed, to walk much, but riding out fatigue six or eight miles a day, and sometimes thirty or forty." And so, "now, retired, and at the age of seventy-six, I am again a hard student . . . and I never go to bed without an hour, or half-hour's previous reading of something moral, whereon to ruminate in the intervals of sleep. But whether I retire to bed early or late, I rise with the sun." This makes me think of Justice Holmes, whose methodical habits and industry and intellectual curiosity seem a replica of Jefferson's. Justice Holmes was sitting in his library one day when Franklin D. Roosevelt called, a few days after his inauguration in 1933, and found him reading Plato, at the age of ninety-two.

"Why do you read Plato, Mr. Justice?"

"To improve my mind, Mr. President," Holmes replied.[2]

And so we are not surprised that with a life that was so vigorous and well applied, both Jefferson and Justice Holmes faced the end of the journey without fear. "There is a fullness of time when men should go, and not occupy too long the ground to which others have the right to advance," Jefferson wrote to Benjamin Rush in 1811. To Abigail Adams, wife of John Adams, he wrote six years later, "But those twenty years! Alas! where are they? . . . Our next meeting must then be in the country to which they have flown—a country for us not now very distant. . . . I heard once a very old friend, who had troubled himself with neither poets nor philosophers, say the same thing in plain prose, that he was tired of pulling off his shoes and stockings at night, and putting them on again in the morning. . . . On the whole, however, perhaps it is wiser and well to be contented with the good things which the master of the feast places before us, and to be thankful for what we have, rather than be thoughtful about what we have not." And Justice Holmes toward the end of his life said about death in a contented and humorous way, the only way in which Death should be looked at, "If the good Lord should tell me I had only five minutes to live, I would say to him, 'All right, Lord, but I'm sorry you can't make it ten.' "[3]

For the sheer genius of being born well and remaining vigorous to the very end of life, God never made a more perfect creature than Ben Franklin. The most astounding thing about Franklin from a physical point of view is that at the age of sixteen, he wrote the sensible, thoughtful *Dogood Papers,* and nine days before his death, at the age of eighty-four, writing to Jefferson in answer to an inquiry about some old question of frontiers between the United States and British settlements on the Bay of Passamaquoddy, he showed a memory more precise than that of many college boys, "I am perfectly clear in the remembrance that the map we used in tracing the boundary was brought to the treaty by the commissioners from England and that it was the same that was published by Mitchell above twenty years

---

[2] Catherine Drinker Bowen, *Yankee from Olympus,* p. 414. Little, Brown and Company.

[3] *Yankee from Olympus,* p. 416.

before." When people speak about the progress of mankind, thinking
we have left the eighteenth-century man far behind us, it makes me
very angry.

We would rather not talk about old age. But a hundred years ago,
Dr. Holmes talked persuasively, gently and humorously about it in
a way that should make us ashamed of ourselves.

*"What is the use of fighting against the season, or the tides,
or the movements of the planetary bodies, or this ebb in the
wave of life that flows through us?"*

BY OLIVER WENDELL HOLMES

My friend, the Professor, began talking with me one day in a dreary
sort of way. I couldn't get at the difficulty for a good while, but at last
it turned out that somebody had been calling him an old man.—He
didn't mind his students calling him *the* old man, he said. That was
a technical expression, and he thought that he remembered hearing it
applied to himself when he was about twenty-five. It may be considered
as a familiar and sometimes endearing appellation. An Irishwoman
calls her husband "the old man," and he returns the caressing expression by speaking of her as "the old woman." But now, said he, just
suppose a case like one of these. A young stranger is overheard talking
of you as a very nice old gentleman. A friendly and genial critic speaks
of your green old age as illustrating the truth of some axiom you had
uttered with reference to that period of life. What *I* call an old man
is a person with a smooth, shining crown and a fringe of scattered
white hairs, seen in the streets on sunshiny days, stooping as he walks,
bearing a cane, moving cautiously and slowly; telling old stories, smiling at present follies, living in a narrow world of dry habits; one that
remains waking when others have dropped asleep, and keeps a little
night-lamp-flame of life burning year after year, if the lamp is not up-
set, and there is only a careful hand held round it to prevent the puffs
of wind from blowing the flame out. That's what I call an old man.

Now, said the Professor, you don't mean to tell me that I have got
to that yet? Why, bless you, I am several years short of the time when
—(I knew what was coming, and could hardly keep from laughing;
twenty years ago he used to quote it as one of those absurd speeches

men of genius will make, and now he is going to argue from it)—several years short of the time when Balzac says that men are—most—you know—dangerous to—the hearts of—in short, most to be dreaded by duennas that have charge of susceptible females.—What age is that? said I, statistically.—Fifty-two years, answered the Professor.—Balzac ought to know, said I, if it is true that Goethe said of him that each of his stories must have been dug out of a woman's heart. But fifty-two is a high figure.

Stand in the light of the window, Professor, said I.—The Professor took up the desired position.—You have white hairs, I said.—Had 'em any time these twenty years, said the Professor.—And the crow's-foot, —*pes anserinus,* rather. The Professor smiled, as I wanted him to, and the folds radiated like the ridges of a half-opened fan, from the outer corner of the eyes to the temples.—And the calipers, said I.—What are the *calipers?* he asked, curiously.—Why, the parenthesis, said I.— *Parenthesis?* said the Professor; what's that?—Why look in the glass when you are disposed to laugh, and see if your mouth isn't framed in a couple of crescent lines,—so, my boy ().—It's all nonsense, said the Professor; just look at my *biceps;*—and he began pulling off his coat to show me his arm. Be careful, said I; you can't bear exposure to the air, at your time of life, as you could once.—I will box with you, said the Professor, row with you, walk with you, ride with you, swim with you, or sit at table with you, for fifty dollars a side.—Pluck survives stamina, I answered.

The Professor went off a little out of humor. A few weeks afterwards he came in, looking very good-natured, and brought me a paper, which I have here, and from which I shall read you some portions, if you don't object. He had been thinking the matter over, he said,—had read Cicero "De Senectute," and made up his mind to meet old age half way. These were some of his reflections that he had written down . . . [*Here follows the "Professor's Paper." I find the most unexpected line from an American author, "you may be expecting to find yourself a grandfather some fine morning; a kind of domestic felicity that gives one a cool shiver of delight to think of, as among the not remotely possible events." The Professor, who is of course Dr. Holmes himself, goes on talking like a medical man about the lesser combustion of carbon after forty-five and repeating a dialogue between himself and*

*Old Age, during which Old Age claims to have made his acquaintance
for five years past, but he has refused to recognize Old Age. The "Professor's Paper" continues.*]

We talked together in this way some time. Then Old Age said again,
—Come, let us walk down the street together,—and offered me a cane,
an eyeglass, a tippet, and a pair of overshoes.—No, much obliged to
you, said I. I don't want those things, and I had a little rather talk
with you here, privately, in my study. So I dressed myself up in a
jaunty way and walked out alone;—got a fall, caught a cold, was laid
up with a lumbago, and had time to think over this whole matter.

. . . —After all, the most encouraging things I find in the treatise,
"De Senectute," are the stories of men who have found new occupations when growing old, or kept up their common pursuits in the
extreme period of life. Cato learned Greek when he was old, and
speaks of wishing to learn the fiddle, or some such instrument (*fid-
ibus*), after the example of Socrates. Solon learned something new,
every day, in his old age, as he gloried to proclaim. Cyrus pointed out
with pride and pleasure the trees he had planted with his own hand.
(I remember a pillar on the Duke of Northumberland's estate at Aln-
wick, with an inscription in similar words, if not the same. That, like
other country pleasures, never wears out. None is too rich, none too
poor, none too young, none too old to enjoy it.) There is a New England story I have heard, more to the point, however, than any of
Cicero's. A young farmer was urged to set out some apple-trees.—No,
said he, they are too long growing, and I don't want to plant for other
people. The young farmer's father was spoken to about it, but he, with
better reason, alleged that apple-trees were slow and life was fleeting.
At last some one mentioned it to the old grandfather of the young
farmer. He had nothing else to do,—so he stuck in some trees. He
lived long enough to drink barrels of cider made from the apples that
grew on those trees. . . .

As to *giving up,* because the almanac or the Family-Bible says that
it is about time to do it, I have no intention of doing any such thing.
I grant you that I burn less carbon than some years ago. I see people
of my standing really good for nothing, decrepit, effete, *la lèvre infé-
rieure déjà pendante,* with what little life they have left mainly concentrated in their epigastrium. But as the disease of old age is epidemic,

endemic, and sporadic, and everybody who lives long enough is sure to catch it, I am going to say, for the encouragement of such as need it, how I treat the malady in my own case.

First. As I feel, that, when I have anything to do, there is less time for it than when I was younger, I find that I give my attention more thoroughly, and use my time more economically than ever before; so that I can learn anything twice as easily as in my earlier days. I am not, therefore, afraid to attack a new study. I took up a difficult language a very few years ago with good success, and think of mathematics and metaphysics by-and-by.

Secondly. I have opened my eyes to a good many neglected privileges and pleasures within my reach, and requiring only a little courage to enjoy them. You may well suppose it pleased me to find that old Cato was thinking of learning to play the fiddle, when I had deliberately taken it up in my old age, and satisfied myself that I could get much comfort, if not much music out of it.

Thirdly. I have found that some of those active exercises, which are commonly thought to belong to young folks only, may be enjoyed at a much later period. . . .

[*After a long excursion on walking, riding, rowing and boxing, etc., the Professor concludes as follows:*]

But now let me tell you this. If the time comes when you must lay down the fiddle and the bow, because your fingers are too stiff, and drop the ten-foot sculls, because your arms are too weak, and, after dallying awhile with eye-glasses, come at last to the undisguised reality of spectacles,—if the time comes when that fire of life we spoke of has burned so low that where its flames reverberated there is only the sombre stain of regret, and where its coals glowed, only the white ashes that cover the embers of memory,—don't let your heart grow cold, and you may carry cheerfulness and love with you into the teens of your second century, if you can last so long.

—*The Autocrat of the Breakfast Table* (VI)

4. DEATH AND IMMORTALITY

Death is an ugly fact, but it is fascinating. It has fascinated men's minds from the Inca Indians to the most modern poets. It is probably the only thing that makes men thoughtful. We dislike it, we abhor it, and yet we are fascinated by the terror of extinction. The greatest conquerors of Chinese history, like Ch'in Shih-hwang who built the Great Wall or Han Wuti who expanded the Chinese Empire to Chinese Turkestan, were gripped by this terror and spent their old days seeking magic formulas for immortality.

There are three ways of meeting this problem. The best way is not to think about it and leave it alone. That was Confucius' way. Philosophical disquisitions on death on the whole are pretty empty and useless. Here I prefer Irwin Edman, who is like Confucius; he doesn't like to think about death, because it is useless to do so. Nothing bores him more than canvassing the possibilities of a future life. He doesn't hail extinction romantically, either, as Browning did. It is just one of the hateful things to him, for "death is one of those enemies against whom all one can do is hate." [4] That is the most intelligent way.

The second answer to death is religion. The basis of all religions is the cold fact of human mortality. One day, coming back from the catacombs on the Appian way and standing in the big Cathedral of St. Paul in Rome, I was struck by the spaciousness and the grandeur of the structure. Having just seen the subterranean passages, where inscriptions on the walls by the early persecuted Christians in the form of prayers to St. Peter and St. Paul have been recently discovered, I could not but be struck by the contrast, and by a great mystery. A handful of fairly illiterate Christians came to the Imperial City; some were crucified, some were decapitated; some were thrown to the lions. And they conquered. It was a fact of history which had to be explained. I began to see and understand how these fishermen could have conquered. They had a great story to tell. I saw the story in its main outline from the point of view of the Roman plebeians and patricians, and realized that it was the story of a scheme for man's salvation. Whether one agrees with the story or not, the scheme of salvation from man's fall to his redemption through vicarious sacrifice was definite, complete, and spiritually an inspiring, heartening message. In the minds of the Christians, the scheme was truly amazing. It was this story which made history, and I said, this was in truth the greatest story ever told. The

[4] *Living Philosophies*, p. 284. Simon and Schuster.

fascinating theme of the story was of course man's death and damnation, and the great, powerful heart-stirring solution was the one word
"Resurrection." I could see mentally written upon the conquering ban-
ner of the Christians the words of St. Paul, "O death, where is thy
sting?" These words conquered Rome.

The third answer to death is through philosophic understanding.
Through a higher understanding of the scheme of things in nature,
one can accept death quite philosophically. It is perhaps more difficult,
but old Alaskan women have been known to go out quietly in the snow
and die when their time comes and when their life is but an added
burden to their families. Many men, like Jefferson and Justice Holmes,
as we have just seen, have been able to take this calm and philosophic
attitude and to face death cheerfully. When Jefferson said he was
thankful for having lived and was quite prepared to make way for
others coming, he talked like many Taoist sages in the books of
Chuangtse, like Tseyu, for instance, who said quite unsentimentally,
"I came to life because it was my time, and I am now parting with it
in the natural course of things." Behind such a simple statement, there
is a complete philosophy which satisfies man's intellect as well as his
heart. No one, east or west, writes more beautifully on the subject of
death than the Taoist Chuangtse. If one can accept such a philosophy
of cosmic change, and know that change is the very law of life, one
can learn to look at death almost impersonally. It is only from such
broad understanding that death can be faced and accepted.

"There is great beauty in the silent universe," says Chuangtse. "There
are manifest laws governing the four seasons without words. There is
an intrinsic principle in the created things which is not expressed. The
Sage looks back to the beauty of the universe and penetrates into the
intrinsic principle of created things. . . . The spirit of the universe
informs all life. Things live and die and change their forms without
knowing the root from which they come. Abundantly it multiplies;
eternally it stands by itself. The greatest reaches do not leave its con-
fines, and the smallest down of a bird in autumn awaits its power to
assume form. The things emerge and submerge, but it remains for ever
without change. The *yin* and the *yang* and the four seasons move in
orderly procession. The things of the creation are nourished by it, with-

out knowing it. This is the root, from which one may survey the universe."

From such a standpoint, therefore: "Life is the companion of death, and death is the companion of life. Who can appreciate the connection between the two? When a man is born, it is but the embodiment of the spirit. When the spirit is embodied, there is life, and when the spirit disperses, there is death. But if life and death are companions to each other, why should I be concerned? Therefore, all things are one. What we love is the mystery of life. What we hate is corruption in death. But the corruptible in its turn becomes mysterious life, and this mysterious life once more becomes corruptible." "How do I know that love of life is not a delusion after all? How do I know but that he who dreads death is not as a child who has lost his way and does not know his way home?" [5]

Here philosophy and religion merge, as they should. When philosophy becomes colored with emotion and teaches a reverent attitude toward the universe, it becomes religion, and when religion does not conflict with a true understanding of nature, it becomes a solid and sensible philosophy of living. Benjamin Franklin had such a philosophy and religion which did not conflict with one another. He faced death in his youth. At the age of twenty-two, he thought he was going to die and wrote his own epitaph, gracefully couched in the phraseology of his trade:

The Body of
B Franklin Printer,
(Like the Cover of an Old Book
Its Contents torn out
And stript of its Lettering & Gilding)
Lies here, Food for Worms.
But the Work shall not be lost;
For it will, (as he believ'd) appear once more,
In a new and elegant Edition
Revised and Corrected,
By the Author.

[5] For all these quotations from Chuangtse on the subject of death, see *The Wisdom of Laotse*, Modern Library, chapters 6, 33, and 50. Reprinted by permission.

Franklin quite believed in a heaven, with rewards and punishments, while Jefferson believed in a kind of immortality but more rationally disbelieved in justice in afterlife for our sins and virtues in this. Franklin's was of course a cheerful kind of eighteenth-century heaven, where he would marry Madame Brillon and they would eat apples roasted with butter and nutmeg and pity those who were not dead. Happy Franklin! Who said that only a fundamentalist had faith? He, if any man, had made peace with God and the universe and with himself. I believe Franklin was never unhappy; it is so difficult to imagine him being so. Read his cheerful letter announcing the death of his brother to the latter's stepdaughter, Miss E. Hubbard.

"His chair was ready first, and he is gone before us."

BY BENJAMIN FRANKLIN

I condole with you. We have lost a most dear and valuable relation. But it is the will of God and nature, that these mortal bodies be laid aside, when the soul is to enter into real life. This is rather an embryo state, a preparation for living.

A man is not completely born until he is dead. Why then should we grieve, that a new child is born among the immortals, a new member added to their happy society? We are spirits. That bodies should be lent us, while they can afford us pleasure, assist us in acquiring knowledge, or in doing good to our fellow creatures, is a kind and benevolent act of God. When they become unfit for these purposes, and afford us pain instead of pleasure, instead of an aid become an encumbrance, and answer none of the intentions for which they were given, it is equally kind and benevolent, that a way is provided by which we may get rid of them. Death is that way. We ourselves, in some cases, prudently choose a partial death. A mangled painful limb, which cannot be restored, we willingly cut off. He who plucks out a tooth, parts with it freely, since the pain goes with it; and he, who quits the whole body, parts at once with all pains and possibilities of pains and diseases which it was liable to, or capable of making him suffer.

Our friend and we were invited abroad on a party of pleasure, which is to last for ever. His chair was ready first, and he is gone before us.

We could not all conveniently start together; and why should you and I be grieved at this, since we are soon to follow, and know where to find him?

—Letter of February 23, 1756

Personally I believe in the immortality of works, of the influence of all we do and all we say on our fellow men, of the effect of our life on others, both now and in the future, whatever that life may be. (Besides that, I believe also in the immortality of the race, which is all that Nature cares for. Science teaches that Nature cares for the immortality of the race, but not of the individuals.) What is immortality anyway? Why all the mystifications? It means nothing to me to believe that Ben Franklin is at this present moment married to Madame Brillon and eating toasted apples in heaven—something which I am either too thick-headed or too intelligent to believe. But it means something very clear to me when it is said that Franklin is immortal today in the lightning rod and the stove he produced, in the American postal service, the American Philosophical Society, yes, and even in the very Republic of the United States itself. Thomas Edison lives for me every time I turn on the switch of an electric light or watch a movie, and Luther Burbank lives for me every time I eat a Burbank pear. The Wright brothers live every time an airplane flies. Is this not enough, O discontented Man?

No matter how important or unimportant we are, how good or wicked or mediocre, we cannot hope to escape the effect our individual lives have upon others. Even the sight of mediocrity produces an effect upon one's students or neighbors. In this sense, not only is Benjamin Franklin immortal, but his parents Josiah and Abiah, too, because they produced something which in turn produced something which affects our life today.

Good, bad, or indifferent, big or small, our influences continue; the things we do and the words we say live after us in the huge stream of life, which goes on forever. Some send out longer waves, and some make only slight ripples on their neighbors or their orphans and affect them, their lives and their beliefs, somehow. But even the slightest ripple in the ocean of life has some effect on its neighboring atoms. And so we go on punishing and rewarding those who live after us. As

for being punished or rewarded in some future life, I am totally unin-
terested. I believe with Emerson and John Dewey that the present life
takes care of that already.

The desire for immortality seems to be a universal wish, expressed
in religion, art, and literature, and even in politics. Men wish that when
they die their names shall be remembered forever, either in their books,
or their words, or on the statues in public squares and upon the lips
of women and children, or in a museum or an institution dedicated
to their memory. Some persons are satisfied with that, and some insist
on a personal if not a physical continuity of their being in the life
after death. Yet an immortal life of the spirit is so far beyond our
comprehension that to predicate further about it seems an impertinence
and shows a lack of the true philosophic spirit. So far human experience tells us that we survive either in our influences and our works
in the broad general stream of humanity, or else we have intimations
of an infinite existence, of which we form a part and to which we go
back upon the end of the present existence. Sometimes the grandeur
of the universe so overwhelms us with its vastness, its mystery, and its
beauty, whether from the light of a distant shimmering star or from
the power of music, that we intuitively perceive our relation and our
kinship to it and cannot but believe that the body of the flesh is but a
manifestation of a more spiritual power and a deeper reality behind
the face of the universe, a Tao, a Logos, an It, or an *Om*. James Russell
Lowell expresses this feeling well in a letter to Miss Grace Norton,
Charles Eliot Norton's sister (March 7, 1878): "One night, the last
time I was ill, I lost all consciousness of my flesh. I was dispersed
through space in some inconceivable fashion, and mixed with the
Milky Way. It was with great labor that I gathered myself again and
brought myself within compatible limits, or so it seemed; and yet the
very fact that I had a confused consciousness all the while of the Milky
Way as something to be mingled with proved that I was there as much
an individual as ever. . . ." Lowell admitted, "Suppose we don't k*now*,
how much *do* we know after all?" But such speculations are necessarily
idle.

I cannot do better than let David Grayson bring the question home
to us in one of the deepest things he wrote. Grayson was describing an
experience when he was in a hospital.

The Man Who Did Not Know He Was Going to Die

BY DAVID GRAYSON

Another man I chanced to meet during these days of my own slow recovery had an indescribable fascination for me. *He was going to die and did not know it.* Everyone about seemed aware of it. It was the bandied news of the corridor. A significant look of the eye, a nod of the head as one went by his door—there in that room is a man who is going to die.

It gave me the strangest sense of tense awareness. I had, in the past, seen men die; I had known the sorrow of the death of dear friends; but death—it is curious when I think of it—had never for me, previous to my experience in the hospital, seemed at all a reality. It was something terrible that happened to other people, and though it may appear shocking in the telling, but it is so, I thought of it somehow as their own fault. Here it had come close to me in many forms as a stark reality: something that might even happen to *me*. In this place it was no longer a phenomenon, but a measurable and daily expectancy. It was this new congeries of observation and intense feeling that so stirred my interest in this man who was going to die—and did not know it!

One day I met him. He had read something I had once written and asked if I would come to see him. I went with the greatest hesitation and reluctance, and yet with an overpowering curiosity. How must a man feel who was about to die? What would he think? How would he look? What would he say? As I walked down the corridor with the nurse who brought the message, these questions came upon me with a vividness and power I cannot describe. In my imagination I saw the poor fellow in bed, emaciated, slow of breath, feebly reaching out his hand to touch mine. I could scarcely control the beating of my heart or the trembling of my knees when I stepped around the screen.

"How are you, sir?" said a steady voice. "Come in. I'm glad to see you."

There he sat in his chair, a stout, rather florid man, in a gay-colored dressing gown. There were flowers on his table—a world of flowers—and pictures of a smiling gray-haired woman and a smiling girl and two little boys. In front of him, on a desk, piles of neatly arranged papers, as though he had just looked up from his daily affairs. It was I who was hesitant and embarrassed: for I could not quickly adjust reality and preconception. It was he who made everything easy and hospitable.

While I sat talking with him a nurse brought in a telegram, which he slit open in the quick, nervous, incidental manner of the business man. He glanced at it and tossed it on the desk, proceeding with his conversation.

It came over me with a kind of shock. What futile urgency—if the man was going to die. Then I remembered, with a wave of pity, that he did not know!

It was not long before I could place him. He was quite a typical American business man—self-confident, positive, vital. He did not tell me in so many words that he was rich: he radiated it. He told me of a "deal" he had just "cleared up" in which he had made a "killing." I found that his secretary came in every morning to take care of "a lot of little matters."

I kept forgetting—but it would come over me suddenly and with a sinking sense of futility, "Why all these deals? What good making any more money? The man is going to die."

The next day when I stopped to see him I found the nurse reading a newspaper aloud, and when he began to talk of the depression in business and the outlook for certain stocks, I kept saying to myself, "Now, what is the use of all that?"

He talked again quite volubly about himself and his affairs: but presently he broke off, and I saw him looking at me with a slow, inscrutable gaze.

"Are you here for long?" he asked.

As I paused I thought his look intensified, and there was something deep down and far back in his narrowing eyes—or did I imagine it?—that was pitiful to see.

"The doctors," said I, "are promising me that I can go home for Christmas."

I shall never forget the pause that followed—my glance drifted away to the picture of the smiling gray-haired woman on his table—nor the peculiar tone of his voice—deep, still—one word:

"Christmas!"

They had all said he did not know, but I knew as well as though he had told me in so many words. He knew! No doubt he had known all along! My whole heart went out to him so that I could scarcely keep the tears from my eyes. I looked at him again. Yes, there was a kind of mediocrity about the man, he had few intellectual resources, but what a fighter! What a fighter! He was playing the game straight through to the end. It seemed to me at the moment as though, of all things in the world, such courage, such steadiness, was most to be admired. He had not thought out a philosophy: he *had it*. He could walk up to death with it.

Telegrams, yes, why not? Deals, yes, why not? A secretary every morning to take his letters, why not? They were not futilities, they were of the essence of the matter. He was refusing to be beaten by the past or crushed by the future. He was living, as a man ought to live, every fiber of him, in the only moment he ever really possesses—this moment! It came to me with intolerable clarity: "Why, we're all going to die and don't know it; and this is what we should do about it."

I cannot tell what the man's religious beliefs were—if he had any. Once or twice during the few days I knew him he seemed on the point of saying something to me—I knew!—but the moment passed. How I should have liked to know! But of this I am certain: he had faith— faith of some kind. Men differ in that: I have mine and you yours. In its essence it is a deep, deep sense of confidence—of calmness—that whatever happens, whatever the process, it is natural, it is universal, it is according to law.

—*Adventures in Solitude* (X)

Chapter V

MAN AS SENTIMENT

I. INADEQUACY OF THE MATERIALISTIC VIEW

SOME wag defined a Beethoven quartet as a scraping of cats' intestines on horses' tails. Now, if I were to take literally the position, I would be able to prove the truth of the statement by chemical and microscopic analysis and other relevant evidences to the satisfaction of any court, and my opponent would have a hard time proving that it isn't. I would be curious to see what kind of evidence my opponent was going to introduce for the jury's examination and by what method he was going to prove his point. I am afraid I would have all the facts and he would have all the feelings. The best he would be able to do would be to play a gramophone record of the quartet and show by the emotional reaction of the audience and the divine ecstasy on their faces that the scraping of the so-called intestines on the alleged tails is nothing, and the feeling that act communicates is everything. I would still maintain that the dried intestines indubitably come from cats and the tails come from horses. But I would also advance to the attack. I would say that his alleged feelings and ecstasies are pretty fuzzy and woolly affairs, unclear, undefined, unmeasurable, that there was no *prima facie* reason why a certain arrangement of a number of vibrations in a certain sequence should be beautiful and others not, that the so-called facts of harmony and dissonance are all subjective, etc. When we got this far, I would be interrupted, and we would be deeply involved in a philosophic discussion of whether subjective evidence would or would not be permissible in court and in the still more troublesome question of whether a feeling is also a fact. (We would have previously agreed to stick only to facts.) I have no idea where the discussion would end.

Of course we have gone through this kind of debate all through the latter half of the nineteenth century and well into the twentieth. Quite

a number of learned and apparently intelligent people took my side
in the above argument. To begin with, there was the Manchester
School of "precise" economics, which produced Karl Marx. There were
Parrington in literary history and Charles Beard in United States
history, and Brooks Adams and Henry Adams worked the formula
to death. The instinct was perhaps admirable; it was a desire for clear,
precise, objective, and scientific facts, and as a method of history, its
merit lay in working solely with provable facts, dismissing—unfortunately—the fuzzier facts as of secondary and quite often of no importance. The inspiration came from the tremendous progress of the natural
sciences; the natural scientists had made such proud progress by showing a dispassionate, objective attitude toward the universe, so it readily
occurred to the historians that they too should learn to be clear and
precise and stick to the provable and the economically demonstrable.
Charles Beard matured and came round to a fuller, if less precise,
realization of the truths and worths and significances of history, but he
did go to the trouble of personally conducting a federal investigation,
ignoble in my opinion, of the investments of the fathers of the American Constitution, to prove that the document represented the triumph
of money power over agricultural individualism. I happen to be intuitively against "my" side and like to think that Hamilton, Madison,
and Jefferson were more interested in creating a great nation on a
stable governmental basis. "Can you *prove* it?" I would be asked. If
by proving is meant proof like investments in the bank and sizes of
estates, I would have to reply, "No." Suddenly I would forget myself,
and I would speak perhaps too eloquently of the nation's past, of the
dreams of the colonists who came in the *Mayflower,* of Roger Williams
and William Penn, of the lands and primeval forests, no, not of a few
paltry thousand acres that belonged to this or that delegate to the Great
Convention, but of a whole continent challenging men's imagination
and powers and energies to convert it into a peaceful habitable country.
I would speak of three million men and women with their dreams
and hopes and purposes; and I would say that the makers of the
Constitution saw this, felt this, that they wanted to build a great nation
upon this earth. And I would see the audience's faces brighten and their
throats catch, and I would say, "There, Americans, feelings are facts
also. They are in you."

Perhaps Henry Adams's case may be studied as an example of what I call disorderly ideas and confusion of thought in the modern man arising from materialistic thinking. He was one of the most intelligent Americans in the nineteenth century, with all its advantages of learning and culture. Yet the labyrinths of despair in which he found himself were representative of man's spiritual journey in the latter half of the nineteenth century. If he had not been intelligent, he would have been quite as contented in animal satisfaction as any others of his generation. But he was too intelligent to be complacent, and not intelligent enough to find any kind of a foothold in life and so to find happiness. Unlimited materialism means an extremely limited view of human existence. Henry Adams tried to find out a law of history analogous to, and strictly in terms of, the laws of physics. He purposed to trace the law of progress, showing the unified existence of man in thirteenth-century Europe and the multiplicity of modern life today. He did this by writing two books—*Mont-Saint-Michel and Chartres* and his autobiographical *Education of Henry Adams*. He never found the laws. The factual reason was that he was so fascinated by the study of the thirteenth century and of his own that he clean forgot what he had set out to demonstrate, but the real reason was that it could never be done, because his theory of interpretation of history as force, motion, and acceleration was false from the very beginning. He could change the phraseology and call the Virgin a force instead of a religious aspiration, a sentiment of man, to suit his purposes, but he could not make the phraseology stick and he knew as well as I know that the adoration of the Virgin is a sentiment and has force in a figurative sense only, in the sense that any idea has force, and he soon got lost. He thought he saw in the dynamo at the Paris Exhibition of 1900 a symbol of force, the modern force, but did he not know well that the dynamo was only a symbol and a good literary figure on which to graft the concept of material force of the modern age? And so when he was reduced to writing *The Prayer to the Dynamo,* it was something to wring tears from the modern man, for that is essentially the last agonizing cry of the man who has lost his faith in both the Virgin and the Dynamo, neither of whom, he knew in his heart, could give him belief; not the first, because he knew he did not believe but only regretted that others of the past had the privilege of doing so, and not the second, because he knew the black cast-iron dynamo was not going to save him or the world but rather represented the blind force eternal. Mark these terrifying words:

Prayer to the Dynamo

BY HENRY ADAMS

We know not whether you are kind,
　　Or cruel in your fiercer mood;
But be you Matter, be you Mind,
We think we know that you are blind,
　　And we alone are good. . . .

What are we then? the lords of space?
　　The master-mind whose tasks you do?
Jockey who rides you in the race?
Or are we atoms whirled apace,
　　Shaped and controlled by you?

Still silence! Still no end in sight!
　　No sound in answer to our cry!
Then, by the God we now hold tight,
Though we destroy soul, life and light,
　　Answer you shall—or die!

We are no beggars! What care we
　　For hopes or terrors, love or hate?
What for the universe? We see
Only our certain destiny
　　And the last word of Fate.

Seize, then, the Atom! rack his joints!
　　Tear out of him his secret spring!
Grind him to nothing!—though he points
To us, and his life-blood anoints
　　Me—the dead Atom-King!

From Henry Adams, *Letters to a Niece and Prayer to the Virgin of Chartres.* Houghton Mifflin Company. Copyright, 1920, by Mabel La Farge. Reprinted by permission.

[*After having said this, the dead Atom-King reverts to prayer to the Virgin, in which he lays bare the "helpless hopelessness of the soul"*]

A curious prayer, dear lady! is it not?
　　Strangely unlike the prayers I prayed to you!
Stranger because you find me at this spot,
　　Here, at your feet, asking your help anew.

Strangest of all, that I have ceased to strive,
　　Ceased even care what new coin fate shall strike.
In truth it does not matter. Fate will give
　　Some answer; and all answers are like.

So, while we slowly rack and torture death
　　And wait for what the final void will show,
Waiting I feel the energy of faith
　　Not in the future science, but in you!

The man who solves the Infinite, and needs
　　The force of solar systems for his play,
Will not need me, nor greatly care what deeds
　　Made me illustrious in the dawn of day.

He will send me, dethroned, to claim my rights,
　　Fossil survival of an age of stone,
Among the cave-men and the troglodytes
　　Who carved the mammoth on the mammoth's bone.

He will forget my thought, my acts, my fame,
　　As we forget the shadows of the dusk,
Or catalogue the echo of a name
　　As we the scratches on the mammoth's tusk.

But when, like me, he too has trod the track
　　Which leads him up to power above control,
He too will have no choice but wander back
　　And sink in helpless hopelessness of soul. . . .

[*And so he continues to the last stanza where he asks the Virgin to
bear, not his own failure, but the failure of God in an excruciating cli-
max of gruesomeness:*]

> Help me to bear! not my own baby load
> But yours; who bore the failure of light,
> The strength, the knowledge and the thought of God.—
> The futile folly of the Infinite!—

—*"Prayer to the Virgin"* [1]

Henry Adams was a pessimist, as we all know, but he was perceptive, and he saw the tragedy of the modern man's having nothing to
believe. After writing the two books, he published them only for
private circulation. What terrifying sadness and disillusion in a man
who concluded that silence and good temper were the marks of sense!
Man has become a "ball of vibrating motions," a "center of super-
sensual chaos," however the mind struggles like a frightened bird to
escape the chaos that engages it, it is in vain.[2] And why? Because
Adams' search for unity had failed and he gave up. The chapter "The
Abyss of Ignorance" in *Education* may be studied as a genesis of
modern despair, where the tortured soul is laid bare on the vivisection
table.[3] Henry Adams' is the case of a fine intellect searching heaven and
earth for a unified system of beliefs and failing to find it. The material-
istically limited conception of the nineteenth century made it impossible for him to arrive at anything but despair.

Someone should have shaken him violently by the shoulder and said
to him, "Harry, you started with the idea of looking only for material
forces and motions. Why are you surprised to find only them? The

---

[1] I could not find a copy of *Mont-Saint-Michel and Chartres* at the tourist shops either
at Mont Saint-Michel or at Chartres. It must have been regarded as irreligious.

[2] "As for himself, according to Helmholz, Ernst Mach, and Arthur Balfour, he was
henceforth to be a conscious ball of vibrations traversed in every direction by infinite
lines of rotation or vibration, rolling at the feet of the Virgin at Chartres, or of
M. Poincaré in an attic at Paris, a center of supersensuous chaos." *The Education of
Henry Adams.* Houghton Mifflin Company.

[3] "Yet the search for a unit of force led into catacombs of thought where hundreds
of thousands of educations had found their end. Generation after generation of painful
and honest-minded scholars had been content to stay in these labyrinths for ever, pursuing ignorance in silence, in company with the most famous teachers of all time. Not
one of them had ever found a logical highroad of escape." *The Education of Henry
Adams.*

trouble with you is that you and your brother Brooks have too much enthusiasm for matter."

I take Henry Adams because he was a product of his age, the latter half of the nineteenth century, when materialism was at its height of fashion, and because two other interesting and notable American figures, whose life span covered almost exactly the same period, offered a sharp rebuttal to his mechanistic theory of history. Henry Adams was born in 1838 and his mental powers failed after 1910; William James lived from 1842 to 1910; and Justice Holmes lived from 1841 to 1935. Thus the three were strictly of the same generation. And the three disagreed about brute matter. If I should be called upon to grade them, Justice Holmes should get 98, William James 80, and Henry Adams 65.

At the end of his life, Adams tried to formulate his theory of history and published privately *A Letter to American Teachers of History*.[4] It was all so sad. He was tremendously impressed by the Second Law of Thermodynamics, because of the universality of its application, a law stating that organized energy tends constantly to disintegrate or fall back into simpler forms. He was worried about this for humanity. If this law was correct, as physically it was, all this complicated energy known as civilization was destined to extinction, perhaps some eons from now, but nevertheless, extinction all the same. After receiving a copy of the *Letter,* William James wrote to his friend an important reply. This letter of James has a very special significance. He wrote it in June, 1910, and two months later he was to return to his home near Cambridge and sink into his chair beside the fire and sob, "It's so good to get home!" and he died a week after. Thus the two letters seem to sum up for us two important and contrasting lines of thought in the preceding seventy years (1840-1910).

He pointed out to Adams where he was wrong on his own ground. First James said that the distribution of energy and the work it produced is just as important as the total volume or duration of flow of energy. Second, James pointed out that, granted the destination of the journey is a zero, the magnificent landscape while we are traveling— and we are all travelers—is worth enjoying none the less, and the present, the interval between the starting point and the vanishing

[4] Later reprinted in *The Degradation of the Democratic Dogma* by his brother Brooks Adams.

point, in other words these few paltry eons when human life exists, is the important thing and has ultimate significance for us.

On the Second Law of Thermodynamics

BAD-NAUHEIM, JUNE 17, 1910.

DEAR HENRY ADAMS,—I have been so "slim" since seeing you, and the baths here have so weakened my brain, that I have been unable to do any reading except trash, and have only just got round to finishing your "letter," which I had but half-read when I was with you at Paris. To tell the truth, it doesn't impress me at all, save by its wit and erudition; and I ask you whether an old man soon about to meet his Maker can hope to save himself from the consequences of his life by pointing to the wit and learning he has shown in treating a tragic subject. No, sir, you can't do it, can't impress God in that way. So far as our scientific conceptions go, it may be admitted that your Creator (and mine) started the universe with a certain amount of "energy" latent in it, and decreed that everything that should happen thereafter should be a result of parts of that energy falling to lower levels; raising other parts higher, to be sure, in so doing, but never in equivalent amount, owing to the constant radiation of unrecoverable warmth incidental to the process. It is customary for gentlemen to pretend to believe one another, and until some one hits upon a newer revolutionary concept (which may be tomorrow) all physicists must play the game by holding religiously to the above doctrine. It involves of course the ultimate cessation of all perceptible happening, and the end of human history. With this general conception as *surrounding* everything you say in your "letter," no one can find any fault—in the present stage of scientific conventions and fashions. But I protest against your interpretation of some of the specifications of the great statistical drift downwards of the original high-level energy. If, instead of criticizing what you seem to me to say, I express my own interpretation dogmatically, and leave you to make the comparison, it will doubtless conduce to brevity and economize recrimination.

To begin with, the *amount* of cosmic energy it costs to buy a certain

distribution of fact which humanly we regard as precious, seems to me
to be an altogether secondary matter as regards the question of history
and progress. Certain arrangements of matter *on the same energy-level*
are, from the point of view of man's appreciation, superior, while
others are inferior. Physically a dinosaur's brain may show as much
intensity of energy-exchange as a man's, but it can do infinitely fewer
things, because as a force of detent it can only unlock the dinosaur's
muscles, while the man's brain, by unlocking far feebler muscles, in-
directly can by their means issue proclamations, write books, describe
Chartres Cathedral, etc., and guide the energies of the shrinking sun
into channels which never would have been entered otherwise—in
short, *make* history. Therefore the man's brain and muscles are, from
the point of view of the historian, the more important place of energy-
exchange, small as this may be when measured in absolute physical
units.

The "second law" is wholly irrelevant to "history"—save that it sets
a terminus—for history is the course of things before that terminus,
and all that the second law says is that, whatever the history, it must
invest itself between that initial maximum and that terminal minimum
of difference in energy-level. As the great irrigation-reservoir empties
itself, the whole question for us is that of the distribution of its effects,
of *which* rills to guide it into; and the size of the rills has nothing
to do with their significance. Human cerebration is the most important
rill we know of, and both the "capacity" and the "intensity" factor
thereof may be treated as infinitesimal. Yet the filling of such rills
would be cheaply bought by the waste of whole sums spent in getting
a little of the down-flowing torrent to enter them. Just so of human
institutions—their value has in strict theory nothing whatever to do
with their energy-budget—being wholly a question of the form the
energy flows through. Though the *ultimate* state of the universe may
be its vital and psychical extinction, there is nothing in physics to
interfere with the hypothesis that the penultimate state might be the
millennium—in other words a state in which a minimum of difference
of energy-level might have its exchanges so skillfully *canalisés* that a
maximum of happy and virtuous consciousness would be the only
result. In short, the last expiring pulsation of the universe's life might
be, "I am so happy and perfect that I can stand it no longer." You

don't believe this and I don't say I do. But I can find nothing in "Energetik" to conflict with its possibility. You seem to me not to discriminate, but to treat quantity and distribution of energy as if they formed one question.

There! that's pretty good for a brain after 18 Nauheim baths—so I won't write another line, nor ask you to reply to me. In case you can't help doing so, however, I will gratify you now by saying that I probably won't jaw back.—It was pleasant at Paris to hear your identically unchanged and "undegraded" voice after so many years of loss of solar energy. Yours ever truly,

WM. JAMES.

[*Post-card*]

NAUHEIM, JUNE 19, 1910.

P. S. Another illustration of my meaning: The clock of the universe is running down, and by so doing makes the hands move. The energy absorbed by the hands and the *mechanical* work they do is the same day after day, no matter how far the weights have descended from the position they were originally wound up to. The *history* which the hands perpetrate has nothing to do with the *quantity* of this work, but follows the *significance* of the figures which they cover on the dial. If they move from O to XII, there is "progress," if from XII to O, there is "decay," etc. etc.

W. J.

[*Post-card*]

CONSTANCE, JUNE 26, [1910].

Yours of the 20th, just arriving, pleases me by its docility of spirit and passive subjection to philosophic opinion. Never, never pretend to an opinion of your own! that way lies every annoyance and madness! You tempt me to offer you another illustration—that of the *hydraulic ram* (thrown back to me in an exam. as a "hydraulic goat" by an insufficiently intelligent student). Let this arrangement of metal, placed in the course of a brook, symbolize the machine of human life. It works, clap, clap, clap, day and night, so long as the brook runs *at all,* and no matter how full the brook (which symbolizes the descending cosmic energy) may be, it works always to the same effect, of raising so many kilogrammeters of water. What the *value* of this work as history may be, depends on the uses to which the water is put in the house which the ram serves.

W. J.

—Letters of William James (II)

There was yet a wiser one, Justice Holmes, whose period of life coincided with that of Adams and James. Henry Adams, professedly a materialist, was really romanticizing history and life all the time. Henry Adams had intellect, without intuition; William James was all intuition; Justice Holmes had both, had wisdom. I mean that quality of mind which gives us a sense of confidence in its all-round view of life both as fact and as ideal, which is confirmed by all of us who find that we have to live. It is a view won, not by romanticizing or theorizing about it, but by taking life by the neck and looking at it stubbornly, critically, honestly and still hopefully. Such a view of life is neither idealistic nor materialistic but real; it is neither classicist nor romanticist but just human. It has an openness and a clear-eyed vision, like someone standing solidly on the earth, without forgetting to look up at the sky. I think Holmes' summary of his own philosophy of life in the speech before the Bar Association of Boston is worth a ton of airy philosophy.[5] "We cannot live our dreams. We are lucky enough if we can give a sample of our best, and if in our heads we can find it has been nobly done. . . . I mean in our ulterior intellectual or spiritual interest, in the ideal part, without which we are but snails or tigers."

No one should be a crass materialist or a starry-eyed idealist. Both are dangers to mankind. Holmes, in his learning and wisdom, saw this. He knew the value of romance in human life. Listen to him when he speaks about "the importance of the uneconomic to man." "If I wished to make you smile I might even ask whether life did not gain an enrichment from neglected opportunities which would be missed in the snug filling out of every chance. But I am not here to press a paradox. I only mean to insist on the importance of the uneconomic to man as he actually feels today. You may philosophize about the honors of leisure as a survival; you may, if you like, describe in the same way, as I have heard them described, the ideals which burn in the center of our hearts. None the less they are there. They are

[5] See Chapter XVI, Section 2.

categorical imperatives. They hold their own against hunger and thirst; they scorn to be classed as mere indirect supports of our bodily needs, which rather they defy; and our friends the economists would do well to take account of them, as some great writers like M. Tarde would take account of them, if they are to deal with man as he is." [7]

2. THE STUFF OF HUMAN EXPERIENCE

No, when we deal with human history or with contemporary human affairs, we are forced back to the obvious fact that man is a bundle of sentiments, of hopes and dreams and longings which are the most potent forces in the ordering of our lives, and if facts include feelings, then these sentiments are the most important facts in human history. There would be no objection to saying that man is spirit, but I think it would be clearer to say that man is sentiment, for if the soul is the functioning of man's personality rather than a mystic substance, then the existence of the human soul is to be sought in our tears and laughter. Give a modern philosopher tears and laughter, and he would not know what to do with them. In fact, he would look rather foolish. Yet sentiment, wise or foolish, constitutes the stuff of our human experience. Take away from man his fond hopes, dreams, and illusions, and he has ceased to live. Of this quality of sentiment, of tenderness particularly, the modern generation of writers shows little; the soft note is seldom heard. The modern writers talk not of sentiments, but of strong, violent, compelling passions. Yet like a low-scented herb, sentiment is always there in an unfrequented corner of our garden for him who has the sense to smell it and the taste to enjoy it. The suppressed cries and sobs of the human heart are usually so overlaid with the cold rationality of conventional life that they seem hardly detectable in social life. Yet I know that they are there. I would wager that the content of human life, life that vibrates with meaning, is ninety per cent wrapped up in such hopes, fancies, and secret, unavowed yearnings of men and women. Go down any alley, into any tenement house, and sentiment is there. Attention to these sentiments

[7] Address at the Dedication of the Northwestern University Law School Building, Chicago, October, 1902. *Collected Legal Papers.* Copyright, 1920, Harcourt, Brace & Company, Inc. Reprinted by permission.

of everyday life, or neglect of them, is merely a matter of literary fashions, reflecting the state of cultivation of men's minds. Some generations prefer the soft-scented lilacs; others prefer the suicidal intoxications of the poppy. Yet common hay is one of the sweetest smells on earth. It is a matter of taste.

I do not know whether we live today in fear of sentiment. We seem to. My thought goes back to the *Autocrat of the Breakfast Table,* essays written when sentiments rather too delicate for modern days were quietly enjoyed by all. The breakfast table is well chosen as a place for light, rambling, and quite often profound observations, but never a place for heated arguments, as might occur after supper. The humanity represented at the boardinghouse is average, and excepting the divinity student and the Autocrat himself, the others, like the young man called John, the lady in black bombazine, the landlady's daughter, and the boy called Benjamin Franklin, are none too intellectual. Nothing sensational happens, unless it is the engagement of the Autocrat and the schoolmistress at the end, but we are shown the quiet sentiments of this peaceful household of boarders. To be sure, it is only at breakfast, but the Autocrat happens to be Oliver Wendell Holmes, father of Justice Holmes, doctor and poet, and "king of New England dinner tables," a charming and vivacious conversationalist. The note of sentiment is best seen in his chapter on "Childhood Recollections." And no wonder, for it is in recollections of childhood that all our unburied dreams come out. It seems the best sentence Thoreau ever wrote was, "We seem to linger in manhood to tell the dreams of our childhood, and they vanish out of memory ere we learn the language." (*Journals,* Feb. 19, 1841.) No wonder that toward the end of his narrative, the old gentleman who was listening drew a long breath, "with such a tremor in it that a little more and it would have been a sob," and when the Autocrat went on to talk of an old love that was long lost and forgotten, the old gentleman drew out a watch, inside which was a faded watch-paper with a date, in small schoolgirl letters. . . .

Childhood Recollections

BY OLIVER WENDELL HOLMES

The firing of the great guns at the Navy-yard is easily heard at the place where I was born and lived. "There is a ship of war come in," they used to say, when they heard them. Of course, I supposed that such vessels came in unexpectedly, after indefinite years of absence,— suddenly as falling stones; and that the great guns roared in their astonishment and delight at the sight of the old war-ship splitting the bay with her cut-water. Now, the sloop-of-war the Wasp, Captain Blakely, after gloriously capturing the Reindeer and the Avon, had disappeared from the face of the ocean, and was supposed to be lost. But there was no proof of it, and, of course, for a time, hopes were entertained that she might be heard from. Long after the last real chance had utterly vanished, I pleased myself with the fond illusion that somewhere on the waste of waters she was still floating, and there were *years* during which I never heard the sound of the great gun booming inland from the Navy-yard without saying to myself, "The Wasp has come!" and almost thinking I could see her, as she rolled in, crumpling the water before her, weather-beaten, barnacled, with shattered spars and threadbare canvas, welcomed by the shouts and tears of thousands. This was one of those dreams that I nursed and never told. Let me make a clean breast of it now, and say, that, so late as to have outgrown childhood, perhaps to have got far on towards manhood, when the roar of the cannon has struck suddenly on my ear, I have started with a thrill of vague expectation and tremulous delight, and the long-unspoken words have articulated themselves in the mind's dumb whisper, *The Wasp has come!* . . .

(I say, then, most of the boarders had left the table about the time when I began telling some of these secrets of mine,—all of them, in fact, but the old gentleman opposite and the schoolmistress. I understand why a young woman should like to hear these simple but genuine experiences of early life, which are, as I have said, the little brown seeds of what may yet grow to be poems with leaves of azure and gold; but when the old gentleman pushed up his chair nearer to me, and slanted round his best ear, and once, when I was speaking of some trifling, tender reminiscence, drew a long breath, with such a tremor in it that a little more and it would have been a sob, why, then I felt there must be something of nature in them which redeemed their seeming insignificance. Tell me, man or woman with whom I am whispering, have you not a small store of recollections, such as these I am uncovering, buried beneath the dead leaves of many summers, perhaps under the unmelting snows of fast returning winters,— a few such recollections, which, if you should write them all out, would be swept into some careless editor's drawer, and might cost a scanty half hour's lazy reading to his subscribers,—and yet, if Death should cheat you out of them, you would not know yourself in eternity?) [*The Autocrat goes on to speak of three "acquaintances" of his childhood, one of which was love.*]

One other acquaintance I made at an earlier period of life than the habit of romancers authorizes.—Love, of course.—She was a famous beauty afterwards.—I am satisfied that many children rehearse their parts in the drama of life before they have shed all their milk-teeth.—I think I won't tell the story of the golden blonde.—I suppose everybody has had his childish fancies; but sometimes they are passionate impulses, which anticipate all the tremulous emotions belonging to a later period. Most children remember seeing and adoring an angel before they were a dozen years old.

(The old gentleman had left his chair opposite and taken a seat by the schoolmistress and myself, a little way from the table.—It's true, it's true,—said the old gentleman.—He took hold of a steel watch-chain, which carried a large, square gold key at one end and was supposed to have some kind of timekeeper at the other. With some trouble he dragged up an ancient-looking, thick, silver, bull's-eye watch. He looked at it for a moment,—hesitated,—touched the inner corner of his right eye with the pulp of his middle finger,—looked at the face of the watch,—said it was getting into the forenoon,—then opened the watch and handed me the loose outside case without a word.—The watch-paper had been pink once, and had a faint tinge still, as if all its tender life had not yet quite faded out. Two little birds, a flower, and, in small school-girl letters, a date,—17..—no matter.—Before I was thirteen years old,—said the old gentleman.—I don't know what was in that young schoolmistress's head, nor why she should have done it; but she took out the watch-paper and put it softly to her lips, as if she were kissing the poor thing that made it so long ago. The old gentleman took the watch-paper carefully from her, replaced it, turned away and walked out, holding the watch in his hand. I saw him pass the window a moment after with that foolish white hat on his head; he couldn't have been thinking of what he was about when he put it on. So the schoolmistress and I were left alone.)

—*The Autocrat of the Breakfast Table* (IX)

I am not certain whether the modern reader will enjoy this piece. It is no more than a tickle, a light nudge in our sensibilities. Modern nerves are so jangled and jazzified that we cannot enjoy a tingle, but only a wallop. The sentiments on which we are fed will have to be considerably more boisterous. A writer for a magazine is told by the editor to pack more "punch" into his article, because the readers need it. But if we have the quiet spirit, the *Autocrat* is as enjoyable as ever, and if we don't, I am afraid the loss is ours. He takes us to the world of Charles Lamb, and I have a notion he will last just as long. The difference is, the world he lived in was a good world, not the external world of his times, seething with political issues and spiritual revolts, but Holmes's own personal, inner world. He believed not only in the Saturday Club and the class of twenty-nine, he believed in "the tolerable certainty of human averages." Those people who can do so, who deal with the tolerable certainty of human averages, seem destined to outlast a generation of fashionable despair. The politics that agitated the souls of Emerson and Thoreau and Theodore Parker passed over him, and Lowell chided him for not throwing himself into the fray [8] —protesting against the Fugitive Slave Law of Massachusetts and the Mexican War—but he had a more sympathetic occupation, the human average. If he could believe in the human average, the average could not be so bad. He was interested in the human soul, and his one strenuous effort was to rescue it, not from God but from Calvin, and restore it to a free and independent and hopeful Americanism. No wonder that he wrote the "Chambered Nautilus" and "The Living

[8] Thoreau in turn rebuked Emerson for staying out of jail, when he himself went to jail as a protest against the law. Isn't it all a difference of degree?

Temple," in which we come as near an appreciation of the noble human soul as we ever can.

3. THE RIGHT TO ROMANCE

One of the most graceful gifts of mankind is the ability to tell fairy tales, not only to say that we wish a pumpkin might become a carriage and mice might become horses to draw it, but to make ourselves believe that these things did happen. No, it can't be; the whole Cinderella story is the result of a crazy imagination, reason says, but where is the heart that will not gladly assist at the moment when the Prince is about to try the glass slipper on Cinderella's foot and lead her off to a grand wedding ceremony? One begins to wonder whether reason or imagination is really perverse; the undeniable fact remains that humanity, generation after generation, in all countries and ages, affirms that the story is not only believable but actually true to life.[9] The modern realist would of course prefer a different treatment; he would picture the rags of Cinderella, her smutty face, the mousy smell of her hair, and her swollen legs; he would make an inventory of the broomsticks in her kitchen, the slop pail, the dishrag, the ash can, and dilate on her hatred of her stepsisters, most of all, hatred of her own mother; the stepsisters would offer an opportunity for a magnificent exhibition of human spite and sheer meanness and filthy language; one of them would by chicanery marry the Prince and torture him ever after, and Cinderella would remain an old maid, talking in stream-of-consciousness drivel bordering on lunacy. This would be offered to us as "real life." I am on the same side with James Branch Cabell and would bet with him that humanity would say no. Such a story would instantly perish.

I believe it is the human being's capacity for dreaming, his unwillingness to accept the gray wall of facts as his prison, his power of pulling down the blinds on present facts and sallying forth to seek the adventure of the unknown and unrealized, that is the ticket to his redemption. James Branch Cabell has made a gallant defense of

[9] The earliest written version of the Cinderella story is in Chinese, dated in the ninth century. See *The Wisdom of China and India*, p. 940. Random House. It has the cruel stepmother and stepsisters and the lost slipper and the handsome prince.

romance against realism in literature, the type of romance that he realized so successfully in *Jurgen*. With gentle irony, with suave and provoking sophistication, with that delightful mixture of gaiety and seriousness which is a manifestation of the true comic spirit, he discourses in *Beyond Life* on the important duty of a novelist to prevaricate gracefully, to lie sedulously and pleasingly about life, to transgress the Second Commandment, and to shoulder the heavy and inescapable obligation of avoiding facts. The demiurge here is the little god, the power of romance that controls men's lives. For without the spirit of romance and a certain amount of artful self-deception, life would be unlivable. If life "as it is" was not relieved by a "life as it ought to be," humanity would have perished long ago. Here is another American master of irony.

The Demiurge: "Gracefully to prevaricate about mankind and human existence was art's signal function."

BY JAMES BRANCH CABELL

—*What is man, that his welfare be considered?—an ape who chatters to himself of kinship with the archangels while filthily he digs for groundnuts. . . .*

—*Yet more clearly do I perceive that this same man is a maimed god. . . . He is under penalty condemned to compute eternity with false weights and to estimate infinity with a yardstick; and he very often does it. . . .*

—*There lies the choice which every man must make—or rationally to accept his own limitations? or stupendously to play the fool and swear that he is at will omnipotent?*

—Dizain des Reines

. . . humanity would seem at an early period to have wrenched comfort from prefiguring man as the hero of the cosmic romance. For it was unpleasantly apparent that man did not excel in physical strength, as set against the other creatures of a planet whereon may be encountered tigers and elephants. His senses were of low development, as compared with the senses of insects: and, indeed, senses possessed by

From *Beyond Life*. Reprinted by permission of the author and originally published by Robert M. McBride & Company.

some of these small contemporaries man presently found he did not share, nor very clearly understand. The luxury of wings, and even the common comfort of a caudal appendage, was denied him. He walked painfully, without hoofs, and, created naked as a shelled almond, with difficulty outlived a season of inclement weather. Physically, he displayed in not a solitary trait a product of nature's more ambitious labor. . . . He, thus, surpassed the rest of vital creation in nothing except, as was beginning to be rumored, the power to reason; and even so, was apparently too magnanimous to avail himself of the privilege.

But to acknowledge such disconcerting facts would never do: just as inevitably, therefore, as the peafowl came to listen with condescension to the nightingale, and the tortoise to deplore the slapdash ways of his contemporaries, man probably began very early to regale himself with flattering narratives as to his nature and destiny. Among the countless internecine animals that roamed earth, puissant with claw and fang and sinew, an ape reft of his tail, and grown rusty at climbing, was the most formidable, and in the end would triumph. It was of course considered blasphemous to inquire into the grounds for this belief, in view of its patent desirability, for the race was already human. So the prophetic portrait of man treading among cringing pleosauri to browbeat a frightened dinosaur was duly scratched upon the cave's wall, and art began forthwith to accredit human beings with every trait and destiny which they desiderated. . . .

And so to-day, as always, we delight to hear about invincible men and women of unearthly loveliness—corrected and considerably augmented versions of our family circle,—performing feats illimitably beyond our modest powers. And so to-day no one upon the preferable side of Bedlam wishes to be reminded of what we are in actuality, even were it possible, by any disastrous miracle, ever to dispel the mist which romance has evoked about all human doings; and to the golden twilight of which old usage has so accustomed us that, like nocturnal birds, our vision grows perturbed in a clearer atmosphere. And we have come very firmly to believe in the existence of men everywhere, not as in fact they are, but 'as they ought to be.'. . .

All is vanity, quoth the son of David, inverting the truth for popular consumption, as became a wise Preacher who knew that vanity is all. For man alone of animals plays the ape to his dreams. That a dog dreams vehemently is matter of public knowledge: it is perfectly possible that in his more ecstatic visions he usurps the shape of his master, and visits Elysian pantries in human form: with awakening, he observes that in point of fact he is a dog, and as a rational animal, makes the best of canineship. But with man the case is otherwise, in that when logic leads to any humiliating conclusion, the sole effect is to discredit logic.

So has man's indomitable vanity made a harem of his instincts, and walled off a seraglio wherein to beget the virtues and refinements and all ennobling factors in man's long progress from gorillaship. As has been suggested, creative literature would seem to have sprung simply from the instinct of any hurt animal to seek revenge,—and 'to get even,' as the phrase runs, in the field of imagination when such revenge was not feasible in any other arena. . . . Then, too, it is an instinct common to brute creatures that the breeding or even the potential mother must not be bitten,—upon which modest basis a little by a little mankind builded the fair code of domnei, or woman-worship, which for so long a while did yeoman service among legis-lators toward keeping half our citizens 'out of the mire of politics,' and which still enables any reputable looking married woman to kill whatsoever male she elects with impunity. . . .

Thus it is that romance, the real demiurge, the first and loveliest daughter of human vanity, contrives all those dynamic illusions which are used to further the ultimate ends of romance. . . .

Always, of course, the chivalrous attitude was an intelligent attitude, in which one spun romances and accorded no meticulous attention to mere facts. . . . For thus to spin romances is to bring about, in every sense, man's recreation, since man alone of animals can, actually, acquire a trait by assuming, in defiance of reason, that he already possesses it. To spin romances is, indeed, man's proper and peculiar function in a world wherein he only of created beings can make no profitable use of the truth about himself. For man alone of animals plays the ape to his dreams. . . .

And still—behold the miracle!—still I believe life to be a personal

transaction between myself and Omnipotence; I believe that what
I do is somehow of importance; and I believe that I am on a journey
toward some very public triumph not unlike that of the third prince in
the fairy-tale. . . . Even to-day I believe in this dynamic illusion. For
that creed was the first great inspiration of the demiurge,—man's big
romantic idea of Chivalry, of himself as his Father's representative in
an alien country;—and it is a notion at which mere fact and reason
yelp denial unavailingly. For every one of us is so constituted that he
knows the romance to be true, and corporal fact and human reason in
this matter, as in divers others, to be the suborned and perjured witnesses of 'realism.'

—*Beyond Life* (II)

4. WHEN THE PRACTICAL MAN BECOMES A LOVER

"Only in some pitiful dreamer, some philosopher, poet, or romancer,
or when the common practical man becomes a lover, does the hard
externality give way," says William James, "and a gleam of insight
into the ejective world . . . the vast world of inner life beyond us, so
different from the outer seeming, illuminate our mind." To illustrate
what he means, James quotes at length the essay by Robert Louis
Stevenson on "The Lantern-bearers," which he regards as deserving
to be immortal. I think it does. Stevenson, too, looks beneath the
external facts and joyously confirms the spark of honor, the fire of
fancy that lies hidden in every common man's breast. "Justice," he
remarks, "is not done to the versatility and the unplumbed childish-
ness of man's imagination." For man, after all, is an imaginative, as
well as a beef-eating animal.[10] "The ground of man's joy is often hard
to hit," and "the man's true life, for which he consents to live, lie[s]
altogether in the field of fancy." It is certainly no accident that Stevenson, like the Autocrat of the Breakfast Table, goes back to the inner
life of boyhood recollections.

[10] "Excite the soul," says Emerson, "and it suddenly becomes virtuous. Touch the deep,
and all these listless, stingy, beef-eating bystanders will see the dignity of the sentiment;
will say, This is good, and all I have I will give for that—" (*Journals*, December 29,
1834). In another entry, Emerson made a final, simple statement, "God defend me from
ever looking at a man as an animal—" (*Journals*, October 20, 1833).

"To miss the joy is to miss all."

BY WILLIAM JAMES

"Toward the end of September," Stevenson writes, "when school-time was drawing near, and the nights were already black, we would begin to sally from our respective villas, each equipped with a tin bull's-eye lantern. The thing was so well known that it had worn a rut in the commerce of Great Britain; and the grocers, about the due time, began to garnish their windows with our particular brand of luminary. We wore them buckled to the waist upon a cricket belt, and over them, such was the rigor of the game, a buttoned top-coat. They smelled noisomely of blistered tin. They never burned aright, though they would always burn our fingers. Their use was naught, the pleasure of them merely fanciful, and yet a boy with a bull's-eye under his top-coat asked for nothing more. The fishermen used lanterns about their boats, and it was from them, I suppose, that we had got the hint; but theirs were not bull's-eyes, nor did we ever play at being fishermen. The police carried them at their belts, and we had plainly copied them in that; yet we did not pretend to be policemen. Burglars, indeed, we may have had some haunting thought of; and we had certainly an eye to past ages when lanterns were more common, and to certain story-books in which we had found them to figure very largely. But take it for all in all, the pleasure of the thing was substantive; and to be a boy with a bull's-eye under his top-coat was good enough for us.

"When two of these asses met, there would be an anxious 'Have you got your lantern?' and a gratified 'Yes!' . . . Four or five would sometimes climb into the belly of a ten-man lugger, with nothing but the thwarts above them—for the cabin was usually locked—or chose out some hollow of the links where the wind might whistle overhead. . . .

"Say that we came [in such a realistic romance] on some such business as that of my lantern-bearers on the links, and described the boys as very cold, spat upon by flurries of rain, and drearily surrounded, all of which they were; and their talk as silly and indecent, which it certainly was. To the eye of the observer they *are* wet and cold and drearily surrounded; but ask themselves, and they are in the heaven of a recondite pleasure, the ground of which is an ill-smelling lantern.

"For, to repeat, the ground of a man's joy is often hard to hit. It may hinge at times upon a mere accessory, like the lantern; it may reside in the mysterious inwards of psychology. . . . It has so little bond with externals . . . that it may even touch them not, and the man's true life, for which he consents to live, lie together in the field of fancy. . . . In such a case the poetry runs underground. The observer (poor soul, with his documents!) is all abroad. For to look at the man is but to court deception. We shall see the trunk from which he draws his nourishment; but he himself is above and abroad in the green dome of foliage, hummed through by winds and nested in by nightingales. And the true realism were that of the poets, to climb after him like a squirrel, and catch some glimpse of the heaven in which he lives. And the true realism, always and everywhere, is that of the poets: to find out where joy resides, and give it a voice far beyond singing.

"For to miss the joy is to miss all. In the joy of the actors lies the sense of any action. That is the explanation, that the excuse."

"To miss the joy is to miss all." Indeed, it is. Yet we are but finite, and each one of us has some single specialized vocation of his own. And it seems as if energy in the service of its particular duties might be got only by hardening the heart toward everything unlike them. Our deadness toward all but one particular kind of joy would thus be the price we inevitably have to pay for being practical creatures. Only in some pitiful dreamer, some philosopher, poet, or romancer, or when the common practical man becomes a lover, does the hard externality give way, and a gleam of insight into the ejective world, as Clifford called it, the vast world of inner life beyond us, so different from that of outer seeming, illuminate our mind. Then the whole scheme of our customary values gets confounded, then our self is riven and its narrow interests fly to pieces, then a new centre and a new perspective must be found.

—"On a Certain Blindness in Human Beings,"
Talks to Teachers on Psychology

Hawthorne, whose main literary occupation may be described as brooding on the human heart, comes to this conclusion in his *American Notebooks,* "The human Heart to be allegorized as a cavern; at the entrance there is sunshine, and flowers growing about it. You step within, but a short distance, and begin to find yourself surrounded with a terrible gloom, and monsters of divers kinds; it seems like Hell itself. You are bewildered, and wander long without hope. At last light strikes upon you. You peep towards it, and find yourself in a region that seems, in some sort, to reproduce the flowers and sunny beauty of the entrance, but all perfect. These are the depths of the heart, or of human nature, bright and peaceful; the gloom and terror may lie deep; but deeper still is the eternal beauty."

5. THE SOUL'S VITAL RAPTURES

Nothing that Santayana wrote, I believe, quite equaled his two essays "Skylarks" and "At Heaven's Gate" in beauty and wisdom and truth. "Skylarks" is not an essay on skylarks but on the human soul itself, on the moments of spontaneity, courage, and trust when the human soul feels itself capable of doing things that at other moments it is powerless to do; the skylarks' song is a symbol of that divine madness which all beggars and prostitutes and common men are capable of attaining and which carries us to the very gates of heaven itself—the moments of redemption that wash away all the sins of our humdrum and troubled existence. For it is only when we can attain the stature of "common brave fools" that we can ever know we have a soul.

"With a simple courage which was half joy in living and half willingness to die"

BY GEORGE SANTAYANA

No, the trilling of larks is not for mankind. Like English poets they sing to themselves of nature, inarticulately happy in a bath of light and freedom, sporting for the sake of sport, turning what doubts they may have into sweetness, not asking to see or to know anything ulterior. They must needs drink the dew amongst these English fields, peeping into the dark little hearts and flushed petals of these daisies, like the heart and cheeks of an English child, or into these buttercups, yellow like his Saxon hair. They could hardly have built their nests far from this maze of little streams, or from these narrow dykes and ditches, arched with the scented tracery of limes and willows. They needed this long, dull, chilly winter in which to gather their unsuspected fund of yearning and readiness for joy; so that when high summer comes at last they may mount with virgin confidence and ardor through these sunlit spaces, to pour their souls out at heaven's gate.

At heaven's gate, but not in heaven. The sky, as these larks rise higher and higher, grows colder and thinner; if they could rise high enough, it would be a black void. All this fluid and dazzling atmosphere is but the drapery of earth; this cerulean vault is only a film round the oceans. As these choristers pass beyond the nether veils of air, the sun becomes fierce and comfortless; they freeze and are dazzled; they must hurry home again to earth if they would live. They must put fuel in their little engines: after all it was flesh and blood in them that were praising the Lord. And accordingly, down they drop to their nests and peck about, anxious and silent; but their song never comes down. Up there they leave it, in the glittering desert it once ravished, in what we call the past. They bore their glad offering to the gate and returned empty; but the gladness of it, which in their palpitation and hurry they only half guessed, passed in and is a part of heaven. In the home of all good, from which their frail souls fetched it for a moment, it is still audible for any ear that ever again can attune itself to that measure. All that was loved or beautiful at any time, or that shall be so hereafter, all that never was but that ought to have been, lives in that paradise, in the brilliant treasure-house of the gods.

How many an English spirit, too modest to be heard here, has now committed its secret to that same heaven! Caught by the impulse of the hour, they rose like larks in the morning, cheerily, rashly, to meet the unforeseen, fatal, congenial adventure, the goal not seen, the air not measured, but the firm heart steady through the fog or blinding fire, making the best of what came, trembling but ready for what might come, with a simple courage which was half joy in living and half willingness to die. Their first flight was often their last. What fell to earth was only a poor dead body, one of a million; what remained above perhaps nothing to speak of, some boyish sally or wistful fancy, less than the song of a lark for God to treasure up in his omniscience and eternity. Yet these common brave fools knew as well as the lark the thing that they could do, and did it; and of other gifts and other adventures they were not envious. Boys and free men are always a little inclined to flout what is not the goal of their present desires, or is beyond their present scope; spontaneity in them has its ebb-flow in mockery. Their tight little selves are too vigorous and too clearly determined to brood much upon distant things; but they are true to their own nature, they know and love the sources of their own strength. Like the larks, those English boys had drunk here the quintessence of many a sunlit morning; they had rambled through these same fields, fringed with hedges and peeping copse and downs purple with heather; these paths and streams had enticed them often; they had been vaguely happy in these quiet, habitable places. It was enough for them to live, as for nature to revolve; and fate, in draining in one draught the modest cup of their spirit, spared them the weary dilution and waste of it in the world. The length of things is vanity, only their height is joy.

Of myself also I would keep nothing but what God may keep of me —some lovely essence, mine for a moment in that I beheld it, some object of devout love enshrined where all other hearts that have a like intelligence of love in their day may worship it; but my loves themselves and my reasonings are but a flutter of feathers weaker than a lark's, a prattle idler than his warblings, happy enough if they too may fly with him and die with him at the gate of heaven.

—"At Heaven's Gate," *Soliloquies in England*

Chapter VI

NEW ENGLAND INTERLUDE

AN interlude means an intermission when some people may hang around the lobby for smoke and unfresh air, while others may sit and quietly listen to pick up and relish some airs that may have gone before or are a promise of what is to come. It seems appropriate here to pause and ponder and speculate about "the flowering of New England" in that brilliant epoch which may be called the Remarkable Decade of 1845–1855.

Within a period of ten years—or if we stretch it either way a little from the publication of Emerson's *Essays: Second Series* in 1844 to the founding of the *Atlantic* in 1857, within a period of fourteen years,— a host of literary works were produced, which may be regarded as first-class literature, some of world importance, and which may be worth as much as the American literary product during the rest of the nineteenth century put together. This flowering of New England was so concentrated. One wonders why. Without these books, American literature would be immeasurably poorer. Of course, the authors who thought and wrote in this period had begun their literary careers before 1844 and continued to write after 1857, but these years were striking enough as landmarks of this flowering of a culture that showed great depth, originality, and diversity of talent. The New England mind had stumbled upon some fertile idea and was thinking hard and with a freedom unknown before. It was pushing forward its spiritual frontiers. Emerson produced his *Essays: Second Series* ('44), *Representative Man* ('50), and *English Traits* ('56); Thoreau produced *A Week on the Concord and Merrimac River* ('49) and *Walden* ('54); Whitman, his *Leaves of Grass* ('55); Melville, *Moby Dick* ('51), besides his minor novels; Hawthorne gave us *Mosses from an Old Manse* ('46), *The Scarlet Letter* ('47), *The House of the Seven Gables* ('51) and his short stories; Holmes wrote The *Autocrat* ('57–'58) for the *Atlantic Monthly,* edited by Lowell; and Lowell wrote

The Bigelow Papers ('48); Francis Parkman produced his *Oregon Trail* ('49). In poetry, Bryant was continuing to write his poems; Whittier was writing *Ichabod* ('50) and other verses of political satire and agitation; and Longfellow published *Evangeline* ('49) and *Hiawatha* ('55). Certainly this is an imposing list. There were minor figures prominent in Unitarianism and transcendentalism, like Theodore Parker, to whom religion and antislavery were about the same thing; William Ellery Channing, the apostle of Unitarianism; Edward Everett, professor of Greek at Harvard, leavening the minds of the college students with Greek culture and German criticism; Margaret Fuller, the intellectual woman of the period, the Miranda of Lowell's *Fable for Critics;* George Ripley with his Transcendental Club; and the eccentric, warm, and abstruse Bronson Alcott, with his new ideas about education, father of Louisa Alcott and characterized by Carlyle as "like Don Quixote, whom nobody can laugh at without loving." There were Unitarianism, transcendentalism, socialism; people's minds were breaking loose from the hold of Calvin, and quite a few joined in the attack; there was political agitation about the Fugitive Slave Law and the Mexican War; there were Alcott's Fruitlands at Harvard and the Brook Farm near West Roxbury, which later became a phalanx of socialist Fourierism. There was what Emerson called in "New England Reformers" a "fertility of projects for the salvation of this world." It seemed that the rustle of God's footsteps could be heard in the late afternoon in Concord or Cambridge. Men's ideas were shaken loose; they were prying and probing at God's universe and some thought they were about to establish heaven, or the perfect human community on earth. Coupled with this intellectual revolution was the intellectual declaration of independence from the Old World, which Emerson led with his Phi Beta Kappa address and which many echoed, Lowell in his *Fable for Critics,* Whitman in his *Democratic Vistas* and Melville in his letters.

One should try to understand the origin of such a remarkable phenomenon. One should see how it came about. The period of spiritual leavening from 1820 to 1850 must be examined a little as the prelude to that final flowering of New England culture which forms the substance of Van Wyck Brook's first (though second in period) volume of his magnificent symphony of the periods of American literature. For this purpose, I think Emerson's "Life and Letters in New England" rewards one's reading richly. He was right in the movement; his own story of Transcendentalism is intrinsically valuable. I think it one of his best written pieces; his characterizations of the different characters are vivid and punctuated with humor; in old age Emerson revealed an unsuspected gift for drawing personal portraits.[1] He possessed the full power of analysis and criticism, and a line like "the young men were born with knives in their brain" shows that he could wield a pen well even when he was not solely occupied with wresting pure thoughts from the Elysian fields. Finally, I think his criticism of socialism and all social reforms like the Brook Farm community project shows a penetrating insight valid still today, while his characterization of Arthur Brisbane's mathematical socialism seems terribly amusing. Mark van Doren calls it "an exercise in social and intellectual history such as few men could have carried through so wittily and triumphantly," and remarks, "It is the history of a culture and as such is a model for other efforts in the field." I myself find the reading of this a sheer delight. For the convenience of the reader I have divided it into three sections here, and omitted a few paragraphs.

Historic Notes of Life and Letters in New England

BY RALPH WALDO EMERSON

> For Joy and Beauty planted it
> With faerie gardens cheered,
> And boding Fancy haunted it
> With men and women weird.

(1) *General influences.* The ancient manners were giving way. There grew a certain tenderness on the people, not before remarked. Children had been repressed and kept in the background; now they were considered, cosseted and pampered. I recall the remark of a witty physician who remembered the hardships of his own youth; he said, "It was a misfortune to have been born when children were nothing, and to live till men were nothing."

---

[1] Emerson probably wrote this in 1867, though it was published posthumously in 1883. It was thus among the last long pieces of his writing before his mental powers began to fail.

There are always two parties, the party of the Past and the party of the Future; the Establishment and the Movement. At times the resistance is reanimated, the schism runs under the world and appears in Literature, Philosophy, Church, State, and social customs. It is not easy to date these eras of activity with any precision, but in this region one made itself remarked, say in 1820 and the twenty years following.

It seemed a war between intellect and affection; a crack in nature, which split every church in Christendom into Papal and Protestant; Calvinism into Old and New schools; Quakerism into Old and New; brought new divisions in politics; as the new conscience touching temperance and slavery. The key to the period appeared to be that the mind had become aware of itself. Men grew reflective and intellectual. There was a new consciousness. The former generations acted under the belief that a shining social prosperity was the beatitude of man, and sacrificed uniformly the citizen to the State. The modern mind believed that the nation existed for the individual, for the guardianship and education of every man. This idea, roughly written in revolutions and national movements, in the mind of the philosopher had far more precision; the individual is the world.

This perception is a sword such as was never drawn before. It divides and detaches bone and marrow, soul and body, yea, almost the man from himself. It is the age of severance, of dissociation, of freedom, of analysis, of detachment. Every man for himself. The public speaker disclaims speaking for any other; he answers only for himself. The social sentiments are weak; the sentiment of patriotism is weak; veneration is low; the natural affections feebler than they were. People grow philosophical about native land and parents and relations. There is an universal resistance to ties and ligaments once supposed essential to civil society. The new race is stiff, heady and rebellious; they are fanatics in freedom; they hate tolls, taxes, turnpikes, banks, hierarchies, governors, yea, almost laws. They have a neck of unspeakable tenderness; it winces at a hair. They rebel against theological as against political dogmas; against mediation, or saints, or any nobility in the unseen.

The age tends to solitude. The association of the time is accidental and momentary and hypocritical, the detachment intrinsic and progressive. The association is for power, merely—for means; the end being the enlargement and independency of the individual. Anciently, society was in the course of things. There was a Sacred Band, a Theban Phalanx. There can be none now. College classes, military corps, or trades-unions may fancy themselves indissoluble for a moment, over their wine; but it is a painted hoop, and has no girth. The age of arithmetic and of criticism has set in. The structures of old faith in every department of society a few centuries have sufficed to destroy. Astrology, magic, palmistry, are long gone. The very last ghost is laid. Demonology is on its last legs. Prerogative, government, goes to pieces day by day. Europe is strewn with wrecks; a constitution once a week. In social manners and morals the revolution is just as evident. In the law courts, crimes of fraud have taken the place of crimes of force. The stockholder has stepped into the place of the warlike baron. The nobles shall not any longer, as feudal lords, have power of life and death over the churls, but now, in another shape, as capitalists, shall in all love and peace eat them up as before. Nay, government itself becomes the resort of those whom government was invented to restrain. "Are there any brigands on the road?" inquired the traveler in France. "Oh, no, set your heart at rest on that point," said the landlord; "what should these fellows keep the highway for, when they can rob just as effectually, and much more at their ease, in the bureaus of office?" . . .

The warm swart Earthspirit which made the strength of past ages, mightier than it knew, with instincts instead of science, like a mother yielding food from her own breast instead of preparing it through chemic and culinary skill—warm Negro ages of sentiment and vegetation—all gone; another hour had struck and other forms arose. Instead of the social existence which all shared, was now separation. Every one for himself; driven to find all his resources, hopes, rewards, society and deity within himself.

The young men were born with knives in their brain, a tendency to introversion, self-dissection, anatomizing of motives. . . .

Germany had created criticism in vain for us until 1820, when Edward Everett returned from his five years in Europe, and brought to Cambridge his rich results, which no one was so fitted by natural grace and the splendor of his rhetoric to introduce and recommend. He made us for the first time acquainted with Wolff's theory of the Homeric writings, with the criticism of Heyne. The novelty of the

learning lost nothing in the skill and genius of his relation, and
the rudest undergraduate found a new morning opened to him in
the lecture room of Harvard Hall.

There was an influence on the young people from the genius of
Everett which was almost comparable to that of Pericles in Athens.
He had an inspiration which did not go beyond his head, but which
made him the master of elegance. If any of my readers were at that
period in Boston or Cambridge, they will easily remember his radiant
beauty of person, of a classic style, his heavy large eye, marble lids,
which gave the impression of mass which the slightness of his form
needed; sculptured lips; a voice of such rich tones, such precise and
perfect utterance, that, although slightly nasal, it was the most mellow
and beautiful and correct of all the instruments of the time. The word
that he spoke, in the manner in which he spoke it, became current
and classical in New England. He had a great talent for collecting
facts, and for bringing those he had to bear with ingenious felicity on
the topic of the moment. Let him rise to speak on what occasion
soever, a fact had always just transpired which composed, with some
other fact well known to the audience, the most pregnant and happy
coincidence. It was remarked that for a man who threw out so many
facts he was seldom convicted of a blunder. He had a good deal of
special learning, and all his learning was available for purposes of the
hour. It was all new learning, that wonderfully took and stimulated
the young men. It was so coldly and weightily communicated from so
commanding a platform, as if in the consciousness and consideration of
all history and all learning—adorned with so many simple and austere
beauties of expression, and enriched with so many excellent digressions
and significant quotations, that, though nothing could be conceived beforehand less attractive or indeed less fit for green boys from Connecticut, New Hampshire and Massachusetts, with their unripe Latin
and Greek reading, than exegetical discourses in the style of Voss and
Wolff and Ruhnken, on the Orphic and Ante-Homeric remains—yet
this learning instantly took the highest place to our imagination in our
unoccupied American Parnassus. All his auditors felt the extreme
beauty and dignity of the manner, and even the coarsest were contented to go punctually to listen, for the manner, when they had found
out that the subject-matter was not for them. In the lecture room, he

abstained from all ornament, and pleased himself with the play of detailing erudition in a style of perfect simplicity. In the pulpit (for he was then a clergyman) he made amends to himself and his auditor for the self-denial of the professor's chair, and, with an infantine simplicity still, of manner, he gave the reins to his florid, quaint and affluent fancy.

. . . He had nothing in common with vulgarity and infirmity, but, speaking, walking, sitting, was as much aloof and uncommon as a star. The smallest anecdote of his behavior or conversation was eagerly caught and repeated, and every young scholar could recite brilliant sentences from his sermons, with mimicry, good or bad, of his voice. This influence went much farther, for he who was heard with such throbbing hearts and sparkling eyes in the lighted and crowded churches, did not let go his hearers when the church was dismissed, but the bright image of that eloquent form followed the boy home to his bed-chamber; and not a sentence was written in academic exercises, not a declamation attempted in the college chapel, but showed the omnipresence of his genius to youthful heads. This made every youth his defender, and boys filled their mouths with arguments to prove that the orator had a heart. This was a triumph of Rhetoric. It was not the intellectual or the moral principles which he had to teach. It was not thoughts. When Massachusetts was full of his fame it was not contended that he had thrown any truths into circulation. But his power lay in the magic of form; it was in the graces of manner; in a new perception of Grecian beauty, to which he had opened our eyes. There was that finish about this person which is about women, and which distinguishes every piece of genius from the works of talent—that these last are more or less matured in every degree of completeness according to the time bestowed on them, but works of genius in their first and slightest form are still wholes. In every public discourse there was nothing left for the indulgence of his hearer, no marks of late hours and anxious, unfinished study, but the goddess of grace had breathed on the work a last fragrancy and glitter.

By a series of lectures largely and fashionably attended for two winters in Boston he made a beginning of popular literary and miscellaneous lecturing, which in that region at least had important results. It is acquiring greater importance every day, and becoming a national

institution. I am quite certain that this purely literary influence was
of the first importance to the American mind.

In the pulpit Dr. Frothingham, an excellent classical and German
scholar, had already made us acquainted, if prudently, with the genius
of Eichhorn's theologic criticism. And Professor Norton a little later
gave form and method to the like studies in the then infant Divinity
School. But I think the paramount source of the religious revolution
was Modern Science. . . .

(2) *Transcendentalists.* I attribute much importance to two papers
of Dr. Channing, one on Milton and one on Napoleon, which were
the first specimens in this country of that large criticism which in
England had given power and fame to the *Edinburgh Review.* They
were widely read, and of course immediately fruitful in provoking
emulation which lifted the style of journalism. Dr. Channing, whilst
he lived, was the star of the American Church, and we then thought,
if we do not still think, that he left no successor in the pulpit. He
could never be reported, for his eye and voice could not be printed,
and his discourses lose their best in losing them. He was made for
the public; his cold temperament made him the most unprofitable
private companion; but all America would have been impoverished
in wanting him. We could not then spare a single word he uttered
in public, not so much as the reading a lesson in Scripture, or a hymn,
and it is curious that his printed writings are almost a history of the
times; as there was no great public interest, political, literary, or even
economical (for he wrote on the Tariff), on which he did not leave
some printed record of his brave and thoughtful opinion. A poor little
invalid all his life, he is yet one of those men who vindicate the power
of the American race to produce greatness.

Dr. Channing took counsel in 1840 with George Ripley, to the point
whether it were possible to bring cultivated, thoughtful people together, and make society that deserved the name. He had earlier talked
with Dr. John Collins Warren on the like purpose, who admitted the
wisdom of the design and undertook to aid him in making the experiment. Dr. Channing repaired to Dr. Warren's house on the appointed evening, with large thoughts which he wished to open. He
found a well-chosen assembly of gentlemen variously distinguished;
there was mutual greeting and introduction, and they were chatting

agreeably on indifferent matters and drawing gently towards their great expectation, when a side-door opened, the whole company streamed in to an oyster supper, crowned by excellent wines; and so ended the first attempt to establish aesthetic society in Boston.

Some time afterwards Dr. Channing opened his mind to Mr. and Mrs. Ripley, and with some care they invited a limited party of ladies and gentlemen. I had the honor to be present. Though I recall the fact, I do not retain any instant consequence of this attempt, or any connection between it and the new zeal of the friends who at that time began to be drawn together by sympathy of studies and of aspiration. Margaret Fuller, George Ripley, Dr. Convers Francis, Theodore Parker, Dr. Hedge, Mr. Brownson, James Freeman Clarke, William H. Channing, and many others, gradually drew together and from time to time spent an afternoon at each other's houses in a serious conversation. With them was always one well-known form,[2] a pure idealist, not at all a man of letters, nor of any practical talent, nor a writer of books; a man quite too cold and contemplative for the alliances of friendship, with rare simplicity and grandeur of perception, who read Plato as an equal, and inspired his companions only in proportion as they were intellectual—whilst the men of talent complained of the want of point and precision in this abstract and religious thinker.

These fine conversations, of course, were incomprehensible to some in the company, and they had their revenge in their little joke. One declared that "It seemed to him like going to heaven in a swing"; another reported that, at a knotty point in the discourse, a sympathizing Englishman with a squeaking voice interrupted with the question, "Mr. Alcott, a lady near me desires to inquire whether omnipotence abnegates attribute?"

I think there prevailed at that time a general belief in Boston that there was some concert of *doctrinaires* to establish certain opinions and inaugurate some movement in literature, philosophy, and religion, of which design the supposed conspirators were quite innocent; for there was no concert, and only here and there two or three men or women who read and wrote, each alone, with unusual vivacity. Perhaps they only agreed in having fallen upon Coleridge and Words-

[2] This was Bronson Alcott.

worth and Goethe, then on Carlyle, with pleasure and sympathy. Otherwise, their education and reading were not marked, but had the American superficialness, and their studies were solitary. I suppose all of them were surprised at this rumor of a school or sect, and certainly at the name of Transcendentalism, given nobody knows by whom, or when it was first applied. As these persons became in the common chances of society acquainted with each other, there resulted certainly strong friendships, which of course were exclusive in proportion to their heat: and perhaps those persons who were mutually the best friends were the most private and had no ambition of publishing their letters, diaries, or conversation.

From that time meetings were held for conversation, with very little form, from house to house, of people engaged in studies, fond of books, and watchful of all the intellectual light from whatever quarter it flowed. Nothing could be less formal, yet the intelligence and character and varied ability of the company gave it some notoriety and perhaps waked curiosity as to its aims and results.

Nothing more serious came of it than the modest quarterly journal called *The Dial* which, under the editorship of Margaret Fuller, and later of some other, enjoyed its obscurity for four years. All its papers were unpaid contributions, and it was rather a work of friendship among the narrow circle of students than the organ of any party. Perhaps its writers were its chief readers: yet it contained some noble papers by Margaret Fuller, and some numbers had an instant exhausting sale, because of papers by Theodore Parker.

Theodore Parker was our Savonarola, an excellent scholar, in frank and affectionate communication with the best minds of his day, yet the tribune of the people, and the stout Reformer to urge and defend every cause of humanity with and for the humblest of mankind. He was no artist. Highly refined persons might easily miss in him the element of beauty. What he said was mere fact, almost offended you, so bald and detached; little cared he. He stood altogether for practical truth; and so to the last. He used every day and hour of his short life, and his character appeared in the last moments with the same firm control as in the mid-day of strength. I habitually apply to him the words of a French philosopher who speaks of "the man of Nature who abominates the steam-engine and the factory. His vast lungs breathe independence with the air of the mountains and the woods.". . .

(3) *Socialists*. These reformers were a new class. Instead of the fiery souls of the Puritans, bent on hanging the Quaker, burning the witch and banishing the Romanist, these were gentle souls, with peaceful and even with genial dispositions, casting sheep's-eyes even on Fourier and his houris. It was a time when the air was full of reform. Robert Owen of Lanark came hither from England in 1845, and read lectures or held conversations wherever he found listeners; the most amiable, sanguine and candid of men. He had not the least doubt that he had hit on a right and perfect socialism, or that all mankind would adopt it. . . .

And truly I honor the generous ideas of the Socialists, the magnificence of their theories, and the enthusiasm with which they have been urged. They appeared the inspired men of their time. Mr. Owen preached his doctrine of labor and reward, with the fidelity and devotion of a saint, to the slow ears of his generation. Fourier, almost as wonderful an example of the mathematical mind of France as La Place or Napoleon, turned a truly vast arithmetic to the question of social misery, and has put men under the obligation which a generous mind always confers, of conceiving magnificent hopes and making great demands as the right of man. He took his measure of that which all should and might enjoy, from no soup-society or charity-concert, but from the refinements of palaces, the wealth of universities, and the triumphs of artists. He thought nobly. A man is entitled to pure air, and to the air of good conversation in his bringing up, and not, as we or so many of us, to the poor smell and musty chambers, cats and fools. Fourier carried a whole French Revolution in his head, and much more. Here was arithmetic on a huge scale. His ciphering goes where ciphering never went before, namely, into stars, atmospheres, and animals, and men and women, and classes of every character. It was the most entertaining of French romances, and could not but suggest vast possibilities of reform to the coldest and least sanguine.

We had an opportunity of learning something of these Socialists and their theory, from the indefatigable apostle of the sect in New York, Albert Brisbane. Mr. Brisbane pushed his doctrine with all the force of memory, talent, honest faith and importunacy. As we listened to his exposition it appeared to us the sublime of mechanical philosophy; for the system was the perfection of arrangement and contrivance. The force of arrangement could no farther go. The merit of the plan was that it was a system; that it had not the partiality and hint-and-fragment character of most popular schemes, but was coherent and comprehensive of facts to a wonderful degree. It was not daunted by distance, or magnitude, or remoteness of any sort, but strode about nature with a giant's step, and skipped no fact, but wove its large Ptolemaic web of cycle and epicycle, of phalanx and phalanstery, with laudable assiduity. Mechanics were pushed so far as fairly to meet spiritualism. One could not but be struck with strange coincidences betwixt Fourier and Swedenborg. Genius hitherto has been shamefully misapplied, a mere trifler. It must now set itself to raise the social condition of man and to redress the disorders of the planet he inhabits. The Desert of Sahara, the Campagna di Roma, the frozen Polar circles, which by their pestilential or hot or cold airs poison the temperate regions, accuse man. Society, concert, cooperation, is the secret of the coming Paradise. By reason of the isolation of men at the present day, all work is drudgery. By concert and the allowing each laborer to choose his own work, it becomes pleasure. "Attractive Industry" would speedily subdue, by adventurous scientific and persistent tillage, the pestilential tracts; would equalize temperature, give health to the globe and cause the earth to yield "healthy imponderable fluids" to the solar system, as now it yields noxious fluids. The hyena, the jackal, the gnat, the bug, the flea, were all beneficent parts of the system; the good Fourier knew what those creatures should have been, had not the mold slipped, through the bad state of the atmosphere; caused no doubt by the same vicious imponderable fluids. All these shall be redressed by human culture, and the useful goat and dog and innocent poetical moth, or the wood-tick to consume decomposing wood, shall take their place. It takes sixteen hundred and eighty men to make one Man, complete in all the faculties; that is, to be sure that you have got a good joiner, a good cook, a barber, a poet, a judge, an umbrella-maker, a mayor and alderman, and so on. Your community should consist of two thousand persons, to prevent accidents of omission; and each community should take up six thousand acres of land. Now fancy the earth planted with fifties and hundreds of these phalanxes side by side—what tillage, what architecture, what refectories, what dormitories, what reading-rooms, what concerts, what lectures, what gardens, what baths! . . . Poverty shall be abolished; deformity, stupidity and crime shall be no more. Genius, grace, art, shall abound, and it is not to be doubted but that in the reign of "Attractive Industry" all men will speak in blank verse.

Certainly we listened with great pleasure to such gay and magnificent pictures. The ability and earnestness of the advocate and his friends, the comprehensiveness of their theory, its apparent directness of proceeding to the end they would secure, the indignation they felt and uttered in the presence of so much social misery, commanded our attention and respect. It contained so much truth, and promised in the attempts that shall be made to realize it so much valuable instruction, that we are engaged to observe every step of its progress. Yet in spite of the assurances of its friends that it was new and widely discriminated from all other plans for the regeneration of society, we could not exempt it from the criticism which we apply to so many projects for reform with which the brain of the age teems. Our feeling was that Fourier had skipped no fact but one, namely Life. He treats man as a plastic thing, something that may be put up or down, ripened or retarded, molded, polished, made into solid or fluid or gas, at the will of the leader; or perhaps as a vegetable, from which, though now a poor crab, a very good peach can by manure and exposure be in time produced—but skips the faculty of life, which spawns and scorns system and system-makers; which eludes all conditions; which makes or supplants a thousand phalanxes and New Harmonies with each pulsation. There is an order in which in a sound mind the faculties always appear, and which, according to the strength of the individual, they seek to realize in the surrounding world. The value of Fourier's system is that it is a statement of such an order externized, or carried outward into its correspondence in facts. The mistake is that this particular order and series is to be imposed, by force or preaching and votes, on all men, and carried into rigid execution. But what is true and good must not only be begun by life, but must be conducted to its issues by life. Could not the conceiver of this design have also believed that a similar model lay in every mind, and that the method of each associate might be trusted, as well as that of his particular Committee and General Office, No. 200 Broadway? Nay, that it would be better to say,

Let us be lovers and servants of that which is just, and straightway every man becomes a center of a holy and beneficent republic, which he sees to include all men in its law, like that of Plato, and of Christ. Before such a man the whole world becomes Fourierized or Christized or humanized, and in obedience to his most private being he finds himself, according to his presentiment, though against all sensuous probability, acting in strict concert with all others who followed their private light.

Yet, in a day of small, sour and fierce schemes, one is admonished and cheered by a project of such friendly aims and of such bold and generous proportion; there is an intellectual courage and strength in it which is superior and commanding; it certifies the presence of so much truth in the theory, and in so far is destined to be fact.

It argued singular courage, the adoption of Fourier's system, to even a limited extent, with his books lying before the world only defended by the thin veil of the French language. The Stoic said, Forbear; Fourier said, Indulge. Fourier was of the opinion of St. Evremond; abstinence from pleasure appeared to him a great sin. Fourier was very French indeed. He labored under a misapprehension of the nature of women. The Fourier marriage was a calculation how to secure the greatest amount of kissing that the infirmity of human constitution admitted. It was false and prurient, full of absurd French superstitions about women; ignorant how serious and how moral their nature always is; how chaste is their organization; how lawful a class. . . .

There is of course to every theory a tendency to run to an extreme, and to forget the limitations. In our free institutions, where every man is at liberty to choose his home and his trade, and all possible modes of working and gaining are open to him, fortunes are easily made by thousands, as in no other country. Then property proves too much for the man, and the men of science, art, intellect, are pretty sure to degenerate into selfish housekeepers, dependent on wine, coffee, furnace-heat, gas-light and fine furniture. Then instantly things swing the other way, and we suddenly find that civilization crowed too soon; that what we bragged as triumphs were treacheries: that we have opened the wrong door and let the enemy into the castle; that civilization was a mistake; that nothing is so vulgar as a great warehouse of rooms full of furniture and trumpery; that, in the circumstances, the best wisdom were an auction or a fire. Since the foxes and the birds have the right of it, with a warm hole to keep out the weather, and no more—a penthouse to fend the sun and rain is the house which lays no tax on the owner's time and thoughts, and which he can leave, when the sun is warm, and defy the robber. This was Thoreau's doctrine, who said that the Fourierists had a sense of duty which led them to devote themselves to their second-best. And Thoreau gave in flesh and blood and pertinacious Saxon belief the purest ethics. He was more real and practically believing in them than any of his company, and fortified you at all times with an affirmative experience which refused to be set aside. Thoreau was in his own person a practical answer, almost a refutation, to the theories of the socialists. He required no Phalanx, no Government, no society, almost no memory. He lived extempore from hour to hour, like the birds and the angels; brought every day a new proposition, as revolutionary as that of yesterday, but different: the only man of leisure in his town; and his independence made all others look like slaves. He was a good Abbot Sampson, and carried a counsel in his breast. "Again and again I congratulate myself on my so-called poverty, I could not overstate this advantage." "What you call bareness and poverty, is to me simplicity. God could not be unkind to me if he should try. I love best to have each thing in its season only, and enjoy doing without it at all other times. It is the greatest of all advantages to enjoy no advantage at all. I have never got over my surprise that I should have been born into the most estimable place in all the world, and in the very nick of time too." There's an optimist for you.

I regard these philanthropists as themselves the effects of the age in which we live, and, in common with so many other good facts, the efflorescence of the period, and predicting a good fruit that ripens. They were not the creators they believed themselves, but they were unconscious prophets of a true state of society; one which the tendencies of nature lead unto, one which always establishes itself for the sane soul, though not in that manner in which they paint it; but they were describers of that which is really being done.

—"Historic Notes of Life and Letters in New England"

Emerson goes on to draw an intimate and in part a humorous picture of the Brook Farm co-operative community, which existed from 1841 to 1847: "Letters were flying not only from house to house, but from room to room. It was a perpetual picnic, a French Revolution in small, an age of Reason in a patty-pan." It was inspiring and disorderly. One man would plow all day, and another would look out of the window all day, thinking he was painting. Perhaps it was like a magnified ultraprogressive secondary school of today, with grown-ups instead of children trying to get the educative value out of flying out of individual personalities. "The ladies took cold on washing day; so it was ordained that the gentlemen-shepherds should wring and hang out clothes; which they punctually did. And it would sometimes occur that when they danced in the evening, clothes-pins dropped plentifully from their pockets." And above all there was the great question of all Utopias; who was to do the dirty work, like cleaning up tables and washing dishes? It was anarchical and stimulating. And Emerson concludes with these words, confident of the broad foundations for a future American culture, that was no longer rude and eccentric, but was beginning to grow a quiet and sustaining power:

"I recall these few selected facts, none of them of much independent interest, but symptomatic of the times and country. I please myself with the thought that our American mind is not now eccentric or rude in its strength, but is beginning to show a quiet power, drawn from wide and abundant sources, proper to a Continent and to an educated people. If I have owed much to the special influences I have indicated, I am not less aware of that excellent and increasing circle of masters in arts and in song and in science, who cheer the intellect of our cities and this country today—whose genius is not a lucky accident, but normal, and with broad foundation of culture, and so inspires the hopes of steady strength advancing on itself, and a day without night."

Chapter VII

LIFE

I. THOREAU AND CONFUCIUS

EMERSON and Thoreau, we know, quoted liberally from Confucius and Mencius. Being a Chinese I do not conceal my delight at discovering any affinity of spirit or exchange of influence between the East and the West. American thinking in Emerson's and Thoreau's times was global though American trade then was not. The Transcendentalists attended to the best of Oriental culture. An idea, like a seed carried by a sea bird across the ocean, was brought and deposited in another continent; in time it sprouted and gave forth new ideas but, while these ideas were encased in some old volume, their potential life was not lost, and fifty or perhaps a hundred years afterward were carried again to the original continent as a return gift. This seems to me to be the story of the psychic transmission of ideas from China and India via Thoreau and back to India. Thoreau had read a lot of Oriental books in Emerson's house and probably those in the Athenaeum of Boston, as is evidenced by the many quotations in *Walden*.[1] When he found in Confucius, that lover of life, something about the values of living, his heart must have been greatly pleased that it coincided exactly with his own. I therefore cannot resist the temptation to introduce here a passage from Confucius which Thoreau so much admired that he copied it out in its entirety. It is not only witty; it bears closely on the subject of the real values of living. I myself have always admired this passage, which may remove for many readers the erroneous impression that Confucius ever allowed himself to be puritanical or pedantic. It is found in Thoreau's unpublished papers.[2]

---

[1] Thomas Cholmondeley's collection of forty-four Oriental books sent from England was received by Thoreau in 1855 after his *Walden* was published.

[2] Reprinted in Arthur Christy, *The Orient in American Transcendentalism*. Columbia University Press.

"Spring being no more ... covered with the bonnet of man-hood, accompanied by five or six men, and six or seven children, I should love to go and bathe in the waters ..."

BY HENRY DAVID THOREAU

I lately read an anecdote of Confucius and his disciples ... Tseu-lou, Thseng-sie, Yan-yeou, Kong-si-hoa, were seated by the side of the Philosopher. The Philosopher said: Make no account of my age more than if I were only a day older than you. Living apart and isolated, then you say: We are not known. If any one knew you, then what would you do?

Tseu-lou replied with a brisk but respectful air: Suppose a kingdom of a thousand war-chariots, hard pressed between other great kingdoms, add even, by enormous armies, and that withal it suffers from want and famine; let Yeou (Tseu-lou) be appointed to its administration, in less than three years I could accomplish that the people of this kingdom should recover a manly courage, and know their condition. The Philosopher smiled at these words.

And you, Khieou, what are your thoughts?

The disciple replied respectfully: Suppose a province of sixty or seventy *li* in extent, or even fifty or sixty *li,* and that Khieou were appointed to its administration, in less than three years I could accomplish that the people should have sufficient. As to the rites and to music, I could entrust the teaching of them to a superior man.

And you, Tchi, what are your thoughts?

The disciple replied respectfully: I will not say that I can do these things; I desire to study. When the ceremonies of the temple of ancestors are performed, and great public assemblies take place, clothed in my robe of azure and other vestments proper for such a place and such ceremonies, I could wish to take part in the quality of a humble functionary.

And you, Tian, what are your thoughts?

The disciple did nothing but draw some rare sounds from his guitar; but these sounds prolonging themselves, he laid it aside, and rising, replied respectfully: My opinion differs entirely from that of my fellow disciples.—The philosopher said: What prevents you from expressing it? Here each one can speak his thought.—The disciple said: Spring being no more, my robe of spring laid aside, but covered with the bonnet of manhood, accompanied by five or six men, and six or seven young people, I should love to go and bathe in the waters of the Y——, to go and take the fresh air in those woody places where they offer sacrifices to heaven to obtain rain, to modulate some airs, and then return to my abode.[3]

The Philosopher applauding these words by a sigh of satisfaction, said: I am of Tian's mind.

The three disciples departed, but Thseng-sie remained yet some time. Thseng-sie said: What ought one to think of the words of these three disciples? The Philosopher said: Each one of them has expressed his opinion; that is all.

The narrator proceeds to tell why the Philosopher smiled; but that is obvious enough. For the most part, when I listen to the conversation of the Reformers, I too am of Tian's mind.

—Unpublished papers

Confucius was of Tian's mind. Thoreau was of Tian's mind, unmistakably. And I am of Tian's mind. Being of Tian's mind, we can move forward and tackle the problems of living, of life, liberty, and the pursuit of happiness, and of all the arts of living which are not only rights but also the high privileges of human life.

2. NO APOLOGY FOR LIVING

"Do not apologize, friend, when you have come into my field. You do not interrupt me. What you have come for is of more importance than corn. Who is it that says I must plow so many furrows this day? *Come friend, and sit here on these clods; we will sweeten the evening with fine words. We will invest our time not in corn, or in cash, but in life.*"

When I first ran across these words by David Grayson, it was incredible to me that a contemporary American could have written them.

[3] Most translations of the Chinese classics attempt to be scholarly by being unclear and stilted, and end up by being incorrect. "The spring being no more" should be "On a late spring day." "The robe of spring laid aside" should be "putting on my newly made spring gown." "But covered with the bonnet of manhood, accompanied by five or six

I have not found in the whole history of American writing any writer so serene except Franklin and Oliver Wendell Holmes. I mean not the calm of mere animal complacency, but the serenity of an intelligence which is broad and strong, which looks at the world honestly and clearly and still enjoys it, and from the plenitude of its inward powers is master of life instead of being a slave to it. Calvinism darkened the first half of the history of American writing, and when its influence was dissolving at about the time of the Brook Farm enthusiasts, when man's spirit was beginning to feel free as it should be, something called Realism with a capital letter came and settled its shadow over the second half, so that from Hawthorne and Melville down to Eugene O'Neill man's thought was preoccupied with sin and the abysses of sin. I do not deny that there was a flutter of the wings of the spirit in Emerson and Thoreau and Alcott and Ripley and the whole lot of them; I do not deny that Emerson had achieved serenity in spirit and in appearance—he had true composure—and that Thoreau truly knew happiness, but the strident note in the latter is quite noticeable and Emerson felt the responsibility of the whole world on

---

men," should be merely "accompanied by five or six grownups." "Six or seven young people" here stands for the simple Chinese phrase "six or seven children." "Modulate some airs and return to my abode" is translated from the simple, clear Chinese three words "Sing on the way home." A proper rendering of this sentence would therefore be, quite simply: "On a late spring day, putting on my newly made spring gown, and accompanied by five or six grownups and six or seven children, I would love to go and bathe in the Yi and enjoy the breeze on the Wuyu Terrace, and then we would sing together on our way home." What really happened, according to the Chinese text, was that Tian had just finished playing on the guitar and, laying it aside *with a bang,* rose and replied, etc., not "these sounds prolonging themselves, he laid it aside." The translator here gratuitously added the word "respectfully," to fit in with the Western notion of Confucian decorum. The reader thus misses the charm of informality which was characteristic of Confucius in intimate circles, and of this particular passage. Tian had shown some hesitation in expressing his ideal because it was different from that of the three others, but what Confucius said in encouraging him was, literally, *"What's the harm?* Each one is saying what he thinks"—not the rather formal "What prevents you from expressing it?" At the end, according to the Chinese text, Confucius merely "said with a sigh, 'Tian is the man for me!' "—not "applauding these words by a sigh of satisfaction, said, etc." I cannot refrain from recording my protest at such translations of the Chinese classics. Here is one example from James Legge's translation of Mencius. Mencius once said that in a battle, "the weather is less important than the terrain, and the terrain is less important than morale," in a language perfectly clear to every child. Legge made Mencius say, "Opportunities of time (vouchsafed by) Heaven are not equal to advantages of situation (afforded by) the earth, and advantages of situation (afforded by) the earth are not equal to the strength (arising from the) accord of men." The Chinese text of this extraordinary circumlocution consists of exactly twelve words!

his shoulders; consequently one could hear the heavy tread and the panting breath even while these two noble spirits were trying to throw off the load of Calvinistic tradition. Thoreau was even squeamish about eating the fish he had caught with his own hands or trapping some animals for Agassiz. Justice Holmes said that Thoreau was a man who insisted on nibbling his asparagus at the wrong end, and Emerson noted in his *Journals* that while walking with his friend he would as soon think of holding Thoreau's hand as holding the arm of an elm tree.

But Grayson is outside, waiting on the corn field, and let us hear him—*under the blue sky*. Listen and feel with him the joy of living. Grayson was more naturalistic than the naturalists, he was natural; more realistic than the realists, he was real; and the natural, unsophisticated man came in the twentieth century, and the sophisticated naturalists comprehended him not. He was talking with a straggler, the professor with his tin botany box (the botany professor probably was in reality his father-in-law). The professor strayed into Grayson's field, without knowing it, and hesitated a little.

"I must make inquiry of the direction of every thoughtful man I meet."

BY DAVID GRAYSON

His walk was slow and methodical, his head and even his shoulders were bent—almost habitually—from looking close upon the earth, and from time to time he stooped, and once he knelt to examine some object that attracted his eye. It seemed appropriate that he should thus kneel to the earth. So he gathered *his* crop and fences did not keep him out nor titles disturb him. He also was free! It gave me at that moment a peculiar pleasure to have him on my land, to know that I was, if unconsciously, raising other crops than I knew. I felt friendship for this old professor: I could understand him, I thought. And I said aloud but in a low tone, as though I were addressing him:

—Do not apologize, friend, when you come into my field. You do not interrupt me. What you have come for is of more importance at this moment than corn. Who is it that says I must plow so many furrows this day? Come in, friend, and sit here on these clods: we will sweeten the evening with fine words. We will invest our time not in corn, or in cash, but in life.—

I walked with confidence down the hill toward the professor. . . . So we talked, or rather he talked, finding in me an eager listener. And what he called botany seemed to me to be life. Of birth, of growth, of reproduction, of death, he spoke, and his flowers became sentient creatures under my eyes.

And thus the sun went down and the purple mists crept silently along the distant low spots, and all the great, great mysteries came and stood before me beckoning and questioning. They came and they stood, and out of the coneflower, as the old professor spoke, I seemed to catch a glimmer of the true light. I reflected how truly everything is in anything. If one could really understand a coneflower he could understand this Earth. Botany was only one road toward the Explanation.

Always I hope that some traveler may have more news of the way than I, and sooner or later, I find I must make inquiry of the direction of every thoughtful man I meet. And I have always had especial hope of those who study the sciences: they ask such intimate questions of nature. Theology possesses a vain-gloriousness which places its faith in human theories; but science, at its best, is humble before nature herself. It has no thesis to defend: it is content to kneel upon the earth, in the way of my friend, the old professor, and ask the simplest questions, hoping for some true reply.

I wondered, then, what the professor thought, after his years of work, of the Mystery; and finally, not without confusion, I asked him. . . . he smiled and said briskly:

"I have been a botanist for fifty-four years. When I was a boy I believed implicitly in God. I prayed to him, having a vision of him— a person—before my eyes. As I grew older I concluded that there was no God. I dismissed him from the universe. I believed only in what I could see, or hear, or feel. I talked about Nature and Reality."

He paused, the smile still lighting his face, evidently recalling to himself the old days. I did not interrupt him. Finally he turned to me and said abruptly,

"And now—it seems to me—there is nothing but God."

As he said this he lifted his arm with a peculiar gesture that seemed to take in the whole world.

For a time we were both silent. When I left him I offered my hand and told him I hoped I might become his friend. So I turned my face toward home. Evening was falling, and as I walked I heard the crows calling, and the air was keen and cool, and I thought deep thoughts.

And so I stepped into the darkened stable. I could not see the out-lines of the horse or the cow, but knowing the place so well I could easily get about. I heard the horse step aside with a soft expectant whinny. I smelled the smell of milk, the musty, sharp odor of dry hay, the pungent smell of manure, not unpleasant. And the stable was warm after the cool of the fields with a sort of animal warmth that struck into me soothingly. I spoke in a low voice and laid my hand on the horse's flank. The flesh quivered and shrunk away from my touch—coming back confidently, warmly. I ran my hand along his back and up his hairy neck. I felt his sensitive nose in my hand. "You shall have your oats," I said, and I gave him to eat. Then I spoke as gently to the cow, and she stood aside to be milked.

And afterward I came out into the clear bright night, and the air was sweet and cool, and my dog came bounding to meet me.—So I carried the milk into the house, and Harriet said in her heartiest tone:

"You are late, David. But sit up, I have kept the biscuits warm."

And that night my sleep was sound.

—*Adventures in Contentment* (III)

I know that the man who talks so intimately about the color and the smell of life, who can appreciate the odor of dry hay and put his loving hand on the horse's twitching flank does not doubt life. Truly, he lives. What a different world from that of the professional phi-losophers! The world may be One, or the world may be Many, but we must get on with the business of living this phenomenal but aesthetically real life. There are any number of loose metaphysical threads of determinism and free will and evil and original sin and the yet undiscovered life after death hanging around, but let no one try to be another Hegel and attempt to comprehend the laws of the whole universe for us, like those "worms" of Clarence Day trying to make over the world according to their self-consciousness! ("Think of

Truth sadly—or madly—eyeing such worms!" says Day.) This business of comprehending the whole universe is a sad and depressing job;
it solidifies thought and gives it an imposing structure, I know, but
more frequently than not—I would go further than that and say without exception—it brings in its train a disease known as fossilization
of the spinal joints until the gay spirit of inquiry departs or dies in
its carcass.

3. THE JOYS OF COMMON LIFE

Let's sit with Grayson once more and relax and bask in his warmth.
Turn to almost any page in that low-priced *David Grayson Omnibus,*
and you are in a different world because the whole book is instinct
with the love of life. Here it is, Grayson's discovery of a book agent.
If you have an eye for the good things of literature, your eye will spot
a good line out of a crowded page of eight hundred words. Here is
an interesting one. " 'The entire set,' he said, 'weighs over ten pounds.
There are 1,162 pages, enough paper if laid down flat, end to end, to
reach half a mile.' " Take him up there, as you may take him up anywhere, and be sure you never know where he will end. He will show
you a pebble, an iceman, a book agent and unravel for you the inner
mystery and beauty of pulsating life beneath the surface of our everyday existence. Somewhere, if you are susceptible to good poetry, your
heart may skip a beat or you may grow cold and numb, and you'll
hear good old Grayson tell you, "Most of us, Anglo-Saxons, tremble
before a tear when we might fearlessly beard a tiger."

*"It was beautiful to see commonplace facts grow phosphor-
escent in the heat of true feelings."*

BY DAVID GRAYSON

I cannot quote his exact language: there was too much of it, but
he made an impressive showing of the amount of literature that could
be had at a very low price per pound. Mr. Dixon was a hypnotist. He
fixed me with his glittering eye, and he talked so fast, and his ideas
upon the subject were so original that he held me spellbound. At first
I was inclined to be provoked: one does not like to be forcibly hypno-

tized, but gradually the situation began to amuse me, the more so when Harriet came in.

"Did you ever see a more beautiful binding?" asked the agent, holding his book admiringly at arm's length. "This up here," he said, pointing to the illuminated cover, "is the Muse of Poetry. She is scattering flowers—poems, you know. Fine idea, ain't it? Coloring fine, too."

He jumped up quickly and laid the book on my table, to the evident distress of Harriet.

"Trims up the room, don't it?" he exclaimed, turning his head a little to one side and observing the effect with an expression of affectionate admiration.

"How much," I asked, "will you sell the covers for without the insides?"

"Without the insides?"

"Yes," I said, "the binding will trim up my table just as well without the insides."

I thought he looked at me a little suspiciously, but he was evidently satisfied by my expression of countenance, for he answered promptly:

"Oh, but you want the insides. That's what the books are for. The bindings are never sold alone."

He then went on to tell me the prices and terms of payment, until it really seemed that it would be cheaper to buy the books than to let him carry them away again. Harriet stood in the doorway behind him frowning and evidently trying to catch my eye. But I kept my face turned aside so that I could not see her signal of distress and my eyes fixed on the young man Dixon. It was as good as a play. Harriet there, serious-minded, thinking I was being befooled, and the agent thinking he was befooling me, and I, thinking I was befooling both of them—and all of us wrong. It was very like life wherever you find it.

Finally, I took the book which he had been urging upon me, at which Harriet coughed meaningly to attract my attention. She knew the danger when I really got my hands on a book. But I made up as innocent as a child. I opened the book almost at random—and it was as though, walking down a strange road, I had come upon an old tried friend not seen before in years. For there on the page before me I read:

"The world is too much with us; late and soon,
Getting and spending we lay waste our powers:
Little we see in Nature that is ours;
We have given our hearts away, a sordid boon!
The sea that bares her bosom to the moon;
The winds that will be howling at all hours,
But are up-gathered now like sleeping flowers;
For this, for everything, we are out of tune;
It moves us not."

And as I read it came back to me—a scene like a picture—the place, the time, the very feel of the hour when I first saw those lines. Who shall say that the past does not live! An odor will sometimes set the blood coursing in an old emotion, and a line of poetry is the resurrection and the life. For a moment I forgot Harriet and the agent, I forgot myself, I even forgot the book on my knee—everything but that hour in the past—a view of shimmering hot housetops, the heat and dust and noise of an August evening in the city, the dumb weariness of it all, the loneliness, the longing for green fields; and then these great lines of Wordsworth, read for the first time, flooding in upon me:

"Great God! I'd rather be
A pagan suckled in a creed outworn:
So might I, standing on this pleasant lea,
Have glimpses that would make me less forlorn;
Have sight of Proteus rising from the sea;
And hear old Triton blow his wreathèd horn."

When I had finished I found myself standing in my own room with one arm raised, and, I suspect, a trace of tears in my eyes—there before the agent and Harriet. I saw Harriet lift one hand and drop it hopelessly. She thought I was captured at last. I was past saving. And as I looked at the agent I saw "grim conquest glowing in his eye!" So I sat down not a little embarrassed by my exhibition—when I had intended to be self-poised.

"You like it, don't you?" said Mr. Dixon unctuously.

"I don't see," I said earnestly, "how you can afford to sell such things as this so cheap."

"They *are* cheap," he admitted regretfully. I suppose he wished he had tried me with the half-morocco.

"They are priceless," I said, "absolutely priceless. If you were the only man in the world who had that poem, I think I would deed you my farm for it."

Mr. Dixon proceeded, as though it were all settled, to get out his black order book and open it briskly for business. He drew his fountain pen, capped it, and looked up at me expectantly. My feet actually seemed slipping into some irresistible whirlpool. How well he understood practical psychology! I struggled within myself, fearing engulfment: I was all but lost.

"Shall I deliver the set at once," he said, "or can you wait until the first of February?"

At that critical moment a floating spar of an idea swept my way and I seized upon it as the last hope of the lost.

"I don't understand," I said, as though I had not heard his last question, "how you dare go about with all this treasure upon you. Are you not afraid of being stopped in the road and robbed? Why, I've seen the time when, if I had known you carried such things as these, such cures for sick hearts, I think I should have stopped you myself!"

"Say, you *are* an odd one," said Mr. Dixon.

"Why do you sell such priceless things as these?" I asked, looking at him sharply.

"Why do I sell them?" and he looked still more perplexed. "To make money, of course; same reason you raise corn."

"But here is wealth," I said, pursuing my advantage. "If you have these you have something more valuable than money."

Mr. Dixon politely said nothing. Like a wise angler, having failed to land me at the first rush, he let me have line. Then I thought of Ruskin's words, "Nor can any noble thing be wealth except to a noble person." And that prompted me to say to Mr. Dixon:

"These things are not yours; they are mine. You never owned them; but I will sell them to you."

He looked at me in amazement, and then glanced around—evidently to discover if there were a convenient way of escape.

"You're all straight, are you?" he asked, tapping his forehead; "didn't anybody ever try to take you up?"

"The covers are yours," I continued as though I had not heard him, "the insides are mine and have been for a long time: that is why I proposed buying the covers separately."

I opened his book again. I thought I would see what had been chosen for its pages. And I found there many fine and great things.

"Let me read you this," I said to Mr. Dixon; "it has been mine for a long time. I will not sell it to you. I will give it to you outright. The best things are always given."

Having some gift in imitating the Scotch dialect, I read:

> "November chill blaws loud wi' angry sugh;
>   The short'ning winter day is near a close;
> The miry beasts retreating frae the pleugh;
>   The black'ning trains o' craws to their repose:
> The toil-worn Cotter frae his labour goes,
>   This night his weekly moil is at an end,
> Collects his spades, his mattock's and his hoes,
>   Hoping the morn in ease and rest to spend,
> And weary, o'er the moor, his course does hameward bend."

So I read "The Cotter's Saturday Night." I love the poem very much myself, sometimes reading it aloud, not so much for the tenderness of its message, though I prize that, too, as for the wonder of its music:

> "Compar'd with these, Italian trills are tame;
>   The tickl'd ear no heart-felt raptures raise."

I suppose I showed my feeling in my voice. As I glanced up from time to time I saw the agent's face change, and his look deepen and the lips, usually so energetically tense, loosen with emotion. Surely no poem in all the language conveys so perfectly the simple love of the home, the quiet joys, hopes, pathos of those who live close to the soil.

When I had finished—I stopped with the stanza beginning:

> "Then homeward all take off their sev'ral way";

the agent turned away his head trying to brave out his emotion. Most of us, Anglo-Saxons, tremble before a tear when we might fearlessly beard a tiger.

I moved up nearer to the agent and put my hand on his knee; then I read two or three of the other things I found in his wonderful book. And once I had him laughing and once again I had the tears in his eyes. Oh, a simple young man, a little crusty without, but soft inside—like the rest of us.

Well, it was amazing once we began talking not of books but of life, how really eloquent and human he became. From being a distant and uncomfortable person, he became at once like a near neighbor and friend. It was strange to me—as I have thought since—how he conveyed to us in a few words the essential emotional note of his life. It was no violin tone, beautifully complex with harmonics, but the clear simple voice of the flute. It spoke of his wife and his baby girl and his home. The very incongruity of detail—he told us how he grew onions in his back yard—added somehow to the homely glamor of the vision which he gave us. The number of his house, the fact that he had a new cottage organ, and that the baby ran away and lost herself in Seventeenth Street—were all, curiously, fabrics of his emotion.

It was beautiful to see commonplace facts grow phosphorescent in the heat of true feeling. How little we may come to know Romance by the cloak she wears and how humble must be he who would surprise the heart of her!

It was, indeed, with an indescribable thrill that I heard him add the details, one by one—the mortgage on his place, now rapidly being paid off, the brother who was a plumber, the mother-in-law who was not a mother-in-law of the comic papers. And finally he showed us the picture of the wife and baby that he had in the cover of his watch; a fat baby with its head resting on its mother's shoulder.

"Mister," he said, "p'raps you think it's fun to ride around the country like I do, and be away from home most of the time. But it ain't. When I think of Minnie and the kid——"

He broke off sharply, as if he had suddenly remembered the shame of such confidences.

"Say," he asked, "what page is that poem on?"

I told him.

"One forty-six," he said. "When I get home I'm going to read that to Minnie. She likes poetry and all such things. And where's that other piece that tells how a man feels when he's lonesome? Say, that fellow knew!"

We had a genuinely good time, the agent and I, and when he finally rose to go, I said:

"Well, I've sold you a new book."

"I see now, mister, what you mean."

I went down the path with him and began to unhitch his horse.

"Let me, let me," he said eagerly.

Then he shook hands, paused a moment awkwardly as if about to say something, then sprang into his buggy without saying it.

When he had taken up his reins he remarked:

"Say! but you'd make an agent! You'd hypnotize 'em."

I recognized it as the greatest compliment he could pay me: the craft compliment.

Then he drove off, but pulled up before he had gone five yards. He turned in his seat, one hand on the back of it, his whip raised.

"Say!" he shouted, and when I walked up he looked at me with fine embarrassment.

"Mister, perhaps you'd accept one of these sets from Dixon free gratis, for nothing."

"I understand," I said, "but you know I'm giving the books to you— and I couldn't take them back again."

"Well," he said, "you're a good one, anyhow. Good-bye again," and then, suddenly, business naturally coming uppermost, he remarked with great enthusiasm:

"You've given me a new idea. *Say,* I'll sell 'em."

"Carry them carefully, man," I called after him; "they are precious."

So I went back to my work, thinking how many fine people there are in this world—if you scratch 'em deep enough.

—*Adventures in Contentment* (IV)

This is typical of Grayson, the sly humor, the wistfulness, the warmth, and the ability to pry loose any crusty senator, millionaire, or shrewd Yankee farmer, prick him gently here and there, and render

him soft and pliable with common emotions—then put him back
where he was before success overtook him. Any time we lose heart,
any time we are lonely, if we take up Grayson we shall recover our
confidence in life and faith in our fellow men. I can say no better
words of him than that he is a good American, that he represents the
sound core of American sentiments and American character. The
character of the American people can well remain on that common
Grayson level without reaching the heights of glorious or inglorious
achievements, and the American nation will be forever safe from conquest without or degeneration within.

To taste the common joys of life, to exhibit human sentiments in
common everyday surroundings and domestic events, to make these
things glow with the heat of true feelings—that is the prime art and
occupation of the true essayist. Charles Lamb has it, and W. H.
Hudson has it. I am speaking of course not of the philosophical essay
or the critical essay but of the literary essay, half narrative and half
reflective, in which the narrative—some simple event or doings—is
the starting point for the writer's reminiscences, musings, and sage
reflections. The essay has nearly died out in American literature now.
This phenomenon, the death of the reflective essay in America, has
troubled me a good deal and set me thinking. It has not died out in
England, thanks to E. M. Forster, E. V. Lucas, W. H. Hudson, and
we may include Arnold Bennett. The reflective mind is always there,
and English scientists often write so well, broadly and deeply. There
is in America today Christopher Morley, and there is the gifted,
witty, and always charming George Jean Nathan, rather like Max
Beerbohm, but who, totally unlike Grayson, doesn't mind the country
but cannot stand its fresh air. But on the whole, the reflective essay
is not in fashion. In speaking about the incomparable Oliver Wendell
Holmes of the *Breakfast Table,* I touched upon this point, or rather
upon the quality and worth of sentiment. For the essay is a state of
mind. It is not just thought but always thought glowing with sentiment. Emerson's essays represent intellectual thought, but whenever
he let in sentiment, especially personal sentiment, there the passage
assumed the true character of an essay. Shall I draw the conclusion
that the present state of American mind is not reflective enough?

Who or what has killed the essay? Perhaps the surface of current

American events is too choppy, too distracting for sage reflections, and detracts from that detachment and serenity of mind which is necessary for reflection. There are other essayists of course, besides those mentioned—Donald Culross Peattie, for example. But on the whole, those columnists who might give us essayists are too bright, too insistent on giving the brilliant shine of phrase, and too much occupied with surface events. There is nothing wrong about surface events as material for the essayist, but it is the inward cogitation and rumination that must go with it which create the mood and the proper temper for the rewarding essay. Heywood Broun, whose happy felicity of style might have given us the true essay, was always aroused by some daily event. It is good to be aroused, to pitch into the battle with all you've got, whether it is a wrong baseball decision, or the murder of Sacco and Vanzetti. But then you don't get the essay.

I have thought of several reasons, and I think two are valid. One lies in the very character of American nerves, which do not want the gentle tingle but demand a wallop, and the best essayist can give you only a gentle nudge in your nerves or perhaps a twitch in your heart-strings—never more than that. It suffices. The other reason is purely commercial, answering the current mania for facts, for news, for special exposé stories, for some particular exciting feature stories that nobody else has got, which would turn us all into newspaper correspondents and authoritative analysts of the whirling events in Japan or Czechoslovakia. Only he who is contented and goes slightly off the trodden path, aloof from the mighty happenings of the day but very close to the thorn bush and the barn and the human heart beating, beating, beating perhaps in some rather sordid surroundings—only he can give us the true essay.

The joys of common life may be said to be the special message and province of David Grayson. Since life which surrounds us is so largely common, that people is wiser and happier who knows how to enjoy it. I have searched here and there for that kind of wisdom in American writings and wish there were more David Graysons. It would give me more faith in the American character, as if it had greater ballast. America, we are told, is a peaceful and happy country, and it is. Why, then, don't we hear more about the joys of the common man and common woman? Somebody is scared, I do not know who.

So many are nervous, and a few are wrecks. Isn't it the duty and privilege of the writers, the fresher minds, to interpret these joys for us, to remind us of them constantly—that there is this joyous common life before us? Is it not the work of the wise human mind to save for us those valuable, essential gifts of life that lie spread before us and that alone make life worth living? Isn't there somewhere always a *faith* in living as such, without thought of more discoveries and inventions? But the mind of America is directed more toward the future than the present. It is for progress and prosperity, which is a different theme altogether. It is always arriving at the next railroad station, never quite contented, never quite satisfied with where it finds itself at the present hour. That, too, is only a state of mind. A prosperous people and a happy people are two different things. My God, what the American people have lost! If they would look around at their country as it is—a peaceful and happy country, as we say, not a prosperous and progressive one—and reap the present hour, and thank God for what their country already is and not what it will be in the next decade! Even their pioneer fathers did stop and pitch a tent, and build a log cabin and raise a home somewhere, didn't they? Or were they forever moving, moving, moving?

Grayson has a lot of this joy and faith in common life, this sheer gratitude for living. To read him is to share his faith in the present, to admire your own doorstep.

"For beauty is inward, not outward. . . . Is it not the prime struggle of life to keep the mind plastic? To see and feel and hear things newly?"

BY DAVID GRAYSON

I love sometimes to have a day alone—a riotous day. Sometimes I do not care to see even my best friends: but I give myself up to the full enjoyment of the world around me. I go out of my door in the morning—preferably a sunny morning, though any morning will do well enough—and walk straight out into the world. I take with me the burden of no duty or responsibility. I draw in the fresh air, odor-laden from orchard and wood. I look about me as if everything were new—and behold everything *is* new. My barn, my oaks, my fences—

I declare I never saw them before. I have no preconceived impressions, or beliefs, or opinions. My lane fence is the end of the known earth. I am a discoverer of new fields among old ones. I see, feel, hear, smell, taste all these wonderful things for the first time. I have no idea what discoveries I shall make!

So I go down the lane, looking up and about me. I cross the town road and climb the fence on the other side. I brush one shoulder among the bushes as I pass: I feel the solid yet easy pressure of the sod. The long blades of the timothy-grass clasp at my legs and let go with reluctance. I break off a twig here and there and taste the tart or bitter sap. I take off my hat and let the warm sun shine on my head. I am an adventurer upon a new earth.

Is it not marvelous how far afield some of us are willing to travel in pursuit of that beauty which we leave behind us at home? We mistake unfamiliarity for beauty; we darken our perceptions with idle foreignness. For want of that ardent inner curiosity which is the only true foundation for the appreciation of beauty—for beauty is inward, not outward—we find ourselves hastening from land to land, gathering mere curious resemblances which, like unassimilated property, possess no power of fecundation. With what pathetic diligence we collect peaks and passes in Switzerland; how we come laden from England with vain cathedrals!

Beauty? What is it but a new way of approach? For wilderness, for foreignness, I have no need to go a mile: I have only to come up through my thicket or cross my field from my own roadside—and behold, a new heaven and a new earth!

Things grow old and stale, not because they are old, but because we cease to see them. Whole vibrant significant worlds around us disappear within the somber mists of familiarity. Whichever way we look the roads are dull and barren. There is a tree at our gate we have not seen in years: a flower blooms in our door-yard more wonderful than the shining heights of the Alps!

It has seemed to me sometimes as though I could see men hardening before my eyes, drawing in a feeler here, walling up an opening there. Naming things! Objects fall into categories for them and wear little sure channels in the brain. A mountain is a mountain, a tree a tree to them, a field forever a field. Life solidifies itself in words. And finally how everything wearies them and that is old age!

Is it not the prime struggle of life to keep the mind plastic? To see and feel and hear things newly? To accept nothing as settled; to defend the eternal right of the questioner? To reject every conclusion of yesterday before the surer observations of to-day?—is not that the best life we know?

—*Adventures in Friendship* (III)

4. THE HEROISM OF COMMON TOIL

The fool looks to an unattainable heaven, the wise man seizes upon the immediate life. The fool looks for a future Paradise, the wise man accepts the imperfect human life on this earth. The fool waits for the next moment, the wise man eats the now. I think the man who can reveal to us the beauties and wonders of the commonplaces of life does a greater service to humanity than the poet who sends us at some rare moments into heavens of ecstatic bliss. And why? Because there are so many commonplace things around us. To discover their beauty, to appreciate their worth, to open our eyes to their human significance is truly the function of the poet and seer.

So much of human life and happiness is subjective that we should be fools not to take advantage of this subjectivity unashamedly and learn to cultivate the seeing eye and the perceptive soul for the beauties that lie around us, and be grateful for it. Of all human vices, the greatest is ingratitude, and we must conclude that the world looks sick because the soul looking on it is sick. Any day, be it shine or rain or snow or a fearful storm, one cannot look out of the window without at least aesthetically feeling the beauty. Let it be raindrops dribbling down a windowpane, or the soft crack of hail upon the glass, or flying leaves, or a sparrow escaping from the storm outside, or the silent fall of the morning sunlight upon a corner of the carpet, or the shimmering outline of a retreating shadow—such ordinary phenomena should rout a man from his mood of pessimism and make him feel ashamed for being less than a dog, which usually knows how to adjust itself to circumstances quite competently. If life is all subjective, why not be subjectively happy rather than subjectively sad?

William James, speaking of the capacity of the soul for such enjoyment, says:

"The occasion and the experience, then, are nothing. It all depends on the capacity of the soul to be grasped, to have its life-currents absorbed by what is given. 'Crossing a bare common,' says Emerson, 'in snow puddles, at twilight, under a clouded sky, without having in my thoughts any occurrence of special good fortune, I have enjoyed a perfect exhilaration. I am glad to the brink of fear.'

"Life is always worth living, if one have such responsive sensibilities. But we of the highly educated classes (so called) have most of us got far, far away from Nature. We are trained to seek the choice, the rare, the exquisite exclusively, and to overlook the common. We are stuffed with abstract conceptions, and glib with verbalities and verbosities; and in the culture of these higher functions the peculiar sources of joy connected with our simpler functions often dry up, and we grow stone-blind and insensible to life's more elementary and general goods and joys." [4]

What, then, is the surface of life in modern American cities like? Is it so tame? Is it suffocating and flat and fast approaching that undesirable heaven which James so dreads? James once went to Chautauqua Lake, an almost Sabbatical city of perfection, and spent a week there, and came out with "Ouf! what a relief!" His reflections are important, for before he was through, he reached a "levelling insight" which to him was a kind of religious inspiration. James would have us believe that, dashed off in a brief essay, it contains one of the most significant perceptions of his life, which, as it were, might redeem his years of teaching abstract philosophy at Harvard. This was his insight into the heroism of common toil, the divinity of muscular labor and his welcome to life's invitation to danger and an adventurous, precipitous living.

[4] "On a Certain Blindness in Human Beings," *Talks to Teachers on Psychology.* Copyright, 1939, Henry James. Permission of Paul R. Reynolds & Son.

Chautauqua Lake: The Heroism of Common Toil ... "the element that gives to the wicked outer world all its moral style"

BY WILLIAM JAMES

A few summers ago I spent a happy week at the famous Assembly Grounds on the borders of Chautauqua Lake. The moment one treads that sacred enclosure, one feels one's self in an atmosphere of success. Sobriety and industry, intelligence and goodness, orderliness and ideality, prosperity and cheerfulness, pervade the air. It is a serious and studious picnic on a gigantic scale. Here you have a town of many thousands of inhabitants, beautifully laid out in the forest and drained, and equipped with means for satisfying all the necessary lower and most of the superfluous higher wants of man. You have a first-class college in full blast. You have magnificent music—a chorus of seven hundred voices, with possibly the most perfect open-air auditorium in the world. You have every sort of athletic exercise from sailing, rowing, swimming, bicycling, to the ball-field and the more artificial doings which the gymnasium affords. You have kindergartens and model secondary schools. You have general religious services and special clubhouses for the several sects. You have perpetually running soda-water fountains, and daily popular lectures by distinguished men. You have the best of company, and yet no effort. You have no zymotic diseases, no poverty, no drunkenness, no crime, no police. You have culture, you have kindness, you have cheapness, you have equality, you have the best fruits of what mankind has fought and bled and striven for under the name of civilization for centuries. You have, in short, a foretaste of what human society might be, were it all in the light, with no suffering and no dark corners.

I went in curiosity for a day. I stayed for a week, held spell-bound by the charm and ease of everything, by the middle-class paradise, without a sin, without a victim, without a blot, without a tear.

And yet what was my own astonishment, on emerging into the dark and wicked world again, to catch myself quite unexpectedly and involuntarily saying: "Ouf! what a relief! Now for something pri-

mordial and savage, even though it were as bad as an Armenian massacre, to set the balance straight again. This order is too tame, this
culture too second-rate, this goodness too uninspiring. This human
drama without a villain or a pang; this community so refined that
ice-cream and soda-water is the utmost offering it can make to the
brute animal in man; this city simmering in the tepid lakeside sun;
this atrocious harmlessness of all things,—I cannot abide with them.
Let me take my chances again in the big outside worldly wilderness
with all its sins and sufferings. There are the heights and depths, the
precipices and the steep ideals, the gleams of the awful and the infinite; and there is more hope and help a thousand times than in this
dead level and quintessence of every mediocrity.". . .

So I meditated. And, first of all, I asked myself what the thing was
that was so lacking in this Sabbatical city, and the lack of which kept
one forever falling short of the higher sort of contentment. And I
soon recognized that it was the element that gives to the wicked outer
world all its moral style, expressiveness and picturesqueness,—the element of precipitousness, so to call it, of strength and strenuousness,
intensity and danger. What excites and interests the looker-on at life,
what the romances and the statues celebrate and the grim civic monu-
ments remind us of, is the everlasting battle of the powers of light with
those of darkness; with heroism, reduced to its bare chance, yet ever
and anon snatching victory from the jaws of death. But in this unspeakable Chautauqua there was no potentiality of death in sight anywhere, and no point of the compass visible from which danger might
possibly appear. The ideal was so completely victorious already that
no sign of any previous battle remained, the place just resting on its
oars. But what our human emotions seem to require is the sight of
the struggle going on. The moment the fruits are being merely eaten,
things become ignoble. Sweat and effort, human nature strained to
its uttermost and on the rack, yet getting through alive, and then
turning its back on its success to pursue another more rare and arduous
still—this is the sort of thing the presence of which inspires us, and
the reality of which it seems to be the function of all the higher forms
of literature and fine art to bring home to us and suggest. . . .

But was not this a paradox well calculated to fill one with dismay?
It looks indeed, thought I, as if the romantic idealists with their

pessimism about our civilization were, after all, quite right. An irremediable flatness is coming over the world. Bourgeoisie and mediocrity, church sociables and teachers' conventions, are taking the place of the old heights and depths and romantic chiaroscuro. . . .

With these thoughts in my mind, I was speeding with the train toward Buffalo, when, near that city, the sight of a workman doing something on the dizzy edge of a sky-scaling iron construction brought me to my senses very suddenly. And now I perceived, by a flash of insight, that I had been steeping myself in pure ancestral blindness, and looking at life with the eyes of a remote spectator. Wishing for heroism and the spectacle of human nature on the rack, I had never noticed the great fields of heroism lying around about me, I had failed to see it present and alive. I could only think of it as dead and embalmed, labelled and costumed, as it is in the pages of romance. And yet there it was before me in the daily lives of the laboring classes. Not in clanging fights and desperate marches only is heroism to be looked for, but on every railway bridge and fire-proof building that is going up today. On freight-trains, on the decks of vessels, in cattle-yards and mines, on lumber-rafts, among the firemen and the policemen, the demand for courage is incessant; and the supply never fails. There, every day of the year somewhere, is human nature *in extremis* for you. And wherever a scythe, an axe, a pick, or a shovel is wielded, you have it sweating and aching and with its powers of patient endurance racked to the utmost under the length of hours of the strain.

As I awoke to all this unidealized heroic life around me, the scales seemed to fall from my eyes; and a wave of sympathy greater than anything I had ever before felt with the common life of common men began to fill my soul. It began to seem as if virtue with horny hands and dirty skin were the only virtue genuine and vital enough to take account of. Every other virtue poses; none is absolutely unconscious and simple, and unexpectant of decoration or recognition, like this. These are our soldiers, thought I, these our sustainers, these the very parents of our life. . . .

If any of you have been readers of Tolstoï, you will see that I passed into a vein of feeling similar to his, with its abhorrence of all that conventionally passes for distinguished, and its exclusive deification of the bravery, patience, kindliness, and dumbness of the unconscious natural man.

Where now is *our* Tolstoï, I said, to bring the truth of all this home to our American bosoms, fill us with a better insight, and wean us away from that spurious literary romanticism on which our wretched culture—as it calls itself—is fed? Divinity lies all about us, and culture is too hide-bound to even suspect the fact. . . .

And there I rested on that day, with a sense of widening of vision, and with what it is surely fair to call an increase of religious insight into life. In God's eyes the differences of social position, of intellect, of culture, of cleanliness, of dress, which different men exhibit, and all the other rarities and exceptions on which they so fantastically pin their pride, must be so small as practically quite to vanish; and all that should remain is the common fact that here we are, a countless multitude of vessels of life, each of us pent in to peculiar difficulties, with which we must severally struggle by using whatever of fortitude and goodness we can summon up. The exercise of the courage, patience, and kindness, must be the significant portion of the whole business; and the distinctions of position can only be a manner of diversifying the phenomenal surface upon which these underground virtues may manifest their effects. At this rate, the deepest human life is everywhere, is eternal. And, if any human attributes exist only in particular individuals, they must belong to the mere trapping and decoration of the surface-show.

Thus are men's lives levelled up as well as levelled down,—levelled up in their common inner meaning, levelled down in their outer gloriousness and show. Yet always, we must confess, this levelling insight tends to be obscured again; and always the ancestral blindness returns and wraps us up, so that we end once more by thinking that creation can be for no other purpose than to develop remarkable situations and conventional distinctions and merits. . . .

This, as I said, became for a time my conviction, and gave me great content.

—"What Makes a Life Significant,"
Talks to Teachers on Psychology

5. THOREAU AND THE VALUES OF LIFE

Among American writers Henry Thoreau may certainly be regarded as one of the few "primary" thinkers who thought about life at first-hand and who had probably most to say about the true values of life. Thoreau was a great writer with limitations, great because he was clearly above the majority of purveyors of secondhand opinions. He was always, from beginning to end, on his own; he was one of the few men who consciously and deliberately went out to experiment and to find out for himself the great realities of human existence and who did not care a twopence what the others say. He was limited, not only as a human spirit but also as a writer, because he was prickly all over and had something of the scold in him, even in *Walden,* which repels rather than convinces. Again, he was great because he was honest, shut up in the prison of his own thoughts, "erect and spotless," sometimes burning with the conviction of St. John the Baptist, and his voice did seem to cry in the wilderness. But that is also his limitation. No voice should cry in the wilderness; a man should come back and talk simply and sweetly and make peace with human society, if that vision he had seen in the desert was truly apocalyptic. I have sometimes wondered what that golden mean is that should mark the harmonious man. It is perhaps to be individualistic without being querulous, and to be urbane without truckling to conventions. Thoreau failed in the former as Emerson succeeded in the latter, and therefore Emerson was the greater man.[5] The mature human spirit is always reconciled with life, but Thoreau's wasn't. It must have been this quality in him that repelled Robert Louis Stevenson at first and made him call Thoreau a "skulker," although later Stevenson retracted this remark. He remained the St. John the Baptist of America, and America might as well be proud that it produced at least one.

You like the man because of his sterling qualities, clean and strong and self-convinced like a New England spruce. So, unlike Whitman, who told Emerson the first edition of his *Leaves of Grass* "sold readily"

---

[5] Also in the scope of their literary powers Emerson was far greater. After writing the *Essays,* he went on to *Representative Men, English Traits,* and *The Conduct of Life,* whereas Thoreau did not progress in thought after *Walden.*

which it didn't, Thoreau was far above cheap publicity (as was also
Herman Melville, who was lonely like him). His *A Week on the
Concord and Merrimack Rivers* had not sold well. Out of the 1000
copies printed, 706 were returned by the publisher, and out of the
remaining 294, 75 were given away. And this was the entry in his
Journals (October 28, 1853): "They are something more substantial
than fame, as my back knows, which has borne them up two flights
of stairs to a place similiar to that to which they trace their origin. . . .
Is it not well that the author should behold the fruits of his labor?. . .
This is authorship; these are the works of my brain. . . . Nevertheless,
in spite of this result, sitting beside the inert mass of my works, I take
up my pen tonight to record what thought or experience I may have
had, with as much satisfaction as ever. Indeed, I believe that this result
is more inspiring than if a thousand had bought my wares. It affects
my privacy less and leaves me freer." The last two lines are not so good,
but that is Thoreau all over again. You respect him for it; he belongs
to the true genre of intellectual creators. The scorn that kept creeping
up in his pages detracts from our pleasure in reading him, but it was
also his strength.

It is a pity that Thoreau gave the impression of growing under the
shadow of Emerson. It is unfortunate that Lowell as a critic failed to
recognize his genius, for his opinion of Thoreau in the *Fable for
Critics,* making merry of him as a servile imitator and follower of
Emerson, must have damaged his reputation.

> There comes——, for instance; to see him's rare sport,
> Tread in Emerson's tracks with legs painfully short;
> How he jumps, how he strains, and gets red in the face,
> To keep step with the mystagogue's natural pace.
> He follows as close as a stick to a rocket,
> His fingers exploring the prophet's each pocket.
> Fie, for shame, brother bard; with good fruit of your own,
> Can't you let Neighbor Emerson's orchards alone?

Whether this was meant for Channing, or for Thoreau (for both had
short legs and both were close to Emerson), Thoreau never quite lived
down the bad joke. Thoreau had lived in Emerson's house as a house-
keeper, and that was the popular acceptance. Emerson himself noted in

his *Journals* (September 1851), "I am very familiar with all his thoughts—they are my own quite originally drest. But if the question be, what new ideas has he thrown into circulation, he has not yet told what that is which he was created to say." It must be surmised from this that Emerson looked upon Thoreau as a rival prophet rather than as a disciple. And Emerson and Thoreau rather irritated each other. Certainly Thoreau was no servile admirer; he was fighting Emerson all the time in their private walks. In 1856, two years after *Walden* was published, Emerson had this to say in his diary, "If I knew only Thoreau, I should think cooperation of good men impossible. Must we always talk for victory, and never once for truth, for comfort, and joy? Centrality he has, and penetration, strong understanding, and the higher gifts,—the insight of the real, or from the real, and the moral rectitude that belongs to it; but all this and all his resources of wit and invention are lost to me, in every experiment, year after year, that I make, to hold intercourse with his mind. Always some weary captious paradox to fight you with, and the time and temper wasted." [6] Thoreau was human; younger and a pencil-maker and surveyor by trade, he was never at home in fashionable society, even in that of the Boston intellectuals. Once he was invited to the Saturday Club at the old Parker House where he was repelled by the smoke of expensive cigars and beat a hasty retreat to the railroad station. He would rather sit on a pumpkin and have it all to himself than be crowded on a velvet cushion, as he tells us in *Walden*.

One might have thought otherwise, that in the Concord and Boston of those days, when the glory of God had descended upon men, such society must have been highly stimulating. But Thoreau was as prickly as a hedgehog bristling with quills and ready to rebuff anyone who came close, as Emerson vainly tried. Emerson himself froze Margaret Fuller and was in turn frozen into silence by her "strange cold-warm, attractive-repelling conversations"; Bronson Alcott talked too much, he talked Emerson to death and talked himself into a "tedious angel," while Emerson in turn tried to talk to Hawthorne, but Hawthorne

---

[6] Emerson's *Journals,* February 29, 1856. Thoreau had the same complaint against Emerson: "P.M.—Talked, or tried to talk, with R. W. E. Lost my time—nay, almost my identity. He, assuming a false opposition where there was no difference of opinion, talked to the wind—told me what I knew—and I lost my time trying to imagine myself somebody else to oppose him." (*Journals*, XI, 188; May 24, 1853.)

shut up like a self-contented, uncommunicative clam so that Emerson was afraid to proceed. A roomful of transcendental angels, each with a gift of the gab, might be too much of a good thing after all.

But Thoreau was the follower of nobody but himself. I am amazed at his "Commencement Part," written as a student graduating from Harvard when he was twenty. Thoreau the thinker is clearly there, the repudiation of the means of living as an end in itself, the picture of the men on earth abusing rather than using the world, the recovery of moral freedom, and the instinctive trust in nature and in the present. "The sea will not stagnate, the earth will be as green as ever, and the air as pure. This curious world which we inhabit is more wonderful than it is convenient; more beautiful than it is useful; it is more to be admired and enjoyed than used." At any rate, this was more thoughtful than many Presidential addresses that I have read, those of Harding especially. Thoreau gave the address on August 16, 1837, and two weeks later Emerson delivered at Harvard the famous address to the Phi Beta Kappa on "The American Scholar," at which Thoreau may have been present. It is possible that Thoreau had read Emerson's "Nature" (his *Essays* were not yet published). Judging by the fairly common experience of young men past and present, Emerson may have greatly stimulated the young Thoreau and confirmed him in his thought track; there was no question about his admiring Emerson's ideas; but when two minds came so close, both on the loose and probing for new keys to God and human life as the minds of men in those days were, and when both men were preachers of the same inspiring individualism and self-reliance, transcendental quills were bound to shoot out in all directions.

Thoreau was the prophet of the individual against the state and a few other things; but above all his whole life was a search for the true scale of values in human life. Much there was in the life of his Concord neighbors that was sham and illusion, triviality and gossip, much that was "groveling" and futility and betrayal of living. Man had lost his moral freedom; he had sold his birthright for a mess of pottage. How we play false to our true nature, lose heart and lead a servile, uninspired existence, truckle to the shams and inanities of convention, and gradually age and die! As we grow old, we live more coarsely, we relax a little in our discipline and cease to obey our finest instincts.

"If within the sophisticated man there is not an unsophisticated one, then he is but one of the Devil's angels," says Thoreau. I have noted a passage as the finest he ever wrote: "We seem to linger in manhood to tell the dreams of our childhood, and they vanish out of memory ere we learn the language." "All men are partially buried in the grave of custom, and of some we see only the crown of the head above the ground. . . . As to preserving potatoes from rotting, your opinion may change from year to year; but as to how to preserve your soul from rotting, I have nothing to learn, but something to practise." (*Letter to Harrison Blake,* February 27, 1853). That passage in *Walden* saying that he long ago lost a hound, a bay horse, and a turtledove has never been fully explained; his turtledove may quite well have been his first love, Ellen Sewall, who rejected his suit (and changed the color of his life), but that it is figurative we are certain. He was forever on the trail of those things which he had lost.[7]

Thoreau was master of the graphic line, the creator of those nervous, tense, sinewy sentences. Next to Emerson, Thoreau is probably the most quotable American author. But both suffered from the same defects as writers. Thoreau was no more master of a paragraph than Emerson; the best they wrote were often half paragraphs. Thoreau is not always easy reading; in fact, I find some of his "Excursions" pieces smoother reading. It seems we can't have both—the master of the sentence and the master of the paragraph; glistening sentences, to fit into a paragraph, must be freshly born; gems cut separately and polished at leisure and then pieced together to form a pattern never quite belong, and however great the artistry in smoothing the corners,

[7] "I long ago lost a hound, a bay horse, and a turtle-dove, and am still on their trail. Many are the travellers I have spoken concerning them, describing their tracks and what they answer to. I have met one or two who had heard the hound, and the tramp of the horse, and even seen the dove disappear behind a cloud, and they seemed anxious to recover them as if they had lost them themselves,"—*Walden,* "Economy." This is exactly like the Chinese sage Mencius talking, who said that if a man had a deformed finger, he would go a hundred miles, out of shame, to have it straightened, but when we have lost "the child's heart" we have not enough shame to go find and retrieve it. Mencius went on to speak of a man losing chickens and dogs and trying to find them. Did Mencius directly inspire this passage? Thoreau made nine or ten references to the Confucian "Four Books" in his *Walden.* It is certain that he read them, apparently in some French translation, for at least the spelling of Confucius as *Khoung-tseu* is French. He was also acquainted with David Collie, *The Chinese Classical Work, Commonly Called the Four Books* (Malacca, 1828).

the reader knows full well that they are imported from other times, other occasions. Both Emerson and Thoreau suffered from the habit of polishing their thoughts in their notebooks and then stringing them together for some occasion or forcing them into paragraphs as the sudden illuminating lines. Bakers know well that a cake must be leavened evenly and thoroughly once and for all, and that constant opening and closing of the oven will only hurt the smooth consistency which makes the perfect cake. Thoreau was a conscientious writer; he polished and repolished too much. And so Thoreau does not flow. Nor does Emerson, except when the subject matter lends him a convenient external contour to follow as in *English Traits*. Both have their "savings banks" in which their spontaneous thoughts are stored up and dipped into to serve the needs of occasions, and it has seemed to me that both their *Journals* contain some of their best writings and richest thoughts—those "initiative, spermative, prophesying, man-making words," as Emerson calls them.

Thoreau's fault was his captiousness.[8] But he sat in his cabin and waited, and there were times when he felt uncommonly prepared for some literary work, when he was braced physically and intellectually. He wrote with his brain and muscles; he created, or rather chiseled, sentences that were simple and strong. There are two Thoreau's, the positive and the negative, the preacher and the scold of social shams and futilities, and the writer with a deep feeling for nature. The second Thoreau is incomparably the better one.

The whole message of *Walden* and of Thoreau, then, is to throw off the veil of business and to discover and to explore man's "Private

---

[8] Thoreau knew his own weakness but was perfectly conscientious about it. He notes in his *Journals* (September 2, 1854), "My faults are:—Paradoxes,—saying just the opposite,—a style which may be imitated. Ingenious. Playing with words,—getting the laugh, not always simple, strong, and broad. Using current phrases and maxims, when I should speak for myself." Emerson analyzes Thoreau's fault and comes to the same conclusion. "Henry Thoreau sends me a paper with the old fault of unlimited contradiction. The trick of his rhetoric is soon learned: it consists in substituting for the obvious word and thought its diametrical antagonist, etc." (*Journals,* August 25, 1843). Thoreau loves to make puns, but his are not always as happy as Lowell's. Some of his belabored puns are: "Even the elephant carries but a small trunk on his journey"; "I love man—kind, but I hate the institutions of the dead unkind"; "There is not a popular magazine in this country that would dare publish a child's thought on important subjects without comment. It must be submitted to the D.D.'s. I would it were submitted to the chicka-deedees."

Sea" by finding out what matters and what does not in life. Thoreau
was astonished and complained that nothing had been said upon this
subject of living.

"It is remarkable that there is little or nothing to be remembered
written on the subject of getting a living; how to make getting a living
not merely honest and honorable, but altogether inviting and glorious;
for if *getting* a living is not so, then living is not. One would think,
from looking at literature, that this question had never disturbed a
solitary individual's musings. . . .

"The title *wise* is, for the most part, falsely applied. How can one
be a wise man, if he does not know any better how to live than other
men? if he is only more cunning and intellectually subtle? Does wisdom work in a treadmill? or does she teach how to succeed *by
example*? Is there any such thing as wisdom not applied to life? Is
she merely the miller who grinds the finest logic?" [9]

"What other liberty is there worth having, if we have not freedom
and peace in our minds,—if our inmost and most private man is but
a sour and turbid pool? Often we are so jarred by chagrins in dealing
with the world, that we cannot reflect. Many men who have had much
intercourse with the world and not borne the trial well affect me as
all resistance, all burr and rind, without any gentleman, or tender and
innocent core left. They have become hedgehogs.

"Ah, the world is too much with us, and our whole soul is stained
by what it works in, like the dyer's hand. . . . If within the old man,
there is not a young man,—within the sophisticated, one unsophisticated,—then he is but one of the devil's angels." [10]

So, in his characteristically strong, vigorous prose, he stated his aims
in going to establish himself at Walden Pond for about two years.

"I went to the woods because I wished to live deliberately, to front
only the essential facts of life, and see if I could not learn what it had
to teach, and not, when I came to die, discover that I had not lived. I
did not wish to live what was not life, living is so dear; nor did I wish
to practise resignation, unless it was quite necessary. I wanted to live
deep and suck out all the marrow of life, to live so sturdily and Spar-
tan-like as to put to rout all that was not life, to cut a broad swath

[9] "Life Without Principle."
[10] *Journals*, October 26, 1853.

and shave close, to drive life into a corner, and reduce it to its lowest terms, and, if it proved to be mean, why then to get the whole and genuine meanness of it, and publish its meanness to the world; or if it were sublime, to know it by experience, and be able to give a true account of it in my next excursion. For most men, it appears to me, are in a strange uncertainty about it, whether it is of the devil or of God, and have *somewhat hastily* concluded that it is the chief end of man here to 'glorify God and enjoy him forever.' " [11]

[11] *Walden* (II).

Chapter VIII

LIBERTY

I. WHY LIBERTY?

LIBERTY is not an end in itself; it is a condition of that higher good, happiness. One may argue that this is perhaps a dangerous doctrine, that if liberty is not an end itself, one may some day surrender it if that higher good, happiness, can be obtained by some other means without it. The answer to this is of course perfectly obvious; it cannot be done. We do not know why it is, but it is just so. No man can be happy unless he is both physically and spiritually free, and sometimes it is even more important to be spiritually than to be physically free. Those who believe that a new society of human happiness can be created by collective distribution of material goods without preserving the fundamental condition of happiness itself, liberty as free men know it and cherish it, delude themselves. May I walk around hell free and alone rather than be led around heaven in chains! Those who advocate the dictatorship either of the proletariat or of the *Führer* are a disgrace to the entire Western tradition of liberalism. Those who lend comfort to the disseminators of such untruths by praising a police state as a democracy have indeed gone a long way from the American tradition.

We must go back to the spiritual fountains of the American faith in the common man, and see just why he deserves that faith, being really as "common" as he is. We have to go back to the ringing words of Emerson, to the mystical but hundred-per-cent confidence in the individual self of Thoreau, and to Jefferson himself, and test the grounds they stood on. And we must not miss that modern American philosopher, Santayana. I quite agree with Henry Hazlitt that "alone among our present writers he is comparable in stature with Emerson."[1] San-

---

[1] "He is not merely our profoundest thinker, but also our most finished artist in prose . . . One cannot compare him even with a writer like Matthew Arnold without recognizing that it is Santayana who has the richer, deeper, and more plastic mind." Henry Hazlitt, *The Forum*, October, 1932.

tayana related the subject of liberty to happiness itself, as Jefferson did. His ideal examination of the subject raises the topic to a realm above mere political dogma and gives human liberty a role as a contributor to the ultimate happiness of man. Santayana's idea of liberty is broadly based on his disenchanted but ever enchanting naturalism, a wholesome, pagan, imaginative conception of the ends of human life.

"The freedom to live well. . . . This liberty to discover and pursue happiness, this liberty to grow wise and to live in friendship with the gods and with one another"

BY GEORGE SANTAYANA

When ancient peoples defended what they called their liberty, the word stood for a plain and urgent interest of theirs: that their cities should not be destroyed, their territory pillaged, and they themselves sold into slavery. For the Greeks in particular liberty meant even more than this. Perhaps the deepest assumption of classic philosophy is that nature and the gods on the one hand and man on the other, both have a fixed character; that there is consequently a necessary piety, a true philosophy, a standard happiness, a normal art. The Greeks believed not without reason, that they had grasped these permanent principles better than other peoples. They had largely dispelled superstition, experimented in government, and turned life into a rational art. Therefore when they defended their liberty what they defended was not merely freedom to live. It was freedom to live well, to live as other nations did not, in the public experimental study of the world and of human nature. This liberty to discover and pursue a natural happiness, this liberty to grow wise and to live in friendship with the gods and with one another, was the liberty vindicated at Thermopylae by martyrdom and at Salamis by victory.

As Greek cities stood for liberty in the world, so philosophers stood for liberty in the Greek cities. In both cases it was the same kind of liberty, not freedom to wander at hazard or to let things slip, but on the contrary freedom to legislate more precisely, at least for oneself, and to discover and codify the means to true happiness. Many of these pioneers in wisdom were audacious radicals and recoiled from no paradox. Some condemned what was most Greek: mythology, athletics, even multiplicity and physical motion. In the heart of those thriving, loquacious, festive little ant-hills, they preached impassibility and abstraction, the unanswerable scepticism of silence. Others practised a musical and priestly refinement of life, filled with metaphysical mysteries, and formed secret societies, not without a tendency to political domination. The cynics railed at the conventions, making themselves as comfortable as possible in the rôle of beggars and mocking parasites. The conservatives themselves were radical, so intelligent were they, and Plato wrote the charter of the most extreme militarism and communism, for the sake of preserving the free state. It was the swan-song of liberty, a prescription to a diseased old man to become young again and try a second life of superhuman virtue. The old man preferred simply to die.

Many laughed then, as we may be tempted to do, at all those absolute physicians of the soul, each with his panacea. Yet beneath their quarrels the wranglers had a common faith. They all believed there was a single solid natural wisdom to be found, that reason could find it, and that mankind, sobered by reason, could put it in practice. Mankind has continued to run wild and like barbarians to place freedom in their very wilderness, till we can hardly conceive the classic assumption of Greek philosophers and cities, that true liberty is bound up with an institution, a corporate scientific discipline, necessary to set free the perfect man, or the god, within us.

Upon the dissolution of paganism the Christian church adopted the classic conception of liberty. Of course, the field in which the higher politics had to operate was now conceived differently, and there was a new experience of the sort of happiness appropriate and possible to man; but the assumption remained unchallenged that Providence, as well as the human soul, had a fixed discoverable scope, and that the business of education, law, and religion was to bring them to operate in harmony. The aim of life, salvation, was involved in the nature of the soul itself, and the means of salvation had been ascertained by a positive science which the church was possessed of, partly revealed and partly experimental. Salvation was simply what, on a broad view, we should see to be health, and religion was nothing but a sort of universal hygiene.

The church, therefore, little as it tolerated heretical liberty, the liberty of moral and intellectual dispersion, felt that it had come into the world to set men free, and constantly demanded liberty for itself, that it might fulfil this mission. It was divinely commissioned to teach, guide, and console all nations and all ages by the self-same means, and to promote at all costs what it conceived to be human perfection. There should be saints and as many saints as possible. The church never admitted, any more than did any sect of ancient philosophers, that its teaching might represent only an eccentric view of the world, or that its guidance and consolations might be suitable only at one stage of human development. To waver in the pursuit of the orthodox ideal could only betray frivolity and want of self-knowledge. The truth of things and the happiness of each man could not lie elsewhere than where the church, summing up all human experience and all divine revelation, had placed it once for all and for everybody. The liberty of the church to fulfil its mission was accordingly hostile to any liberty of dispersion, to any radical consecutive independence, in the life of individuals or of nations.

When it came to full fruition this orthodox freedom was far from gay; it was called sanctity. The freedom of pagan philosophers too had turned out to be rather a stiff and severe pose; but in the Christian dispensation this austerity of true happiness was less to be wondered at, since life on earth was reputed to be abnormal from the beginning, and infected with hereditary disease. The full beauty and joy of restored liberty could hardly become evident in this life. Nevertheless a certain beauty and joy did radiate visibly from the saints; and while we may well think their renunciations and penances misguided or excessive, it is certain that, like the Spartans and the philosophers, they got something for their pains. Their bodies and souls were transfigured, as none now found upon earth. If we admire without imitating them we shall perhaps have done their philosophy exact justice. Classic liberty was a sort of forced and artificial liberty, a poor perfection reserved for an ascetic aristocracy in whom heroism and refinement were touched with perversity and slowly starved themselves to death.

Since those days we have discovered how much larger the universe is, and we have lost our way in it. Any day it may come over us again that our modern liberty to drift in the dark is the most terrible negation of freedom. Nothing happens to us as we would. We want peace

and make war. We need science and obey the will to believe, we love
art and flounder among whimsicalities, we believe in general comfort
and equality and we strain every nerve to become millionaires. After
all, antiquity must have been right in thinking that reasonable self-
direction must rest on having a determinate character and knowing
what it is, and that only the truth about God and happiness, if we
somehow found it, could make us free. But the truth is not to be found
by guessing at it, as religious prophets and men of genius have done,
and then damning every one who does not agree. Human nature, for
all its substantial fixity, is a living thing with many varieties and
variations. All diversity of opinion is therefore not founded on ignorance; it may express a legitimate change of habit or interest. The
classic and Christian synthesis from which we have broken loose was
certainly premature, even if the only issue of our liberal experiments
should be to lead us back to some such equilibrium. Let us hope at
least that the new morality, when it comes, may be more broadly based
than the old on knowledge of the world, not so absolute, not so meticulous, and not chanted so much in the monotone of an abstracted sage.

—"Classic Liberty," *Soliloquies in England*

2. "DEMOCRACY" VERSUS "DEMOCRATSKY"

It is necessary to see first the significance of liberty in the context
of the world thought and world politics of today. There has been a
modern apostasy from liberty that to me personally is shocking. Under
the influence of collectivistic thought, some so-called liberals tend to
forget, neglect, and compromise with the rights of the individual.
This comes out in various forms, but the root of the trouble seems
to be that their belief in liberty is not deep enough and strong enough.
The love of liberty is not an exclusively American tradition; the love
of personal liberty is innate, if anything is innate, but the American
nation seems by its tradition and popular instinct to stand more sig-
nally than other nations for this ideal. I tremble in my shoes when
I hear some American fellow travelers talk. An intelligent reporter
writes a book about Soviet Russia and conveys the impression that the
fact that millions of slaves starve and die and lose their freedom in

Siberian camps leaves him entirely unmoved. Social good is the important thing. Put everybody under surveillance, but secure them their bread and butter and abolish poverty. And these people call themselves the spiritual descendants of Thomas Jefferson, who should turn in his grave.

What frightened Jefferson was that, on his return from Europe, he heard the dinner tables of New York and Washington buzzing with what he insisted on calling "monarchist" talk. So soon—in 1790? Doubts, betrayals of the heart are common, and it was human to forget. So our hearts often betray us today and we begin to forget once more. Lincoln says well that there are only two eternal principles in politics: "That is the issue that will continue in this country when these poor tongues of Judge Douglas and myself shall be silent. It is the eternal struggle between these two principles—right and wrong—throughout the world. They are the two principles that have stood face to face from the beginning of time; and will ever continue to struggle. The one is the common right of humanity, and the other the divine right of kings. *It is the same principle in whatever shape it develops itself."* [2] What would Lincoln say today? I am sure he would rise again in debate and with his precise logic and simple eloquence show the worshipers of Stalin's democracy to be the renegades that they are. "Lincoln's gray eyes would flash fire when speaking against slavery . . . when speaking of liberty," we are told by Herndon. Either your eyes flash fire, or they don't. Either the citizens of a police state are slaves, or they are not. Either Stalin has the divine right of kings, or he hasn't. The issue cannot be avoided. Some intellectuals affect to be able to see the difference between *Vive le roi!* and *Long live Stalin!* I cannot.

How do I account for such false liberalism today? Perhaps it is because certain Americans seem to me to believe that freedom of thought is the very lifeblood of an American because he is born an American, but that other peoples, the peoples of Eastern Europe and of China, the college students of Prague, for example, do not mind having their religious and intellectual freedoms gagged, provided these totalitarian regimes secure them a better "living." I think that such Americans err on this point, that they do not believe in liberty hard

<hr>

[2] Lincoln's debate with Douglas, "Reply at Alton." Italics are mine. In this particular instance, he was speaking of the oppression by one race of another race, the Negroes.

enough, and that those who consider liberty unimportant for others will lose their title as champions of liberty at home.

Part of the confusion is due to words, especially the word "democracy," probably the most abused and misused word today. Democracy is the most confused word in use today, because Soviet Communists, as different from Mussolini's Fascists, know it is a good word to use and because it was part of Lenin's political strategy to confuse the democracies. Stalin's totalitarianism pays a subtle tribute to democracy by donning the latter's costume and speaking its language and is therefore the more dangerous. If we don't look out, one of these mornings we will read in the papers that democracy was first discovered by Catherine the Great, not by Thomas Jefferson.

We can at once dismiss the confusing question whether a democracy, under whatever name, without faith in the individual and without liberty, can be called a democracy. Jefferson defined the problem well: there are only two types of government in all the world, those that trust the people and those that fear them.

It might clarify the situation at once if instead of talking about democracy, we would talk about liberty. You can argue whether Soviet Russia is a democracy, but Gromyko himself could not argue that there is liberty in Russia. I think Henry Wallace was dishonest when he spoke of Soviet Russia as a "directed democracy." Why, we ask, by the same token was not Hitler's Reich also a "directed democracy"? Lenin has succeeded beyond his expectations in confusing us. There are so many counterfeits of democracy today that when a correspondent spoke of the "democratic forces" of China, or the "democratic army" of Iran, with a familiar American accent, I felt a shudder and a shock. I would not mind if Molotov had said it—but an American!

So vitiated is the word "democracy" by adulterated use that it would make for clarity if we either dropped the word and presented the issue as one of liberty rather than of democracy, or if we must continue to use it, created a new word for democracy without liberty and reserved the good old word for democracy *with* liberty. For democracy cannot mean one thing and its antithesis at the same time; we must have sympathy for the poor newspaper readers who are trying to think straight on the basic problems, which are hard enough without this unfortunate confusion of terms. We must honestly admit that there are two articles by the same name today, Soviet democracy and American democracy, antithetical to each other from the very bases up. It would greatly make for clarity if the former be called "democratsky," and its elements, its peculiar administration, its army, its techniques, etc., be described by the adjective "democratov," instead of "democratic." Thus if an American fellow traveler wishes to speak of the Chinese Communist regime as a "democratsky" or as a "democratov" regime, everybody would know exactly what it means. So also we could safely report the "democratov" elections in Czechoslovakia and the "democratov revolution" in Indo-China, and everybody would be happier.

How useful are words! The world still lacks a name for a new article, Soviet imperialism, which is totally different from British imperialism in technique, ideology, and procedure. To call it merely red imperialism adds to the confusion, for the human mind hangs on by habit to its usual associations of the word "imperialism." Imperialism has gone on to new evolutionary forms, and we still call it by its old name. What is that subtle dialectic by which Communists in Eastern Europe are persuaded that Russians may love their own country but Yugoslavs may not, under penalty of being liquidated as guilty of "deviation from internationalism"? If it is befuddled thinking to be loyal to one's country and the correct Leninist-Stalinist thesis to be loyal to Moscow, clearly, then, every Yugoslav is expected to lay down his life for Russia, the Russians themselves, to be quite fair and consistent, also pledging the same. I really am amazed at this dialectic. Meanwhile, Russians may make a heroic struggle to love themselves, perhaps even glorify themselves, but for Lithuanians and Poles to "love thy neighbor" would be enough. The outside democratic world has to go a long way to catch up with these subtleties. As an aid to clearer thinking, to get away from the vitiated terms, any new word for the new article—to coin a word of the Russian type, "sovimpism" —would be preferable to the good, old imperialism of England which to copy is to traduce. Then we would also need the necessary complement to this sovimpist as we need a masochist to enjoy the pain inflicted by the sadist; the word "fosterist" probably would do. But unless we do something about this confusion of words, we will be fighting not Russia but an antiquated vocabulary of our own.

I have digressed, purposely, to note the significance of the word "liberty" in the context of the present-day world. As I say, there is an unalterable, inescapable antithesis in the theory and practice of modern government, the Hitler-Stalinist fear of the people and the Jeffersonian trust in the people. It does not matter what the form of administration is; it may be a monarchy, a republic, a totalitarian government, a socialist guild republic, or an anarchy. Human ingenuity is such that you can get anything you want, give it any name you want, fool the people enough for a time to make them believe that they have got what really they haven't, and fool other people enough to desire what those people haven't got but the outsiders think that they have, by juggling with words.

3. THE COMMON MAN

It goes without saying that we can't even talk of liberty unless we are willing to assume that the common man deserves it, unless we have faith in the individual human being with all his imperfections. It is not an easy thesis to establish. As Jefferson expressed it, it was a mystical faith, unproved and untried yet, and through his trust in the instincts of the colonists as he found them, he was willing to try it. We all know that historically the American Republic was adopted only as an experiment, though that experiment has now proved to be successful. It was a first trial; the French Republic had not been born. The founders of the American Republic were compelled to face the naked formula: either the common man must be trusted to govern himself, or he has to be ruled by others. The Republic was founded on faith, but it would be more nearly correct to describe it as a good hunch that the common man could govern himself. Thus faith in the worth and sovereignty of the individual is the very bottom and central foundation of democracy.

Faith in the individual was implicit in the land of the Pilgrim's pride. But, as far as I am aware, it took a long, long time for that faith to be justified by a conscious philosophy, the philosophy of Emerson. It was a difficult thing to do. Why believe that the common man and woman are worth our trust? The fathers of the American Republic bet on democracy as one would bet on a horse. Of the American colonists' desire for national liberty and independence there was no doubt; it was not a bet, it was an imperative desire. But about individual liberty and trust in the common man or fear of the common man, there was considerable wavering and dissension. So Jefferson and the Federalists had a fight. If Jefferson won and was elected President, it was because the sentiment of the American people confirmed him, because after throwing out the English who wanted to govern for them, they did not want others of their own nation, a particular class, to govern for them—in other words, when they said they wanted to govern themselves, they meant to govern themselves.

The proposition was audacious. By 1792 the French Revolution had broken out, and there was every semblance of mob rule. But Jefferson believed that the special circumstances of the country and the special qualities of its people could make democracy work. And so, I believe, the whole character of the American Republic today is profoundly influenced at that critical stage when Jefferson and the people of America won. Because that experiment succeeded through the inherent qualities of the race, we speak and read every day today of the common man and hear of the common man, forgetting that at that time trust in the common man was an experiment after all.

Abraham Lincoln said that God must love the common people because He made so many of them. That was a clever, religious statement, by which I mean a statement which is true not because it is true but because we already choose to believe it anyway. Philosophically, of course, it does not have a leg to stand on. God made many more fish in the Pacific Ocean than men on the American continent. He also made many more flies and ants, not to speak of bacteria. I haven't got statistics about bacteria, and nobody else has, but of course the figures are astronomical. So God must love bacteria more than man. But even if He does, we choose not to believe it. God made some of them so they can even survive subzero temperature and boiling water. A philosophical proof of the common man thesis evidently cannot be maintained. The establishment of the philosophical proof is difficult, because the parts never measure up to the whole and the philosophers who express their love and trust in their fellow men quite often go to the bank or the market or the subway and are sadly disillusioned. To express love for man in the singular and disappointment in men in the plural, as so many writers do in their private letters and journals, is to deprive this love of all its real content and is of no practical consequence to the philosopher himself. That is the inherent difficulty to be solved.

Emerson's essay on "Nominalists and Realists" and his lecture on "New England Reformers" were published in 1844. At about this time. there was a sudden philosophic assertion of the mystic sovereignty of the individual. One would like to think that it was all Emerson's influence but cannot be quite sure that it was. The time for the ripening of that faith, for a conscious, imperious assertion of that faith, had come. Emerson had already given in 1837 his "The American Scholar" address, America's "intellectual Declaration of Independence," as Oliver Wendell Holmes called it. He began to sound the note of "self-trust" which he continued to sound all his life. "The deeper he dives into his privatest, secretest presentiment, to his wonder he finds this is the most acceptable, most public, and universally true." "The private life of one man shall be a more illustrious monarchy, more formidable to its enemy, more sweet and serene in its influence to its friend, than any kingdom in history." "Another sign of our times . . . is the new importance given to the single person . . . man shall treat with man as a sovereign state with a sovereign state . . . it is for you to know all; it is for you to dare all." Young men who heard it were stirred. The next year Emerson gave the "Divinity School Address." Thank God for all the Wesleys and Oberlins and saints and prophets "but say, 'I also am a man.' " The young divines who heard this were again stirred. In 1841 he published his essay on "Self-Reliance." "Nothing is at last sacred but the integrity of your own mind." "Let a man then know his worth, and keep things under his feet. Let him not peep or steal, or skulk up and down with the air of a charity boy, a bastard, or an interloper in the world which exists for him." And in 1844 came the two essays above mentioned, which, read together, provide a complete philosophic justification of the common man as far as it is possible to do so.

As I say, the times were ripe; these ideas pervaded the general atmosphere of transcendentalism. Emerson says in his *Journals* that a Mrs. B. said, with a wave of her hand, "Transcendentalism means *a little beyond*," and some State Street people suspected that it would invalidate contracts. As a matter of fact, it means practically the distribution of Godhead in individuals. Transcendentalists or not, the writers of the times caught its meaning. Melville, quite transcendental in his own way, said in 1851 in *Moby Dick,* "If, then, to meanest mariners, and renegades and castaways, I shall hereafter ascribe high qualities, though dark; weave round them tragic graces; if even the most mournful, perchance the most debased, among them all, shall at times lift himself to the exalted mounts; if I shall touch that workman's arm with some ethereal light; if I shall spread a rainbow over his disastrous set of sun; then against all moral critics bear me out in it, thou Spirit of Equality, which has spread one royal mantle of humanity over all my kind! Bear me out in it, thou great democratic God!" [3] About this time he wrote to Nathaniel Hawthorne, "So when you see or hear of my ruthless democracy on all sides, you may possibly feel a touch of a shrink, or something of that sort. It is but nature to be shy of a normal who boldly declares that a thief in jail is as honorable a personage as General George Washington." As quoted already, Thoreau wrote to Harrison Blake, March 27, 1848, "I am simply what I am, or I begin to be that . . . Do what you love. Know your own bone; gnaw at it, bury it, unearth it, and gnaw it still." And Whitman said in the "Song of Myself" in 1855, "I exist as I am—that is enough." Did Emerson influence them all? Against Whitman's own testimony, I think he got his mystic view of individual identity from Emerson's "Nominalists and Realists." The only distant approach to a philosophical occupation in Whitman was the problem of individual identity and the aggregate, the en masse, but that was the problem Emerson had dealt with explicitly and satisfactorily. There is of course something peculiarly Whitmanesque in his sexual interpretation of it—"Always a knit of identity—always distinction—always a breed of life." Whitman's magnification of his ego—"I dote on myself—there is that lot of me, all so luscious"—and taking himself "the exact dimensions of Jehovah" is more braggadocio of a virile young man than philosophy. We do not know whether he was being mystical or misty. But Whitman tried to express the importance of the individual, as far as he could make it articulate, in *Democratic Vistas.*

[3] *Moby Dick,* chap. XXVI.

"For after the rest is said—after the many time-honored and really true things for subordination, experience, rights of property, etc., have been listened to and acquiesced in—after the valuable and well-settled statement of our duties and relations in society is thoroughly conned over and exhausted—it remains to bring forward and modify everything else with the idea of that Something a man is (last precious consolation of the drudging poor), standing apart from all else, divine in his own right, and a woman in hers, sole and untouchable by any canons of authority, or any rule derived from precedent, state-safety, the acts of legislatures, or even from what is called religion, modesty, or art. The radiation of this truth is the key of the most significant doing of our immediately preceding three centuries, and has been the political genesis and life of America. Advancing visibly, it still more advances invisibly. Underneath the fluctuations of the expressions of society, as well as the movements of the politics of the leading nations of the world, we see steadily pressing ahead and strengthening itself, even in the midst of immense tendencies toward aggregation, this image of completeness in separation, of individual personal dignity, of a single person, either male or female, characterized in the main, not from extrinsic acquirements or position, but in the pride of himself or herself alone; and, as an eventual conclusion and summing up (or else the entire scheme of things is aimless, a cheat, a crash), the simple idea that the last, best dependence is to be upon humanity itself, and its own inherent, normal, full-grown qualities without any superstitious support whatever...."

In "Nominalists and Realists" Emerson provides the metaphysical basis for his theory of the individual. From an examination of the relation of parts to the whole, he comes to the conclusion that "every man is wanted, and no man is wanted much" and that "we fancy men are individuals; so are pumpkins; but every pumpkin in the field goes through every point of pumpkin history." Emerson was fully conscious of the difficulties of generalizing about man in the abstract and men in the particular in this two-faced universe; "I loved man, if men seemed to me mice and rats," he said toward the end. He takes the position of a recluse who imagines his own ideas of man. Then the recluse "goes into a mob, a banking house, into a mechanic's shop, into a mill, into a laboratory, into a ship, into a camp, and in each new place he is no better than an idiot." He makes the discovery that all types of men are needed in this universe and all, if true each to his own genius, "take turns at the top." He sees well enough that all individuals, geniuses, great leaders and all, are imperfect, however noble and inspiring the thought of man in the abstract may be. Then he philosophizes: "Nature will not be Buddhist: she resents generalizing, and insults the philosopher with a million of fresh particulars . . . Nick Bottom cannot play all the parts, work it how he may; there will be somebody else, and the world will be round . . . She would never get anything done, if she suffered admirable Crichtons and universal geniuses. She loves better a wheelwright who dreams all night of wheels, and a groom who is part of his horse; for she is full of work, and these are her hands." Therefore, "if John was perfect, why are you and I alive? As long as any man exists, there is some need of him; let him fight for his own." But while "we have insisted on the imperfection of individuals, our affections and our experience urge that every individual is entitled to honor, and a very generous treatment is sure to be paid." "If we cannot make voluntary and conscious steps in the admirable science of universals, let us see the parts wisely, and infer the genius of nature from the best particulars with a becoming charity." Actually, he speaks of the "incarnation" and distribution of "godhead" in individuals with a touch of Hindu idealism or German romanticism. In his *Journals* he says, "God manifest in the flesh of every man is a perfect rule of social life. Justify yourself to an infinite Being in the ostler and dandy and stranger, and you shall never repent. . . . Very fitly therefore I assert that every man is a partialist; that nature secures him as an instrument by self-conceit, preventing the tendencies to religion and science; and now further assert, that, each man's genius being nearly and affectionately explored, he is justified in his individuality, as his nature is found to be immense; and now I add that every man is a universalist also, and, as our earth, whilst it spins on its own axis, spins all the time around the sun through the celestial spaces, so the least of its rational children, the most dedicated to his private affair, works out, though as it were under a disguise, the universal problem. We fancy men are individuals; so are pumpkins; but every pumpkin in the field goes through every point of pumpkin history."

Thus the conundrum of the universal and the particular was solved by Emerson. This emphasis on the particular, this robust sense of the stuff of immediate experience, I find is a fundamental trait of American thinking. Emerson the monist and William James the pluralist were really very much alike; both were torn between love for the concrete particular fact and the abstract unity and universality of being, and both came to the same conclusion of the importance of the individual. Students of philosophy will do well to note the passage where Emerson, as a monist and preacher of the over-soul, says, "Therefore I assert that every man is a partialist," on which we may say his theory of individualism is based. Emerson's monism never went through the thinning process of classification to discover a universal substance; he worshiped rather the particular fact as a unit representative of the whole in the sense that all the molecules of a piece of iron act as individual magnets when that iron becomes a magnet.

It is, however, in his lecture on "New England Reformers" that we hear the challenging, revivifying words of Emerson as an apostle of the dignity of the individual. Here Emerson himself became a lodestone of American thinking. It must be this vivifying message of the importance of the private individual, this power to release the faith of every man in himself, this assertion that "men are better than they seem" which account for Emerson's perpetual potent influence on each generation. It was this gift of inspiring and releasing fresh energy and reinstating man on his old throne that made Lowell write to Charles Eliot Norton on hearing Emerson's lecture, "All through it I felt something in me that cried, 'Ha, ha, to the sound of the trumpets!'" Man, in fact, was discovered again. It was Emerson's declaration that "a nobler life, a better manhood, a purer purpose, wooed every listening soul" that made George William Curtis describe his lecture in the following words in the "Editor's Easy Chair" of *Harper's:* "At the desk stood the lecturer and read his manuscript, and all but the boys sat silent and enthralled by the musical spell. . . . Some thought him very queer. All laughed at the delightful humor or the illustrative anecdote that sparkled for a moment upon the surface of his talk; and some sat inspired with unknown resolves, soaring upon lofty hopes as they heard. . . . And when the words were spoken and the lecturer sat down, the Easy Chair sat still and heard the rich cadences lingering in the air, as the young priest's heart throbs with the long vibrations when the organist is gone. . . . Grave parents were quoted as saying, 'I don't go to hear Mr. Emerson; I don't understand him. But my daughters do.'"[4]

The following consists of extracts from the second half of the lecture on "New England Reformers." I have made here a rather long selection because of the central importance of the subject in American thought.

"Only by obedience to his genius, only by the freest activity in the way constitutional to him, does an angel seem to rise before a man and lead him by the hand out of all the wards of the prison."

BY RALPH WALDO EMERSON

I resist the skepticism of our education and of our educated men. I do not believe that the differences of opinion and character in men are organic. I do not recognize, beside the class of the good and the wise, a permanent class of skeptics, or a class of conservatives, or of malignants, or of materialists. I do not believe in two classes. You remember the story of the poor woman who importuned King Philip of Macedon to grant her justice, which Philip refused: the woman exclaimed, "I appeal:" the king, astonished, asked to whom she appealed: the woman replied, "From Philip drunk to Philip sober." The text will suit me very well. I believe not in two classes of men, but in man in two moods, in Philip drunk and Philip sober. I think, according to the good-hearted word of Plato, "Unwillingly the soul is deprived of truth." Iron conservative, miser, or thief, no man is but by a supposed necessity which he tolerates by shortness or torpidity of sight. The soul lets no man go without some visitations and holydays of a diviner presence. It would be easy to show, by a narrow scanning of any man's biography, that we are not so wedded to our paltry performances of every kind but that every man has at intervals the grace to scorn his performances, in comparing them with his belief of what he should do;—that he puts himself on the side of his enemies, listening gladly to what they say of him, and accusing himself of the same things. . . .

[4] Reprinted by permission of *Harper's Magazine*.

Nothing shall warp me from the belief that every man is a lover of truth. There is no pure lie, no pure malignity in nature. The entertainment of the proposition of depravity is the last profligacy and profanation. There is no skepticism, no atheism but that. Could it be received into common belief, suicide would unpeople the planet. It has had a name to live in some dogmatic theology, but each man's innocence and his real liking of his neighbor have kept it a dead letter. I remember standing at the polls one day when the anger of the political contest gave a certain grimness to the faces of the independent electors, and a good man at my side, looking on the people, remarked, "I am satisfied that the largest part of these men, on either side, mean to vote right." I suppose considerate observers, looking at the masses of men in their blameless and in their equivocal actions, will assent, that in spite of selfishness and frivolity, the general purpose in the great number of persons is fidelity. . . .

And as a man is equal to the Church and equal to the State, so he is equal to every other man. The disparities of power in men are superficial; and all frank and searching conversation, in which a man lays himself open to his brother, apprises each of their radical unity. When two persons sit and converse in a thoroughly good understanding, the remark is sure to be made, See how we have disputed about words! Let a clear, apprehensive mind, such as every man knows among his friends, converse with the most commanding poetic genius, I think it would appear that there was no inequality such as men fancy, between them; that a perfect understanding, a like receiving, a like perceiving, abolished differences; and the poet would confess that his creative imagination gave him no deep advantage, but only the superficial one that he could express himself and the other could not; that his advantage was a knack, which might impose on indolent men but could not impose on lovers of truth; for they know the tax of talent, or what a price of greatness the power of expression too often pays. I believe it is the conviction of the purest men that the net amount of man and man does not much vary. Each is incomparably superior to his companion in some faculty. His want of skill in other directions has added to his fitness for his own work. Each seems to have some compensation yielded to him by his infirmity, and every hinderance operates as a concentration of his force.

These and the like experiences intimate that man stands in strict connection with a higher fact never yet manifested. There is power over and behind us, and we are the channels of its communications. . . . This open channel to the highest life is the first and last reality, so subtle, so quiet, yet so tenacious, that although I have never expressed the truth, and although I have never heard the expression of it from any other, I know that the whole truth is here for me. . . .

If the auguries of the prophesying heart shall make themselves good in time, the man who shall be born, whose advent men and events prepare and foreshow, is one who shall enjoy his connection with a higher life, with the man within man; shall destroy distrust by his trust, shall use his native but forgotten methods, shall not take counsel of flesh and blood, but shall rely on the Law alive and beautiful which works over our heads and under our feet. Pitiless, it avails itself of our success when we obey it, and of our ruin when we contravene it. Men are all secret believers in it, else the word justice would have no meaning: they believe that the best is the true; that right is done at last; or chaos would come. It rewards actions after their nature, and not after the design of the agent. 'Work,' it saith to man, 'in every hour, paid or unpaid, see only that thou work, and thou canst not escape the reward: whether thy work be fine or coarse, planting corn or writing epics, so only it be honest work, done to thine own appro-bation, it shall earn a reward to the senses as well as to the thought: no matter how often defeated, you are born to victory. The reward of a thing well done, is to have done it.'

As soon as a man is wonted to look beyond surfaces, and to see how this high will prevails without an exception or an interval, he settles himself into serenity. He can already rely on the laws of gravity, that every stone will fall where it is due; the good globe is faithful, and carries us securely through the celestial spaces, anxious or resigned, we need not interfere to help it on: and he will learn one day the mild lesson they teach, that our own orbit is all our task, and we need not assist the administration of the universe. Do not be so impatient to set the town right concerning the unfounded pretensions and the false reputation of certain men of standing. They are laboring harder to set the town right concerning themselves, and will certainly succeed. Suppress for a few days your criticism on the insufficiency of this or

that teacher or experimenter, and he will have demonstrated his insufficiency to all men's eyes. In like manner, let a man fall into the
divine circuits, and he is enlarged. Obedience to his genius is the
only liberating influence. We wish to escape from subjection and a
sense of inferiority, and we make self-denying ordinances, we drink
water, we eat grass, we refuse the laws, we go to jail: it is all in vain;
only by obedience to his genius, only by the freest activity in the way
constitutional to him, does an angel seem to arise before a man and
lead him by the hand out of all the wards of the prison.

That which befits us, embosomed in beauty and wonder as we are,
is cheerfulness and courage, and the endeavor to realize our aspirations.
The life of man is the true romance, which when it is valiantly conducted will yield the imagination a higher joy than any fiction.

—"New England Reformers," *Essays: Second Series*

4. THE STATE AND THE INDIVIDUAL

Thoreau was, in a very special sense, the prophet of the individual
and defender of the individual against the state. The recluse of
Walden seemed to the citizens of Concord rather queer. On a summer
morning he would sit in his sunny doorway from sunrise until noon,
rapt in reverie, amid the pines and hickories and sumachs, until by
the sun falling in his west window or by the noise of some traveler's
wagon on the distant highway he was reminded that it was past
noon. He had aimed at being a cedar post, wet and cold and pleasantly
tickled by lichens slowly spreading over him; there he was like an
Indian yogi or like Chuangtse's sage who had a bird's nest over his
head and a willow growing out of his armpit. In one of the most
extraordinary statements Thoreau ever made, in his letter to Harrison
Blake, December 6, 1856, he said ". . . generally, I take events as unconcernedly as a fence post. . . . Could I not be content, then, to be a
cedar post, which lasts twenty-five years? Would I not rather be that
than the farmer that set it? or he that preaches to the farmer? and
go to the heaven of posts? I think I should like that as well as any
would like it. But I should not care if I sprouted into a living tree,
put forth leaves and flowers, and bore fruit." This was a little too
much for the average American intelligence, and James Russell

Lowell as an editor once deleted a line from Thoreau's essay on "shesuncook" where he said, "It (the pine tree) is as immortal as I am and perhaps will go to a higher heaven, there to tower above me." [5]

Thoreau might have seemed to his neighbors, as did many eccentrics of his time, on the "lunatic fringe" of reformers, socialists, amateur prophets, mesmerists, phrenologists, etc. The land was as full of apostles as the woods were full of coons and chipmunks. But Thoreau was probing deep into life. While Darwin was proving man's animal ancestry, Emerson and Thoreau, by the intuitive, transcendental approach, were establishing man's kinship with nature. While his neighbors thought him peculiar, Thoreau knew that he lived and that sitting there from morning until noon amid pine trees or being the captain of huckleberry parties was the way man should live. Having established this absolute inner conviction, it is natural that he took passing events as unconcernedly as a fence post. Therefore, when Emerson declared man equal to the state, equal to the church, and equal to every other man as a sovereign state was equal to another sovereign state, Thoreau went further. He assumed a still higher point of view for looking at the state. "I do not wish to quarrel with any man or nation. I do not wish to split hairs, to make fine distinctions, or set myself up as better than my neighbors. I seek rather, I may say, even an excuse for conforming to the laws of the land. I am but too ready to conform to them. . . . Seen from a lower point of view, the Constitution, with all its faults, is very good; the law and the courts are very respectable; even this State and this American government are, in many respects, very admirable, and rare things, to be thankful for, such as a great many have described them; but seen from a point of view a little higher, they are what I have described them; seen from higher still, and the highest, who shall say what they are, or that they are worth looking at or thinking of at all?" ("Civil Disobedience.")

[5] The impression the Concordian philosophers made on the farmers of the neighborhood was well described by Kate Douglas Wiggin, who as a girl of thirteen saw Emerson and Alcott and who knew Elizabeth Peabody well. She described a fellow passenger on the way to Concord as saying to her, "Be you one of them Phy-loss-er-fers? The woods is chuck full of em now. I went in the hall the other day just a-purpose to hear 'em charnt with their eyes shet. I'd jest like to see one of 'em grubbin' stumps out of an old timber patch." *My Garden of Memory*, p. 148. Copyright, 1923, Houghton Mifflin Company. Reprinted by permission.

Thoreau's importance today is therefore his hard and earnest assertion, clear and strong as a trumpet blast, that the individual is more
important than the state, even if he did seem extreme in taking that
position. What he felt was not an idiosyncrasy but a fundamental
truth in consonance with the American instinct, which so many today,
in opposition to that fine instinct, often forget. He carried his doctrine
into practice. He refused allegiance to the state of Massachusetts, and
"quietly declared war with the State" when the Fugitive Slave Law
angered him. When the Negro Burns was arrested and returned to
slavery, his thoughts breathed "murder to the State." Once he refused
to pay tax for the support of a clergyman and was ready to go to jail
for it, but "unfortunately" somebody paid it for him. Then he flatly
refused to pay the poll tax of a dollar and fifty cents. One morning
as he was going to a shoemaker's to get a shoe which was being
mended, he was arrested and put in jail. He stayed in jail one night,
for somebody again paid the tax for him. The next morning he proceeded to get the shoes and, having put them on, joined a huckleberry
party going to one of the highest hills, two miles off, and "then the
State was nowhere to be seen."

What Thoreau did was nobody's business but his own. What he
did belonged to himself and to the hour. But the truth behind that
act of voluntarily going to jail for even one night was portentous. As
Henry Seidel Canby says, he legislated "for eternity." The following
is one of the most important testaments of American democracy.

*"There will never be a really free and enlightened State un-
til the State comes to recognize the individual as a higher
and independent power."*

BY HENRY DAVID THOREAU

"The authority of government, even such as I am willing to submit
to,—for I will cheerfully obey those who know and can do better than
I, and in many things even those who neither know nor can do so
well,—is still an impure one: to be strictly just, it must have the sanc-
tion and consent of the governed. It can have no pure right over my
person and property but what I concede to it. The progress from an

absolute to a limited monarchy, from a limited monarchy to a democracy, is a progress toward a true respect for the individual. Even the Chinese philosopher * was wise enough to regard the individual as the basis of the empire. Is a democracy, such as we know it, the last improvement possible in government? Is it not possible to take a step further towards recognizing and organizing the rights of man? There will never be a really free and enlightened State until the State comes to recognize the individual as a higher and independent power, from which all its own power and authority are derived, and treats him accordingly. I please myself with imagining a State at last which can afford to be just to all men, and to treat the individual with respect as a neighbor; which even would not think it inconsistent with its own repose if a few were to live aloof from it, not meddling with it, nor embraced by it, who fulfilled all the duties of neighbors and fellowmen. A State which bore this kind of fruit, and suffered it to drop off as fast as it ripened, would prepare the way for a still more perfect and glorious State, which also I have imagined, but not yet anywhere seen.

—"Civil Disobedience"

Thoreau's extreme personal example will seldom be imitated in America, just as few Americans would "prefer grasshoppers to preachers" as he did. But of course Thoreau had a disciple in India, no less a person than Mahatma ("Great Soul") Gandhi. It is always easier for an Oriental than an American to understand Thoreau, because Thoreau's scale of values is closer to the Oriental one. Much of Thoreau's spiritual nourishment came from India itself.

The story of Thoreau's influence on Gandhi is an interesting chapter in the interchange of world thought. In 1841 Thoreau wrote after reading *The Laws of Manu* in Emerson's house, "That title, 'The Laws of Menu with the Gloss of Colluca,' comes to me with such a volume of sound as if it had swept unobstructed over the plains of Hindostan; and when my eye rests on yonder birches, or the sun in the water, or the shadows of trees, it seems to signify the laws of them all." He went to the woods in 1845 and came out of them in 1847. In 1849 he wrote "Resistance to Civil Government" ("Civil Disobedience"). In 1907, some sixty years later, Gandhi read the paper

* Confucius.

in South Africa. In reply to an inquiry by Henry S. Salt, a biographer of Thoreau, Gandhi wrote, "My first introduction to Thoreau's writings was, I think, in 1907, or later, when I was in the thick of the passive resistance struggle. A friend sent me the essay on Civil Disobedience. It left a deep impression upon me. I translated a portion for the readers of *Indian Opinion* in South Africa, which I was then editing, and I made copious extracts for the English part of that paper. The essay seemed to be so convincing and truthful that I felt the need of knowing more of Thoreau, and I came across your Life of him, his *Walden,* and other essays, all of which I read with great pleasure and equal profit." [6]

Gandhi was no mere yogi; he was a man who believed that spiritual truths, if true, should be applied even to politics. The dichotomy between religion and politics, so curious an American custom, was not there. So out of a statement of a theoretic truth, Gandhi launched forth into one of the world's most significant nonviolent movements.

I believe it is the following passages in the paper on "Civil Disobedience" which influenced Gandhi's thinking and led him to his conclusion. It has the elements of (1) defying the law, (2) a "peaceful revolution," that could be bloodless, (3) absence of hatred of the law agent as a person, and (4) the idea of a nation going to jail en masse as a means of protest and rectifying wrongs and injustices.

"I know this well . . . if ten honest *men only, ay, if one HONEST man, in this State of Massachusetts . . . were actually to withdraw from this copartnership, and be locked up in the county jail therefor . . ."*

BY HENRY DAVID THOREAU

Unjust laws exist: shall we be content to obey them, or shall we endeavor to amend them, and obey them until we have succeeded, or shall we transgress them at once? . . .

If the injustice is part of the necessary friction of the machine of government, let it go, let it go: perchance it will wear smooth,—certainly the machine will wear out. If the injustice has a spring, or a

---

[6] Henry S. Salt, *Company I Have Kept,* London, Allen & Unwin, 1930, pp. 100-101, quoted in Arthur Christy, *The Orient in American Transcendentalism,* p. 266.

pulley, or a rope, or a crank, exclusively for itself, then perhaps you may consider whether the remedy will not be worse than the evil; but if it is of such a nature that it requires you to be the agent of injustice to another, then, I say, break the law. Let your life be a counter friction to stop the machine. What I have to do is to see, at any rate, that I do not lend myself to the wrong which I condemn. . . .

I do not hesitate to say, that those who call themselves Abolitionists should at once effectually withdraw their support, both in person and property, from the government of Massachusetts, and not wait till they constitute a majority of one, before they suffer the right to prevail through them. I think that it is enough if they have God on their side, without waiting for that other one. Moreover, any man more right than his neighbors constitutes a majority of one already.

I meet this American government, or its representative, the state government, directly, and face to face, once a year—no more—in the person of its tax-gatherer; this is the only mode in which a man situated as I am necessarily meets it; and it then says distinctly, Recognize me; and the simplest, the most effectual, and, in the present posture of affairs, the indispensablest mode of treating with it on this head, of expressing your little satisfaction with and love for it, is to deny it then. My civil neighbor, the tax-gatherer, is the very man I have to deal with,—for it is, after all, with men and not with parchment that I quarrel,—and he has voluntarily chosen to be an agent of the government. How shall he ever know well what he is and does as an officer of the government, or as a man, until he is obliged to consider whether he shall treat me, his neighbor, for whom he has respect, as a neighbor and well-disposed man, or as a maniac and disturber of the peace, and see if he can get over this obstruction to his neighborliness without a ruder and more impetuous thought or speech corresponding with his action. I know this well, that if one thousand, if one hundred, if ten men whom I could name,—if ten *honest* men only,—ay, if *one* HONEST man, in this State of Massachusetts, *ceasing to hold slaves,* were actually to withdraw from this copartnership, and be locked up in the county jail therefor, it would be the abolition of slavery in America. For it matters not how small the beginning may seem to be: what is once well done is done forever. But we love better to talk about it: that we say is our mission. Reform keeps many scores of newspapers in its service, but not one man. If my esteemed neighbor, the State's ambassador, who will devote his days to the settlement of the question of human rights in the Council Chamber, instead of being threatened with the prisons of Carolina, were to sit down the prisoner of Massachusetts, that State which is so anxious to foist the sin of slavery upon her sister,—though at present she can discover only an act of inhospitality to be the ground of a quarrel with her,—the Legislature would not wholly waive the subject the following winter.

Under a government which imprisons any unjustly, the true place for a just man is also a prison. . . . A minority is powerless while it conforms to the majority; it is not even a minority then; but it is irresistible when it clogs by its whole weight. If the alternative is to keep all just men in prison, or give up war and slavery, the State will not hesitate which to choose. If a thousand men were not to pay their tax-bills this year, that would not be a violent and bloody measure, as it would be to pay them, and enable the State to commit violence and shed innocent blood. This is, in fact, the definition of a peaceable revolution, if any such is possible. If the taxgatherer, or any other public officer, asks me, as one has done, "But what shall I do?" my answer is, "If you really wish to do anything, resign your office." When the subject has refused allegiance, and the officer has resigned his office, then the revolution is accomplished. But even suppose blood should flow. Is there not a sort of blood shed when the conscience is wounded? Through this wound a man's real manhood and immortality flow out, and he bleeds to an everlasting death. I see this blood flowing now. . . .

I have paid no poll-tax for six years. I was put into a jail once on this account, for one night; and, as I stood considering the walls of solid stone, two or three feet thick, the door of wood and iron, a foot thick, and the iron grating which strained the light, I could not help being struck with the foolishness of that institution which treated me as if I were mere flesh and blood and bones, to be locked up. I wondered that it should have concluded at length that this was the best use it could put me to, and had never thought to avail itself of my services in some way. I saw that, if there was a wall of stone between me and my townsmen, there was a still more difficult one to climb or break through before they could get to be as free as I was. I did not for a moment feel confined, and the walls seemed a great waste of stone and mortar. I felt as if I alone of all my townsmen had paid my tax. They plainly did not know how to treat me, but behaved like persons who are underbred. In every threat and in every compliment there was a blunder; for they thought that my chief desire was to stand the other side of that stone wall. I could not but smile to see how industriously they locked the door on my meditations, which followed them out again without let or hindrance, and *they* were really all that was dangerous. As they could not reach me, they had resolved to punish my body; just as boys, if they cannot come at some person against whom they have a spite, will abuse his dog. I saw that the State was half-witted, that it was timid as a lone woman with her silver spoons, and that it did not know its friends from its foes, and I lost all my remaining respect for it, and pitied it.

—"Civil Disobedience"

5. JEFFERSONIAN DEMOCRACY

If I were asked who in my opinion is the greatest American philosopher, I would answer Thomas Jefferson—unless we have mistaken ideas about a "philosopher." We are apt to think of a philosopher as a man, in John Dewey's phrase, shut up in "a well-equipped gymnasium wherein to engage in dialectical exercises." If we mean by the greatest philosopher the man who produced the biggest idea and influenced the whole tone of American thought by it, I think that the honor cannot but go to Jefferson. The general assumption in America that the common man is the important man in the republic is so well established today that we think it is natural and forget that it was an issue hotly discussed by the founders of the republic at the Federal Convention and elsewhere—the issue whether the common man could be trusted to govern himself. How much that tone has changed may be realized if we read as if in a speech by a senator today the following words:

"Take mankind as they are, and what are they governed by? Their passions. . . . One great error is that we suppose mankind more honest than they are. Our prevailing passions are ambition and interest; and it will ever be the duty of a wise government to avail itself of those passions, in order to make them subservient to the public good. . . .

All communities divide themselves into the few and the many. The first are the rich and well-born; the other the mass of the people . . . turbulent and changing, they seldom judge or determine right. Give, therefore, to the first class a distinct, permanent share in the Government."

That was Alexander Hamilton speaking at the Federal Convention. A senator today speaking in these terms in public would be regarded by his friends as insane. That is a proper gauge of Jefferson's influence on American thought. The common man, like democracy, has become a word to conjure with, to which even its enemy must pay tribute today, thanks to Jefferson.

The issue was a fundamental one. From the beginning, it was stated by Jefferson very clearly as one between faith in the people and fear of the people; it was never so sharpened as in those days. "I am not among those who fear the people. They, and not the rich, are our dependence for continued freedom," announced Jefferson in a letter to Samuel Kercheval, July 12, 1816. "The sickly, weakly, timid man, fears the people, and is a Tory by nature. The healthy, strong and bold, cherishes them, and is formed a Whig by nature," he wrote to Lafayette toward the end of his life. "Men by their constitutions are naturally divided into two parties," he wrote to Henry Lee a year later, in 1824, "1. Those who fear and distrust the people, and wish to draw all powers from them into the hands of the higher classes. 2. Those who identify themselves with the people, have confidence in them, cherish and consider them as the most honest and safe, although not the most wise depository of the public interests." And the last letter of his life, written less than two weeks before his death, contains these striking words, "All eyes are opened, or opening, to the rights of man. The general spread of the light of science has already laid open to every view the palpable truth, that the mass of mankind has not been born with saddles on their backs, nor a favored few booted and spurred, ready to ride them legitimately, by the grace of God." (Letter to Roger C. Weightman, June 24, 1826.)

Jefferson was a hard nut for economic historians to crack. The issue between Jeffersonism and Hamiltonism was clearly the issue between liberty and property. Jefferson was a landed aristocrat, and his rich property (his "class ideology") should have influenced his opinions, while Hamilton was only an aspirant, a "British snob" as Jefferson called him. Perhaps here a point of human psychology beyond the ken of economic historians already came into play, for Hamilton probably had the psychology of an "adventurer" as Henry Adams called him. What can an economic historian do, staring the facts in the face? Talking about the rich, one remembers that Jefferson inherited 1,900 acres and 83 slaves. His wine cellar was celebrated. When Mrs. Jefferson's father died, she inherited 40,000 acres of land and 135 slaves.[7] Jefferson was right, however: one's political beliefs have much to do with one's temperament—the "sickly, weakly, timid man, fears the people." A philosophy is only a temperament; it is the development of an idea, and the idea is always subjective, though its development is always dialectical; it takes life and power only in the mind of a man who is by temperament receptive to it. Jefferson was constitutionally a democrat, and his temperament of a democrat (in those days called a "republican") overruled his wine cellar and his tens of thousands of acres of land. His life was devoted to one idea, the idea of intellectual, religious, and political liberty. So one of the greatest aristocrats of Virginia fought the landed aristocracy and the clergy of Virginia. The aristocracy hated him because he was for abolition and the Episcopalian bishops hated him because he thought "God hath created the mind free." By introducing the Virginia "Act for Establishing Religious Freedom," he made it impossible for the Established (Episcopal) Church of Virginia to throw Presbyterian, Baptist, and Methodist ministers into jail.[8]

It is not true that because Jefferson owned a hundred slaves he condoned slavery in the Declaration of Independence. According to his *Autobiography,* among the parts drafted by him and struck out by the Congress was this passage, the omission of which made it so difficult for Daniel Webster and even for Abraham Lincoln to find guidance in the matter of the abolition of slavery: "He has waged cruel war against human nature itself, violating its most sacred rights of life and liberty in the persons of a distant people who never offended him, captivating and carrying them into slavery in another hemisphere, or to incur miserable death in their transportation hither. This piratical

[7] See Saul K. Padover, *Jefferson,* pp. 27, 31.
[8] Claude G. Bowers, *Jefferson and Hamilton,* p. 104.

warfare, the opprobrium of *infidel* powers, is the warfare of the *Christian* King of Great Britain. Determined to keep open a market where men should be bought and sold, he has prostituted his negative for suppressing every legislative attempt to prohibit or to restrain this execrable commerce." That is to say, for Jefferson, men meant all men, including Negroes, and the "sacred rights of life and liberty" belong to them as well as to white men, the violation of which constitutes a "war against human nature."

A closer study of Jefferson's letters to his family and to his friends will show us the temperament and character of the man, from which his philosophy arose. One of the most charming ones was his letter to his younger daughter Maria (Polly), his favorite (April 11, 1790), when she was of the age of twelve and he the Secretary of State, "Where are you, my dear Maria? how do you do? How are you occupied? . . . Tell me whether you see the sun rise everyday? How many pages a day do you read in *Don Quixote?* how far are you advanced in him? . . . how many hours a day you sew? whether you have an opportunity of continuing your music? whether you know how to make a pudding yet, to cut out a beefsteak, to sow spinach? or to set a hen? Be good, my dear, as I have always found you . . . try to let everybody's fault be forgotten, as you would wish yours to be . . ." And to his elder daughter Martha (Patsy) Jefferson, Mrs. Randolph (December 23, 1790), "This is a scolding letter for you all. I have not received a scrip of a pen from home since I left it. I think it so easy for you to write me one letter every week, which will be but once in the three weeks for each of you, when I write one every week, who have not one moment's repose from business, from the first to the last moment of the week. Perhaps you think you have nothing to say to me. It is a great deal to say you are well; or that one has a cold, another a fever, etc.; besides there is not a sprig of grass that shoots uninteresting to me; nor anything that moves from yourself down to Bergère and Grizzle [shepherd dogs]." Several times I find in his letters, as in one to Martha, the injunction which must have been his practical philosophy, "If you find yourself in difficulty, and doubt how to extricate yourself, do what is right, and you will find it the easiest way to get out of the difficulty" (letter of April 7, 1787). His passion had always been "my family, my farm, and my books." "An honest man can find no pleasure in the exercise of power over his fellow citizens," he wrote to John Melish (January 13, 1813). One of the best things he wrote, as well as the most interesting was his message to the inhabitants of Abermarle County when he had retired from public office (April 3, 1809), "Long absent on duties which the history of a wonderful era made incumbent on those called to them, the pomp, the turmoil, the bustle and splendor of office, have drawn but deeper sighs for the tranquil and irresponsible occupations of private life, for the enjoyment of an affectionate intercourse with you, my neighbors and friends, and the endearments of family love, which nature has given us all, as the sweetener of every hour. . . . Of you, then, my neighbors, I may ask, in the face of the world, 'Whose ox have I taken, or whom have I defrauded? Whom have I oppressed, or of whose hand have I received a bribe to blind mine eyes therewith?'" Somehow, these letters come closer than his political statements, to giving us a picture of Jefferson the democrat at home and in his own county. It was this essentially democratic temperament that made democracy possible in America. Seeing the generation of Washington and Franklin and Jefferson, one must say that in those days God not only made men free, He made them pretty well.

The character of Hamilton the man may be best seen in an interesting anecdote contained in a letter from Jefferson to Benjamin Rush, January 16, 1811, when the latter was trying to arrange for a reconciliation of John Adams and Jefferson, in which he succeeded. Jefferson's letter was on the whole a defense of Adams's moderate position. "While he [Adams] was Vice-President, and I Secretary of State, I received a letter from President Washington, then at Mount Vernon, desiring me to call together the Heads of departments, and to invite Mr. Adams to join us (which, by-the-bye, was the only instance of that being done) in order to determine on some measure which required despatch; and he desired me to act on it, as decided, without again recurring to him. I invited them to dine with me, and after dinner, sitting at our wine, having settled our question, other conversation came on, in which a collision of opinion arose between Mr. Adams and Colonel Hamilton, on the merits of the British constitution, Mr. Adams giving it as his opinion, that, if some of its defects and abuses were corrected, it would be the most perfect constitution of government ever devised by man.

Hamilton, on the contrary, asserted, that with its existing vices, it
was the most perfect model of government that could be formed; and
that the correction of its vices would render it an impracticable government. And this you may be assured was the real line of difference between the political principles of these two gentlemen. Another incident
took place on the same occasion, which will further delineate Mr.
Hamilton's political principles. The room being hung around with
a collection of the portraits of remarkable men, among them were
those of Bacon, Newton and Locke, Hamilton asked me who they
were. I told him they were my trinity of the three greatest men the
world had ever produced, naming them. He paused for some time:
'the greatest man,' said he, 'that ever lived, was Julius Cæsar.' Mr.
Adams was honest as a politician, as well as a man; Hamilton honest
as a man, but, as a politician, believing in the necessity of either force
or corruption to govern men."

The two philosophies, Hamiltonian and Jeffersonian, resolved themselves, as Jefferson said, into two basic attitudes, fear of the people and
faith in the people. Neither of them could be proved except by history;
faith in the people, as well as fear of them, was essentially an instinct,
a hunch. Jefferson had a hunch that the people could be trusted to
govern themselves, and it was the wisest and most important hunch
any American in history ever had the luck of having. Perhaps we can
state it another way by saying that both philosophies were motivated
by two different fears, Hamilton's fear of the people and Jefferson's
fear of a class permanently established in the government. Jefferson
distrusted government as much as Hamilton distrusted the common
people.[9] Because Jefferson distrusted a ruling class in the government,

[9] Perhaps Jefferson's instinctive distrust of government was as characteristically American as his confidence in the common people. Carl L. Becker says in "The American
Political Tradition," "For us, state and government are one thing, and that thing
merely a number of men whom we choose as our agents to do for us certain necessary
and prosaic things. We choose them and hope for the best, but we limit their terms
of office and always reserve the right to turn the rascals out for good reasons, or even
for no reason at all, if we feel like it. No, we do not regard the government as an
enemy; but for all that we more or less agree with Thomas Paine, who said that whereas
society springs from men's virtues, government springs from their vices, and is therefore a necessary evil. Our characteristic and traditional attitude is to view with alarm
any new and unusual activity on the part of the government, and to point with pride
to the new and unusual things that the people have done, and will always do on their
own initiative if the government only refrains from undue meddling and minds its

the people of the United States today need not be afraid of their government, while if Hamilton who feared the people had succeeded, today the United States government would not be afraid of its people.

Why did Jefferson fear privilege? He had brought with him from Europe not only the philosophy of the Enlightenment but also a personal knowledge of social and economic evils of that continent, which had much to do with his distrust of a privileged class. Once at a dinner, Madison tells us, somebody argued against an elected executive and in favor of a hereditary ruler. Jefferson stood up and remarked sarcastically but humorously that he had heard of a "University somewhere in which the professor of Mathematics was hereditary."

For Jefferson had a close knowledge of the European kings of his days, who were either fools or lunatics. It was in fact a rather devastating picture. "While in Europe," he wrote to Governor John Langdon (March 5, 1810), "I often amused myself with contemplating the characters of the then reigning sovereigns of Europe. Louis the XVI was a fool, of my own knowledge, and in despite of the answers made for him at his trial. The King of Spain was a fool, and of Naples the same. They passed their lives in hunting, and despatched two couriers a week, one thousand miles, to let each other know what game they had killed the preceding days. The King of Sardinia was a fool. All these were Bourbons. The Queen of Portugal, a Braganza, was an idiot by nature. And so was the King of Denmark. Their sons, as regents, exercised the powers of government. The King of Prussia, successor to the great Frederick, was a mere hog in body as well as in mind. Gustavus of Sweden, and Joseph of Austria, were really crazy, and George of England, you know, was in a straight waistcoat. There remained, then, none but old Catharine, who had been too lately picked up to have lost her common sense. In this state Bonaparte found Europe; and it was this state of its rulers which lost it with scarce a struggle. These animals had become without mind and powerless; and so will every hereditary monarch be after a few generations. Alexander, the grandson of Catharine, is as yet an exception. He is able to hold his own. But he is only of the third generation. His race is not

---

own business." Reprinted from *Freedom and Responsibility in the American Way of Life*, by Carl L. Becker, by permission of Alfred A. Knopf, Inc. Copyright, 1945, by Alfred A. Knopf, Inc.

yet worn out. And so endeth the book of Kings, from all of whom the Lord deliver us, and have you, my friend, and all such good men and true, in His holy keeping."

From all these observations, Jefferson came to the all-important conclusion that since privilege led to corruption and force could not be relied upon in government, the central foundation of a good government lay in the education and free information of the people. "I am not a friend to a very energetic government," he wrote characteristically to Madison from Paris (December 20, 1787) in that important letter offering his criticism of the draft of the Constitution. "It is always oppressive. It places the governors indeed more at ease, at the expense of the people. . . . Nor will any degree of power in the hands of government prevent insurrections." He pointed to insurrections in France and Turkey and asked Madison to consider these examples. "And say, finally, whether peace is best preserved by giving energy to the government, or information to the people. This last is the most certain, and the most legitimate engine of government. Educate and inform the whole mass of people. . . . They are the only sure reliance for the preservation of our liberty."

It is important to know what Jefferson's ideas of democracy are, and I have attempted to summarize them under the following heads.[10] The lessons of republicanism were not learned thoroughly then, they are not learned thoroughly now; they were not heeded in his days by some people, they are not heeded today when we are talking about a world democracy. Some Americans, like Charles Beard, have suggested that a close study of *The Federalist* and the United States Constitution should be of help to those talking about World Federalism, which is a very valuable and practical suggestion.[11] By an accidental confusion of terms, the World Federalists are the Jeffersonians today, while the Hamiltonism of the United Nations Organization, as it is at present constituted, would shock Hamilton himself. At least Hamilton believed in the Union and in the principle of the majority. How the

[10] Jefferson's principal writings are his letters, and he was a conscientious, prodigious correspondent. The fullest collection of his letters in an easily obtainable edition is in *The Life and Selected Writings of Jefferson,* Modern Library, where the letters are chronologically arranged.

[11] See the Preface, Charles A. Beard, *The Enduring Federalist,* Doubleday and Company, 1948.

framers of the United Nations Charter at San Francisco could fall so low in their Bourbonism as to adopt the unheard-of and unknown and untried principle of unanimity in place of majority is a clear index of retrogression of the world's thought since World War I. If we expect the United Nations to work, we must follow the principles of democracy; otherwise it will remain a shop front without reality for a world organization which in scientific terms cannot be otherwise described than as a plutocracy. Jefferson said firmly that the only alternative to the principle of majority is force. We have chosen force.

(*1*) *The people are the only safe depository of power.* Trying to define republicanism in his letter to John Taylor (May 28, 1816), Jefferson said, "Were I to assign to this term a precise and definite idea, I would say, purely and simply, it means a government by its citizens in mass, acting directly and personally, according to rules established by the majority; and that every other government is more or less republican, in proportion as it has in its composition more or less of this ingredient of the direct action of its citizens." Again, "On this view of the import of the term *republic,* instead of saying, as has been said, 'that it may mean anything or nothing,' we may say with truth and meaning, that governments are more or less republican, as they have more or less of the element of popular election and control in their composition; and believing, as I do, that the mass of the citizens is the safest depository of their own rights and especially, that the evils flowing from the duperies of the people, are less injurious than those from the egoism of their agents, I am a friend to that composition of government which has in it the most of this ingredient." He made his position clear in a letter to Monsieur A. Coray, a Greek doctor and philologist (October 31, 1823), "And true it is that the people, especially when moderately instructed, are the only safe, because the only honest, depositories of the public rights, and should therefore be introduced into the administration of them in every function to which they are sufficient; they will err sometimes and accidentally, but never designedly, and with a systematic and persevering purpose of overthrowing the free principles of the government. Hereditary bodies, on the contrary, always existing, always on the watch for their own aggrandizement, profit of every opportunity of advancing the privileges of their order, and encroaching on the rights of the people."

Both Jefferson and Stalin knew that the small landholders are the strongest supports of the people's liberty, and they acted accordingly, to cherish them or to crush them, as their objects might be—to promote or to destroy the people's liberty. Jefferson believed in a graduated income tax and in the redistribution of land, "only taking care to let their subdivisions go hand in hand with the natural affections of the human mind." He believed that "the earth is given as a common stock for man to labor and live on. If for the encouragement of industry we allow it to be appropriated, we must take care that other employment be provided to those excluded from the appropriation. If we do not, the fundamental right to labor the earth returns to the unemployed." Then he adds, "The small landholders are the most precious part of a state" (letter to Madison, October 28, 1785). To John Jay he wrote (August 23, 1785), "Cultivators of the earth are the most valuable citizens. They are the most vigorous, the most independent, the most virtuous, and they are tied to their country, and wedded to its liberty and interests, by the most lasting bonds."

(2) *The people's self-government by direct action.* Jefferson insisted on the idea of "dividing the country into wards." "No, my friend," he wrote to Joseph C. Cabell, his co-worker in establishing the University of Virginia (February 2, 1816), "the way to have safe and good government, is not to trust it all to one, but to divide it among the many, distributing to each one exactly the functions he is competent to . . . It is by dividing and subdividing these republics from the great national one down through all its subordinations, until it ends in the administration of every man's farm by himself; by placing under every one what his own eye may superintend, that all will be done for the best. . . . As Cato, then, concluded every speech with the words, 'Carthago delenda est,' so do I every opinion, with the injunction, 'divide the counties into wards.' I am sure they will have the will, to fortify us against the degeneracy of our government, and the concentration of all its powers in the hands of the one, the few, the well-born or the many." He went into more detail in the letter to John Tyler (May 26, 1810), "I have indeed two great measures at heart, without which no republic can maintain itself in strength. 1. That of

general education, to enable every man to judge for himself what will secure or endanger his freedom. 2. To divide every county into hundreds, of such size that all the children of each will be within reach of a central school in it. But this division looks to many other fundamental provisions. Every hundred, besides a school should have a justice of the peace, a constable and a captain of militia . . . and all other elections should be made in the hundreds separately, and the votes of all the hundreds be brought together." Concerning the difficulty of getting the people to attend election meetings where the divisions are too large, he wrote to Samuel Kercheval (July 12, 1816), "The mayor of every ward, on a question like the present, would call his ward together, take the simple yea or nay of its members, convey these to the county court, who would hand on those of all its wards to be the proper general authority; and the voice of the whole people would be thus fairly, fully, and peaceably expressed, discussed, and decided by the common reason of the society. If this avenue be shut to the call of sufferance, it will make itself heard through that of force, and we shall go on, as other nations are doing, in the endless circle of oppression, rebellion, reformation; and oppression, rebellion, reformation, again; and so on forever. . . ."

(3) *The rule of the majority, the vital principle of republics.* In his Inauguration Address of 1801 Jefferson counted among the essential principles of the American government, "absolute acquiescence in the decisions of the majority—the vital principle of republics, from which there is no appeal but to force, the vital principle and immediate parent of despotism." He wrote to the great naturalist, Alexander von Humboldt (June 13, 1817), "The first principle of republicanism is, that the *lex majoris partis* (law of the majority) is the fundamental law of every society of individuals of equal rights; to consider the will of the society enounced by the majority of a single vote, as sacred as if unanimous, is *the first of all lessons in importance, yet the last which is thoroughly learnt.* [Italics are mine.] This law once disregarded, no other means remains but that of force, which ends necessarily in despotism."

Jefferson knew, if the framers of the United Nations Charter did not know, that since the history of man began no two men can completely agree on a number of subjects; that the question has to be

settled somehow, by accepting like intelligent and civilized people the
decisions of the majority or as the only alternative by knocking the
other fellow out. There is no third alternative. Nobody except a fool
or a visionary has believed in unanimity of opinion. Unanimity of
cabinet opinion in the English government is merely a fiction established by the theory of collective responsibility of the cabinet and is
itself based on differences of opinion expressed in the cabinet meeting
itself before the will of the majority is made known. The Big Five
wanted the principle of unanimity only because each wanted to maintain for himself the authority of the despot and have his will, whenever he liked it, override the will of the majority of the United Nations.

The United Nations Charter is of course antidemocratic. It is a
simple formula of world plutocracy; first, to take all power out of the
hands of the delegates of the nations by depriving the General Assembly of all powers except the power of talking and recommending and
by concentrating the real power in the Security Council, and then to
paralyze the Security Council itself by the principle of unanimity and
the veto. Now the Big Five are about as unanimous as five hedgehogs
in an underground hole on a winter night; they huddle together for
warmth and self-assurance as far as they dare without feeling each
other's quills and separate again as soon as they come into contact
with one another. If somebody tells me that these five hedgehogs are
going to keep peace for the world, well . . . or if they are going to
keep peace among themselves and leave the world alone as long as
they keep that foolhardy principle of unanimity . . . what indeed can
one say? We don't need the Big Five to keep peace for the small
nations; they don't need it. What the world needs is that the Big Five
keep peace *among themselves* and *leave the small nations alone*. Having caused the world two big World Wars and caused all peoples to
suffer on their account, are the Big Powers not yet ashamed of themselves, and can they arrogantly sit in the Security Council and presume
to judge and "help" the small nations, who are rumored to threaten
world peace by their lack of education and low standard of living?
If a third war devastates and ruins the world, it will be brought about
by the better "educated" and better "fed" nations, not by the Indo-
nesians or the Burmese or the Eskimos. Education, I thought, meant
the ability to reflect upon oneself. On the other hand, I quite realize

that to follow the rule of the majority and allow the opinions of the nations who are not themselves to count would mean losing their power to rule the world as they like it. But to defy the common sense of democratic rule and expect such an organization ever to work shows a sad lack of clear thinking, and how can a nation call itself educated unless its representatives can learn to think clearly? I am quite sure that some day, as soon as the Big Powers have educated themselves the hard way, a truly democratic world peace organization will come to exist, for I am convinced that the small nations are not standing in the way. . . . But ideologically, the five hedgehogs are only a mythical transformation of the three hedgehogs who thought they were going to live forever and would cut up the world in their infinite wisdom for our benefit. They never meant democracy or anything remotely approaching it. That is why we are where we are today.

(4) *Freedom of belief and of the press.* Part of the process of democratic acceptance of the majority is the freedom of discussion and of belief. The "Act for Establishing Religious Freedom" (1779) in Virginia, which Jefferson drafted and sponsored, expresses it well. . . . "and finally, that truth is great and will prevail if left to itself, that she is the proper antagonist to error, and has nothing to fear from the conflict, unless by human interposition disarmed of her natural weapons, free argument and debate, errors ceasing to be dangerous when it is permitted freely to contradict them." Regarding the freedom of the press, he said in the Second Inaugural Address, "Nor was it uninteresting to the world, that an experiment should be fairly and fully made, whether freedom of discussion, unaided by power, is not sufficient for the propagation and protection of truth . . . No inference is here intended, that the laws, provided by the State against false and defamatory publications, should not be enforced . . . but the experiment is noted, to prove that since truth and reason have maintained their ground against false opinions in league with false facts, the press, confined to truth, needs no other restraint."

Jefferson was a man of faith. "I like the dreams of the future better than the history of the past," he wrote to John Adams in 1816. He knew his country well. "But ours," he said in the same letter, "will be the follies of enthusiasm, not of bigotry, not of Jesuitism. Bigotry is the disease of ignorance, of morbid minds; enthusiasm of the free and

buoyant. Education and free discussion are the antidotes of both."
Then he waxed somewhat buoyant himself. "We are destined to be
a barrier against the returns of ignorance and barbarism. Old Europe
will have to lean on our shoulders, and to hobble along by our side,
under the monkish trammels of priests and kings, as she can." As a
prophet, he was not far wrong though Europe today has thrown off
the monkish trammels of priests and kings; the totalitarian despot, his
old enemy, wears a different robe today . . . He could not have foreseen. Nor could he have believed that there are so many renegades
among the intellectuals of America itself. But I like best the first letter
he wrote to John Adams after their reconciliation (January 21, 1812),
when the two retired Presidents could ruminate on their past experience of forty years and forecast on the future of America.

"And I believe we shall continue to growl, to multiply and prosper."

BY THOMAS JEFFERSON

A letter from you calls up recollections very dear to my mind. It
carries me back to the times when, beset with difficulties and dangers,
we were fellow laborers in the same cause, struggling for what is most
valuable to man, his right of self-government. Laboring always at the
same oar, with some wave ever ahead, threatening to overwhelm us,
and yet passing harmless under our bark, we knew not how we rode
through the storm with heart and hand, and made a happy port. Still
we did not expect to be without rubs and difficulties; and we have had
them. . . . In your day, French depredations; in mine, English, and
the Berlin and Milan decrees; now, the English orders of council, and
the piracies they authorize. When these shall be over, it will be the
impressment of our seamen or something else; and so we have gone
on, and so we shall go on, puzzled and prospering beyond example
in the history of man. And I do believe we shall continue to growl,
to multiply and prosper until we exhibit an association, powerful, wise
and happy, beyond what has yet been seen by men."

—Letter to John Adams, January 12, 1812

Chapter IX

THE PURSUIT OF HAPPINESS

I. THE BLUE BIRD

I HAVE always been impressed by the fact that the most studiously avoided subject in western philosophy is that of happiness. It would be wonderful if there existed a philosophy devoted entirely to a study of the aims, methods and possibilities of attaining happiness in this present life. Common sense tells us that happiness is what everybody is striving for, and yet with all the past and present wisdom of men no one has attempted to tell us how to get there. The goal of religion is salvation, not happiness. Philosophy occupies itself with truth, not happiness. Moralists talk about duty, not happiness. Those who have money to spend seek after pleasures, not happiness. Socialists, whose aim is the greatest happiness of the greatest number, occupy themselves with economics, not happiness. Lovers who have sometimes caught that blue bird, squeeze it too tightly for joy, and find it dead on their hands. The only man who knows about happiness is a man with a pipe in his mouth—if he would only write a book and tell people about it! Shall I try to rush in where angels fear to tread? It is always tempting to write on a subject that nobody writes about.

It is certainly curious; I almost cannot believe it. I have before me a fair collection of books by the wittiest and wisest American minds —Emerson, Mark Twain, Will Rogers, William James, John Dewey, Tom Paine, scholars, poets, naturalists, literary critics—all impressive volumes of learning and philosophy. With a great many, the subject of happiness never enters their heads, so busy are they with their respective fields. Some circumvent it, some pass it by without once taking a second look, and some pause to reflect upon it, without calling it by the right name (James calls it what makes life "vitally significant"). Even Santayana disappoints me here; with his sweet acceptance of life, he has less to say on the subject than I expected.

210 ON THE WISDOM OF AMERICA

Thoreau went straight for it, and very nearly got hold of it. He went in the right direction, but he went too far, and when he constantly protested against our reading of newspapers and going to the post-office for mail, I know that he had not made peace with common life as we live it. True, there is the happiness of solitude, of simple labor, of communion with nature. Yet to be happy only when one is alone would hardly fit the life of the common men and women. Most of us are happiest when we get a lot of mail and when we go to the movie theater and when we are in company. When philosophy does not square with life, it is like a radio which goes off beam. Though it misses it only by a fraction, it is useless for us. Perhaps the reason the subject has not been better understood is because moralists and philosophers are apt to start out with some favorite *a priori* theory of what happiness should be. They are determined that life shall agree with their particular theory, rather than their theory with life.

Perhaps the reason why we have been consistently fooling ourselves, training ourselves to look upon the attainment of happiness as an ancient and unsolved riddle, is that we started with the wrong leg. Accidents will happen. Surely it is an accident of history that today hundreds of thousands, perhaps even millions, of happy, hard-working honest Americans who usually face life quite cheerily and are able to take it, still believe in a dark, vengeful and constantly jealous Jehovah, with all the demons and the Legion of Darkness in league against them. Surely it is equally an accident, due to the same tradition, that our eyes have been turned away from the present world. Sound business men, real estate agents, Fuller brush salesmen and farmers and laborers all take the present life pretty seriously, but the moment they reflect or attempt to be spiritual, they become unworldly, look for salvation, and run out on all the principles that have motivated their life. The first thought of anyone who makes a claim to thoughtfulness is to deny that he has a body. This willful ignoring of our bodily existence, in the light of all modern physiology and psychology, would be ridiculous if it were not so pathetic. The idea is that human beings are, or should be, transcendental souls, with appetites only for the spiritual truths of beauty and justice, or if there are any other kinds of appetites their existence should be ignored or considered beneath notice. Sometimes a pastor pretends that we should have no hunger except for spiritual wisdom and no thirst except for truth. His audience knows, however, that they have other than spiritual thirsts. When the pastor descends from his pulpit, he feels a different kind of thirst, too, and asks for a "spirit" of some kind—"just one glass," of course—no, not lemon juice, that would be too worldly! And so we go on with this comedy of living the sensorial life and talking as if we were disembodied and disenchanted angels.

I think the church must take a great deal of blame for this unreal and mistaken type of spirituality. That is why so few clergymen are poets, or make an attempt to be poetic in the pulpit, why so few of them pay tribute to the glory of this God-created earth. Very few clergymen dilate on the glories of an Arizona sunset, on the sweet scent of lilacs, or the notes of the mocking bird—which is their business if their professional duty is to praise God and teach us to have a thankful heart for His great bounty. I do not care how scientists explain colors, but I know that the grass is green, the sky is blue, the clouds are white, the mountain sides are purple, the dawn is russet and the evening glow is golden—not just golden, but shimmeringly, bewitchingly golden. Someone might be grateful for all this and express his thankfulness for living, and if that some one claimed he believed in God, he should be the first to express his wonder and admiration for all the glories of this sensorial life. Authors, artists and shoemakers are displeased when people do not like their products. God could hardly feel pleased when we show contempt for His handiwork which is the present earth. When we despise food, we despise our God-made palate, and when we disparage the sense of sound, we certainly show no respect for the Creator of our ear-drums and those three delicate ear-bones!

On the other hand, orthodox Christian theology makes this mistake because its eyes are fixed upon heaven and not upon this earth—a rather hasty and sweeping mistake. I think theologians are hasty and sweeping in their condemnation of the present life as something to escape from and bear with for the present, before they let their eyes dwell on a sunset or even remind themselves that they have seen one. I understand that this other-worldiness of point of view took its rise in the days of the decadent Roman Empire, as a powerful protest against mere sensuality of living. That was how a handful of intrepid but fairly illiterate persons conquered the mighty Roman Empire at last. But then, life was generally hard in those days for the majority of people, and heaven was conceived as a haven of rest to ease the groanings and muscular pains of galley slaves. It was an aspiration that came from a desire for "surcease of trouble." In other words, many of the plebeians must have felt pretty tired of struggle in this life. But suppose we are not galley slaves, suppose we are not exactly groaning upon this earth, suppose that we even desire and welcome struggle, because there is comparatively greater opportunity for the common man today, what then? Suppose that it is good for the eyes to see the light of the sun, that a walk in a late autumn afternoon is good for the body and for the soul, suppose that the mere eating of a fruit does make one happy, and waking up from a perfect sleep does make the world look completely cheerful and reliable because you yourself are competent to do the jobs you are facing today? Surely God has not created the present life in vain. Of all the blasphemers of God, these people blaspheme life, they blaspheme the earth and its Creator, they blaspheme all their neighbors and their parents who gave birth to them and took such pains to bring them up *to live in this world*.

We see how the question of human happiness, of proper enjoyment of this life, escaped us from the very outset—in fact, was not even properly considered. Happiness in this sensorial existence was ruled out beforehand, while the picture of happiness in the Hereafter remains contradictory and confused—sometimes full of sensual delights, like seeing the pearly gates of an opulent city (a pawnbroker's dream), and sometimes non-sensual and ethereal and vague and unhypothecated. One arrives at an *impasse* of nothingness, so far as the quest for happiness is concerned. Perhaps it would be simpler to say, as I have said, that the goal of religion is not happiness but salvation—salvation *for* what we are not certain, but salvation *from* what we know—from this wicked present life.

Why has religion done that? Why have not only Christianity but also other religions done the same? The reason is that human happiness is always elusive, and often short-lived, that it is unreliable and impermanent. The happiness that comes from eating a good meal or wearing a new garment does not last. Religion makes its appeal to permanence and security in a happiness that lasts to eternity. (As a matter of fact, "eternity" is an exaggeration not warranted by experience.) For the first thing we must note about happiness is its completely elusive quality. There are happy *moments* in our lives and other unhappy moments which quickly succeed them. That was why the fathers of the American Republic talked about the right to the *pursuit* of happiness only; while they were sure of the right to life and liberty. They were not sure that happiness was attainable by every man; they felt that neither God nor their Constitution could vouch for happiness, but only would confirm the right to, and provide the opportunity for, its pursuit for every American citizen. (Nevertheless, it was very thoughtful of the philosophical Jefferson to put it in as one of the three rights, in place of the old trinity of the rights of life, liberty and property.)

Happiness has always seemed like a blue bird, and consists of moments. Such moments when we can be positive about being happy are, for instance, when we have had a really good dinner, when a friend we haven't seen for a long time suddenly turns up to chat for a whole evening, when a couple marches up the aisle to the wedding altar, when we have cleared all debts and after paying the income tax find there is still a comfortable margin left, when we hear that a wicked man has died or that we have the good opinion of somebody we respect, when we have spent a day of successful labor and our eyes feel drowsy and our muscles are pleasantly tired and there is no guest to prevent us from straightway going to bed. A moment later, happiness may be gone, and we start chasing it again. The bride driving away with her husband at the wheel may have a sudden unaccountable misgiving or even fear. The friend who has turned up seems changed, and there is an all but detectable decrease in his enthusiasm for life. The good opinion of our neighbor does not seem so reassuring when we search our hearts in the dead of the night. As for clearing all debts, you thought you had a fair margin left, but you had forgotten an item of $175.65. With the single exception of the man with the pleasantly tired muscles after a good day's work, not one is assured of a sound sleep that night. The very excitement of the occasion is disturbing and the human mind starts wondering again, thinks up imperfections, makes comparisons, and the man is saved and falls into a sound sleep only if he possesses a philosophy to laugh at himself. That is about the point where philosophy comes in.

If there could be a science of human happiness, I firmly believe that it should begin by being merely descriptive, contenting itself with describing or cataloguing our moments of happiness before analyzing them and drawing conclusions as to what makes men happy. One might learn to be open-minded, not caring what conclusion it leads to. I think that proceeding in this manner, one might have a fairly reliable guide as to what happiness is and how to attain it. If we reject a pompous theoretical approach and are objective and observant, we may be amazed to find, at the very first effort at thinking, that happiness is a common portion of our daily life, instead of the mysterious riddle which it is supposed to be. For instance, we might catch ourselves saying "I am happy" when we eat well. Such an observation of our commonest moments might lead to an important discovery of the source and nature of true happiness. The wise old Preacher of the Old Testament who certainly had made an experiment with life in search of happiness and had even "made a test of folly and madness" stumbled upon the same conclusion. "Therefore go, eat thy bread with joy, and drink thy wine with a merry heart." He had found that women failed him. If he was King Solomon, with his three thousand wives, I can understand why.

2. PHYSIOLOGICAL PEACE

If we proceed then without the mystification of the theologians and philosophers, we shall find happiness a simple fact, fairly manageable and reducible to a humanly applicable formula; happiness is peace, peace of body and peace of mind. It is a condition of satisfaction with oneself and with the surrounding one finds oneself in, and perhaps with one's purpose in life. Usages of the word suggest that we are all after that condition of peace and satisfaction of our material and spiritual wants. There is a Chinese word, *p'ing-an,* which seems to sum up the wish of every home and the end of living of all families. On New Year's Day every wall and every door is pasted with that word written very large on red paper (or some other word to the same effect). This word, which is untranslatable, bridges the difference between peace and happiness and makes the two identical. It means the feeling when a man is bodily and spiritually at ease. The usage of the English word "happy" reflects also a state of satisfaction with one's mental and bodily conditions. When you take your guest to his room in your house and install him there for three weeks, you say, "I think you can be happy here," meaning that you think he will have everything he wants. Or when you send him away and take him to the station, you may find the car overcrowded, but somehow you are able to find a seat near the window for him. There is not much elbow room, but the car is well heated, and your friend is nicely tucked away in a corner. You ask him, "Are you happy now?" meaning whether he is satisfied with his place, has got his magazines and other things and there are no obviously obnoxious neighbors facing him. If he has all those conditions and has in his pocket a good detective story that will last the journey, he will probably answer, "Yes, I am perfectly happy, and many·thanks."

We want our wants satisfied before we can have happiness; that seems axiomatic. No one who is dissatisfied can be happy; no one who is restless or frustrated in his life purpose can have happiness or peace; no one who does not know what he wants can have peace, and a person who does not want anything cannot have the satisfaction of having his wants fulfilled, either. All animals seem perfectly happy because all animals have their wants satisfied and provided by nature —or they die. The problem of human happiness comes up only because man has more complicated wants, perhaps an ambition, a desire to find a life purpose, and these wants are less easy to satisfy. Man is superior to animals because he has higher wants, and perhaps knows greater happiness than the animals, but I don't know. What we often forget in this complex civilization of human society is that basically we cannot get away from our bundle of blood and nerves and muscles, that our nerves and our muscles function by the usual physiological laws of our being, and that we are higher animals, but animals with a body still. Happiness often seems to me the perfect functioning of our endocrine glands. Modern doctors often tell their patients that the trouble with them is that they don't function physiologically—that probably, in the over-civilized life of today, they have moved too far away from the primary essential factors of ordinary, healthy living.

I am aware that happiness comes from the feeling of satisfaction in work done, in something achieved. I am aware that work is often mental as well as physical, and that happiness comes to those who have their work successfully completed, irrespective of what kind. But it would seem that the material must be the basis for the spiritual well-being, that no matter how high-minded we are, the ancient laws of our being, the physiological requirements of our nerves and muscles, may not be ignored or defied. The basis of happiness that is sure and attainable by almost every man is through the body, and particularly through the senses; the spiritual uplift can come later.

Emerson observes: "I know no means of calming the fret and perturbation into which too much sitting, too much talking, brings me, so perfect as labor. I have no animal spirits; therefore, when surprised by company and kept in a chair for many hours, my heart sinks, my brow is clouded and I think I will run for Acton woods, and live with the squirrels henceforward. But my garden is nearer, and my good hoe, as it bites the ground, revenges my wrongs, and I have less lust to bite my enemies. I confess I work at first with a little venom, lay to a little unnecessary strength. But by smoothing the rough hillocks, I smooth my temper; by extracting the long roots of the piper-grass, I draw out my own splinters; and in a short time I can hear the bobolink's song and see the blessed deluge of light and color that rolls around me." (*Journals,* June 12, 1839.) That is true wisdom.

When a man gets frightened or unhappy about the United Nations or the problems of world peace, and wants to recover his happiness, the best thing to do is to find some choked kitchen drain and try to clear it. There is hardly a man on earth who is not proud when he sees the water go down the sink smoothly with a clear gurgle as the result of his morning's labor. Or, instead of committing suicide over the tragedy of Czechoslovakia, one should find out if there isn't a shaky chair in the house and see if he can't fix it and make it safe to sit on again. After all, one can save the future of Czechoslovakia only by saving oneself and keeping oneself happy and alive first. The sovereign remedy for world chaos seems to be to provide every household with a hammer and a monkey wrench and a plentiful supply of nails. I can almost hear Confucius say, save the chair and the house is saved; save the house and the nation is saved; save the nation and the world is saved. A parent is wise to tell his boy, "Go out and tinker with those faulty spark plugs," when he finds him restless and unhappy in the house. He will find that his boy has snapped out of his moodiness when he returns triumphantly with the spark plugs in order. The same parent is often not wise enough to snap out of his own despair over his own personal problems.

The glory of a shoemaker who has completed making a good proud pair of shoes! The bliss of a farmer who has successfully completed digging a marsh ditch! What mystic delight can excel the pleasure of a pair of stretched legs after a good day's work? David Grayson in his chapter on "Marsh Ditch" in *Adventures in Contentment* communicates that sheer excitement of digging a drainage ditch and the sense of sheer animal happiness and content after labor even better than Thoreau's description of his digging on the "Beanfield" in *Walden*. I suspect the "high-minded" reader will have left this chapter by this time, but I wonder how much that high-minded person knows about the laws of human life. I am not sure but that he may be brooding over the universe at this moment. I do not envy him.

"There is a poem in stretched legs. . . . Happiness, I have discovered, is nearly always a rebound from hard work. . . . For happiness must be tricked!"

BY DAVID GRAYSON

——How surely, soundly, deeply, the physical underlies the spiritual. This morning I was up and out at half-past four, as perfect a morning as I ever saw: mists yet huddled in the low spots, the sun coming up over the hill, and all the earth fresh with moisture, sweet with good odors, and musical with early bird-notes.

It is the time of the spring just after the last seeding and before the early haying: a catch-breath in the farmer's year. I have been utilizing it in digging a drainage ditch at the lower end of my farm. A spot of marsh grass and blue flags occupies nearly half an acre of good land and I have been planning ever since I bought the place to open a drain from its lower edge to the creek. . . . This morning, after hastening with the chores, I took my bag and my spade on my shoulder and set off (in rubber boots) for the ditch. . . . So I dug. There is something fine in hard physical labor, straight ahead: no brain used, just muscles. I stood ankle-deep in the cool water: every spadeful came out with a smack, and as I turned it over at the edge of the ditch small turgid rivulets coursed back again. I did not think of anything in particular. I dug. A peculiar joy attends the very pull of the muscles. I drove the spade home with one foot, then I bent and lifted and turned with a sort of physical satisfaction difficult to describe. At first I had the cool of the morning, but by seven o'clock the day was hot enough! I opened the breast of my shirt, gave my sleeves another roll, and went at it again for half an hour, until I dripped with perspiration.

"I will knock off," I said, so I used my spade as a ladder and climbed out of the ditch. Being very thirsty, I walked down through the marshy valley to the clump of alders which grows along the creek. I followed a cow-path through the thicket and came to the creek side, where I knelt on a log and took a good long drink. Then I soused my head in the cool stream, dashed the water upon my arms and came up dripping and gasping! Oh, but it was fine!

So I came back to the hawthorn tree, where I sat down comfortably and stretched my legs. There is a poem in stretched legs—after hard digging—but I can't write it, though I can feel it! I got my bag and took out a half loaf of Harriet's bread. Breaking off big crude pieces, I ate it there in the shade. How rarely we taste the real taste of bread! We disguise it with butter, we toast it, we eat it with milk or fruit. We even soak it with gravy (here in the country where we aren't at all polite—but very comfortable), so that we never get the downright delicious taste of the bread itself. I was hungry this morning and I ate my half loaf to the last crumb—and wanted more. Then I lay down for a moment in the shade and looked up into the sky through the thin outer branches of the hawthorn. A turkey buzzard was lazily circling cloud-high above me: a frog boomed intermittently from the little marsh, and there were bees at work in the blossoms.

——I had another drink at the creek and went back somewhat reluctantly, I confess, to the work. It was hot, and the first joy of effort had worn off. But the ditch was to be dug and I went at it again. One becomes a sort of machine—unthinking, mechanical: and yet intense physical work, though making no immediate impression on the mind, often lingers in the consciousness. I find that sometimes I can remember and enjoy for long afterward every separate step in a task.

It is curious, hard physical labor! One actually stops thinking. I often work long without any thought whatever, so far as I know, save that connected with the monotonous repetition of the labor itself—down with the spade, out with it, up with it, over with it—and repeat. And yet sometimes—mostly in the forenoon when I am not at all tired —I will suddenly have a sense as of the world opening around me—a sense of its beauty and its meanings—giving me a peculiar deep happiness, that is near complete content——

Happiness, I have discovered, is nearly always a rebound from hard work. It is one of the follies of men to imagine that they can enjoy mere thought, or emotion, or sentiment! As well try to eat beauty! For happiness must be tricked! She loves to see men at work. She loves sweat, weariness, self-sacrifice. She will be found not in palaces but lurking in cornfields and factories and hovering over littered desks: she crowns the unconscious head of the busy child. If you look up suddenly from hard work you will see her, but if you look too long she fades sorrowfully away.

——Down toward the town there is a little factory for barrel hoops and staves. It has one of the most musical whistles I ever heard in my life. It toots at exactly twelve o'clock: blessed sound! The last half-hour at ditch-digging is a hard, slow pull. I'm warm and tired, but I stick down to it and wait with straining ear for the music. At the very first note of that whistle I drop my spade. I will even empty out a load of dirt half way up rather than expend another ounce of energy; and I spring out of the ditch and start for home with a single desire in my heart—or possibly lower down. And Harriet, standing in the doorway, seems to me a sort of angel—a culinary angel!

Talk of joy: there may be things better than beef stew and baked potatoes and homemade bread—there may be——

—*Adventures in Contentment* (VI)

3. THE TONIC EFFECT OF WORK

What David Grayson calls "a poem in stretched legs," William James, the psychologist, calls "the effects of a well-toned apparatus." Happiness is very often a state of animal well-being; without wanting to be brutal about it, we may say that the happiness that we are capable of in this life is very often "animal happiness." If there is greater happiness than lying in the sun, I'd like to be told. I do not mean idleness. The "animal well-being" is a condition when our nerves function perfectly and are ready for work and can tackle a job on hand competently. Since our nerves cannot function, in fact are restless, unless we have something to do, the toning effect is the result of a man occupying himself with some work which he likes to do. In other words, happiness comes from work and from the feeling of joy and peace when a job is well done.

This work may be mental, as well as manual. Thoreau describes the state of animal well-being when he was ready to start his literary work: "We sometimes experience a mere fullness of life, which does not find any channels to flow into . . . I feel myself uncommonly prepared for *some* literary work . . . I am braced both physically and intellectually . . . I feel that the juices of the fruits which I have eaten, the melons and apples, have ascended to my brain and are stimulating it. They give me a heady force. Now I can write nervously." (*Journals,* Sept. 7, 1851.) Thoreau said that writing should be done by "the whole man," and he himself wrote with his brain and muscles. "When after feeling dissatisfied with life, I aspire to something better, am more scrupulous, more reserved and continent, as if expecting somewhat, suddenly I find myself full of life as a nut of meat—am overflowing with a quiet, genial mirthfulness. I think to myself, I must attend to my diet; I must get up earlier and take a morning walk; I must have done with luxuries and devote myself to my muse. So I dam up my stream, and my waters gather to a head. I am freighted with thought." (*Journals,* Oct. 26, 1853.)

The distinction between manual work and mental work is not absolute. It did not matter that Benjamin Franklin sometimes sat naked after breakfast to do his morning work; he was functioning perfectly and he was enjoying his intellectual labors. In either case, the joy of making things, producing things, and getting something done which we may be proud of, is the best reward of this life. Whether it is the farmer watching the progress of sowing his potato fields or the author seeing the work grow under his hands, the pleasure and the satisfaction are the same. No hand laborer is worthy of his name unless he uses his head also, and I know of no author who does not delight in the physical act of writing, whether it be pounding the typewriter and seeing his lines emerge from the paper platen, or hearing the steady scratch of the pen on the paper in continuous progress. A real author must come to enjoy the hours of his labor and all the familiar physical conditions associated with it, including the pen, the notebook, the familiar desk, and even the pot of paste and scissors. Unless he enjoys doing all the manual work associated with authorship, he does not belong to the profession. So Van Wyck Brooks describes his own writing habits and the joy of the physical act of writing:

"Allston liked Michael Angelo's phrase, which he said was also true of him,—'It is only well with me when I have a chisel in my hand.' In two or three notes he refers to his methods:

"I always begin my writing day by copying all the work of the day before, making a few slight changes. This warms me up and gives me momentum. It is like winding a top. Sometimes, nowadays, when I have finished my copying, the top begins to spin of itself. . . . Thus my notes are all deposits of feeling, and this feeling returns when I take up my notes in the course of my work. May heaven save me from typing notes and dictating to secretaries. It is this that produces the chalk-like style of most historical writers. Good writing is felt writing, and this effect is cheaply bought at any extravagant expenditure of time and effort." [1]

No, you don't get away from the physical. Even the suit one wears has something to do with one's writing. "I never used to throw away any of my own old suits until I had finished another book," says Oliver Allston. "When I set to work on ——, I was wearing a grey tweed suit of which I was particularly fond; and, before I had finished the second chapter, the suit and the book had somehow grown together in my mind. I should not have dreamed of sitting down to write in any other coat or trousers. That was the book in the middle of which I had a serious breakdown. I went on wearing the suit, hoping it would bring back my luck; and when I was able to work again the suit was in

---

[1] Taken from *The Opinions of Oliver Allston*, by Van Wyck Brooks, copyright, 1941, Van Wyck Brooks, published by E. P. Dutton & Company, Inc., New York, and J. M. Dent & Sons, London.

tatters. But 'let back and sides go bare, go bare,' would I have thrown away that suit? Not for all the treasure on Cocos Island. I kept the suit and finished the book, and I always felt that my old grey coat had turned the trick for me." [2]

So much unhappiness, it seems to me, is due to nerves, and bad nerves are the result of having nothing to do, or doing a thing badly, unsuccessfully, or incompetently. Of all the unhappy people in the world, the unhappiest are those who have not found something they want to do. The proportion of people who go to mental hospitals is the measure of people who worry and do not work, not of people who work and do not worry. Nobody dies of hard successful work; one dies only of unmanageable work, purposeless work, work of a nature that drowns a man's nerves as the sea drowns a man's body. This is a dangerous thing to say in America; too many die of heart attacks, of over-strain of their nervous system. But the truth is not known. One can die of hard work in the sense that one can die of over-eating, or even of walking, as in a Marathon race. But this is unfair to the idea of the normal function of working, eating or walking. Americans don't die of hard work, as I understand the sense of the word; they die, so many of them, of running a Marathon race with their nervous systems to see who is going to outlast whom. The ordinary laws of

[2] *Op. cit.,* p. 31. Ellery Queen, too, wears a particular jacket when he is writing. There is a lively passage describing how he, the author, works before his typewriter "spits good hot words." "Mark that the process involved in preparing to conceive a book is technically different from that involved in preparing to bear it. In the latter stage, there are typewriters to examine and clean, ribbons to change, pencils to sharpen, clean paper to be arranged at the precise distance from the arm at which the least exertion is called forth, notes or outlines to be propped at the exactly acute angle to the machine, and so forth. The situation at the outset of the conceptual stage is quite deplorably different. . . . He is fired with energetic intentions. He paces his rug like a general, marshalling his mental forces. . . . Now observe him twenty minutes later. His legs jump. His brows work fiercely. His hands are helpless fists. He leans against a wall, seeking the cool plaster. He darts to a chair, perches on its edge with hands clasped, as if imploringly, between his knees. He jumps up, fills his pipe, sets it down, lights a cigarette, puffs twice, it goes out, it remains between his lips. He nibbles his finger-nails. He rubs his head. He explores a dental cavity. He pinches his nose. He plunges his hands into his jacket pockets. He kicks a chair. He glances at the headline of a morning newspaper on his desk but glances away heroically. He goes to the window and soon becomes interested in the scientific aspects of a fly crawling up the screen. He fingers the tobacco grains in his right pocket. . ." *Ten Days' Wonder* (Little, Brown and Company). Talk of an author's work being "spiritual." It is all physical as far as I can see. The animal functions or *it don't.*

our animal being are not to be defied. But, short of defying common sense, true happiness comes to him who does his work well, followed by a relaxing and refreshing period of rest. True happiness comes from the right amount of work for the day.

In this connection, a special problem confronts the privileged women of America. As wealth grows in a country, a privileged idle class also grows up, but in America it has brought into being a class of privileged, idle and unhappy women. It is the class of women about whom Lillian Hellman and Clare Boothe write in their plays and Dorothy Parker in her stories, the class which Pearl Buck calls the "gunpowder women." James Truslow Adams describes the historic growth of the strange phenomenon of the separation of life between men and women in America from the eighteen fifties onward.

"A new sort of loneliness"
BY JAMES TRUSLOW ADAMS

There also came into American life a new sort of loneliness, that in the relationship of husband and wife. . . .

The American woman in innumerable cases had to busy herself about something, and in a world where all around her was humming with activity, get away from the loneliness and monotony of the house. Except for the very unusual woman, or one who was willing in those days to be known more or less as a "crank," business, the professions and politics were barred fields. So countless ordinary but lonely and social and active-minded women began to make a world of their own. It is noteworthy that the West, where perhaps loneliness was most intense, was the section in which, in the 1850's, the movement was started organizing Women's Clubs of the modern type. Woman, starved in so many ways emotionally and intellectually, discovered "culture" and beauty. "The lones" gave birth to Browning Clubs and the House Beautiful. It may all have been somewhat crude but woman had found new interests and new incentives, and a new self-importance which was reassuring. Men might be laying the material foundations of personal or national life with amazing speed, but woman had found a job in building the intellectual and aesthetic life. Mr. John Doe might be acquiring a rising importance as president of the local grocery company or lumber concern or running for Congress, but Mrs. Doe might now become president of the Ladies Literary Society and begin to feel herself a leader in the social and cultural life of the same community.

The gulf between the man's world and the woman's widened still further. If the wife could not follow the husband into business and politics, neither could the husband follow the wife into "culture.". . . In his absorption in the game of getting ahead he may have had twinges of conscience about not doing enough for his wife, and felt that he was drifting away from the "little woman." When, however, she became active in a woman's mental and social world from which he was himself excluded, the score was evened. He felt he could devote all the time he wanted to business, whiskey and talking business with his men friends so long as his wife was not alone but enjoying herself in "society," having her tea and listening to some neighboring woman read a paper on *Sordello*. That curious separation of the sexes socially and intellectually which was so long to be characteristic of the American had begun.

—*The American* [2a]

So Pearl Buck, in examining the condition of these American women, makes clear the curse of privilege and asks work for the "gunpowder women" as the sovereign remedy for their unhappiness. "The most tragic person in our civilization is the middle-aged woman whose duties in the home are finished, whose children are gone, and who is in her mental and physical prime and yet feels there is no more need for her. She is that most unfortunate of persons, idle because nothing is demanded or expected of her, and yet unable to be happy because she is idle. . . . When I consider this handicap of privilege, then, which has produced these gunpowder women in my country, I cannot find a single word of blame for them. I know that men would never have risen to their present pre-eminence in all fields if they had had such a handicap—if, in short, they had not had the advantage of the compulsory discipline of work. . . . No, without the discipline of regular labor, of fixed hours, of competitive standards,

[2a] Reprinted by courtesy of the publisher, Charles Scribner's Sons.

the man would be where the woman is now." With true psychological insight, she comes to the conclusion, "Work is the one supreme privilege which will really make them free. . . . There is everything for her to do. If she wants a small job, let her look around her village or her neighborhood. If she wants a big job, let her look around her state or think as largely as her nation, or even realize that there is a world beyond. Not to see the infinite number of things to be done is to prove the damage that privilege does to the perceptions; not to do after she sees is to prove the damage already done to her will." [3]

It is the great psychologist C. G. Jung who advises these nervous city women, "Go to the country. Raise children, raise pigs and raise carrots." I doubt that the pleasure of a woman who sees her carrots grow is excelled by that of an artist in seeing his completed painting, or of an author in seeing the product of his pen inside book covers. In all cases, it is the happiness of producing things and of seeing one's work well done. It is axiomatic that among the inmates of an insane asylum you never find a successful carrot-grower.

4. THE SECRET OF CONTENTMENT

There is room for a philosophy after all, the philosophy of contentment. I have already quoted the Professor at the Breakfast Table as saying, "The great end of living is to harmonize man with the order of things." The Professor, I take it, does not call upon us to re-establish the order of things to harmonize with man, which would be a very big order, but to harmonize man with that order of things as he finds it to be, and—here is the central point—of what he finds in himself. In less pretentious language, the great end of any man's existence is to find his place in life—and that is the secret of contentment. Life is again like the picture of a man who finds himself in an overcrowded railroad car. If he has found his place in that crowded car, he is happy and contented; if not, he isn't. There are busybodies who neglect to do that, but rather think it to be their duty to take that carload of people in hand and reform the passengers—to object to a neighbor's protruding legs, to tell him to put his coat in some other place, to

[3] Pearl Buck, *Of Men and Women*. The John Day Company. Copyright, 1941, by Pearl S. Buck.

demand the opening or shutting of windows as he feels hot or cold, and to hush some one behind who perhaps talks too loud, his "hushing" being louder than the talking. He does not know that order will establish itself in five minutes by every man finding a place for himself, and that if he is not to be a restless nervous wreck at the end of the journey his first duty is to find his own place in that temporary community.

The Americans, at least the New Yorkers, impress foreigners as nervous and restless. They are a nation characterized by intense nervous energy, compared with the people of the Old World. Some business executives imagine that they are happiest when the three telephones on their desk keep ringing at the same time. It is assurance that they are a "success." They deceive themselves. Whoever does that loses the calm which is the first sign of a man who has got hold of life, has found himself. Multifarious motions do not constitute success by any means. A successful man—and therefore a happy man—is merely one who has found what he wants in life and has got it.

The secret of contentment is the discovery by every man of his own powers and limitations, finding satisfaction in a line of activity which he can do well, plus the wisdom to know that his place, no matter how important or successful he is, never counts very much in the universe. A man may very well be so successful in carving a name for himself in his field that he begins to imagine himself indispensable or omnipotent. He is eaten up by some secret ambition, and then good-by to all contentment. Sometimes it is more important to discover what one cannot do, than what one can do. So much restlessness is due to the fact that a man does not know what he wants, or he wants too many things, or perhaps he wants to be somebody else, to be anybody except himself. The courage of being one's genuine self, of standing alone and of not wanting to be somebody else! The Chinese people are perhaps best at this matter of contentment. Both Emerson and Thoreau quoted the Chinese philosopher Mencius. "The philosopher said, 'From an army of three divisions one can take away its general, and put it in disorder; from the man the most abject and vulgar one cannot take away his thought.' " [4]

---

[4] *Walden*, "Conclusion." This is from Confucius in a garbled translation, "You can capture the commander-in-chief of three armies, but you cannot overcome a private man's will." *Chih*, in Chinese, is definitely "will" and not "thought." The idea of the

One of the best lines from Grayson is the following: "One thing I am coming to learn in this world, and that is to let people haggle along with their lives as I haggle along with mine." That, I believe, embodies a whole philosophy of life, not easily arrived at except by one who has pondered and thought a great deal about the human drama. "I long ago decided," he said in the chapter "I Whistle" in *The Friendly Road,* "to try to be fully what I am and not to be anything or anybody else." And once he reflected, "I remember how, once in my life, I wasted untold energy trying to make over my dearest friends. There was Harriet, for example, dear, serious, practical Harriet. I used to be fretted by the way she was forever trying to clip my wing feathers—I suppose to keep me close to the quiet and friendly and unadventurous roost! We come by such a long, long road, sometimes, to the acceptance of our nearest friends for exactly what they are. Because we are so fond of them we try to make them over to suit some curious ideal of perfection of our own—until one day we suddenly laugh aloud at our own absurdity (knowing that they are probably trying as hard to reconstruct us as we are to reconstruct them!) and thereafter we try no more to change them, we just love 'em and enjoy 'em!" [5]

Once Grayson quoted Marcus Aurelius to the Stanley boy in a farmer's family where he had put up for the night:

" 'Listen,' I said, 'to what this old Roman philosopher said'—and I held the book up to the lamp and read aloud:

" ' "You can be invincible if you enter into no contest in which it is not in your power to conquer. Take care, then, when you observe a man honored before others or possessed of great power, or highly esteemed for any reason, not to suppose him happy and be not carried away by the appearance. For if the nature of the good is in our power, neither envy nor jealousy will have a place in us. But you yourself will not wish to be a general or a senator or consul, but a free man, and there is only one way to do this, to care not for the things which are not in our power." '

---

infinite capacity of the individual was developed by Mencius. His philosophy is Emersonian, or Emerson's philosophy is Mencian in this respect, and Mencius' influence on young men has always been like that of Emerson. Emerson quotes the central Mencian doctrine of developing one's inborn expansive spirit, the "vast-flowing vigor," in the essay on "Experience" and recommends it.

[5] *The Friendly Road,* p. 416.

" 'That,' said Mr. Stanley triumphantly, 'is exactly what I've always said, but I didn't know it was in any book. I always said I didn't want to be a senator or a legislator, or any other sort of office-holder. It's good enough for me right here on this farm.' "

I have let this chapter become almost a Grayson chapter, for he has good and important things to say on the subject of happiness and other writers have so little.

"Contentment . . . comes as the infallible result of great acceptances, great humilities."

BY DAVID GRAYSON

Joy of life seems to me to arise from a sense of being where one belongs, as I feel right here; of being foursquare with the life we have chosen. All the discontented people I know are trying sedulously to be something they are not, to do something they cannot do. In the advertisements of the country paper I find men angling for money by promising to make women beautiful and men learned or rich—over-night—by inspiring good farmers and carpenters to be poor doctors and lawyers. . . .

Contentment, and indeed usefulness, comes as the infallible result of great acceptances, great humilities—of not trying to make ourselves this or that (to conform to some dramatized version of ourselves), but of surrendering ourselves to the fullness of life—of letting life flow through us. To be used!—that is the sublimest thing we know.

It is a distinguishing mark of greatness that it has a tremendous hold upon real things. I have seen men who seemed to have behind them, or rather within them, whole societies, states, institutions: how they come at us, like Atlas bearing the world! For they act not with their own feebleness, but with a strength as of the Whole of Life. They speak, and the words are theirs, but the voice is the Voice of Mankind.

I don't know what to call it: being right with God or right with life. It is strangely the same thing; and God is not particular as to the name we know him by, so long as we know Him. Musing upon these secret things, I seem to understand what the theologians in their darkness have made so obscure. Is it not just this at-one-ment with life which sweetens and saves us all?

In all these writings I have glorified the life of the soil until I am ashamed. I have loved it because it saved me. The farm for me, I decided long ago, is the only place where I can flow strongly and surely. But to you, my friend, life may present a wholly different aspect, variant necessities. Knowing what I have experienced in the city, I have sometimes wondered at the happy (even serene) faces I have seen in crowded streets. There must be, I admit, those who can flow and be at one with that life, too. And let them handle their money, and make shoes, and sew garments, and write in ledgers—if that completes and contents them. I have no quarrel with any one of them. It is, after all, a big and various world, where men can be happy in many ways.

For every man is a magnet, highly and singularly sensitized. Some draw to them fields and woods and hills, and are drawn in return; and some draw swift streets and the riches which are known to cities. It is not of importance what we draw, but that we really draw. And the greatest tragedy in life, as I see it, is that thousands of men and women never have the opportunity to draw with freedom; but they exist in weariness and labor, and are drawn upon like inanimate objects by those who live in unhappy idleness. They do not farm: they are farmed. . . .

Thus flowing with life, self-surrendering to life a man becomes indispensable to life, he is absolutely necessary to the conduct of this universe. And it is the feeling of being necessary, of being desired, flowing into a man that produces the satisfaction of contentment.

—*Adventures in Friendship* (IV)

5. HOW TO BE SWEET THOUGH SOPHISTICATED

It is all a frame of mind, this enjoyment of living. Wine may be the means of drowning sorrow, or a matter of habitual craving, or the proper occasion for feeling just a little elated, a little better than usual. Things don't give us anything except what we bring to the enjoyment of them. One may be a habitual cynic, taking pleasure in his cynicism, or a shallow optimist, or a sentimentalist, each frame of mind being as subjective as the others. How to select our spectacles through which to look at life is all a matter of personal choice. A frame of mind may become habitual and fixed, and then it becomes for that man a philosophy of life, an attitude toward it. A wise man would be careful not to let any particular frame of mind settle down into a permanent attitude, knowing that once he has got it, he will take a stubborn pleasure in it. A crusty old fool will delight in being just a crusty old fool, and a young sophisticated cynic will wallow in his cynicism. (Even in a picture, Lionel Barrymore's old crustiness palls on me.)

Jefferson said, "I like the dreams of the future better than the history of the past." That, we may say, is a Jeffersonian frame of mind. He chose to wear those spectacles without quite knowing how he came by that philosophy. How does anyone know how he comes by any philosophy or favorite way of looking at life? Justice Holmes somehow found his philosophy in the formula that "the rule of joy and the law of duty seem to me all one. I confess that altruistic and cynically selfish talk seem to me about equally unreal." Again, "The joy of life is to put out one's power in some natural and useful or harmless way." Justice Holmes found these things out after a long lifetime of wise living.

Franklin was a hedonist, an optimist, an amateur moralist. He looked at life without illusion and without disillusion. He expressed the idea of the *free choice,* of two ways of looking at life in the little essay, "The Handsome and Deformed Leg," which is typically Franklinian and which I find fresh as ever today. There is fashion in ideas as in dress, and Franklin suggests that a person's philosophy of life may have been caught "by Imitation and is unawares grown into a Habit." Franklin, I believe, was suffering from gout and had one of his legs bandaged up when he wrote this humorous piece.

The Handsome and Deformed Leg

by Benjamin Franklin

There are two Sorts of People in the World, who with equal Degrees of Health, & Wealth, and the other Comforts of Life, become, the one happy, and the other miserable. This arises very much from the different Views in which they consider Things, Persons, and Events; and the Effect of those different Views upon their own Minds.

In whatever Situation Men can be plac'd, they may find conveniencies & Inconviencies: In whatever Company; they may find Persons & Conversation more or less pleasing. At whatever Table, they may meet with Meats & Drinks of better and worse Taste, Dishes better & worse dress'd: In whatever Climate they will find good and bad Weather: Under whatever Government, they may find good & bad Laws, and good & bad Administration of those Laws. In every Poem or Work of Genius they may see Faults and Beauties. In almost every Face & every Person, they may discover fine Features & Defects, good & bad Qualities.

Under these Circumstances, the two Sorts of People above mention'd fix their Attention, those who are to be happy, on the Conveniencies of Things, the pleasant Parts of Conversation, the well-dress'd Dishes, the Goodness of the Wines, the fine Weather; &c., and enjoy all with Chearfulness. Those who are to be unhappy, think & speak only of the contraries. Hence they are continually discontented themselves, and by their Remarks sour the Pleasures of Society, offend personally many People, and make themselves everywhere disagreable. If this Turn of Mind was founded in Nature, such unhappy Persons would be the more to be pitied. But as the Disposition to criticise, & be disgusted, is perhaps taken up originally by Imitation, and is unawares grown into a Habit, which tho' at present strong may nevertheless be cured when those who have it are convinc'd of its bad Effects on their Felicity; I hope this little Admonition may be of Service to them, and put them on changing a Habit, which tho' in the Exercise it is chiefly an Act of Imagination yet has serious Consequences in Life, as it brings on real Griefs and Misfortunes. For as many are offended by, & nobody well loves this Sort of People. . . .

An old philosophical friend of mine was grown, from experience, very cautious in this particular, and carefully avoided any intimacy with such people. He had, like other philosophers, a thermometer to show him the heat of the weather, and a barometer to mark when it was likely to prove good or bad; but, there being no instrument invented to discover, at first sight, this unpleasing disposition in a person, he for that purpose made use of his legs; one of which was remarkably handsome, the other, by some accident, crooked and deformed. If a Stranger, at the first interview, regarded his ugly Leg

more than his handsome one, he doubted him. If he spoke of it, &
took no notice of the handsome Leg, that was sufficient to determine
my Philosopher to have no further Acquaintance with him. Every
body has not this two-legged Instrument, but every one with a little
Attention, may observe Signs of that carping, fault-finding Disposition,
& take the same Resolution of avoiding the Acquaintance of those
infected with it. I therefore advise those critical, querulous, discon-
tended, unhappy People, that if they wish to be respected and belov'd
by others, & happy in themselves they should *leave off looking at the
ugly Leg.*

—"The Handsome and Deformed Leg"

Professor Irwin Edman wrote an essay, "How to Be Sweet though
Sophisticated," in the heyday of the Hemingway cult in the nineteen
twenties when American youth ostentatiously paraded death, sex, and
despair.[6] It was in Franklinian terms a bad fashion, a childish fashion,
and youth took it up. The discovery of sex, the daring to be frank
about it, the sudden sense of disillusion, and the desire to be known
as a "tough guy," all fairly normal characteristics of adolescence, were
thought of as sophisticated wisdom. Edman, a wise head on young
shoulders then, queried all this, like a professor correcting an undergraduate's paper, and as always happens after such corrections, no matter how good-humoredly it is done, the paper looks a little silly, or trite,
or woefully misinformed. The ancient American, as Benjamin Franklin shows us, brooded on happiness, the modern sophisticated American loves to brood on unhappiness and despair.

*"One of the worst sins Dante could think of was to sulk in
the sunlight. To those who did he assigned the eternal
punishment of wallowing in the mud."*

BY IRWIN EDMAN

One can learn as much about the prevailing temper of a generation
by studying its contempts as by remembering its loves. It is indeed

From *Adam, the Baby and the Man from Mars.* Houghton Mifflin Company. Copyright, 1929, Irwin Edman. Reprinted by permission.

[6] "*Ernest Hemingway.* Half of our novelists are boys, determined to be boys. They
will not hear of any other prospect."—Van Wyck Brooks, *Opinions of Oliver Allston,*
p. 300.

very difficult in our time to tell what we love, the old objects of our adoration having been riddled with suspicion, and love itself, in the skeptical hands of our contemporary wise men, having come into disrepute. To the Spartan, the ideal of life was represented by the warrior, disciplined and taut. To the medieval, the ideal of the good life was typified by the martyr, the ascetic or the saint. In the Renaissance one wished to be something like Castiglione's courtier, a polished fusion of the gentleman, the scholar, the soldier and the man of the world. The contemporary hero, the mythical pattern in the imitation of whom we would live, remains as yet undefined. We have no hero; what is more to the point, we suspect hero worship. . . .

Science has ceased to be the esoteric possession of experts in a laboratory; it has become the popular jargon of the men in the street or at least of the women in the salon. We know enough about glands to be incredulous of our own or of anybody else's melancholy. When we are depressed we know that it is probably not the cosmos in general but the thyroid in particular that is wrong with us. . . . Love, again, may among adolescents parade its ancient recognizable rhetoric. But we know better. We see through the disguise, ornate and thin, by which lust conceals itself—even from itself. Every schoolboy, almost, has read Freud. Every adult can quote Havelock Ellis. Our devotion may seem deep, but its depths are in the seamier profundities of our psyches. And as for that eternity with which we credit every passing affection—well, we smile ourselves at that outmoded sentimentalism. . . .

So having discarded the old myths, we have gradually been forming a hero-myth of our own. . . . Enter the Modern. It makes no difference whether it be a man or a woman. In either case, the ideas, like the figure and headdress, will be much the same. He will not talk of love or admit it. He will not believe in the Good Life or be publicly seen leading it. He will have no nonsense about religion or believe that relic of primitive mentality still exists. He will be "anæsthetized to all that Jesus or that Plato prized." He will have little patience with politeness or allow himself to practice it. He will try to be a tough mind gayly indifferent in a tough world. The last obscenity he will permit himself will be nobility. The last weakness he will indulge in will be to be sweet or soft. He will talk like a character out of Ernest Hemingway, act like one of Aldous Huxley's bizarre London intelligentsia

—or pretend he does—and try to think in such terms as James Joyce's heroines use in their more untrammeled moments. . . .

It is now in the best circles indecent to be decent, shameful to be shy, offensive to be courteous, suspicious to be simple. Many of our newly smart would rather be found murdering their children than being kind to their parents. They would prefer to be damned for rudeness than to be snickered at for courtesy. They suspect even themselves for any outworn noble sentiment they may happen to experience, any unpremeditated act of kindness they may do, any spontaneous impulse of affection to which they may give way. . . .

It is not merely fear of what people will say, but fear of what one will think of one's self that makes it difficult in our time to be at once a "tough mind" and a gentle heart. All the new realism of thinking and writing and conversation have made us self-skeptical. Any one acquainted with the new psychiatry knows why. That gesture we intended to be generous we know to be timid or vain. The kindness we tried to utter we are told is a defense against our own weakness, a fear of not being kind. Enthusiasm is a symptom of prolonged adolescence. Rapture is a psychological debauch that is a vulgar truancy from reason.

Now it would seem to be high time to find out whether this sort of thing has not gone too far. The sophisticates themselves, I suspect, feel that it has. How else is one to account for the joy with which in our most advanced circles, intelligentlemen, intelligentlewomen hail any naïveté in literature or art. . . . As for the respectable bourgeois rabble whom our sophisticated despise, these comfortable bumpkins cannot get enough of the traditional simple virtues and simple souls. Write them a story, as an Englishman did recently, of a brave father come down in the world, fighting the good fight against slimy obstacles for the love of his pure and devoted son, and you will have hundreds of thousands at your feet and at your publisher's. And what of the whole English-speaking world that quotes with glee the childlike whimsicalities of "Christopher Robin" and "Winnie-the-Pooh."

The question indeed comes down to this: Is it possible to be at once sweet and sophisticated? In our generation can one be at once honest and kindly, intelligent and courteous, informed and gay? . . . These are rhetorical questions and they are intended to be such. This observer at least wishes to bear humble testimony to the conviction that contemporary wisdom has overreached itself. It is submitted that it is the easiest thing in the world, even the contemporary world, to find life agreeable, and to live it agreeably. . . .

Sophistication demands honesty; it does not require ill temper. There is a kind of wisdom called mellowness and the history of literature is amiably strewn with its exemplars. Montaigne is the prince of these; his essays are the perfectly urbane expression of a man who kept his mind clear and his blood sweet. He knew as well as the latest contemporary futilitarian knows how much there is to bewail in the world. At its best life is short; half of its felicities are illusions and the other half are fatal in their consequences. There is little of which we can be certain, and much of which we must be regretful or ashamed.

But it is not clear now as it was to Montaigne that ill temper is hardly the mood with which to live pleasantly, nor the spirit which reason will commend to adopt toward the world. The light may have gone out of Heaven and meaning out of the earth. We may be fated animals crawling anxiously through the palpitation brief and confused, that we call life. But that chaotic interval is at moments clear with wonder or beauty, and even the disorder of our current societies permits moments of delight. These are clearly on the debit side of the ledger, and a realism that denies the doughnut in affirming the hole is both jaundiced and dishonest.

Nor is it any more honest or reasonable to be continually suspicious of our pleasures, our kindnesses or our raptures because the laboratory has been revealing the machinery by which these operate. Love, we are told, is merely a matter of glandular secretions. But to admit the truth of this physiological fact is far from denying that love exists. There may be a thousand subconscious reasons why we aid a friend in distress or sacrifice our life and energies for some lost or forlorn ideal. The causes of the late war may be demonstrated to have been sordid and mean, but even the most cynical will not deny that thousands of men gave their lives in the generous belief that they were not. It matters not what produces our raptures or our loves or loyalties. Even the most hardened can hardly contest their existence.

To know the material origins of our flights is not to deny their being or their value. To recognize the horrors and evils in the texture of existence is not to blind us to all the loveliness and liveliness there is to enjoy and to commemorate under the sun. It may be said indeed that the essence of being adult rather than childish is to cease to be sulky and irritable at finding life and existence to be what they are. It means among other things to be able to face life steadily and without illusion—but also without disillusion. . . .

A persistent satire upon life is hardly more adult than a persistent prettifying of it. One of the worst sins Dante could think of was to sulk in the sunlight. To those who did he assigned the eternal punishment of wallowing in the mud. . . . One might set up as a conceivable ideal for our generation the combination of the tough mind and the gentle heart. The tough mind will be undismayed by any fact or any horror; it will not be misled by any pleasure or mirage. It will know that man is neither an ape nor an angel, but a precarious and harassed animal living in an uncertain, sometimes abominable, sometimes exquisite world.

—*Adam, the Baby and the Man from Mars*

Chapter X

THE ARTS OF LIVING

I. THE ART OF DOING NOTHING

SOMETHING like a sense of remorse has been weighing upon me ever since I wrote about the tonic effect of work in the last chapter. To talk to Americans about the joy of work is like preaching industry to the bees. Even if it is true, it may be woefully misunderstood. One may commend "hard work" and some reader may imagine that I am commending a Marathon race with a man's own nervous system. For if there is anything unnatural in American life, it is this perpetual straining of the nervous fibre, this inability to accept quiet, the unwillingness to let the world alone for a while, the failure to insist on the right to unemployment for certain hours of the day. Pushing, ambitious young men actually are not ashamed to tell their boss that they worked on certain documents up to one o'clock on Saturday night, drove out to Cleveland and back on Sunday just for the fun of it and took a cat nap before changing and dressing for the concert that night. Such a young man evidently aims at becoming a Vice-President! Perhaps this has become natural in American life. But in no country in the world except the United States has man so wronged himself. What is natural in nature has become unnatural in man, and what is unnatural has become natural. God created all animals to play as well as to hunt for a living; only men make slaves of men. One soon forgets to listen to the wind in the pine forest, or watch the robin on the lawn. Life, even human life, was never meant that way.

What does man want in life? Does he want to change the universe? Time flows for ever; the past cannot be recaptured and the future is uncertain; only the day, the present hour, is a solid good. Perhaps the best way to thank God for the gift of living is to appreciate the present hour, to sit quietly and hear your own breathing and look out on the universe *and be content*. One can see time flow sometimes; one does not have to do something to pass the time; time can pass by itself. And there is infinite pleasure in watching the color of the day change from hour to hour and being able to say to oneself, "I have passed a perfect leisurely afternoon." Such perfect afternoons are entirely possible. There is no intrusion upon one's solitude—not one telephone call, no television—one sees from the window only a child falling and bruising her leg, nothing serious, and young lovers and middle-aged couples sitting quietly on benches under trees. The world goes by. It is enough.

Or perhaps you have spent three hours in the garden, trimming branches or saving some young sprouts, or clearing the weeds and improving the garden path under a cloudless sky, and you have just come in and lit a pipe. You have been left alone, free and careless, with the passage of time, and in those hours of freedom and utter disregard for all that happens in the outside world, you have won a majesty and dignity you have seldom felt before. You have regained possession of yourself. How rarely one dares to steal such a perfect day and snatch freedom from time itself! The day passes and you are one day older. Tomorrow there is work; let's put a solid wall of sleep between the two. It is a good human life.

I lived for ten years in New York, and observed the well-known phenomenon of hustling American life. Everybody is hustling down into the subway and hustling out from it again. Of course the subway is always crowded and uncomfortable; men's bodies have no rest and their nerves and faces are taut. The sidewalks are too narrow for leisurely sauntering; there are no boulevards with trees; people sit on the edge of rotating or rotatable discs before lunch counters and give themselves fifteen minutes for lunch, and women's high-heeled shoes key up every nerve in their soles and calves. Now what is the explanation? The Americans don't want comfort? But they preach material comforts. Then I remember that America is a youthful nation, that youth is held at a premium; an exuberant show of energy governs the pattern of their lives. Perhaps it would be truer to say that everybody is trying to be young than to say that everybody is trying to be rich. I am almost sure that this is the explanation, that the ideal of youthful energy is at the bottom of it all. Traveling in all countries, one comes to note the word "energy" as the most characteristic of the

American people and the American nation. Youth, energy, hope, keenness are the characteristic notes of the American people. Certainly the
material results justify such a general state of mind. And why not?
The Americans have energy; why should they not be a little exuberant?

Yet hurry and hustle do take away from the reflective life. I feel
that there is too much hurry and not enough reflection and contemplation in American life and thought. The deep contemplative life has
something to do with the development of great reflective and non-
conformist personalities. It would indeed be ironic if the securing of
the greatest material freedom should produce also a tendency toward
conformity and mitigate against the production of great individuals.
Hurry toward a material objective does take away from the reflective
spirit and the capacity for contemplation. Maturity of spirit is the
one quality of mind that, like wine, cannot be produced in a hurry.
The breadth of spirit, the delight of insight, and the full and free
luxuriant flowering of thought in writing, well conditioned, giving
that stimulating sparkle and mellowed body in its draughts of thought,
and satisfying our highest demands—these are the qualities which,
like wine, must mellow for decades in dark, cool, undisturbed cellars.
Perhaps the hurry of American life is not conducive to such spiritual
hibernation.

The capacity for reflection comes from a state of mind, made
possible by the physical habit of doing nothing at certain hours of the
days. John Livingston Lowes writes charmingly of this habit of keeping still.

"Leisure, which is not to be confused with empty time, but which is time through which free, life-enhancing currents flow ..."

BY JOHN LIVINGSTON LOWES

For we live in an age and a land above all things marked by hurried
motion. I happened to come from Pittsburgh to New York the other
day, at the rate of fifty miles an hour. Every few minutes another train
flashed by in the opposite direction. On a hundred thousand miles of

rails the same flying shuttles were hurtling back and forth. The taxi which took me from one station to another in New York was numbered (they know better now) one million seven hundred thousand and odd, and the other million or so were trying simultaneously to hurl themselves along the streets. And under the street, packed trains, a couple of minutes or so apart, were crashing back and forth in the din of steel on steel flung back from walls of stone. . . . The word of the hour is the word of my headline—'drive.' To carry on the business of college, church, or hospital, we initiate a 'drive.' Even in religion, education, and philanthropy we tend to think and act in terms of energy translated into tense and often fevered motion. . . .

For one of the consequences of this modern malady of ours is that the gracious things which lend to life and human intercourse the beauty of serenity and comeliness are gone, or on the wane. 'The wisdom of a learned man,' wrote the author of Ecclesiasticus long centuries ago, 'cometh by opportunity of leisure,' and not wisdom only, but grace, and gentle breeding, and amenity, and poise come so, and only so. And leisure (which is not to be confused with empty time, but which is time through which free, life-enhancing currents flow)— leisure in these days is something to be sought and cherished as a rare and priceless boon; leisure to think, and talk, and write, and read— lost arts else, all of them. 'John Wesley's conversation is good,' said Dr. Johnson to Boswell once, 'but he is never at leisure. He is always obliged to go at a certain hour. This is very disagreeable to a man who loves to fold his legs and have out his talk, as I do.' The sainted John Wesley in the rôle of a modern 'hustler' is a little humorous, and Samuel Johnson did a certain amount of work himself. But an age that loved, on occasion, to fold its legs, and have its talk out, and its book out, and its delightful familiar letters out, may not have been one hundred per cent efficient (in our devastating modern phrase), but it did have shelter to grow ripe, and it did have leisure to grow wise, and more than our own driving, restless period, it did possess its soul. 'He hasteth well,' wrote Chaucer, whom business could not make dull, 'who wisely can abide,' and we first learn to live when we

> . . . claim not every laughing Hour
> For handmaid to [our] striding power . . .

To usher for a destined space
(*Her own sweet errands all forgone*)
The too imperious traveller on.

'We are great fools,' says Montaigne: ' "He spends his life in idleness,"
we say, "I've *done* nothing to-day." What! Have you not *lived*? That
is not only the most fundamental, but the most illustrious of your
occupations.'

Our salvation, then, lies in the refusal to be forever hurried with
the crowd, and in our resolution to step out of it at intervals, and drink
from deeper wells. 'Il se faut reserver une arrière boutique, toute nostre,
toute franche'—'we ought to reserve for ourselves an *arrière boutique*,
a back shop, all our own, all free, in which we may set up our own
true liberty and principal retreat and solitude.'

—*Of Reading Books*

Professor Lowes, in the above commencement address to Radcliffe
college girls in 1924, quoted William James's famous lecture made
before the same college in 1899. James had called American girls with
their characteristic energy "bottled lightning," and Professor Lowes
added, "That was twenty-five years ago. Today, be they masculine or
feminine, we dub such persons dynamos. And the human dynamo is
fast becoming our ideal." William James's lecture on "The Gospel of
Relaxation" will always be remembered as the outstanding contribution
on this subject. The following selection is very much condensed.

Bottled Lightning

BY WILLIAM JAMES

Many years ago a Scottish medical man, Dr. Clouston, a mad-
doctor as they call him there, or what we should call an asylum
physician (the most eminent one in Scotland), visited this country,
and said something that has remained in my memory ever since.
"You Americans," he said, "wear too much expression on your faces.
You are living like an army with all its reserves engaged in action.
The duller countenances of the British population betoken a better

scheme of life. They suggest stores of reserved nervous force to fall back upon, if any occasion should arise that requires it.". . .

And all Americans who stay in Europe long enough to get accustomed to the spirit that reigns and expresses itself there, so unexcitable as compared with ours, makes a similar observation when they return to their native shores. They find a wild-eyed look upon their compatriots' faces, either of too desperate eagerness and anxiety or of too intense responsiveness and good-will. It is hard to say whether the men or the women show it most. It is true that we do not all feel about it as Dr. Clouston felt. Many of us, far from deploring it, admire it. We say: "What intelligence it shows! How different from the stolid cheeks, the codfish eyes, the slow, inanimate demeanor we have been seeing in the British Isles!" Intensity, rapidity, vivacity of appearance, are indeed with us something of a nationally accepted ideal. . . . In a weekly paper not very long ago I remember reading a story in which, after describing the beauty and interest of the heroine's personality, the author summed up her charms by saying that to all who looked upon her an impression as of "bottled lightning" was irresistibly conveyed. Bottled lightning, in truth, is one of our American ideals, even of a young girl's character! . . .

Now what is the cause of this absence of repose, this bottled-lightning quality in us Americans? . . . The American over-tension and jerkiness and breathlessness and intensity and agony of expression are primarily social, and only secondarily physiological, phenomena. They are *bad habits,* nothing more or less, bred of custom and example, born of the imitation of bad models and the cultivation of false personal ideals. . . . I suspect that neither the nature nor the amount of our work is accountable for the frequency and severity of our breakdowns, but that their cause lies rather in those absurd feelings of hurry and having no time, in that breathlessness and tension, that anxiety of feature and that solicitude for results, that lack of inner harmony and ease, in short, by which with us the work is so apt to be accompanied, and from which a European who should do the same work would nine times out of ten be free. . . .

It is your relaxed and easy worker, who is in no hurry, and quite thoughtless most of the while of consequences, who is your efficient worker; and tension and anxiety, and present and future, all mixed up together in our mind at once, are the surest drags upon steady progress and hindrances to our success. . . .

My advice to students, especially to girl-students, would be somewhat similar. Just as a bicycle-chain may be too tight, so may one's carefulness and conscientiousness be so tense as to hinder the running of one's mind. Take, for example, periods when there are many successive days of examination impending. One ounce of good nervous tone in an examination is worth many pounds of anxious study for it in advance. If you want really to do your best in an examination, fling away the book the day before, say to yourself, "I won't waste another minute on this miserable thing, and I don't care an iota whether I succeed or not." Say this sincerely, and feel it; and go out and play, or go to bed and sleep, and I am sure the results next day will encourage you to use the method permanently.

—"The Gospel of Relaxation," *Talks to Teachers on Psychology*

2. FRIENDSHIP AND CONVERSATION

Of the arts of leisure, of enjoying the present hour, friendship and conversation come first. It seems wise for me, a Chinese talker, to refrain from talking on the subject of talking, when there is such a galaxy of great talkers as Oliver Wendell Holmes, James Russell Lowell, and Christopher Morley to talk to us about the grand style of talking and incidentally of friendship and of *not* answering letters. I need only repeat that Dr. Holmes was himself a great conversationalist and that his subjects ranged from horses and insanity to "a girl's face or figure—which?" I wonder why that American Montaigne stands almost alone. None has touched his loquaciousness since, and so few are willing to write on all the interesting topics that have to do with man's daily life and the arts of living. Once when he was starting the second series of his "Breakfast Table" talks under the guise of the "Professor," his other literary self, the Autocrat, expressed the doubt that he could have anything left to say after the Autocrat had said it all, or said so much already, and the Professor answered that "life can coin thought somewhat faster than I can count it off in words. Here am I, the Professor,—a man who has lived long enough to have plucked the flowers of life and come to the berries,—which are not always sad-colored, but sometimes golden-hued as the crocus of April, or rosy-cheeked as the damask of June; a man who staggered against books as a baby, and will totter against them, if he lives to decrepitude; with a brain as full of tingling thoughts, such as they are, as a limb which we call "asleep," because it is so particularly awake, is of pricking points; presenting a keyboard of nerve-pulps, not as yet tanned or ossified, to the finger-touch of all outward agencies; knowing something of the filmy threads of this web of life in which we insects buzz awhile, waiting for the gray old spider to come along; contented enough with daily realities, but twirling on his finger the key of a private Bedlam of ideals; in knowledge feeding with the fox oftener than with the stork,—loving better the breadth of a fertilizing inundation than the depth of a narrow artesian well; finding nothing too small for his contemplation in the markings of the *grammatophora subtilissima,* and nothing too large in the movement of the solar system towards the star Lambda of the constellation Hercules;—and the question is, whether there is anything left for me, the Professor, to suck out of creation, after my lively friend has had his straw in the bung-hole of the Universe!" (*The Professor at the Breakfast Table.*)

That is what I call the grand style of talking. We do not have to tell Dr. Holmes to let himself go; he always does that.

Since human society began, with men getting together around campfires, or sitting on top of beer barrels with pipe in hand, or lounging in the leather chairs of a club room, that intercourse of spirits, that free and easy exchange and friction and sending back and forth of thoughts which is called a conversation, has always been one of the great pleasures of life. Here is Dr. Holmes talking, or rather "jawing" at his ambling ease, on the society of men and the art of conversation.

"You see wisdom in slippers and science in a short jacket."
BY OLIVER WENDELL HOLMES

We get into a way of thinking as if what we call an "intellectual man" was, as a matter of course, made up of nine tenths, or thereabouts, of book-learning, and one tenth himself. But even if he is actually so compounded, he need not read much. Society is a strong solution of books. It draws the virtue out of what is best worth reading, as hot water draws the strength of tea-leaves. If I were a prince, I would hire or buy a private literary tea-pot, in which I would steep all the leaves of new books that promised well. The infusion would do for me without the vegetable fibre. You understand me; I would have a person whose sole business should be to read day and night, and talk to me whenever I wanted him to. I know the man I would have: a quick-witted, out-spoken, incisive fellow; knows history, or at any rate has a shelf full of books about it, which he can use handily, and the same of all useful arts and sciences; knows all the common plots of plays and novels, and the stock company of characters that are continually coming on in new costume; can give you a criticism of an octavo in an epithet and a wink, and you can depend on it; cares for nobody except for the virtue there is in what he says; delights in taking off big wigs and professional gowns, and in the disembalming and unbandaging of all literary mummies. Yet he is as tender and reverential to all that bears the mark of genius,—that is, of a new influx of truth or beauty,—as a nun over her missal. In short, he is one of those men that know everything except how to make a living. Him would I keep on the square next my own royal compartment on life's chessboard. To him I would push up another pawn, in the shape of a comely and wise young woman, whom he would of course take,—to wife. For all contingencies I would liberally provide. In a word, I would, in the plebeian, but expressive phrase, "put him through" all the material part of life; see him sheltered, warmed, fed, button-mended, and all that, just to be able to lay on his talk when I liked,—with the privilege of shutting it off at will.

A Club is the next best thing to this, strung like a harp, with about a dozen ringing intelligences, each answering to some chord of the macrocosm. They do well to dine together once in a while. A dinner-party made up of such elements is the last triumph of civilization over barbarism. Nature and art combine to charm the senses; the equatorial zone of the system is soothed by well-studied artifices; the faculties are off duty, and fall into their natural attitudes; you see wisdom in slippers and science in a short jacket.

The whole force of conversation depends on how much you can take for granted. Vulgar chess-players have to play their game out;

nothing short of the brutality of an actual checkmate satisfies their dull apprehensions. But look at two masters of that noble game! White stands well enough, so far as you can see; but Red says, Mate in six moves;—White looks,—nods;—the game is over. Just so in talking with first-rate men; especially when they are good-natured and expansive, as they are apt to be at table. That blessed clairvoyance which sees into things without opening them,—that glorious license, which, having shut the door and driven the reporter from its key-hole, calls upon Truth, majestic virgin! to get off from her pedestal and drop her academic poses, and take a festive garland and the vacant place on the *medius lectus,*—that carnival-shower of questions and replies and comments, large axioms bowled over the mahogany like bomb-shells from professional mortars, and explosive wit dropping its trains of many-colored fire, and the mischief-making rain of *bon-bons* pelting everybody that shows himself,—the picture of a truly intellectual banquet . . . All lecturers, all professors, all schoolmasters, have ruts and grooves in their minds into which their conversation is perpetually sliding. Did you never, in riding through the woods of a still June evening, suddenly feel that you had passed into a warm stratum of air, and in a minute or two strike the chill layer of atmosphere beyond? Did you never, in cleaving the green waters of the Back Bay,—where the Provincial blue-noses are in the habit of beating the "Metropolitan" boat-clubs,—find yourself in a tepid streak, a narrow, local gulf-stream, a gratuitous warm-bath a little underdone, through which your glistening shoulders soon flashed, to bring you back to the cold realities of full-sea temperature? Just so, in talking with any of the characters above referred to, one not unfrequently finds a sudden change in the style of the conversation. The lacklustre eye, rayless as a Beacon-Street door-plate in August, all at once fills with light; the face flings itself wide open like the church-portals when the bride and bridegroom enter; the little man grows in stature before your eyes, like the small prisoner with hair on end, beloved yet dreaded of early childhood; you were talking with a dwarf and an imbecile,—you have a giant and a trumpet-tongued angel before you!—Nothing but a streak out of a fifty-dollar lecture.

—*The Autocrat of the Breakfast Table* (III)

Samuel McChord Crothers brings out clearly the pleasure of conversation as a process whereby one can see thoughts being adjusted or being born, as an antidote against incrustation of ideas, and as a meeting of two fallible minds, which is what a conversation should be.

"*Two Infallibilities, each speaking* ex cathedra, *could not converse . . .*"

BY SAMUEL McCHORD CROTHERS

So the philosophic mind is liable to become "broody." It is then no longer content to produce fresh thoughts. It must hatch out a complete system of its own. The philosopher in this mood is irritable beyond the wont of ordinary mortals. When another philosopher approaches he flies at him, for he suspects that he has come to destroy his metaphysical nest-eggs.

A glance at a philosophical library will show how many huge volumes have been the result of this mood. A philosopher is at his best when he is thinking a new thought, he is at his worst when he is defending his old thoughts against all comers. This is a sore trial to his temper and does not really improve his intellect. Now and then we find one who keeps on thinking, without caring very much what becomes of his thoughts. He knows that there are more where they come from. Then you have a Plato whose philosophy takes the form, not of a system, but of a conversation among friends.

The beauty of a conversation is that the other side always has a chance. There is no finality as the friendly speech goes on in a series of polite half-contradictions. "What you were saying just now was very interesting and was quite true in its way. It reminds me of an experience which I once had which shows that the subject may be looked at in a different way."

The natural man, or rather the natural boy, puts these contradictions more bluntly. Huckleberry Finn and his compeers begin the conversation with "You lie!" which leads to the clever repartee "You're another!"; after which they feel acquainted.

As we grow more maturely civilized, these sharp antagonisms are softened until they become merely a pleasing variety; or, in Milton's phrase, "brotherly dissimilitudes not vastly disproportionable." In order to have a conversation with you, it is not necessary for me to assume that the truth is not in you, but only that you have approached the truth from a somewhat different angle. You had overstated one side in order that I might make the needed correction.

Two Infallibilities, each speaking *ex cathedra,* could not converse; they could only fulminate. After the first round they would relapse into sullen silence. When we start out with the easy assurance of mutual fallibility, we can go on indefinitely setting each other right. Thinking comes to be a coöperative industry in which we share the profits. We not only reason, but we reason together.

In free conversation the truth slips out that would be carefully concealed in a formal document. We perceive not only what was done but the "moving why they did it."

—Among Friends

I must say, however, that conversation at American dinner tables is more often impossible than possible. It is impossible at a cocktail party, of course, but even at dinner the long table usually kills it. For strange to say, you can talk only when you are free not to talk; conversation is something which oozes, or drops in driblets, or suddenly gushes forth in a wild, generous torrent, one of those things that cannot be compelled, cannot be made to order, and cannot be premeditated. The hostess is of course the person who should be on the lookout to see where it flows comfortably, where it has dwindled to driplets, and where there is promise of a likely torrent. Is it an ever so slight change in the hue of a person's eyes, or a more than usual glitter shining from behind the half-drawn curtain of the window of the soul, behind which you see words, phrases, ideas, and expressions, diabolical or otherwise (the eyebrow tells that) in a state of phosphorescent glow, just about ready to sally forth, to be born and given the body of sound? What chances are there for such when a dinner party goes above seven or eight? By a sort of automatic fission you have two or three knots of compulsory and competitive conversations instead of one spontaneous, sparkling generous flow. My spirit is vexed then. I try to do two or three things at the same time, none of which I can do well. I try to hear, to overhear, and to keep myself talking, for fear of seeming impolite, to search for a possible fish bone between my teeth, and at the same time to worry whether it is possible to ask for coffee when others are having dessert. Of course you may sit next to a very pretty young woman and the filet of sole tastes so much richer and you are more brilliant than usual, but you may also run smack into a snob who abruptly and completely shuts off all possible flow of conversation because you obviously have a fifty-cent tie. And there at the other end of the table sits an old man with impressive white hair talking in a low, comfortable rippling flow with a girl of eighteen with keen eyes and verve, whose soft ripples of laughter are wafted across the table over the delectable fumes of hot goulash with an exotic Spanish sauce. When conversation so breaks up by fission, you cannot remain silent, and you cannot sit back and just listen. Any time, I would rather chew the chicken and listen and see the arc lights of mind confronting mind shoot across the table in a sort of haphazard fashion. You yourself don't shoot until some invisible arc light plays directly upon you and kindles in you something that goes out from you in the flash of a second, quickly responsive, sympathetic, and fitting your role in the general play of such atomic forces.

Letter writing is but a continuation of conversation among friends, and therefore has all the wayward disorderliness and unpredictability of a good conversation. You make believe, you exaggerate, you overstate, and you are not on your guard because a sentence that might be misinterpreted by the public will not be so misunderstood by a friend. The background of contradictory things you have said on other occasions insures you against that. James Russell Lowell, who was himself one of the best letter-writers of America, tells how letters should not be written. In a letter to Miss Norton (April 6th, 1869), he says, ". . . Authors, my altogether dear woman, can't write letters. At best they squeeze out an essay now and then, burying every natural sprout in a dry and dreary *sand-flood,* as unlike as possible to those delightful freshets with which your heart overflows the paper. *They* are thinking of their punctuation, of crossing their *t's* and dotting their *i's,* and cannot forget themselves in their correspondent, which I take to be the true recipe for a letter."

To Mrs. Francis Shaw, Lowell talked gracefully about the duty to owe our best friends some letters.

250 ON THE WISDOM OF AMERICA

"What is the use of loving people if they can't let us owe them a letter?"

Elmwood, Jan. 11, 1853.

My Dear Sarah,—

You know that I promised solemnly to write you a letter from Switzerland, and therefore, of course, I didn't do it. These epistolary promises to pay always do (or at least always ought to) come back protested. A letter ought always to be the genuine and natural flower of one's disposition—proper both to the writer and the season—and none of your turnip japonicas cut laboriously out of a cheap and flabby material. Then, when you have sealed it up, it comes out fresh and fragrant. I do not like shuttle-cock correspondences. What is the use of our loving people if they can't let us owe them a letter? if they can't be sure we keep on loving them if we don't keep sending an acknowledgment under our hands and seals once a month? As if there were a statute of limitations for affection! The moment Love begins to think of Duty, he may as well go hang himself with his own bow-string. All this means that if I should never write you another letter (which is extremely likely), and we should never meet again till I drop in upon you some day in another planet, I shall give an anxious look at myself in the mirror (while I am waiting for you to come down), and shall hear the flutter of your descending wings with the same admiring expectation as I should now listen for your foot upon the stairs. . . .

—James Russell Lowell, *Letters*

On the very human subject of not answering letters Christopher Morley has written a piece of delightful fooling, warm and affectionate, which shows the essayist at his best.

On Unanswering Letters

by Christopher Morley

There are a great many people who really believe in answering letters the day they are received, just as there are people who go to the

From *Essays,* copyright, 1928, Christopher Morley. Published by J. B. Lippincott Company.

movies at nine o'clock in the morning; but these people are stunted and queer.

It is a great mistake. Such crass and breathless promptness takes away a great deal of the pleasure of correspondence.

The psychological didoes involved in receiving letters and making up one's mind to answer them are very complex. If the tangled process could be clearly analyzed and its component involutions isolated for inspection we might reach a clearer comprehension of that curious bag of tricks, the efficient Masculine Mind.

Take Bill F., for instance, a man so delightful that even to contemplate his existence puts us in good humor and makes us think well of a world that can exhibit an individual equally comely in mind, body and estate. Every now and then we get a letter from Bill, and immediately we pass into a kind of trance, in which our mind rapidly enunciates the ideas, thoughts, surmises and contradictions that we would like to write to him in reply. We think what fun it would be to sit right down and churn the ink-well, spreading speculation and cynicism over a number of sheets of foolscap to be wafted Billward.

Sternly we repress the impulse for we know that the shock to Bill of getting so immediate a retort would surely unhinge the well-fitted panels of his intellect.

We add his letter to the large delta of unanswered mail on our desk, taking occasion to turn the mass over once or twice and run through it in a brisk, smiling mood, thinking of all the jolly letters we shall write some day.

After Bill's letter has lain on the pile for a fortnight or so it has been gently silted over by about twenty other pleasantly postponed manuscripts. Coming upon it by chance, we reflect that any specific problems raised by Bill in that manifesto will by this time have settled themselves. And his random speculations upon household management and human destiny will probably have taken a new slant by now, so that to answer his letter in its own tune will not be congruent with his present fevers. We had better bide a wee until we really have something of circumstance to impart.

We wait a week.

By this time a certain sense of shame has begun to invade the privacy of our brain. We feel that to answer that letter now would be an indelicacy. Better to pretend that we never got it. By and bye Bill will write again and then we will answer promptly. We put the letter back in the middle of the heap and think what a fine chap Bill is. But he knows we love him, so it doesn't really matter whether we write or not.

Another week passes by, and no further communication from Bill. We wonder whether he does love us as much as we thought. Still— we are too proud to write and ask.

A few days later a new thought strikes us. Perhaps Bill thinks we have died and he is annoyed because he wasn't invited to the funeral. Ought we to wire him? No, because after all we are not dead, and even if he thinks we are, his subsequent relief at hearing the good news of our survival will outweigh his bitterness during the interval. One of these days we will write him a letter that will really express our heart, filled with all the grindings and gear-work of our mind, rich in affection and fallacy. But we had better let it ripen and mellow for a while. Letters, like wines, accumulate bright fumes and bubblings if kept under cork.

Presently we turn over that pile of letters again. We find in the lees of the heap two or three that have gone for six months and can safely be destroyed. Bill is still on our mind, but in a pleasant, dreamy kind of way. He does not ache or twinge us as he did a month ago. It is fine to have old friends like that and keep in touch with them. We wonder how he is and whether he has two children or three. Splendid old Bill!

By this time we have written Bill several letters in imagination and enjoyed doing so, but the matter of sending him an actual letter has begun to pall. The thought no longer has the savour and vivid sparkle it had once. When one feels like that it is unwise to write. Letters should be spontaneous outpourings: they should never be undertaken merely from a sense of duty. We know that Bill wouldn't want to get a letter that was dictated by a feeling of obligation.

Another fortnight or so elapsing, it occurs to us that we have entirely forgotten what Bill said to us in that letter. We take it out and con it over. Delightful fellow! It is full of his own felicitous kinks of whim, though some of it sounds a little old-fashioned by now. It seems a bit stale, has lost some of its freshness and surprise. Better not answer it just yet, for Christmas will soon be here and we shall have to write then anyway. We wonder, can Bill hold out until Christmas without a letter?

We have been rereading some of those imaginary letters to Bill that have been dancing in our head. They are full of all sorts of fine stuff. If Bill ever gets them he will know how we love him. To use O. Henry's immortal joke, we have days of Damon and Knights of Pythias writing those uninked letters to Bill. A curious thought has come to us. Perhaps it would be better if we never saw Bill again. It is very difficult to talk to a man when you like him so much. It is much easier to write in the sweet fantastic strain. We are so inarticulate when face to face. If Bill comes to town we will leave word that we have gone away. Good old Bill! He will always be a precious memory.

A few days later a sudden frenzy sweeps over us, and though we have many pressing matters on hand, we mobilize pen and paper and literary shock troops and prepare to hurl several battalions at Bill. But, strangely enough, our utterance seems stilted and stiff. We have nothing to say. *My dear Bill,* we begin, *it seems a long time since we heard from you. Why don't you write? We still love you, in spite of all your shortcomings.*

That doesn't seem very cordial. We muse over the pen and nothing comes. Bursting with affection, we are unable to say a word.

Just then the 'phone rings. "Hello?" we say.

It is Bill, come to town unexpectedly.

"Good old fish!" we cry, ecstatic. "Meet you at the corner of Tenth and Chestnut in five minutes."

We tear up the unfinished letter. Bill will never know how much we love him. Perhaps it is just as well. It is very embarrassing to have your friends know how you feel about them. When we meet him we will be a little bit on our guard. It would not be well to be betrayed into any extravagance of cordiality.

And perhaps a not altogether false little story could be written about a man who never visited those most dear to him, because it hurt him so to say good-bye when he had to leave.

—Essays

3. FOOD AND WINE

I have found much to admire in American civilization, and equally much that has been a disappointment. Among the disappointments is the American, and western, war with the senses. The very term "the lower senses" implies a note of contempt, of disparagement, meaning that there is a higher one, though what that higher one is no one has made quite clear.

One of the most notoriously underrated and disparaged senses is that of taste, or eating. We denounce it as one of the "lower" carnal senses, and then keep on eating apologetically, pretending it is beneath our notice. What actually happens is that you either forget your philosophy and enjoy your gravy, or remember your philosophy and with a sense of humiliation swallow it. Most of us do the former. Such a "philosophy," having no practical application, therefore becomes "idle" as in fact academic philosophy has been proud of being all along.

An Oriental differs from this. He agrees that the life of the senses is all we know and all we are likely to know, but if this is the case, why not take the senses seriously? Let me give an example of Oriental enthusiasm about food. The greatest ancient Chinese poet, Ch'u Yuan (343–290 B.C.), was once in great despondency, so much so that he was struggling with the question of committing suicide. He therefore wrote a poem to persuade himself that it was good to live. In "The Great Summons," he urged his Soul to come back and not depart from his body. He pictured to his Soul the fearful caverns and wildernesses to be traveled in death; but he also used a more seductive device —he reviewed for his Soul the many good things of this earthly life, like food and wine and beautiful girls and music. One of the most convincing arguments for his Soul to remain in this earthly abode was the vast and rich variety of food possible:

> *O Soul, come back to joys beyond telling!*
> *Where thirty cubits high at harvest-time*
> *The corn is stacked;*
> *Where pies are cooked of millet and bearded-maize.*
> *Guests watch the steaming bowls*

And sniff the pungency of peppered herbs.
The cunning cook adds slices of bird-flesh,
Pigeon and yellow heron and black-crane.
They taste the badger-stew.
O Soul, come back to feed on foods you love!

Next are brought
Fresh turtle, and sweet chicken cooked in cheese
Pressed by the men of Ch'u.
And pickled suckling-pig
And flesh of whelps floating in liver-sauce
With salad of minced radishes in brine;
All served with that hot spice of southernwood
The land of Wu supplies.
O Soul, come back to choose the meats you love! [1]

Ch'u Yuan goes on with a more extended list of all the glories of
living.

I have not been able to find much similar writing in English prose
or poetry. If the Americans are good eaters, their poets have not turned
it into account. Of all American writers, the author of "The Autocrat
of the Breakfast Table" was the one most likely to discourse on steaks,
mutton chops and the mixing of salads. On food he was silent; and he
even "blushed to say" that he drank black tea. Holmes, the urbane *bon
vivant,* the lover of liquids, might have given some expression to the
ecstasies of eating either oyster stew or lobster salad. But he didn't, even
though he lived in Boston.

What shame, what sense of humiliation, due I believe to a Puritan
conscience, has prevented some great writer from writing a satisfactory
description of a good dinner, heartily eaten by men with taste, with
finesse, with love and respect and enthusiasm for the fuming wonders
on the table? I would not look for it in Emerson anyway. Bronson
Alcott couldn't have it in his Con-Sociate Family. As for Thoreau, he
was afraid to dash the hopes of a morning with a cup of coffee! "I
believe," he wrote in *Walden,* "that water is the only drink for a wise

[1] Reprinted from *Translations from the Chinese* by Arthur Waley, by permission of
Alfred A. Knopf, Inc. Copyright, 1919, 1941, by Alfred A. Knopf, Inc.

man; wine is not so noble a liquor; and think of dashing the hopes of a morning with a cup of warm coffee, or of an evening with a dish of tea!" He was so occupied with his "higher laws"! "Not that food which entereth the mouth defileth a man, but the appetite with which it is eaten. It is neither the quality nor the quantity, but the devotion to sensual savors; when that which is eaten is not a viand to sustain our animal, or inspire our spiritual life, but food for the worms that possess us . . . The wonder is how they, how you and I, can live this slimy beastly life, eating and drinking."

"Cookery is the greatest art in the world—next to poetry, and much better appreciated," says Grayson. "Think how easy it is to find a poet who will turn you a presentable sonnet, and how difficult it is to find a cook who will turn you an edible steak." [2]

Grayson was a poet, though he didn't know it. Would not American life be richer if there were more Graysons to call our attention to the good things of this life, common things which we already have, and be thankful for them? Where is the masterpiece on Thanksgiving, yet to be written in the style of Ch'u Yuan?

There is really a paradox about living for Christians. The orthodox attitude seems to be, "We suffer on earth, but we are going to enjoy ourselves in heaven"—or so most Christians believe. The Christian teaching seems often to be, avoid pleasures on earth and ye may not have to avoid them in heaven. Emerson once wrote about a preacher's conception of heaven, "We are to have *such* a good time as the sinners have now. . . . You sin now, we shall sin by and by; we would sin now, if we could; not being successful, we expect our revenge tomorrow." [3] The Mohammedans do the same; they delay their enjoyment of the senses till they are in heaven, where they are promised good wine, luscious fruits, savory meats and a bevy of beautiful dancing houris with dimpled cheeks. This seems bad sense; it seems simpler, and safer, to eat one guinea-fowl now on earth than wait for two in heaven tomorrow. Can one not combine laying up treasures in heaven with playing up pleasures on earth? Benjamin Franklin was wiser than most Americans. He looked forward to sharing heaven with Madame Brillon where they would eat "apples of Paradise toasted with butter

[2] *Adventures in Understanding,* III.
[3] Essay on "Compensation."

and nutmeg," but that did not prevent him from eating a hearty break-fast with "four dishes of tea with cream, one or two buttered toasts and slices of hung beef."

I sometimes think it would be wonderful if we could have a sixth and a seventh sense, as shown by the bat or the emperor moth or the homing pigeon. But to have five, and then artificially to cut them down to three or four does not seem to me the mark of wisdom. A man might just as well put out his eyes in order the better to contemplate spiritual laws! The whole war with the senses seems so senseless. It can quite well be that some of the most talkative western philosophers have never known the use of their tongues. And any writer who talks about the wonders of smell (of certain flowers, for instance) in recalling the emotions and pictures of childhood without including the smell of fresh, home-made bread or biscuits must be something of an impostor, or through forgetfulness he leaves a wide crack in his cuirass for my attack.

It is impossible to read any volume of Grayson and escape Harriet's pumpkin pies. The subject may turn up almost any time—at the end of a mountain walk, upon the return from a stay of weeks in a hospital; I forget whether it helped his appreciation of Marcus Aurelius, but it may well have. I think we have been quite consistently spiritual so far, and can take five minutes to watch Grayson eating on his return from the hospital.

The Pumpkin Pie

by David Grayson

At dinner on that unforgettable occasion there appeared in all its glory the most perfect pumpkin pie that ever I saw in my life. It was like a full moon, crimped about with little flaky clouds of piecrust, and being just from the oven—I *hate* clammy pies!—it gave off the ambrosia of the gods. Nowhere else on earth, save in New England, has pumpkin pie reached the final stage of perfection: for in New England, by one of those daring incongruities or disharmonies that mark the highest art, it is often not made of pumpkin at all, but of squash.

There it was, then, reposing in all its refulgence of golden glory upon our largest dinner plate. Little brown and yellow bubbles had worked upon its surface a kind of autumnal pattern, and the crinkled rim of crust about it was exactly of the right color to tempt the eye, for it promised to melt in the mouth.

"A wonderful pie," said I to Harriet.

"Wait until you taste it," said she.

So she drew the knife across it and cut out and lifted a generous slice—I give my word it was all of two inches thick!—and having placed it carefully upon a little plate, passed it along to me. There it was, a deep, luscious yellow, shading to orange, all warm and moist and rich and full of ravishing odors.

"This surely," said I, "is one of the great moments of life."

"Ridiculous," said Harriet, "eat it, eat it!"

"Slowly, slowly," said I, "one thing at a time. This is no occasion for usurpation by any one of the senses. This is not merely for tasting but for smelling and seeing, and, I think, for touching also——"

"Don't touch it! Eat it!"

"I expect also," said I, "if one's hearing were sufficiently acute—say as good as a honeybee's—he could also find keen enjoyment in listening to what is going on inside of this delectable pie——"

"I never saw your like," interrupted Harriet.

"All the faint little bubblings and boilings and dissolvings and settlings left over from the oven. He could see, too, if his eyes were perfect, the delicate aroma, the veritable spirit—one might call it the animate mist—rising from this pie——"

"Stop, stop!"

"As I said, the animate mist of the pie, charged with the spices of Araby, rising out of its delicious hidden recesses——"

"When *are* you going to eat that pie?"

"When I have enjoyed it sufficiently beforehand," said I to Harriet. "When I have reached the appropriate place in the ritual. Let me ask you this: is there any point in taking less enjoyment out of nature than one is capable of doing? Why walk on one leg when you have two? Or use one sense when you have five? In this degenerate and greedy age, are we grown to be savages, willing to bolt our beauty?"

"And," interposed Harriet with spirit, "philosophize until our pie is cold."

"And," continued I, "merely eat our pie?"

I found myself waving my fork in the air. The last remark of Harriet much impressed me; it was extremely sensible. So I fell to —as the unctuous older writers used to say—and without further excursions into philosophy or poetry ate every crumb of my triangle of pie.

I have thought since how I could express the sensations of that blissful moment, and have decided that language is a beggarly medium, wholly incapable, whether with adjectives, verbs, or nouns, of giving even a hazy conception of what I was experiencing. My only recourse is to ask any possible reader of these lines to think back, carefully, along the whole course of his life and recall the moment of his greatest gustatory adventure, the most poignant thrill that the art of cookery ever gave him, and let me assure him that my experience at dinner with that perfect pumpkin pie was equal to, or possibly greater than, his noblest moment.

"Well," said I, lifting at length my napkin, "this has been one of the notable incidents of my career."

"Ridiculous!" commented Harriet.

"I shall never forget it," said I. "Heaven has no greater bliss for the souls of the saved!"

With such evidences as these, how can I doubt the completeness of my recovery?

—*Adventures in Solitude* (XV)

Holmes with his jovial humor, however, had a good deal to say about wine.

"There are forms and stages of alcoholic exaltation which, in themselves, and without regard to their consequences, might be considered as positive improvements of the persons affected. When the sluggish intellect is roused, the slow speech quickened, the cold nature warmed, the latent sympathy developed, the flagging spirit kindled,—before the trains of thought become confused, or the will perverted, or the muscles relaxed,—just at the moment when the whole human zoöphyte flowers out like a full-blown rose, and is ripe for the subscription-paper or the contribution-box,—it would be hard to say that a man was, at that very time, worse, or less to be loved, than when driving a hard bargain with all his meaner wits about him. The difficulty is, that the alcoholic virtues don't wash; but until the water takes their colors out, the tints are very much like those of the true celestial stuff." (*The Autocrat of the Breakfast Table.*)

He went on with his defense of sensible drinking by warning his hearers not to insult "the first miracle wrought by the Founder of our religion."

"Among the gentlemen that I have known, few, if any, were ruined by drinking. My few drunken acquaintances were generally ruined before they became drunkards. The habit of drinking is often a vice, no doubt,—sometimes a misfortune,—as when an almost irresistible hereditary propensity exists to indulge in it,—but oftenest of all a *punishment*.

"Empty heads,—heads without ideas in wholesome variety and sufficient number to furnish food for the mental clockwork,—ill-regulated heads, where the faculties are not under the control of the will,—these are the ones that hold the brains which their owners are so apt to tamper with, by introducing the appliances we have been talking about. Now, when a gentleman's brain is empty or ill-regulated, it is, to a great extent, his own fault; and so it is simple retribution . . ."

The happiest comment seems to be the following, with its inimitable digressions:

"Let us praise it for its color and fragrance and social tendency."

BY OLIVER WENDELL HOLMES

—All this, however, is not what I was going to say. Here am I, suppose, seated—we will say at a dinner-table—alongside of an intelligent Englishman. We look in each other's faces,—we exchange a dozen words. One thing is settled: we mean not to offend each other, —to be perfectly courteous,—more than courteous; for we are the entertainer and the entertained, and cherish particularly amiable feelings to each other. The claret is good; and if our blood reddens a little with its warm crimson, we are none the less kind for it.

—I don't think people that talk over their victuals are like to say anything very great, especially if they get their heads muddled with strong drink before they begin jabberin'.

The Bombazine uttered this with a sugary sourness, as if the words had been steeped in a solution of acetate of lead.—The boys of my time used to call a hit like this a "side-winder."

—I must finish this woman.—

Madam,—I said,—the Great Teacher seems to have been fond of talking as he sat at meat. Because this was a good while ago, in a far-off place, you forget what the true fact of it was,—that those were real dinners, where people were hungry and thirsty, and where you met a very miscellaneous company. Probably there was a great deal of loose talk among the guests; at any rate, there was always wine, we may believe.

Whatever may be the hygienic advantages or disadvantages of wine, —and I for one, except for certain particular ends, believe in water, and, I blush to say it, in black tea,—there is no doubt about its being the grand specific against dull dinners. A score of people come together in all moods of mind and body. The problem is, in the space of one hour, more or less, to bring them all into the same condition of slightly exalted life. Food alone is enough for one person, perhaps,— talk, alone, for another; but the grand equalizer and fraternizer, which works up the radiators to their maximum radiation, and the absorbents to their maximum receptivity, is now just where it was when

The conscious water saw its Lord and blushed,

—when six great vessels containing water, the whole amounting to more than a hogshead-full, were changed into the best of wine. . . .

The longer I live, the more I am satisfied of two things: first, that the truest lives are those that are cut rose-diamond-fashion, with many facets answering to the many-planed aspects of the world about them; secondly, that society is always trying in some way or other to grind us down to a single flat surface. It is hard work to resist this grinding-down action.—Now give me a chance. Better eternal and universal abstinence than the brutalities of those days that made wives and mothers and daughters and sisters blush for those whom they should have honored, as they came reeling home from their debauches! Yet better even excess than lying and hypocrisy; and if wine is upon all

our tables, let us praise it for its color and fragrance and social tendency, so far as it deserves, and not hug a bottle in the closet and pretend not to know the use of a wine-glass at a public dinner! I think
you will find that people who honestly mean to be true really contradict themselves much more rarely than those who try to be "consistent." But a great many things we say can be made to appear
contradictory, simply because they are partial views of a truth, and
may often look unlike at first, as a front view of a face and its profile
often do.

—The Professor at the Breakfast Table (II)

4. TEA AND TOBACCO

A man has no right to tamper with his machine, described by the
Autocrat as the seventy-year clock. Tic-tac! tic-tac! it goes, sounding
the beat of life. In general this clock is pretty well made; it is set at
birth, and if not unduly tampered with, runs for seventy years without more than minor readjustments. Comparing it with a Swiss watch,
a radio set, or a gramophone, one cannot complain of the workmanship. When a man tampers with his clock, whether by inordinate
consumption of liquor or by inordinate ambition and hard work, the
sin is the same. The clock begins to rattle, loses its even rhythm, skips
a beat. That is the time when the clock gets nervous and develops
hypochondria and complains of its maker. The clock gets sick, and
in its morbid states of depression, all looks dark around it, and the
sweet serenity of its pendulum movement becomes a lackadaisical,
automatic, meaningless drift as if it were hanging on to life by compulsion, or else it gets into a sudden mad and hurried pace as if
consciously to help itself run down the sooner.

But one has every right to all contrivances, appliances, conveniences,
and helps to tranquillity of spirit. Clearly, human civilization has provided two of these helps: tea and tobacco. It is such a pity that Americans do not know that peace of mind and tranquillity of spirit achieved
by a cup of good lungching tea. It is doubtful whether the threepenny
tea tax during the American War of Independence when the "Mistresses of Families" in Boston pledged themselves to banish tea from
their own tables, was the sole cause of this insensitivity to this pleasure

of the spirit. True, as Agnes Repplier says,[4] that trumpery threepence was the match which ignited the Revolutionary fire. The students of Harvard College resolved to use no more of the "pernicious herb." But that perhaps is not the whole story. If they didn't stop it, they would have drunk black English tea anyway. It is altogether a different thing we are talking about.

John Adams drank a tankard of hard cider every morning, so I am informed, and though he loved tea, I doubt he would have been satisfied with less than a tankard. No, tea drinking belongs to another realm of the spirit, a realm of slow sips and the good company of like-minded friends devoted to banishment of worries. We may as well forget about it here.

But there is the pipe, which is the Red Indian's gift to civilization.

Among the moderns, I find Christopher Morley is the one who consistently keeps up the essayist tradition of looking along the wayside for the little things of everyday life and rendering them enjoyable with meaning. Here is Christopher Morley on "The Last Pipe."

"I define life as a process of the Will-to-Smoke."

BY CHRISTOPHER MORLEY

The sensible man smokes (say) sixteen pipefuls a day, and all differ in value and satisfaction. In smoking there is, thank heaven, no law of diminishing returns. I may puff all day long until I nigresce with the fumes and soot, but the joy loses no savor by repetition. It is true that there is a peculiar blithe rich taste in the first morning puffs, inhaled after breakfast. (Let me posit here the ideal conditions for a morning pipe as I know them.) After your bath, breakfast must be spread in a chamber of eastern exposure, let there be hominy and cream, and if possible, brown sugar. There follow scrambled eggs, shirred to a lemon-yellow with toast sliced in triangles, fresh, unsalted butter, and Scotch bitter marmalade. Let there be without fail a platter of hot bacon, curly, juicy, fried to the debatable point where softness is overlaid with the faintest crepitation of crackle, of crispyness. If hot

From *Essays,* copyright, 1928, Christopher Morley. Published by J. B. Lippincott Company.

[4] *To Think of Tea!* p. 127.

Virginia corn pone is handy, so much the better. And coffee, two-thirds hot milk, also with brown sugar. It must be permissible to call for a second serving of the scrambled eggs; or, if this is beyond the budget, let there be a round of judiciously grilled kidneys, with mayhap a sprinkle of mushrooms, grown in chalky soil. That is the kind of breakfast they used to serve in Eden before the fall of man and the invention of innkeepers with their crass formulæ.

After such a breakfast, if one may descend into a garden of plain turf, mured about by an occluding wall, with an alley of lime trees for sober pacing: then and there is the fit time and place for the first pipe of the day. Pack your mixture in the bowl; press it lovingly down with the cushion of the thumb; see that the draught is free—and then for your *säckerhets tändstickor!* A day so begun is well begun, and sin will flee your precinct. Shog, vile care! The smoke is cool and blue and tasty on the tongue; the arch of the palate is receptive to the fume; the curling vapor ascends the chimneys of the nose. Fill your cheeks with the excellent cloudy reek, blow it forth in twists and twirls. The first pipe! . . .

This is the schedule I vouch for:

> After breakfast: 2 pipes
> At luncheon: 2 pipes
> Before dinner: 2 pipes
> Between dinner and bed: 10 to 12 pipes
> (Cigars and cigarettes as occasion may require.)

The matter of smoking after dinner requires consideration. If your meal is a heavy, stupefying anodyne, retracting all the humane energies from the skull in a forced abdominal mobilization to quell a plethora of food into subjection and assimilation, there is no power of speculation left in the top storeys. You sink brutishly into an armchair, warm your legs at the fire, and let the leucocytes and phagocytes fight it out. At such times smoking becomes purely mechanical. You imbibe and exhale the fumes automatically. The choicest aromatic blends are mere fuel. Your eyes see, but your brain responds not. The vital juices, generous currents, or whatever they are that animate the intelligence, are down below hatches fighting furiously to annex and drill into submission the alien and distracting mass of food that you have taken on board. They are like stevedores, stowing the cargo for portability. A little later, however, when this excellent work is accomplished, the bosun may trill his whistle, and the deck hands can be summoned back to the navigating bridge. The mind casts off its corporeal hawsers and puts out to sea. You begin once more to live as a rational composition of reason, emotion, and will. The heavy dinner postpones and stultifies this desirable state. Let it then be said that light dining is best: a little fish or cutlets, white wine, macaroni and cheese, ice cream and coffee. Such a régime restores the animal health, and puts you in vein for a continuance of intellect.

Smoking is properly an intellectual exercise. It calls forth the choicest qualities of mind and soul. It can only be properly conducted by a being in full possession of the five wits. For those who are in pain, sorrow, or grievous perplexity it operates as a sovereign consoler, a balm and balsam to the harassed spirit; it calms the fretful, makes jovial the peevish. Better than any ginseng in the herbal, does it combat fatigue and old age. Well did Stevenson exhort virgins not to marry men who do not smoke.

Now we approach the crux and pinnacle of this inquirendo into the art and mystery of smoking. That is to say, the last pipe of all before the so-long indomitable intellect abdicates, and the body succumbs to weariness.

No man of my acquaintance has ever given me a satisfactory definition of *living*. An alternating systole and diastole, says physiology. Chlorophyl becoming xanthophyl, says botany. These stir me not. I define life as a process of the Will-to-Smoke: recurring periods of consciousness in which the enjoyability of smoking is manifest, interrupted by intervals of recuperation.

Now if I represent the course of this process by a graph (the coordinates being Time and the Sense-of-by-the-Smoker-enjoyed-Satisfaction) the curve ascends from its origin in a steep slant, then drops away abruptly at the recuperation interval. This is merely a teutonic and pedantic mode of saying that the best pipe of all is the last one smoked at night. It is the penultimate moment that is always the happiest. The sweetest pipe ever enjoyed by the skipper of the *Hesperus* was the one he whiffed just before he was tirpitzed by the poet on that angry reef.

The best smoking I ever do is about half past midnight, just before "my eyelids drop their shade," to remind you again of your primary school poets. After the toils, rebuffs, and exhilarations of the day, after piaffing busily on the lethal typewriter or *schreibmaschine* for some hours, a drowsy languor begins to numb the sense. In dressing gown and slippers I seek my couch; Ho, Lucius, a taper! and some solid, invigorating book for consideration. My favorite is the General Catalogue of the Oxford University Press. . . .

With due care I fill, pack, and light the last pipe of the day, to be smoked reverently and solemnly in bed. The thousand brain-murdering interruptions are over. The gentle sibilance of air drawn through the glowing nest of tobacco is the only sound. With reposeful heart I turn to some favorite entry in my well-loved catalogue. . . .

One o'clock is about to chime in the near-by steeple, but my pipe and curiosity are now both going strong. . . .

But I dare not force my hobbies on you further. One man's meat is another's caviar. I dare not even tell you what my favorite tobaccos are, for recently when I sold to a magazaine a very worthy and excellent poem entitled "My Pipe," mentioning the brands I delight to honor, the editor made me substitute fictitious names for my dearly loved blends. He said that sound editorial policy forbids mentioning commercial products in the text of the magazine.

But tobacco, thank heaven, is not merely a "commercial product." Let us call on Salvation Yeo for his immortal testimony:

"When all things were made none was made better than this; to be a lone man's companion, a bachelor's friend, a hungry man's food, a sad man's cordial, a wakeful man's sleep, and a chilly man's fire, sir; while for stanching of wounds, purging of rheum, and settling of the stomach, there's no herb like unto it under the canopy of heaven."

And by this time the bowl is naught but ash. Even my dear General Catalogue begins to blur before me. Slip it under the pillow; gently and kindly lay the pipe in the candlestick, and blow out the flame. The window is open wide: the night rushes in. I see a glimpse of stars . . . a distant chime . . . and fall asleep with the faint pungence of the Indian herb about me.

—Essays

5. HOBBIES

Every man has his hobby. It may be hiking, boating, riding or any other kind of sport. Of these, I believe walking is the oldest known to man, the most natural and conducive to health, and still the best. The pleasure of walking, of putting one leg forward, then the other, while requiring no skill, has a pleasure of smooth rhythm, of calming satisfaction, of intensified activity of the lungs and the whole bodily system, which is more allied to tea and tobacco as a means of spiritual comfort and release. In addition, of course, there is always the charm of the untrodden path, the smell of the hedgerow and the distant view of hills, or a meandering river or peaceful forests, as the case may be.

Again, for describing voluptuously the pleasure of putting a few miles behind us by alternately shifting our legs, we have to go to Christopher Morley. In the beginning of the essay on "The Art of Walking" he reminds us of a good number of great English writers who were also great walkers. The list is impressive. Wordsworth was perhaps one of the greatest walkers, hiking through France to the Alps, Italy and back. In 1797 Coleridge tramped from Nether Stowey to Racedown, a full 40 miles, to meet William and Dorothy Wordsworth. De Quincey describes a 40-mile all-night walk from Bridgewater to Bristol. Goldsmith tramped the Continent for two years. And we can go on with Hazlitt, Tennyson, Fitzgerald, Matthew Arnold, Carlyle, Kingsley, Meredith, Richard Jeffries, and the great walker Leslie Stephen; in our own times, W. H. Davies, Hilaire Belloc, E. V. Lucas, etc. "Now your true walker is mightily 'curious in the world,'" says Morley, "and he goes upon his way zealous to sate himself with a thousand quaintnesses. When he writes a book he fills it full of food, drink, tobacco, the scent of sawmills on sunny afternoons, and arrivals at inns late at night." In the conclusion Morley soliloquizes in his own vein, which it would be unfair to describe as less than rapturous. The selection is useful also for including material on Vachel Lindsay, otherwise not easy to get.

"In our old trousers and our easy shoes, with pipe and stick, we can do fifteen miles between lunch and dinner, and glorify the ways of God to man."

BY CHRISTOPHER MORLEY

Ungenerous hosts have cozened Vachel by begging him to recite his poems at the beginning of each course, in the meantime getting on with their eating; but despite the naïveté of his eagerness to sing, there is a plain and manly simplicity about Vachel that delights us all. We like to know that here is a poet who has wrestled with poverty, who never wrote a Class Day poem at Harvard, who has worn frayed collars or none at all, and who lets the barber shave the back of his neck. We like to know that he has tramped the ties in Georgia, harvested in Kansas, been fumigated in New Jersey, and lives contented in Illinois. Four weeks a year he lives as the darling of the cisalleghany Browning Societies, but he is always glad to get back to Springfield and resume his robes as the local Rabindranath. If he ever buys an automobile I am positive it will be a Ford. Here is *homo americanus,* one of ourselves, who never wore spats in his life.

But even the plain man may see visions. Walking on crowded city streets at night, watching the lighted windows, delicatessen shops, peanut carts, bakeries, fish stalls, free lunch counters piled with crackers and saloon cheese, and minor poets struggling home with the Saturday night marketing—he feels the thrill of being one, or at least two-thirds, with this various, grotesque, pathetic, and surprising humanity. The sense of fellowship with every other walking biped, the full-blooded understanding that Whitman and O. Henry knew in brimming measure, comes by gulps and twinges to almost all. That is the essence of Lindsay's feeling about life. He loves crowds, companionship, plenty of sirloin and onions, and seeing his name in print. He sings and celebrates the great symbols of our hodge-podge democracy: ice-cream soda, electrical sky-signs, Sunday-school picnics, the movies, Mark Twain. In the teeming ooze and ocean bottoms of our atlantic humanity he finds rich corals and rainbow shells, hospitality, reverence, love, and beauty.

This is the sentiment that makes a merry pedestrian, and Vachel has scrutineered and scuffled through a dozen states, lightening larders and puzzling the worldly. Afoot and penniless is his technique—"stopping when he had a mind to, singing when he felt inclined to"—and begging his meals and bed. I suppose he has had as many free meals as any American citizen; and this is how he does it, copied from his little pamphlet used on many a road:

RHYMES TO BE TRADED FOR BREAD

Being new verses by Nicholas Vachel Lindsay, Springfield, Illinois, June, 1912, printed expressly as a substitute for money.

This book is to be used in exchange for the necessities of life on a tramp-journey from the author's home town, through the West and back, during which he will observe the following rules:

(1) Keep away from the cities.
(2) Keep away from the railroads.
(3) Have nothing to do with money. Carry no baggage.
(4) Ask for dinner about quarter after eleven.
(5) Ask for supper, lodging, and breakfast about quarter of five.
(6) Travel alone.
(7) Be neat, truthful, civil, and on the square.
(8) Preach the Gospel of Beauty.

In order to carry out the last rule there will be three exceptions to the rule against baggage. (1) The author will carry a brief printed statement, called "The Gospel of Beauty." (2) He will carry this book of rhymes for distribution. (3) Also he will carry a small portfolio with pictures, etc., chosen to give an outline of his view of the history of art, especially as it applies to America. . . .

The motors have done this for us at least, that as they have made the highways their own beyond dispute, walking will remain the mystic and private pleasure of the secret and humble few. For us the byways, the footpaths, and the pastures will be sanctified and sweet. Thank heaven there are still gentle souls uncorrupted by the victrola and the limousine. In our old trousers and our easy shoes, with pipe and stick, we can do our fifteen miles between lunch and dinner, and glorify the ways of God to man.

And sometimes, about two o'clock of an afternoon (these spells come most often about half an hour after lunch), the old angel of peregrination lifts himself up in me, and I yearn and wamble for a season afoot. When a blue air is moving keenly through bare boughs this angel is most vociferous. I gape wanly round the lofty citadel where I am pretending to earn the Monday afternoon envelope. The filing case, thermostat, card index, typewriter, automatic telephone: these ingenious anodynes avail me not. Even the visits of golden nymphs, sweet ambassadors of commerce, who rustle in and out of my room with memoranda, mail, manuscripts, aye, even these light-foot figures fail to charm. And the mind goes out to the endless vistas of streets, roads, fields, and rivers that summon the wanderer with laughing voice. Somewhere a great wind is scouring the hillsides; and once upon a time a man set out along the Great North Road to walk to Royston in the rain. . . .

Grant us, O Zeus! the tingling tremor of thigh and shank that comes of a dozen sturdy miles laid underheel. Grant us "fine walking on the hills in the direction of the sea"; or a winding road that tumbles down to some Cotswold village. Let an inn parlor lie behind red curtains, and a table be drawn toward the fire. Let there be a loin of cold beef, an elbow of yellow cheese, a tankard of dog's nose. Then may we prop our Bacon's Essays against the pewter and study those mellow words: "Certainly it is heaven upon earth to have a man's mind move in charity, rest in providence, and turn upon the poles of truth." *Haec studia pernoctant nobiscum, peregrinantur, rusticantur.*

—Essays

Chapter XI

NATURE

I. SOCIETY AND NATURE

WHEN one's senses are fully awakened, however, the true feast is neither food nor wine, nor the salutary aroma of tobacco, but nature itself. Only people who live on cement streets and carpeted floors can ever forget the inherent drama in nature and, by mere habits of city living, become nature-blind. The drama of nature is so rich, intense and variegated and it envelops our being so completely by touching the air we breathe and the colors we see, that it seems as astounding for a man not to feel it as for a fog-bound Londoner not to be aware of the fog. To one who is not nature-blind, any hour in the open will be drama enough, and the drama is fast and always changing. Beauty is merely nature in action. For what is this heaven and earth except a vast play of forces, of rays shooting, waves vibrating, colors changing, vapors rising, mists descending, clouds sailing, waters falling, the sun setting, the moon rising, grass growing and all things aspiring to live in the light of the sun? Not a moment passes but the subtle and delicate balance of forces is changed, the very air we breathe changes its odor as it passes over the country, shadows move, colors deepen or brighten, and woolly masses of clouds race against one another at different speeds and pile up or disperse like children at play, reminding us of the original of Michelangelo's *Creation*. A lot of Taoist priests have learned to watch this drama with unending pleasure and to "play with the sun and the moon, and gambol with the winds and clouds." The mystery of the universe is that we don't know it.

Perhaps half an hour in bed watching such drama is enough for a lesson, provided one has a bedroom window looking out on a valley in the East. Preferably the stage should be set with an outline of hills on the horizon, or still better, a line of hills running out to the sea. Your eyes are fixed on the formation of clouds in that lightening dawn heralding the approach of the morning sun. You know the earth has been asleep and in the next quarter of an hour the day is coming. How does the day come? The clouds feel it first. Not only are they going to experience a transmogrification of colors. They know they are going to start their journey for the day. Their very form depends on that delicate balance of air pressure and temperature, and is subtly responsive to its changes. Gradually, but quite perceptibly, the mists rise in response to the change in temperatures, while masses above still slumber on in their woolly sleep. All of a sudden the sky glows into a bright shimmer, and while your eyes have been momentarily turned elsewhere, the light of the sun strikes the valley and the hill tops with shafts of resplendent brightness. All hues change; the sky pales and the red crags and purple hills come out with greater clearness. The air begins to move and the march of the clouds begins. Where there was doom and death, there is now light and life. No one can witness this first shaft of the morning sun over a village and be unmoved. Sultan or pauper, scientist or grocer, our life depends upon it. That it is so beautiful to look at is a gratuitous gift of the Creator which makes me strongly suspect that God never meant to make men slave bread-earners merely, that all evidences considered, the universe is suspected of being designed as a pleasure garden.

Is modern man getting further away from nature? I doubt it. In spite of all that gloomy critics say about human degeneracy, I do not think that is the present trend of civilization. Civilization does not degenerate till it begins to adore effeminate living, and there is too much evidence of the worship of sports in America, of even physical toughness, and there are too many temptations and facilities for out-door living for me to accept the thesis that the American man or woman is becoming soft. Unless my observations betray me, there is more danger of overdevelopment of the body than of the mind in American schools and colleges. Even if we grant that driving in a car is an evil and is calculated to promote the progressive degeneration of the leg muscles, as some obtuse anthropologists have said, still one must admit that sitting or lounging lazily in the back seat of a car is better than in a soft-lighted hotel lounge, and that once on a road, there is always a chance that a man may be enticed into getting out and taking a five-minute walk in the woods and accidentally bump into a dogwood or find a maple leaf in his pocket. One of the greatest

contributions of the motor car to contemporary civilization is that it
brings the country closer to us and enables many city workers to have
homes in the country. Nothing is more obvious than the fact that
nature is the best healer of souls and that animal happiness, which is
a natural everyday fact common to birds and animals, has assumed
the proportions of a mystery and a philosophic riddle only when we
have lost touch with nature. "Last night a walk to the river with
Margaret [Fuller], and saw the moon broken in the water, interrogating, interrogating," wrote Emerson in an isolated entry in his notebooks. Those Transcendentalists were really good at opening their
pores to the silent influence of nature and recovering their health and
sanity of spirit. With Emerson and with a modern motor car, there
is no longer any excuse for a man not knowing the country today.

It is always a question of human society versus nature. Emerson
says in the essay on "Nature," "Cities give not the human senses room
enough. . . . My house stands in low land, with limited outlook, and
on the skirt of the village. But I go with my friend to the shore of
our little river, and with one stroke of the paddle I leave the village
politics and personalities, yes, and the world of villages and personalities, behind, and pass into a delicate realm of sunset and moonlight,
too bright for spotted man to enter without novitiate and probation."
Again he wrote (February 8, 1836), "Society seems noxious. I believe
that against these baleful influences Nature is the antidote. The man
comes out of the wrangle of the shop and office, and sees the sky and
the woods, and is a man again. He not only quits the cabal, but he
finds himself. But how few men see the sky and the woods!" So one
afternoon he went with Henry Thoreau to the cliff. The April weather
was misty, but warm and pleasant, and he seemed to "drink in gladness." At night he went out into the dark and saw a glimmering star
and heard a frog, and Nature seemed to say to him, "Well, do not
these suffice? Ponder it, Emerson, and not like the foolish world,
hanker after thunders and multitudes and vast landscapes, the sea
or Niagara." (*Journals,* April 26, 1838.) Or he went with John Very,
the mystic poet, to Edmund Hosmer's and Walden Pond. As he sat
on the bank of the Drop or God's Pond and saw the amplitude of the
little water and noted how the water seemed made for the wind and
the wind seemed made for the water, he said to his companion, "I
declare this world is so beautiful that I can hardly believe it exists."

It was always the effect of nature in changing the scale of values of life, in making him see the infinite smallness of man and his petty affairs, in seeing the stars "pouring satire on the pompous business of the day" (*Journals,* July 26, 1837). In the divine pleasures of walks on a June night, on a tedious and homely country road which night had transformed into Italy or Palmyra, he could put his life before him as a fact and stand aloof from its honor and shame. Man's life in the cities and its preoccupations always produced a warped sense of proportion, and his spirit became cramped. "I am afraid there is no morning in Chestnut Street," he says; "it is all full of rememberers, they shun each other's eyes, they are all wrinkled with memory of the tricks they have played, or mean to play, each other, of petty arts and aims all contracting and lowering their aspect and character." (*Journals,* September, 1854.)

Poets, we think, are often insane. Thoreau talked with a stranger woodchuck for over half an hour, and one of the longest entries in his *Journals* was about chasing a lost pig. Thoreau reflected, "But really he is no more obstinate than I. I cannot but respect his tactics and his independence. He will be he, and I may be I. . . . He has a strong will. He stands upon his idea." Whitman went tramping completely naked through the thickets and down a stream when he was staying with John Burroughs in New Jersey, and he thought he never got so close to Nature and Nature never got so close to him because his nakedness matched Nature's own. "It was too lazy, soothing, and joyous-equable to speculate about. Yet I might have thought somehow in this vein: Perhaps the *inner* never lost rapport we hold with earth, light, air, trees, etc., is not to be realized through eyes and mind only, but through the whole corporeal body, which I will not have blinded or bandaged any more than the eyes." (*Specimen Days,* Aug. 27, 1877.) But the sense is clearer when we read Whitman's *Song of Myself:*

I think I could turn and live with animals, they are so placid and
     self-contain'd;
I stand and look at them long and long.
They do not sweat and whine about their condition;
They do not lie awake in the dark and weep for their sins;
They do not make me sick discussing their duty to God;

Not one is dissatisfied—not one is demented with the mania of
  owning things;
Not one kneels to another, nor to his kind that lived thousands of
  years ago;
Not one is respectable or industrious over the whole earth.

  The point seems to be: when it comes to perfect health and a simple,
harmonious life, it is very much open to question whether human
beings have any advantage over the animals. It seems that, in the
over-civilized artificial life of a human community, man has often
drifted too far away from the simple laws of our natural being, and
the result is petty fears, petty jealousies, frustrated ambitions and—
unhappiness. This seems to suggest that we may borrow that freshness and moral rectitude from Nature by living in closer contact with
her, and recover that state of health and simplicity and content which
was our inherited right as animals until we lost it through civilization. Poets, thinkers, and writers have testified to this time and again.
"Really to see the sun rise or go down every day, so to relate ourselves
to a universal fact, would preserve us sane forever," Thoreau wrote in
Life Without Principle. "Surely, joy is the condition of life," he said
in *Excursions*—he means that joy is the condition of life in nature.
He could not hear the song of a cockerel without being reminded
that the universe was healthy and well, and drawing spiritual strength
from it. "In society you will not find health, but in nature. Unless our
feet at least stood in the midst of nature, all our faces would be pale
and livid. Society is always diseased, and the best is the most so.
There is no scent in it so wholesome as that of the pines, nor any
fragrance so penetrating and restorative as the life-everlasting in high
pastures. To him who contemplates a trait of natural beauty no harm
nor disappointment can come. The doctrines of despair, of spiritual
or political tyranny or servitude, were never taught by such as shared
the serenity of nature. . . . The spruce, the hemlock, and the pine will
not countenance despair. . . . Surely joy is the condition of life."
  One morning David Grayson went up a hill to track the scent of a
clump of pine-trees, and found himself sitting upon the floor cleanly
carpeted with brown pine-needles while all about was hung a tapestry
of green, and "At that moment, like a flame for clearness, I understood some of the deep and simple things of life, as that we are to be

like the friendly pines, and the elm trees, and the open fields, and reject no man, judge no man. Once, a long time ago, I read a sober treatise by one who tried to prove with elaborate knowledge that, upon the whole, good was triumphant in this world, and that probably there was a God, and I remember going out dully afterward upon a hill, for I was weighed down with a strange depression, and the world seemed to me a hard, cold, narrow place where good must be heavily demonstrated in books. And as I sat there the evening fell, a star or two came out in the clear blue sky, and suddenly it became all simple to me, so that I laughed aloud at that laborious big-wig for spending so many futile years in seeking doubtful proof of what he might have learned in one rare hour upon my hill. . . . As I came away from that place I knew I should never again be quite the same person I was before. . . . After I have been out about so long on such an adventure as this, something lets go inside of me, and I come out of the mountain—and yet know deeply that I have been where the bush was burning; and have heard the Voice of the Fire." [1]

2. THIS SENSE-FILLED EARTH

Perhaps academic philosophers never understood the problem of happiness, and never could, because of their refusal to notice that we have sensory organs for enjoying this life, because they were strictly "out of their senses." A philosopher, in a moment of intellectual lapse, may forgetfully agree with you that human happiness consists some-times of lying in the sun, but you see the sense of inhibition on his face and you know that when he is ready to *think,* his Reason will rebel against all this and he will cry down the folly and lack of in-tellectual perception of the unphilosophically-minded fellows like our-selves. Does the professor enjoy a hot bath and a good rub down, I wonder? Do not his pores open and luxuriate in warm sunshine ex-actly like ours? Is he not aware of physiology and biology and will he never admit that there is no way of getting out of this system of nerves, pores, sweat glands and instincts, in short, of this bodily heritage of ours which is more than a million years old? Since phi-losophy itself tells us that one hundred per cent of our knowledge comes from sensory experience itself, a philosophy which will not deal

[1] *Great Possessions,* III.

with the facts of sensory experience but will exile it beyond the occupation of one's mind must, *ipso facto,* be of no consequence to human life whatsoever.

"Vice," says Grayson, "is ever the senses gone astray." The emaciation of the true values of human life comes from the fact that "we experience described emotions," and "think prepared thoughts," that "we do not hear, but overhear" and live a poor, sad, second-rate existence. In other words, the true appreciation of things has gone out of us because, perhaps living too long in the city, our senses have lost contact with this sentient universe vibrant with colors and sights and sounds.

"The senses are the tools by which we lay hold upon the world: they are the implements of consciousness and growth. So long as they are used upon the good earth—used to wholesome weariness—they remain healthy, they yield enjoyment, they nourish growth; but let them once be removed from their natural employment and they turn and feed upon themselves, they seek the stimulation of luxury, they wallow in their own corruption, and finally, worn out, perish from off the earth which they have not appreciated." [1a]

William James, a trained physiologist and psychologist, was closer to the facts of human life when he counseled occasional retreat to the primitive existence on the "non-thinking, purely sensorial level." The English essayist, W. H. Hudson,[2] had described such an experience when he rode up the Patagonian wastes, which presented the appearance of a prehistoric bare desert, with no trees, animals or human beings in sight. Such a vast and completely silent desert created a weird effect on his mind. He was alone with the universe, confronted with empty time and space. He felt a state of "intense watchfulness, or alertness rather, with suspension of the higher intellectual faculties." His thinking had stopped; thought had become impossible. He had reverted to the mental state of the pure savage. As a matter of fact, it must have been like the state of a hunted deer, or a bloodhound, when the animal was alert with his whole being. He was the whole, sensorial animal again. Hudson spoke of a "strong feeling of elation." [3]

[1a] David Grayson, *Adventures in Contentment,* VI
[2] He was born of American Massachusetts parents in Argentina, and later lived in England.
[3] From *Idle Days in Patagonia,* by W. H. Hudson. Published by E. P. Dutton & Company, Inc., N. Y., and J. M. Dent & Sons, London.

William James commenting on this, says, "I am sorry for the boy or girl, or man or woman, who has never been touched by the spell of this mysterious sensorial life, with its irrationality, if you so like to call it, but [with] its vigilance and its supreme felicity. The holidays of life are its most significant portions because they are, or at least should be, covered with just this kind of magically irresponsible spell." [4]

But we need not take the extreme experience of Hudson as a case of mystic return to the savage state of our sensorial being. Every one has felt, and many poets have expressed, the feeling of sheer delight and happiness and emancipation when we return to Nature's world, when we open the pores of our sensory being and let Nature sink its impress on it. There is no mystery about such an experience. The ancient man is always in us, except that we seldom give our whole sensorial outfit free play. The way to get "close to nature" is simply to lie down on the ground and feel the smell of new broken soil and let the wind blow over your uncovered head, wafting the mingled smell of the thorny bush and lilac and pine. I give here three examples of how Whitman, through his sense of color, Thoreau through his sense of sound, and Grayson, through his nose, recovered a feeling of health and strength and an inner mystic happiness of reunion with Nature.

Whitman wrote in *Specimen Days: "Oct. 20 (1877).* A clear, crispy day—dry and breezy air, full of oxygen. Out of the sane, silent, beauteous miracles that envelop and fuse me—trees, water, grass, sunlight, and early frost—the one I am looking at most today is the sky. It has that delicate, transparent blue, peculiar to autumn, and the only clouds are little or larger white ones, giving their still and spiritual motion to the great concave. All through the earlier day (say from 7 to 11) it keeps a pure, yet vivid blue. But as noon approaches the color gets lighter, quite gray for two or three hours—then still paler for a spell, till sundown—which last I watch dazzling through the interstices of a knoll of big trees—darts of fire and a gorgeous show of light yellow, liver color and red, with a vast silver glaze askant on the water —the transparent shadows, shafts, sparkle, and vivid colors beyond all the paintings ever made.

"I don't know what or how, but it seems to me mostly owing to these

---

[4] "On a Certain Blindness in Human Beings," *Talks to Teachers on Psychology.* Copyright, 1939, Henry James. Permission Paul R. Reynolds & Son.

skies, (every now and then I think, while I have of course seen them every day of my life, I never really saw the skies before,) I have had this autumn some wondrously contented hours—may I not say perfectly happy ones? As I've read, Byron just before his death told a friend that he had known but three happy hours during his whole existence. Then there is the old German legend of the king's bell, to the same point. While I was out there by the wood, that beautiful sunset through the trees, I thought of Byron's and the bell story, and the notion started in me that I was having a happy hour. . . .

"What is happiness, anyhow? Is this one of its hours, or the like of it?—so impalpable—a mere breath, an evanescent tinge? I am not sure —so let me give myself the benefit of the doubt. Hast Thou, pellucid, in Thy azure depths, medicine for case like mine? (Ah, the physical shatter and troubled spirit of me the last three years.) And dost Thou subtly, mystically now drip it through the air invisibly upon me?"

Thoreau heard the distant drum beats at night and felt that the sound of the drums gave him an unspeakable unhappiness. "How can I go on, who have just stepped over such a bottomless skylight in the bog of my life. . . . It (a strain of music) teaches us again and again to trust the remotest and finest as the divinest instinct, and makes a dream our only real existence." When he heard the wind singing over telegraph wires it was to him the "Aeolian harp" of heaven. He wrote again and again on the philosophical import of the creak of crickets, an import which, because of our senses gone astray, we are seldom privileged to feel.

"First observe the creak of crickets. It is quite general amid these rocks. The song of only one is more interesting to me. It suggests lateness, but only as we come to a knowledge of eternity after some acquaintance with time. It is only late for all trivial and hurried pursuits. It suggests a wisdom mature, never late, being above all temporal considerations, which possesses the coolness and maturity of autumn amidst the aspiration of spring and the heats of summer. To the birds they say: 'Ah! you speak like children from impulse; Nature speaks through you; but with us it is ripe knowledge. The seasons do not revolve for us; we sing their lullaby.' So they chant, eternal, at the roots of the grass. It is heaven where they are, and their dwelling need not be *heaved* up. Forever the same, in May and in November (?). Serenely wise, their song has the security of prose. They have drunk

no wine but the dew. It is no transient love-strain, hushed when the
incubating season is past, but a glorifying of God and enjoying of him
forever. They sit aside from the revolution of the seasons. Their strain
is unvaried as Truth. Only in their saner moments do men hear the
crickets. . . ." (*Journals,* May 22, 1854.)

David Grayson's books seem to be a symphony of praise of this
sense-filled world and of the senses of smell, taste and hearing, particularly the sense of smell. His father, who was deaf, could smell an
Indian half a mile away, by snuffing the scent of the Indian's moccasin
leather and camp-fire wood. Grayson inherited this extraordinary sense
of smell himself; the first four chapters of *Great Possessions* are entirely
devoted to the odors of the earth.

The Well-flavored Earth

BY DAVID GRAYSON

For these many years, since I have lived here in the country, I
have had it in my mind to write something about the odor and taste
of this well-flavored earth. The fact is, both the sense of smell and the
sense of taste have been shabbily treated in the amiable rivalry of the
senses. Sight and hearing have been the swift and nimble brothers,
and sight especially, the tricky Jacob of the family, is keen upon the
business of seizing the entire inheritance, while smell, like hairy
Esau, comes late to the blessing, hungry from the hills, and willing to
trade its inheritance for a mess of pottage.

I have always had a kind of errant love for the improvident and
adventurous Esaus of the Earth—I think they smell a wilder fragrance
than I do, and taste sweeter things—and I have thought, therefore,
of beginning a kind of fragrant autobiography, a chronicle of all the
good odors and flavors that ever I have had in my life. . . .

My father before me had a singularly keen nose. I remember well
when I was a boy and drove with him in the wild North Country,
often through miles of unbroken forest, how he would sometimes break
a long silence, lift his head with sudden awareness, and say to me:

"David, I smell open fields."

In a few minutes we were sure to come to a settler's cabin, a log barn,
or a clearing. Among the free odors of the forest he had caught, afar
off, the common odors of the work of man.

When we were tramping or surveying in that country, I have seen him stop suddenly, draw in a long breath, and remark:

"Marshes," or, "A stream yonder."

Part of this strange keenness of sense, often noted by those who knew that sturdy old cavalryman, may have been based, as so many of our talents are, upon a defect. My father gave all the sweet sounds of the world, the voices of his sons, the songs of his daughters, to help free the Southern slaves. He was deaf.

It is well known that when one sense is defective the others fly to the rescue. . . .

I recall once on a wild Northern lake, when we were working along the shore in a boat, how he stopped suddenly and exclaimed:

"David, do you hear anything?"—for I, a boy, was ears for him in those wilderness places.

"No, Father. What is it?"

"Indians."

And, sure enough, in a short time I heard the barking of their dogs and we came soon upon their camp, where, I remember, they were drying deer meat upon a frame of poplar poles over an open fire. He told me that the smoky smell of the Indians, tanned buckskin, parched wild rice, and the like, were odors that carried far and could not be mistaken. . . . I think I inherited from my father something of the power of enjoyment he had from that sense, though I can never hope to become the accomplished smeller he was.

I am moved to begin this chronicle because of my joy this morning early—a May morning!—just after sunrise, when the shadows lay long and blue to the west and the dew was still on the grass, and I walked in the pleasant spaces of my garden. . . .

I went from clump to clump of the lilacs testing and comparing them with great joy and satisfaction. They vary noticeably in odor; the white varieties being the most delicate, while those tending to deep purple are the richest. Some of the newer double varieties seem less fragrant —and I have tested them now many times—than the old-fashioned single varieties which are nearer the native stock. . . .

I have felt the same defect in the cultivated roses. While the odors are rich, often of cloying sweetness, or even, as in certain white roses, having a languor as of death, they never for me equal the fragrance of the wild sweet rose that grows all about these hills, in old tangled fence rows, in the lee of meadow boulders, or by some unfrequented roadside. No other odor I know awakens quite such a feeling—light like a cloud, suggesting free hills, open country, sunny air; and none surely has, for me, such an after-call. A whiff of the wild rose will bring back in all the poignancy of sad happiness a train of ancient memories—old faces, old scenes, old loves—and the wild thoughts I had when a boy. The first week of the wild-rose blooming, beginning here about the twenty-fifth of June, is always to me a memorable time.

I was a long time learning how to take hold of nature, and think now with some sadness of all the life I lost in former years. The impression the earth gave me was confused: I was as one only half awake. A fine morning made me dumbly glad, a cool evening, after the heat of the day, and the work of it, touched my spirit restfully; but I could have explained neither the one nor the other. Gradually as I looked about me I began to ask myself, "Why is it that the sight of these common hills and fields gives me such exquisite delight? And if it is beauty, why is it beautiful? And if I am so richly rewarded by mere glimpses, can I not increase my pleasure with longer looks?"

I tried longer looks both at nature and at the friendly human creatures all about me. I stopped often in the garden where I was working, or loitered a moment in the fields, or sat down by the roadside, and thought intently what it was that so perfectly and wonderfully surrounded me; and thus I came to have some knowledge of the Great Secret. It was, after all, a simple matter, as such matters usually are when we penetrate them, and consisted merely in shutting out all other impressions, feelings, thoughts, and concentrating the full energy of the attention upon what it was that I saw or heard at that instant.

At one moment I would let in all the sounds of the earth, at another all the sights. So we practice the hand at one time, the foot at another, or learn how to sit or to walk, and so acquire new grace for the whole body. Should we do less in acquiring grace for the spirit? It will astonish one who has not tried it how full the world is of sounds commonly unheard, and of sights commonly unseen, but in their nature, like the smallest blossoms, of a curious perfection and beauty....

What a new and wonderful world opened to me then! My takings of nature increased tenfold, a hundredfold, and I came to a new acquaintance with my own garden, my own hills, and all the roads and fields around about—and even the town took on strange new meanings for me. I cannot explain it rightly, but it was as though I had found a new earth here within the old one, but more spacious and beautiful than any I had known before. I have thought, often and often, that this world we live in so dumbly, so carelessly, would be more glorious than the tinsel heaven of the poets if only we knew how to lay hold upon it, if only we could win that complete command of our own lives which is the end of our being.

For it is only the sense of the spirit of life, whether in nature or in other human beings, that lifts men above the beasts and curiously leads them to God, who is the spirit both of beauty and of friendliness. I say truly, having now reached the point in my life where it seems to me I care only for writing that which is most deeply true for me, that I rarely walk in my garden or upon the hills of an evening without thinking of God. It is in my garden that all things become clearer to me, even that miracle whereby one who has offended may still see God; and this I think a wonderful thing. In my garden I understand dimly why evil is in the world, and in my garden learn how transitory it is.

—Great Possessions (I)

What is true of the sense of smell is true of all the other senses of sight, hearing, taste, and touch. We cannot go through all these. But I cannot refrain from letting Helen Keller tell us about the wonders of seeing and knowing how to use our eyes. Her essay "Three Days to See" is, I think, an American gem and would be worth reproducing in full, but here are extracts.[5]

Three Days to See

BY HELEN KELLER

Sometimes I have thought it would be an excellent rule to live each day as if we should die tomorrow. Such an attitude would emphasize sharply the values of life. We should live each day with a gentleness, a vigor, and a keenness of appreciation which are often lost when time stretches before us in the constant panorama of more days and months

[5] Published in *The Atlantic Monthly,* January, 1933, and reprinted in *The Essay Annual, 1933,* edited by Erich A. Walter.

and years to come. There are those, of course, who would adopt the epicurean motto of "Eat, drink, and be merry," but most people would be chastened by the certainty of impending death. . . .

Only the deaf appreciate hearing, only the blind realize the manifold blessings that lie in sight. . . . I have often thought it would be a blessing if each human being were stricken blind and deaf for a few days at some time during his early adult life. Darkness would make him more appreciative of sight; silence would teach him the joys of sound.

Now and then I have tested my seeing friends to discover what they see. Recently I was visited by a very good friend who had just returned from a long walk in the woods, and I asked her what she had observed. "Nothing in particular," she replied. I might have been incredulous had I not been accustomed to such responses, for long ago I became convinced that the seeing see little.

How was it possible, I asked myself, to walk for an hour through the woods and see nothing worthy of note? I who cannot see find hundreds of things to interest me through mere touch. I feel the delicate symmetry of a leaf. I pass my hands lovingly about the smooth skin of a silver birch, or the rough shaggy bark of a pine. In spring I touch the branches of trees hopefully in search of a bud, the first sign of awakening Nature after her winter's sleep. I feel the delightful, velvety texture of a flower, and discover its remarkable convolutions; and something of the miracle of Nature is revealed to me. Occasionally, if I am very fortunate, I place my hand gently on a small tree and feel the happy quiver of a bird in full song. I am delighted to have the cool waters of a brook rush through my open fingers. To me a lush carpet of pine needles or spongy grass is more welcome than the most luxurious Persian rug. To me the pageant of seasons is a thrilling and unending drama, the action of which streams through my finger tips. . . .

Perhaps I can best illustrate by imagining what I should most like to see if I were given the use of my eyes, say, for just three days. . . . If, by some miracle, I were granted three seeing days, to be followed by a relapse into darkness, I should divide the period into three parts.

On the first day, I should want to see the people whose kindness and gentleness and companionship have made my life worth living. First I should like to gaze long upon the face of my dear teacher, Mrs. Anne Sullivan Macy, who came to me when I was a child and opened the outer world to me. I should want not merely to see the outline of her face, so that I could cherish it in my memory, but to study that face and find in it the living evidence of the sympathetic tenderness and patience with which she accomplished the difficult task of my education. I should like to see in her eyes that strength of character which has enabled her to stand firm in the face of difficulties, and that compassion for all humanity which she has revealed to me so often. . . .

And I should like to look into the loyal, trusting eyes of my dogs— the grave, canny little Scottie, Darkie, and the stalwart, understanding Great Dane, Helga, whose warm, tender, and playful friendships are so comforting to me.

On that busy first day I should also view the small simple things of my home. I want to see the warm colors in the rugs under my feet, the pictures on the walls, the intimate trifles that transform a house into home. . . .

In the afternoon of that first seeing day, I should take a long walk in the woods and intoxicate my eyes on the beauties of the world of Nature, trying desperately to absorb in a few hours the vast splendor which is constantly unfolding itself to those who can see. On the way home from my woodland jaunt my path would lie near a farm so that I might see the patient horses ploughing in the field (perhaps I should see only a tractor!) and the serene content of men living close to the soil. And I should pray for the glory of a colorful sunset. . . .

In the night of that first day of sight, I should not be able to sleep, so full would be my mind of the memories of the day.

The next day—the second day of sight—I should arise with the dawn and see the thrilling miracle by which night is transformed into day. I should behold with awe the magnificent panorama of light with which the sun awakens the sleeping earth.

This day I should devote to a hasty glimpse of the world, past and present. I should want to see the pageant of man's progress, the kaleidoscope of the ages. How can so much be compressed into one day? Through the museums, of course. [She goes on to describe how she would see the history of man in the New York Metropolitan Museum of Art and the Museum of Natural History.]

The evening of my second day of sight I should spend at a theater or at the movies. Even now I often attend theatrical performances of all sorts, but the action of the play must be spelled into my hand by a companion. . . . I cannot enjoy the beauty of rhythmic movement except in a sphere restricted to the touch of my hands. I can vision only dimly the grace of a Pavlowa, although I know something of the delight of rhythm, for often I can sense the beat of music as it vibrates through the floor. I can well imagine that cadenced motion must be one of the most pleasing sights in the world. I have been able to gather something of this by tracing with my fingers the lines in sculptured marble; if this static grace can be so lovely, how much more acute must be the thrill of seeing grace in motion. . . .

The following morning, I should again greet the dawn, anxious to discover new delights, for I am sure that, for those who have eyes which really see, the dawn of each day must be a perpetually new revelation of beauty.

This, according to the terms of my imagined miracle, is to be my third and last day of sight. . . . Today I shall spend in the workaday world of the present, amid the haunts of men going about the business of life. And where can one find so many activities and conditions of men as in New York? So the city becomes my destination.

I start from my home in the quiet little suburb of Forest Hills, Long Island. Here, surrounded by green lawns, trees, and flowers, are neat little houses, happy with the voices and movements of wives and children, havens of peaceful rest for men who toil in the city. I drive across the lacy structure of steel which spans the East River, and I get a new and startling vision of the power and ingenuity of the mind of man. Busy boats chug and scurry about the river—racy speed boats, stolid, snorting tugs. If I had long days of sight ahead, I should spend many of them watching the delightful activity upon the river.

I look ahead, and before me rise the fantastic towers of New York, a city that seems to have stepped from the pages of a fairy story. What an awe-inspiring sight, these glittering spires, these vast banks of stone and steel—structures such as the gods might build for themselves! This animated picture is a part of the lives of millions of people every day. How many, I wonder, give it so much as a second glance? Very few, I fear. Their eyes are blind to this magnificent sight because it is so familiar to them. . . .

Now I begin my rounds of the city. First, I stand at a busy corner,

merely looking at people, trying by sight of them to understand something of their lives. I see smiles, and I am happy. I see serious determination, and I am proud. I see suffering, and I am compassionate....

From Fifth Avenue I make a tour of the city—to Park Avenue, to
the slums, to factories, to parks where children play. I take a stay-at-
home trip abroad by visiting the foreign quarters. Always my eyes are
open wide to all the sights of both happiness and misery so that I may
probe deep and add to my understanding of how people work and
live. My heart is full of the images of people and things. My eye passes
lightly over no single trifle; it strives to touch and hold closely each
thing its gaze rests upon. Some sights are pleasant, filling the heart
with happiness; but some are miserably pathetic. To these latter I do
not shut my eyes, for they, too, are part of life. To close the eye on
them is to close the heart and mind.

My third day of sight is drawing to an end. Perhaps there are many
serious pursuits to which I should devote the few remaining hours,
but I am afraid that on the evening of that last day I should again run
away to the theater, to a hilariously funny play, so that I might appreciate the overtones of comedy in the human spirit.

At midnight my temporary respite from blindness would cease, and
permanent night would close in on me again.

—"Three Days to See"

3. THE WONDER OF IT ALL

Yet one might go further and probe into nature's secret mystery, for
nature is spirit and must be seen with the eyes of the spirit also. I have
actually seen people who look upon nature as a catalogue of things to
be numbered, labeled and remembered, who have never allowed their
minds to step into the realm of wonder, and who therefore in my
opinion have never really seen nature at all. There was a man who
was told about the Eighth Wonder of the world—a desert in moonlight. On returning from a moonlit desert with his friend, he asserted
that he saw only sands. The question is, which is the Eighth Wonder?

Emerson was capable of wonder. He was not a naturalist, or a
specialist, but a philosopher who saw life steadily and saw it whole.
He had read about geology and botany, but acquaintance with the

teachings of science only increased his sense of wonder at the universe. I believe a first-rate scientist is never a man condemned to knowledge without insight, sticking to his facts like a mole and unable to look beyond the facts to their meaning, their mystery, and their glory. Emerson wrote in his *Journals*:

" 'Miracles have ceased.' Have they indeed? When? They had not ceased this afternoon when I walked into the wood and got into bright, miraculous sunshine, in shelter from the roaring wind. Who sees a pine-cone, or the turpentine exuding from the tree, or a leaf, the unit of vegetation, fall from its bough, as if it said, 'the year is finished,' or hears in the quiet, piny glen the chickadee chirping his cheerful note, or walks along the lofty promontory-like ridges which, like natural causeways, traverse the morass, or gazes upward at the rushing clouds, or downward at a moss or a stone and says to himself, 'Miracles have ceased'? Tell me, good friend, when this hillock on which your foot stands swelled from the level of the sphere by volcanic force; pick up that pebble at your foot; look at its gray sides, its sharp crystal, and tell me what fiery inundation of the world melted the minerals like wax, and, as if the globe were one glowing crucible, gave this stone its shape. There is the truthspeaking pebble itself, to affirm to endless ages the thing was so. Tell me where is the manufactory of this air, so thin, so blue, so restless, which eddies around you, in which your life floats, of which your lungs are but an organ, and which you coin into musical words. I am agitated with curiosity to know the secret of nature. Why cannot geology, why cannot botany speak and tell me what has been, what is, as I run along the forest promontory, and ask when it rose like a blister on heated steel? Then I looked up and saw the sun shining in the vast sky, and heard the wind bellow above and the water glistened in the vale. These were the forces that wrought then and work now. Yes, there they grandly speak to all plainly, in proportion as we are quick to apprehend." (*Journals*, November 6, 1837.)

Among Emerson's generation, writing on the subject of nature, I still find Holmes the most satisfying. Holmes had a mental sweep and an expansive imagination rarely equaled, as seen in the following examples, where he writes of the mountain and the sea, and of Nature creeping to the cities.

"The mountains have a grand, stupid, lovable tranquillity; the sea has a fascinating, treacherous intelligence."

BY OLIVER WENDELL HOLMES

—I have lived by the sea-shore and by the mountains.—No, I am not going to say which is best. The one where your place is is the best for you. But this difference there is: you can domesticate mountains, but the sea is *feræ naturæ*. You may have a hut, or know the owner of one, on the mountain-side; you see a light half-way up its ascent in the evening, and you know there is a home, and you might share it. You have noted certain trees, perhaps; you know the particular zone where the hemlocks look so black in October, when the maples and beeches have faded. All its reliefs and intaglios have electrotyped themselves in the medallions that hang round the walls of your memory's chamber. —The sea remembers nothing. It is feline. It licks your feet,—its huge flanks purr very pleasantly for you; but it will crack your bones and eat you, for all that, and wipe the crimsoned foam from its jaws as if nothing had happened. The mountains give their lost children berries and water; the sea mocks their thirst and lets them die. The mountains have a grand, stupid, lovable tranquillity; the sea has a fascinating, treacherous intelligence. The mountains lie about like huge ruminants, their broad backs awful to look upon, but safe to handle. The sea smooths its silver scales until you cannot see their joints,—but their shining is that of a snake's belly, after all.—In deeper suggestiveness I find as great a difference. The mountains dwarf mankind and fore-shorten the procession of its long generations. The sea drowns out humanity and time; it has no sympathy with either; for it belongs to eternity, and of that it sings its monotonous song forever and ever.

Yet I should love to have a little box by the sea-shore. I should love to gaze out on the wild feline element from a front window of my own, just as I should love to look on a caged panther, and see it stretch its shining lengths, and then curl over and lap its smooth sides, and by-and-by begin to lash itself into rage and show its white teeth and spring at its bars, and howl the cry of its mad, but, to me, harmless fury.—And then,—to look at it with that inward eye,—who does not love to shuffle off time and its concerns, at intervals,—to forget who is

President and who is Governor, what race he belongs to, what language he speaks, which golden-headed nail of the firmament his particular planetary system is hung upon, and listen to the great liquid metronome as it beats its solemn measure, steadily swinging when the solo or duet of human life began, and to swing just as steadily after the human chorus has died out and man is a fossil on its shores? . . .

I don't know anything sweeter than this leaking in of Nature through all the cracks in the walls and floors of cities. You heap up a million tons of hewn rocks on a square mile or two of earth which was green once. The trees look down from the hill-sides and ask each other, as they stand on tiptoe,—"What are these people about?" And the small herbs at their feet look up and whisper back,—"We will go and see." So the small herbs pack themselves up in the least possible bundles, and wait until the wind steals to them at night and whispers, —"Come with me." Then they go softly with it into the great city,— one to a cleft in the pavement, one to a spout on the roof, one to a seam in the marbles over a rich gentleman's bones, and one to the grave without a stone where nothing but a man is buried,—and there they grow, looking down on the generations of men from mouldy roofs, looking up from between the less-trodden pavements, looking out through iron cemetery-railings. Listen to them, when there is only a light breath stirring, and you will hear them saying to each other,— "Wait awhile!" The words run along the telegraph of those narrow green lines that border the roads leading from the city, until they reach the slope of the hills, and the trees repeat in low murmurs to each other,—"Wait awhile!" By-and-by the flow of life in the streets ebbs, and the old leafy inhabitants—the smaller tribes always in front— saunter in, one by one, very careless seemingly, but very tenacious, until they swarm so that the great stones gape from each other with the crowding of their roots, and the feldspar begins to be picked out of the granite to find them food. At last the trees take up their solemn line of march, and never rest until they have encamped in the market-place. Wait long enough and you will find an old doting oak hugging a huge worn block in its yellow underground arms; that was the cornerstone of the State-House. Oh, so patient she is, this imperturbable Nature!

—The Autocrat of the Breakfast Table (XI)

In the matter of nature writing, I think that the moderns are far better than the people of a century ago. Some naturalists are of course professionals and somewhat beneath contempt as far as their nature writing goes. I am scandalized to read what Donald Culross Peattie says about some of these specialists, and Peattie knows what he is talking about. The disease of specialization, of sheer accumulation of facts, has eaten into this realm of study also. "Many collectors of insects will now take specimens of only one family. The span of human life does not permit a specialist to dally with bees if his business be wasps. It is my contention," continues Peattie in *An Almanac for Moderns* ("September Twenty-first"), "that specialization should be left to those who are not mentally gifted at generalization. The specialist is to be called upon for precise information. But there is still a place for the all-around naturalist." [6] Still, modern nature writers are far more accurate, the world they open up to us is wider, more full of wonder, and there are some extremely good writers, of whom Peattie is one.

Perhaps I may venture to say that Thoreau's *Walden* is overrated; it is too labored. I would risk a private opinion that compared with *Walden,* Peattie's *A Prairie Grove* is a superior literary work, superior not only in accuracy of information and wider scientific knowledge, but as writing and in breadth of insight and learning, and in philosophy backed by a true scientist's imagination. Perhaps Peattie studied Thoreau; there is a certain nervous energy and tenseness in his short sentences that remind me of the transcendentalist. On the other hand, Peattie, almost alone among modern writers, has the virtue of brevity and compressed strength. He usually hits the target in the space of a few paragraphs, and sometimes gives us an illuminating biography of a certain naturalist on one page. I am sure he cuts and polishes his sentences, as Thoreau did. But he is the master of the single page, as in his justly famous *Almanac for Moderns.*

Peattie's *A Prairie Grove* seems to me unique. It is a study of the Illinois prairies and groves, backed by fragments of memoirs, letters, and county histories and personal observation. No history of any state has ever been written with such a majestic breadth of vision. Peattie denies that he is writing history and says he is just remembering, but his remembering covers a wide range from the glacial period, to the country known by the Indians, and to the coming of the first white settlers. It contains therefore a unique mixture of historical, geological, biological, scenic, and philosophic wisdom, with the result that it gives us an intimate knowledge of the land, the nature, and the natural life and forces of that region as no history book can. One gets a more decent respect for the United States when written about as they are by men like Peattie and John Muir. For in the United States there is much greatness in the sheer sweep of nature in time and in space, against which the human species comes in to play only a comparatively short role. Peattie gives that unique feeling.

Perhaps the following selection from *A Prairie Grove* will show the author's incisive, power-charged, and thought-bearing style, and give the reader a deeper, loving knowledge of the land from the human point of view and yet curiously detached from it. The land thus has a life of its own. He is talking about the prairie grass after the glacial period as the Indians found it.

"The Illinois prairie grass; I felt this most uncorrupted earth beneath me, and all its cleanly, raw, hard strength."

BY DONALD CULROSS PEATTIE

Root touched root across this empire. The harsh edged leaves locked fingers, and the thoughtless west wind bore the pollen to the feathery purple stigmas of the husk-cupped flowers. In the jointed culms were water and salts, in the herbage was strength for the grazing herds, in the starch-filled seeds harvest for the mice. To the small rodents grass was forest. To the bison it was life certain underneath their hooves. Here the cock prairie chicken strutted before his wives, here in trust the lark sparrow laid her clutch of little eggs scrawled on the end with the illegible brown rune of her species, and the rattlers had a care for their frail spines when the elk walked by, terrible in branch and rut.

You may have seen Nebraska prairie, but that is low grass, bunch grass, a scattered, a semidesertic formation. You may have seen meadows, full of timothy and bluegrass, orchard grass and daisies. Those are introduced species; those are tamed Old World immigrants. The aboriginal high-grass prairie is nearly gone now. And it was something else.

It grew taller than a certain traveler who has left us his notes, taller than this man when he sat in his saddle. It grew so thick it flung the plowshares up when they came to break it. When it burned, they say, it filled the sky with its smoke; the smoke blew through the forest belt, and when the Dakotah were rounding up the game, the Ottawa in the woods of Michigan smelt that great hunt in the air.

But we have come to subdue the grasses, to conquer the empire of locked roots. The furrows lie even and open now, in spring and fall. The geometry of fields rules the landscape. It is a land turned to use, and I do not say it is not a good use, but some purity is gone. For the fallowed field does not grow up again to prairie. Thistles and burdock come up instead; we have the tares with our wheat, and nothing wholly wild is left.

But after long hunting I have found, upon the edge of my island grove, one slim paring of forgotten virgin prairie. I knew it first because the thistles had stopped stabbing at my knees, and there was nothing here so gentle as daisies. It was not tall as the banished high grass, but it was unsullied by a single foreign weed. Between field and field of grain, it grew with a varied flourish; close set, coarse-stemmed, the rank flowers sprang amid the whistling grasses. Nothing grew there because it was useful; it was itself, complete, sufficient, claiming the land by the most ancient of rights.

I sat down there and looked away from the farms. I lay down and looked up at the sky. I felt this most uncorrupted earth beneath me, and all its cleanly, raw, hard strength. I knew the prairie was once all thus, and I tried to remember how that must have been. There would have been no feeling of fences around me, but only forest and grass, grass and forest, and rivers winding through. Even now was left to me that baked rosin odor of the compass plants; I saw the irritable tribal toil of the ants in their enormous mound, and in my ears the crackling of the locusts' wings and the distant anger of the crows were like primordial Amerind language.

What had happened on this natural stage? There are histories to tell me that, eyewitnesses who wrote in languages I understand. But on this turf and in the grove behind me the red men had a camp and a portage. That portage, to them but one of thousands, was, by the great accident that predestines any pattern we may see, directly in the road of history. Men of my own race had to come here. They were searching a passage to the China Seas, they were bringing the totem of a pale Manitou. Or they were men with lesser aims and common hungers, bringing only their right to grow where they stood and fling their seeds where they had cleared.

The bell of the church a mile north on the road rang down the fields. It is a good sound, even to unbelievers, but it broke some dream. So I stood up, the grass rising no higher than my knees. You are not so tall today, you prairie, as we are, and we shall never make you grow again, except in our thoughts.

—A Prairie Grove (III)

Characteristically, the author says, in concluding the early prehistoric part, "Humans have to take their place where it falls in the fauna. But there is no plot; this is not a novel, not a historical romance, not a popularization of history. I say that I am remembering, remembering for the trees and the great grass province and the passenger pigeons and the wild swans. I say that the coming of our species was an event, perhaps an impermanent one in the greater story. So my characters are transient, even shadowy. Individual character does not matter to Nature. In the end she absorbs all individualities; she knows only races and their rise and fall. But the ideas of our species are the human scent we leave upon the wild turf. They drift and linger on the airs after we have gone, and are the things most worth remembering about us."

The following is a brief sketch of the prairie world of the Indians as the first white man found it.

"And in all historic time there has never been abundance like it. There was an amply filled solitude, a yet undestroyed balance in all the land then."

BY DONALD CULROSS PEATTIE

So the first white men found it, the wooded ridge just lifted from the steppe and the swamp. A faint ridge, but one strategic, fateful, because it lay across the way men had to take, pressing westward and southward, seeking a way from the Lakes to the Gulf, seeking a portage. Here, finding its way down through the cramped and twisted drainage that the glaciers had confused, the Kilimick runs northward, toward the lakes. Further west, the Seignelay flows southward to the Father of Waters. In the spring floods, in the rarer rising of the autumn waters, a chain of sloughs connected them; a light canoe could push through the wild rice and the reed grass—so subtle is this scenery, where the faint boss of the land, less tall than a tall tree, divides the waters of the continent.

The land is drained now; the canoes are gone. Our human imprints erase natural landmarks. The eye accustomed to broken scenery finds this midland monotonous. Run by, fly by, do not stop, swift traveler; there is nothing here to interest you; you have said it yourself; you read no meaning; you hear no thunder in the great empty burning arch of the sky.

Only gradually the lingerer grows conscious of fine shadings, of great meanings in slight symbols. At last he can hear the great voice that speaks softly; he can see the swell and fall upon the flank of a statue carved out in a whole continent's marble.

The Illinois came here, not foreknowing this grove's destined role, but placing their summer camp strategically, on the crossroads of the forest game and the prairie game. The human animal, the red man, was a carnivore, who hunted, like the wolves in packs, the other beasts about him. An obligate nomad, he went where the game went, and on foot he chased his food, his clothing and his implements that arrogantly fled before him. He followed the game southward, harrying, in winter, marching in the trail of its dung, streaking after it like the cowbirds that flew to sit upon the rumps of the buffalo and devour the ticks and flies.

With an elk tine the women dug a seed hole for the maize. In a raccoon skin the jugglers carried medicine, and when the wild swans went over, a storm of arrows shot from arches bent to breaking struck across their flyway and brought them plummeting to earth. Then the girls must set them away in brine against the winter famine. Swan feathers blew about the camp then, and with owl's feathers and heron's plumes and metallic glitter of teal and mallard and goldeneye, they went to make the magic of the medicine lodge; they winged the arrows, trailed in splendor from the calumet, or were thrust in the greased black hair.

Here was a species whose talons were arrows, whose speed was in their cunning, whose strength was the prairie fires they lighted that ran without need of breath or water, and so outran the stumbling herd of heaving flanks and lolling tongues. They ate as the beasts ate, ravenous and gorging in hours of abundance; they all knew famine in its season, and like carnivores they had to eat then the memory of old feasts. They took some thought against the morrow, but never enough. Yet in the midst of abundance, they were not wasteful; they were too ignorant to kill for sport. The animals too, they thought, had souls; they must not be insulted or their spirits broken; the herbs were in the earth's keeping, and when they gathered their simples they asked her pardon. "I take these thy hairs, Nokomis, grandmother, and I thank you and ask your pardon."

One must not think that they were sentimental; they took what they needed because they saw that all things take what they need. Why not, in a world so rich?

And in all historic time there has never been abundance like it. Not in the temperate world, where men are restless, where the speeding years flash past the gay dress and the nakedness of the seasons. It was a very long time ago that Greece lost her forests and that the circular hunt of the Tartars swept the great game from the Asian steppes. But in our own yesterdays the elk still lifted confident antlered heads unafraid of a bullet; the mast of the forest fed ten million pigeons; trees fell only from rot or wind. Ducks still built their nests neighbor to men, that now must hide them away in a last borderland of reeds. There was an amply filled solitude, a yet undestroyed balance in all the land then. It was a balance kept by harsh laws past our reconstructing. Yet all things enjoyed then the right to live, and to death they were submissive without thought. Amidst such prodigality there was little need to plant, and the buffalo calved in the deep grass without tending.

We have substituted another life, one that without our mastery upon it runs back to weak forms, dry udders, thorns without fruit, and the smutted kernel. It is our way, and it is a great way, with a sweet traditional taste to it, and I love the barnyard with its fowl out of Asia, the haymow with its fermenting grasses brought here from the cultural sources of our civilization. I like the starlings and the sheep and the horses mighty and diffident; I like the white little hams of the children squatting down to entice the geese with grain. These are our belongings; this is our flesh; this way must we go.

But lift your hand from the land, or let the outraged earth turn on you—and the wild comes back, an embittered wild. There was never a tempest that so darkened heaven as the great dust storms blown from lands tortured into too much bearing. Strip the ancient herbs away, the lance-tall grasses with their pennant chaff, and in revenge the thistles spring—rabble running where the old kings stood. There will be crows here to pick the last grain we sow. But never again the pigeons, the bison, the man holding his fingers to the sun.

—*A Prairie Grove* (VI)

I cannot refrain from including part of the description of the flight of pigeons witnessed by the Goodner family and reported by Alexander Wilson and Audubon. It is exciting in its suggestion of the sheer power and extravagance of nature.

The Flight of Pigeons

BY DONALD CULROSS PEATTIE

The pigeons did not come every year to the grove, but only at rare and unforgettable intervals. They came when the mast in the Michigan forests gave out. Alexander Wilson calculated that a pigeon daily ate half a pint of acorns or beechnuts, and that a flock consumed seventeen million four hundred and twenty-four bushels in a day; Audubon makes it eighteen million. Wilson said that he saw a column a mile broad, every bird in it moving at the rate of a mile a minute. He watched it for four hours, which means that at his conservative estimate of three pigeons in a square yard, the ribbon of wings was two hundred and forty miles long and contained two thousand two hundred and thirty million, two hundred and seventy-two thousand passenger pigeons. This was but a single band, and of these birds not one today is living.

They are so gone that all we hear of them is fabulous. Alexander Wilson was standing one day at a pioneer's door when there was a tremendous roar out of the sky; the sun was so instantly darkened that he took this happening for a tornado and expected to see the trees torn up. "It is only the pigeons," said the frontiersman. Audubon saw a hawk pounce on a pigeon flight; the birds beneath it plummeted almost to earth like the funnel of a twister, and every bird coming after them executed the same figure, dashing into the vortex and by an unseen force shot out of it again. Everyone speaks of the roar of the wings; it plowed the forest boughs into billows. Their droppings fell like shot through the leaves till the ground was covered with them, and the voices forever called upon each other. Imagine the tender contented throaty plaint of the barnyard pigeon amplified by a million voices to a portentous crying thunder torn with the speed of flight. Imagine all your county under forest and all that forest one vast pigeon roost; in such quantities they nested or they rested.

If the evidence lay only on the word of a few, it might not be credible, but the agreement among the skeptical and the rivals is too telling. "The boughs of the trees were constantly breaking under the weight of the birds." "You could hear a pigeon roost miles away." "It was the grandest sight I ever saw to watch them streaming across the sky." "The sun was dark for hours when they went over."

They say that their wings flashed in the sun; the soft rose breasts, the delicate blue heads, the wings changeable green and blue and bronze all had pearl-like luster. The luster is gone from the sad museum specimen that looks at a curious public with a glass eye. But there is Audubon's plate, painted from the life with every nacreous gleam of a pinion, and the dour soul who is embarrassed by Audubon can read the testimony of the cautious Wilson, who makes the pigeon sound as though Audubon's brush had understated it.

—A Prairie Grove

4. THE POWER AND THE GLORY

John Muir was equally happy in his love of nature in all its rude grandeur, and in his gift of writing. He, too, saw more wondrous sights, in the Sierra Nevadas and the Yosemite, than Thoreau was ever privileged to see. And he saw them all alone. One of the most exciting passages is his description of a storm in the mountain forests of the Sierra, watched, as few men ancient or modern would watch, from the top of a swinging Douglas spruce during the height of the storm and enjoyed all the more for it.

"It occurred to me that it would be a fine thing to climb one of the trees to obtain a wider outlook and get my ear close to the Æolian music of its topmost needles."

BY JOHN MUIR

One of the most beautiful and exhilarating storms I ever enjoyed in the Sierra occurred in December, 1874, when I happened to be exploring one of the tributary valleys of the Yuba River. The sky and the ground and the trees had been thoroughly rain-washed and were dry again. The day was intensely pure, one of those incomparable bits of California winter, warm and balmy and full of white sparkling sunshine, redolent of all the purest influences of the spring, and at the same time enlivened with one of the most bracing wind-storms conceivable. Instead of camping out, as I usually do, I then chanced to be stopping at the house of a friend. But when the storm began to sound, I lost no time in pushing out into the woods to enjoy it. For on such occasions Nature has always something rare to show us, and the danger to life and limb is hardly greater than one would experience crouching deprecatingly beneath a roof.

It was still early morning when I found myself fairly adrift. Delicious sunshine came pouring over the hills, lighting the tops of the pines, and setting free a steam of summery fragrance that contrasted strangely with the wild tones of the storm. The air was mottled with pine-tassels and bright green plumes, that went flashing past in the sunlight like birds pursued. But there was not the slightest dustiness, nothing less pure than leaves, and ripe pollen, and flecks of withered bracken and moss. I heard trees falling for hours at the rate of one every two or three minutes; some uprooted, partly on account of the loose, water-soaked condition of the ground; others broken straight across, where some weakness caused by fire had determined the spot. The gestures of the various trees made a delightful study. Young Sugar Pines, light and feathery as squirrel-tails, were bowing almost to the ground; while the grand old patriarchs, whose massive boles had been tried in a hundred storms, waved solemnly above them, their long, arching branches streaming fluently on the gale, and every needle thrilling and ringing and shedding off keen lances of light like a diamond. The Douglas Spruces, with long sprays drawn out in level tresses, and needles massed in a gray, shimmering glow, presented a most striking appearance as they stood in bold relief along the hilltops. The madroños in the dells, with their red bark and large glossy leaves tilted every way, reflected the sunshine in throbbing spangles like those one so often sees on the rippled surface of a glacier lake. But the Silver Pines were now the most impressively beautiful of all. Colossal spires 200 feet in height waved like supple goldenrods chanting and bowing low as if in worship, while the whole mass of their long, tremulous foliage was kindled into one continuous blaze of white sun-fire. The force of the gale was such that the most steadfast monarch of them all rocked down to its roots with a motion plainly perceptible when one leaned against it. Nature was holding high festival, and every fiber of the most rigid giants thrilled with glad excitement.

I drifted on through the midst of this passionate music and motion, across many a glen, from ridge to ridge; often halting in the lee of a rock for shelter, or to gaze and listen.

Toward midday, after a long, tingling scramble through copses of hazel and ceanotus, I gained the summit of the highest ridge in the neighborhood; and then it occurred to me that it would be a fine thing to climb one of the trees to obtain a wider outlook and get my ear close to the Æolian music of its topmost needles. But under the circumstances the choice of a tree was a serious matter. One whose instep was not very strong seemed in danger of being blown down, or of being struck by others in case they should fall; another was branchless to a considerable height above the ground, and at the same time too large to be grasped with arms and legs in climbing; while others were not favorably situated for clear views. After cautiously casting about, I made choice of the tallest of a group of Douglas Spruces that were growing close together like a tuft of grass, no one of which seemed likely to fall unless all the rest fell with it. Though comparatively young, they were about 100 feet high, and their lithe, brushy tops were rocking and swirling in wild ecstasy. Being accustomed to climb trees in making botanical studies, I experienced no difficulty in reaching the top of this one, and never before did I enjoy so noble an exhilaration of motion. The slender tops fairly flapped and swished in the passionate torrent, bending and swirling backward and forward, round and round, tracing indescribable combinations of vertical and horizontal curves, while I clung with muscles firm braced, like a bobolink on a reed.

In its widest sweeps my tree-top described an arc of from twenty to thirty degrees, but I felt sure of its elastic temper, having seen others of the same species still more severely tried—bent almost to the ground indeed, in heavy snows—without breaking a fiber. I was therefore safe, and free to take the wind into my pulses and enjoy the excited forest from my superb outlook. The view from here must be extremely beautiful in any weather. Now my eye roved over the piny hills and dales as over fields of waving grain, and felt the light running in ripples and broad swelling undulations across the valleys from ridge to ridge, as the shining foliage was stirred by corresponding waves of air. Oftentimes these waves of reflected light would break up suddenly into a kind of beaten foam, and again, after chasing one another in regular order, they would seem to bend forward in concentric curves, and disappear on some hillside, like sea-waves on a shelving shore. The quantity of light reflected from the bent needles was so great as to make whole groves appear as if covered with snow, while the black shadows beneath the trees greatly enhanced the effect of the silvery splendor.

Excepting only the shadows there was nothing somber in all this wild sea of pines. On the contrary, notwithstanding this was the winter season, the colors were remarkably beautiful. The shafts of the pine and libocedrus were brown and purple, and most of the foliage was well tinged with yellow; the laurel groves, with the pale undersides of their leaves turned upward, made masses of gray; and then there was many a dash of chocolate color from clumps of manzanita, and jet of vivid crimson from the bark of the madroños, while the ground on the hillsides, appearing here and there through openings between the groves, displayed masses of pale purple and brown.

The sounds of the storm corresponded gloriously with this wild exuberance of light and motion. The profound bass of the naked branches and boles booming like waterfalls; the quick, tense vibrations of the pine-needles, now rising to a shrill, whistling hiss, now falling to a silky murmur; the rustling of laurel groves in the dells, and the keen metallic click of leaf on leaf—all this was heard in easy analysis when the attention was calmly bent.

The varied gestures of the multitude were seen to fine advantage, so that one could recognize the different species at a distance of several miles by this means alone, as well as by their forms and colors, and the way they reflected the light. All seemed strong and comfortable, as if really enjoying the storm, while responding to its most enthusiastic greetings. We hear much nowadays concerning the universal struggle for existence, but no struggle in the common meaning of the word was manifest here; no recognition of danger by any tree; no deprecation; but rather an invincible gladness as remote from exultation as from fear.

I kept my lofty perch for hours, frequently closing my eyes to enjoy

the music by itself, or to feast quietly on the delicious fragrance that
was streaming past. The fragrance of the woods was less marked than
that produced during warm rain, when so many balsamic buds and
leaves are steeped like tea; but, from the chafing of resiny branches
against each other, and the incessant attrition of myriads of needles,
the gale was spiced to a very tonic degree. And besides the fragrance
from these local sources there were traces of scents brought from afar.
For this wind came first from the sea, rubbing against its fresh, briny
waves, then distilled through the redwoods, threading rich ferny
gulches, and spreading itself in broad undulating currents over many
a flower-enameled ridge of the coast mountains, then across the golden
plains, up the purple foot-hills, and into these piny woods with the
varied incense gathered by the way. . . .

When the storm began to abate, I dismounted and sauntered down
through the calming woods. The storm-tones died away, and, turning
toward the east, I beheld the countless hosts of the forests hushed and
tranquil, towering above one another on the slopes of the hills like a
devout audience. The setting sun filled them with amber light, and
seemed to say, while they listened, "My peace I give unto you."

As I gazed on the impressive scene, all the so-called ruin of the storm
was forgotten, and never before did these noble woods appear so fresh,
so joyous, so immortal.

—*The Mountains of California* (X)

5. PANTHEISTIC REVELRY

The Transcendentalists did not merely escape from the city to look
at nature, nor did they only make objective and accurate observations,
as many modern naturalists do. These outings partook of the nature
of a true communion with the moon, the stars and the Earth Spirit.
They went out to find God in Nature, to know His lurking places, to
hear the song of the wood thrush and be uplifted and inspired, to
banish all triviality and be reinstated in man's true dominion, as
Thoreau did; or to let Nature's influence pass through into their souls
or to hear a spiritual message, as Emerson did.

There was a definite touch of mystic reunion with the earth, a sense
of kinship with nature, in the writings of Thoreau and Emerson,

which many rationalists will not be able to understand. It was not so much a return to nature, as being at one with nature. Some extraordinary images must either baffle or greatly impress the modern reader. I cannot say which of the two was the greater mystic, Emerson or Thoreau—both of them have it in full measure. Thus, visiting the Jardin des Plantes at Paris, Emerson noted an occult relation between the scorpion and man. "I feel the centipede in me—cayman, carp, eagle, fox. I am moved by strange sympathies." "Come out of your warm, angular house, resounding with few voices," he wrote elsewhere in his *Journals* (May 11, 1838) "into the chill grand, instantaneous night, with such a presence as a full moon in the clouds, and you are struck with a poetic wonder. In the instant you leave far behind human relations, wife, mother and child, and live only with the savages—water, air, light, carbon, lime and granite. . . . I become a moist, cold element. 'Nature grows over me.' Frogs pipe; waters far off tinkle; dry leaves hiss; grass bends and rustles, and I have died out of the human world and come to feel a strange, cold, aqueous, terraqueous, aerial, ethereal sympathy and existence. I sow the sun and moon for seeds." Deep draughts of nature these Transcendentalists quaffed. Poetry is so akin to wonder that we are no longer surprised that this was the time when the New England culture flowered. Perhaps we cannot grow, cannot live and feel truly, without some touch of divine madness.

Thoreau, we know, said that he would be contented to be a fence post feeling with joy the sensation of lichen gradually spreading over him. He would not mind being a woodchuck, and once he had a silent encounter with one round the corner of Hubbard's Grove. He took a twig a foot long and played with it. "We sat looking at one another about half an hour, 'till we began to feel mesmeric influences. . . . I sat down by his side within a foot. I talked to him *quasi* forest lingo, baby talk, at any rate in a conciliatory tone, and thought that I had some influence on him." And he concluded, "I think I might learn some wisdom of him." (*Journals,* April 16, 1852.) He wanted not to observe nature from the outside, but "to be nature looking into nature with such easy sympathy as the blue-eyed grass in the meadow looks in the face of the sky." (Letter to Mrs. Lucy Brown, July 21, 1841.) He seemed to see more his own kith and kin in the lichens on the rocks than in any books. "I am of kin to the sod," he wrote to Harrison Blake (May 2, 1848), "and partake largely of its dull patience, in winter expecting the sun of spring. . . . I am too easily contented with a slight and almost animal happiness. My happiness is a good deal like that of the woodchucks." That, I say, is a yogi writing.

Any time I would prefer the mysticism of a yogi to the cold deductions of a bat-eyed materialist. I have a suspicion that if one of them falls further short of the truth, it is the materialist and not the yogi. The radio and the radar, the bat's flight at night, the sense of direction of the homing pigeon, and the mysterious attraction of the female emperor moths for the male moths (seemingly without the aid of the five senses, according to Fabre) have considerably altered our picture of even this sensuous world, and at the same time have shaken faith in our poorly delimited sense organs. Perhaps we can hear and see only what is good enough for us; meanwhile there exists in the universe a vast symphony of waves, a phantasmagoria of colors which are beyond our ken.

From pantheistic communion with nature to religion is only a short step. It is no accident that Emerson gave his best, truest definition of religion on the top of a mountain. "Here, among the mountains, the pinions of thought should be strong, and one should see the errors of men from a calmer height of love and wisdom. What is the message that is given me to communicate next Sunday?" the latter wrote in July, 1832. "Religion in the mind is not credulity, and in the practice is not form. It is life. It is the order and soundness of a man. It is not something *to be got,* to be *added,* but is a new life of those faculties you have. It is to do right. It is to love, it is to serve, it is to think, it is to be humble" (*Journals,* July 6, 1832). No better definition of religion have I read. That was the good of going to the mountains.

Happiness comes unexpectedly, so perhaps religion also, without one straining for it. Religion perhaps is not something to be "got" as the expression goes, or caught like a baseball. Nobody got religion, nobody got wisdom, and nobody got happiness. These things grow inside one.[7] One may perhaps go to look for happiness on a June

---

[7] John Jay Chapman said to William James, "My dear James, whatever religion may be, it is a *passive* experience. . . . Let him not try to assist or foment it. Religion is a thing that encloses, envelops, and unifies, affects both the mind and the muscles, the inner and the outer—the digestion and the dreams of a man. The only way to assist religion is to be passive, indifferent—all the bars down. Every snare you set to catch it scares the bird." *John Jay Chapman and His Letters,* edited by M. A. Howe. Houghton Mifflin Company. Copyright, 1937, M. A. DeWolfe Howe. Reprinted by permission.

night with a full moon and unexpectedly find religion there. Who knows? Perhaps religionists would call this entering into religion by the back door, but the universe is really so big it is hard to tell what is the front door and what the back door. Who knows? Anyway, this close contact with nature seems to represent a return to simplicity and health and joy, to a true sense of proportions and a sound scale of values, to a fuller aesthetic appreciation of beauties and a sense of reverence for the mystery and the grandeur and the power of nature. If the front door is closed, the back door of the universe seems ever open for the receptive mind which knows the true breadth of the dominions of the spirit. In Emerson we see how the feeling for nature and poetry and religion are really fused into one. That was how he produced what I think is one of the greatest religious poems ever written by man, a characteristically panthestic revelry.

The Problem

BY RALPH WALDO EMERSON

> I like the church; I like the cowl;
> I love a prophet of the soul;
> And on my heart monastic isles
> Fall like sweet strains, or pensive smiles:
> Yet not for all his faith can see
> Would I that cowlèd churchman be.
>
> Why should the vest on him allure,
> Which I could not on me endure?
> Not from a vain or shallow thought
> His awful Jove young Phidias brought,
> Never from lips of cunning fell
> The thrilling Delphic oracle;
> Out from the heart of nature rolled
> The burdens of the Bible old;
> The litanies of nations came,
> Like the volcano's tongue of flame,
> Up from the burning core below,
> The canticles of love and woe:

The hand that rounded Peter's dome
And groined the aisles of Christian Rome
Wrought in a sad sincerity;
Himself from God he could not free;
He builded better than he knew;
The conscious stone to beauty grew.

Know'st thou what wove yon woodbird's nest
Of leaves, and feathers from her breast?
Or how the fish outbuilt her shell,
Painting with morn each annual cell?
Or how the sacred pine tree adds
To her old leaves new myriads?
Such and so grew these holy piles,
Whilst love and terror laid the tiles.
Earth proudly wears the Parthenon,
As the best gem upon her zone,
And Morning opes with haste her lids
To gaze upon the Pyramids;

O'er England's abbeys bends the sky,
As on its friends, with kindred eye;
For out of Thought's interior sphere
These wonders rose to upper air;
And Nature gladly gave them place,
Adopted them into her race,
And granted them an equal date
With Andes and with Ararat.

These temples grew as grows the grass;
Art might obey, but not surpass.
The passive Master lent his hand
To the vast soul that o'er him planned;
And the same power that reared the shrine
Bestrode the tribes that knelt within.
Ever the fiery Pentecost
Girds with one flame the countless host,
Trances the heart through chanting choirs,

And through the priest the mind inspires.
The word unto the prophet spoken
Was writ on tables yet unbroken;
The word by seers or sibyls told,
In groves of oak, or fanes of gold,
Still floats upon the morning wind,
Still whispers to the willing mind.
One accent of the Holy Ghost
The heedless world hath never lost.
I know what say the fathers wise,
The Book itself before me lies,
Old *Chrysostom,* best Augustine,
And he who blent both in his line,
The younger *Golden Lips* or mines,
Taylor, the Shakespeare of divines.
His words are music in my ear,
I see his cowlèd portrait dear;
And yet, for all his faith could see,
I would not the good bishop be.

—Poems

I do not think it is important whether a man enters religion by the front door or the back door, so long as he enters. For only as he enters does he find peace. If to find God by the garden path is the back door, then by all means go down the garden path. Emerson, by his contemplation of nature, came to say, rhapsodically, "In the wood, God was manifest, as he was not in the sermon—In the cathedralled larches the ground-pine crept him, the thrush sung him, the robin complained him, the catbird mewed him, the anemone vibrated him," etc. That is mysticism if you like, but St. Francis of Assisi was a mystic; so was Jesus. We have no approach to heaven save by the lower senses, and so far the back door to religion seems the safest. If we can arrive at the position in which Jesus admired the lilies of the valley and St. Francis loved the birds as God's own creatures, we have stumbled upon the very source from which all religions took their rise, and will no longer be contented as secondhand believers.

Chapter XII

GOD

OF all the subjects in this modern individualistic society, sex and religion are regarded as the most private of a man's beliefs, in both cases because of a discrepancy between belief and profession. If a man has an affair, it is his own private business, and if a man interprets his religion in his own way, that is his own business, too. Freedom of belief means you can believe anything you like, provided you don't at the same time use the freedom of speech to let others know what you believe. What is meant by the word "private" is then that sex or religion is strictly your own affair until you carry it to a point where you trespass upon the public instinct or tend to threaten a public institution, namely, the church or marriage. Society has an instinct too, a fundamentally healthy instinct of what is good for itself and of the foundations of public order. On the other hand, this instinct, of course conservative, is for preserving things as they are and have been and is inimical to the exercise of critical thought. In the case of religion, any deviation from the original path is sensed as public danger and cries of "atheism!" go up against him who seeks God by his own individual path. This is nonsense, for I have found few thinkers, very few indeed, who do not believe in the existence of God. In the vast majority of cases, atheism simply means *"against-my-kind-of-theism,"* and each sect regards itself as the sacred guardian of the orthodox view of divinity.

For example, Emerson, at the age of thirty-five, was invited by the graduating class of the Harvard Divinity School to give an address. He accepted the invitation, went and gave the famous "Divinity School Address," the essence of which was that "God is, not was, that He speaketh, not spake." "Men have come to speak of the revelation as somewhat long ago given and done, as if God were dead." He urged the budding clergymen to "go alone," to break away from tradition, to seek the presence of God by exploring the moral nature of man, and to have the courage to say, "I also am a man." Outside of that, there was nothing more shocking than the sweet admonition, "The time is coming when all men will see that the gift of God to the soul is not a vaunting, overpowering, excluding sanctity, but a sweet, natural goodness, a goodness like thine and mine, and that so invites thine and mine to be and to grow." Of course it threw Harvard into consternation, because it threw Boston into consternation. The head of the Divinity School made a public statement that Emerson had been invited to speak not by the school authorities but by the students, thus essentially agreeing with an old woman, a neighbor of John Jay Chapman's grandmother, that the preacher of the Boston Second Church had gone mad. Emerson was not invited to speak at Harvard again for twenty-seven years. Oh, dear Harvard, why did it have to be near Boston, where President Lowell later assisted in the condemnation of Sacco and Vanzetti? I suppose Boston was no worse than any other city; the same thing would have happened in any Hoosier town. Why could not Harvard throw off the shackles of mortality, be not in any town at all, and live in pure air as a spirit alone and recover its spiritual freedom? The point I am coming to is that I have found a note in Emerson's *Journals* after the row over the address. The address was given on July 15, 1838, and on October 19, Emerson wrote in his private notebook, "It is plain from the noise that there is atheism somewhere; the only question is now, Which is the atheist?"

That is America's social difficulty, the right of every man to believe in God in his own way and the social duty not to talk about it to others. The correct thing in good company is, talk about God, but if you have anything to say, don't say it. Six years before, Emerson had already resigned from the pastorate, finding it necessary to quit the ministry to be a good minister. The point was a point of ritual. He had come to believe that the Last Supper was never meant to be a perpetual celebration, and after much wrangling with his conscience, he found it obligatory to resign since he could no longer administer the Holy Communion with conviction. Emerson had discovered for himself a

greater message, the infinitude of the private man.[1] Emerson shocked
not only Brattle Street and Boston, but all New England when he
told them that there was the divine in us, a doctrine as old as the
Bible and the Upanishads. I do not know what else the New Testament taught except that we are sons of God. But this was so shocking
to his Cambridge and Bostonian contemporaries that they could not
quite take it. All Brattle Street and State Street Christians cried
indignantly, "Do you mean to say that what the Bible says is true?
You infidel and atheist!"

A liberal church! When shall we have it? When will America be
able to break the incrustation of creeds, when will the garden of faith
be watered with the spring of a liberal spirit of free inquiry and man
anew, with the assistance of the saints, set out to discover fresh, glowing beauties of divine truths, with the added joy of that pursuit? If
the professionals will allow religion to grow and become perennially
fresh with one tenth of the enthusiasm with which a man renovates
his Buick or Studebaker, religion can become vital again, which of
course it isn't, and the professionals know it. But the prospect of such
renovation is dim. Things have not changed since Benjamin Franklin
wrote his speech asking the Great Convention to pass the Constitution
of the United States. "It is therefore that, the older I grow, the more
apt I am to doubt my own judgment of others. Most men, indeed, as
well as most sects in religion, think themselves in possession of all
truth, and that wherever others differ from them, it is so far error.
Steele, a Protestant, in a dedication tells the Pope that the only difference between our two churches in their opinions of the certainty of
their doctrine, is, the Romish Church is infallible and the Church of
England is *never in the wrong*. But, though many private Persons
think almost as highly of their own infallibility as of that of their
sect, few express it so naturally as a certain French lady, who, in a
little dispute with her sister, said, 'But I meet with nobody but myself
that is *always* in the right.' 'Je ne trouve que moi qui aie toujours
raison.' "

---

[1] "In all my lectures I have taught one doctrine, namely the infinitude of private man.
This the people accept readily enough, and even with a loud commendation, as long as
I call the lecture Art or Politics, or Literature, or the Household, but the moment I call
it religion they are shocked . . ." (*Journals*, April 7, 1840).

Freedom of belief is therefore a funny thing. It has become resolved practically into the formula: I believe what I think, and you have all the freedom to believe what you think, but don't you ever let me know what you think or I shall regard you as an enemy of the faith and of the republic. And so the dilemma of the modern church must continue to remain forever. Hasn't someone discovered that God is being overprotected?

2. OUR LOW NOTIONS OF GOD

Of all the disharmonies of belief, or disharmonies between private belief and public profession, the one regarding God is the saddest and produces the most inner discomfort. This is why modern intellectuals sometimes envy the pagan world, where man's inner belief and outer forms of public worship are in harmony. It is also the one that is least likely to benefit from critical thinking; I rather think that the deadlock of silence, each man having his own private belief and respecting that of others, will persist. What is wrong? To be sure, the revolt against Calvinism is a great part of the story. Calvin's doctrine of total depravity was and is so much at variance with the modern respect for and understanding of the body, or shall we say at variance with the modern, flamboyant parade of the flesh, that a conflict between outer belief and inner conviction is produced. And so the wonderful "one-hoss shay" of Oliver Wendell Holmes, the "deacon's masterpiece," did not *break down* in parts; the marvelous dovetailing of the parts of the mechanism in that impressive logical structure of Calvin's was perfect, and every part was as strong as the other, but one day in November, 1855, as the poem tell us, the whole thing just melted down—it was worn out with age. The only unsatisfactory thing about silence is that the phantom one-hoss shay is assumed to go on forever, and no one will quite say publicly that it has disappeared, melted, evaporated.

One Sunday morning in my New York apartment, I turned on the radio and was curious to hear the kind of preaching that was going on on the air. I passed by the Beethoven symphony singing the glory of God and heard an angry, canting snuffle, quaking and damning and ranting at sin like that of a Billy Sunday reborn. It was all there, from

Calvin himself. But I didn't like Calvin and thought of Coolidge and merely said to myself, "Oh, he is against it," and switched to Beethoven. I think I was not alone. There is so much exclusive contemplation of sin at divine service that any man seen coming out of church ought to be ashamed of himself, as someone has said. If a man will say to me, "Come with me to the church, and you will feel a better man," I will go with him. But if I know I am going to come out of the church feeling more wicked than before and despise myself for it, I won't. No, that tone of a quack vociferating at a country fair to sell a patent medicine won't do. You cannot sell religion nowadays by scaring people with hell and damnation; a sweeter clinical manner is required. Besides, we are already so much surrounded by the complexes of modern psychologists, and we can do without the additional guilt complex of the preacher. To be sure, the preacher does not create in you the guilt complex of original sin without providing a remedy easy to take, but the plain truth is that you cannot scare people into loving the wrathful God of Calvin.

The matter is perhaps a little more ancient than Calvin; its roots go back to the pretty low notions that man had some two thousand years ago and passed on to us. There is an atavism in some of our deepest community beliefs. Man moves on, but the old beliefs of ages gone by still hang on, very much alive. God was at first conceived to love the smell of fresh blood when man ate raw flesh. But long after man had discovered fire, God was still conceived to love blood, raw and uncooked. The best way man thought and still sometimes thinks to please God is to offer the blood of someone; God is supposed to be a cannibal like man himself. Hundreds of thousands of years passed before man started the new idea that God, like men, perhaps relished roasts. Clarence Day's prehistoric prophet meditates again on the kind of gods the simians will create for themselves. It is good to get a little aloof.

The Gods of the Simian Race

BY CLARENCE DAY

Imagine you are watching the Bandarlog at play in the forest. As you behold them and comprehend their natures, now hugely brave and boastful, now full of dread, the most weakly emotional of any intelligent species, ever trying to attract the notice of some greater animal, not happy indeed unless noticed,—is it not plain they are bound to invent things called gods? Don't think for the moment of whether there are gods or not; think of how sure these beings would be to invent them. (Not wait to find them.) Having small self-reliance they can not bear to face life alone. With no self-sufficingness, they must have the countenance of others. It is these pressing needs that will hurry the primates to build, out of each shred of truth they can possibly twist to their purpose, and out of imaginings that will impress them because they are vast, deity after deity to prop up their souls.

What a strange company they will be, these gods, in their day, each of them an old bearded simian up in the sky, who begins by fishing the universe out of a void, like a conjurer taking a rabbit out of a hat. (A hat which, if it resembled a void, wasn't there.) And after creating enormous suns and spheres, and filling the farthest heavens with vaster stars, one god will turn back and long for the smell of roast flesh, another will call desert tribes to "holy" wars, and a third will grieve about divorce or dancing.

All gods that any groups of simians ever conceive of, from the woodenest little idol in the forest to the mightiest Spirit, no matter how much they may differ, will have one trait in common: a readiness to drop any cosmic affair at short notice, focus their minds on the far-away pellet called Earth, and become immediately wholly concerned, aye, engrossed, with any individual worshipper's woes or desires,—a readiness to notice a fellow when he is going to bed. This will bring indescribable comfort to simian hearts; and a god that neglects this duty won't last very long, no matter how competent he may be in other respects.

Reprinted from *This Simian World*, by Clarence Day, by permission of Alfred A. Knopf, Inc. Copyright, 1920, 1948 by Katherine B. Day and Clarence Day.

But one must reciprocate. For the maker of the Cosmos, as they see him, wants noticing too; he is fond of the deference and attention that simians pay him, and naturally he will be angry if it is withheld;— or if he is not, it will be most magnanimous of him. Hence prayers and hymns. Hence queer vague attempts at communing with this noble kinsman.

To desire communion with gods is a lofty desire, but hard to attain through an ignobly definite creed. Dealing with the highest, most wordless states of being, the simians will attempt to conceive them in material form. They will have beliefs, for example, as to the furnishings and occupations in heaven. And why? Why, to help men to have religious conceptions without themselves being seers,—which in any true sense of "religious" is an impossible plan. . . .

What are the handicaps this race will have in building religions? The greatest is this: they have such small psychic powers. The over-activity of their minds will choke the birth of such powers, or dull them. The race will be less in touch with Nature, some day, than its dogs. It will substitute the compass for its once innate sense of direc-tion. It will lose its gifts of natural intuition, premonition, and rest, by encouraging its use of the mind to be cheaply incessant.

This lack of psychic power will cheat them of insight and poise; for minds that are wandering and active, not receptive and still, can sel-dom or never be hushed to a warm inner peace.

One service these restless minds however will do: they eventually will see through the religions they themselves invented.

But ages will be thrown away in repeating this process.

A simian creed will not be very hard thus to pierce. When forming a religion, they will be in far too much haste, to wait to apply a strict test to their holy men's visions. Furthermore they will have so few visions, that any will awe them; so naturally they will accept any vision as valid. Then their rapid and fertile inventiveness will come into play, and spin the wildest creeds from each vision living dust ever dreamed.

They will next expect everybody to believe whatever a few men have seen, on the slippery ground that if you simply try believing it, you will then feel it's true. Such religions are vicarious; their prophets alone will see God, and the rest will be supposed to be introduced to him by the prophets. These "believers" will have no white insight at all of their own.

Now, a second-hand believer who is warmed at one remove—if at all—by the breath of the spirit, will want to have exact definitions in the beliefs he accepts. Not having had a vision to go by, he needs plain commandments. He will always try to crystallize creeds. And that, plainly, is fatal. For as time goes on, new and remoter aspects of truth are discovered, which can seldom or never be fitted into creeds that are changeless.

Over and over again, this will be the process: A spiritual personality will be born; see new truth; and be killed. His new truth not only will not fit into too rigid creeds, but whatever false finality is in them it must contradict. So, the seer will be killed.

His truth being mighty, however, it will kill the creeds too.

There will then be nothing left to believe in—except the dead seer.

For a few generations he may then be understandingly honored. But his priests will feel that is not enough: he must be honored uncritically: so uncritically that, whatever his message, it must be deemed the Whole Truth. Some of his message they themselves will have garbled; and it was not, at best, final; but still it will be made into a fixed creed and given his name. Truth will be given his name. All men who thereafter seek truth must find only his kind, else they won't be his "followers." (To be his co-seekers won't do.) Priests will always hate any new seers who seek further for truth. Their feeling will be that their seer found it, and thus ended all that. Just believe what he says. The job's over. No more truth need be sought.

It's a comforting thing to believe cosmic search nicely settled.

Thus the mold will be hardened. So new truths, when they come, can but break it. Then men will feel distraught and disillusioned, and civilizations will fall.

Thus each cycle will run. So long as men intertwine falsehoods with every seer's visions, both perish, and every civilization that is built on them must perish too.

—This Simian World (XVI, XVII)

3. ESSAY ON BLACK

The plain truth is, of course, that modern Christianity is too often painted in black, and the modern man does not like black. You cannot sell salvation unless you sell conviction of sin first, just as you cannot sell a medicine unless you first sell conviction of a disease. By sheer instinct, missionaries have been doing just that all over Africa, Asia, and the South Pacific islands; the greater the consciousness of nudity, the bigger the sale of calico, and so the skirts in Tahiti get longer and longer while those in New York get shorter and shorter. Concomitantly, the consciousness of sin grows thinner and thinner in New York while it grows stronger and stronger in Tahiti, and if the missionaries are right, Tahiti must one day become the bastion of religion. I won't go so far as an economic historian, to interpret this as the natural movement of calico. Still—the "Bikini" bathing suit comes back to New York with a sudden vengeance.

We are only occupied with the problem of modern consciousness. By that, I mean the problem of the average man's attitude toward religion or toward the church. That is where the clergyman, if he has any experimental spirit, must conduct the test. Pending a Gallup poll on man's private religious beliefs with regard to the articles of the creed, we may study, from letters and journals, what those beliefs of men and women of the past were. And so it seems immensely more important to me to find out what Mrs. Emerson thought than what her husband thought; that is, what she said to her husband in the privacy of her household, casually, truthfully. Lidian Emerson is not just Lidian Emerson here; she, I believe, was the average woman, religious by instinct, willing to believe, but confused. Emerson notes in his *Journals* a short line, which ought to frighten all clergymen, "Lidian says it is wicked to go to church on Sundays." [2] For if Lidian spoke there her own feelings merely, it is nothing; if she said what many other women felt and feel then and now, it is everything. And

[2] Entry of December 3, 1838. In the "Divinity Address," Emerson mentions merely a "devout person" as saying this. "It is already beginning to indicate character and religion to withdraw from the religious meetings. I have heard a devout person, who prized the Sabbath, say in bitterness of heart, 'On Sundays, it seems wicked to go to church.'"

if it is everything, then the question is, what made Lidian Emerson and a lot of others feel the way she did? The consensus seems to point to one thing—something in black. That was the impression, according to the witty Benjamin Franklin, which a white man's church sermon made on an Indian who happened to go into a church service and could not understand the sermon in English. What the Indian saw was "a figure in black" who began to talk to the people "very angrily." But we will let Franklin tell the story; it is from one of Franklin's best satires. Conrad Weiser, an Indian interpreter, was telling Franklin the story of how he talked with Canassatego who could not make head or tail of a Sunday sermon which he heard, except that he surmised the purpose was to cheat him on the price of a beaver.

Canassatego's Impression of a White Man's Sermon

BY BENJAMIN FRANKLIN

Conrad answered all his Questions; and when the Discourse began to flag, the Indian, to continue it, said, "Conrad, you have lived long among the white People, and know something of their Customs; I have been sometimes at Albany, and have observed, that once in Seven Days they shut up their Shops, and assemble all in the great House; tell me what it is for? What do they do there?" "They meet there," says Conrad, "to hear and learn *good Things.*" "I do not doubt," says the Indian, "that they tell you so; they have told me the same; but I doubt the Truth of what they say, and I will tell you my Reasons. I went lately to Albany to sell my Skins and buy Blankets, Knives, Powder, Rum, &c. You know I us'd generally to deal with Hans Hanson; but I was a little inclin'd this time to try some other Merchant. However, I call'd first upon Hans, and asked him what he would give for Beaver. He said he could not give any more than four Shillings a Pound; 'but,' says he, 'I cannot talk on Business now; this is the Day when we meet together to learn *Good Things,* and I am going to the Meeting.' So I thought to myself, 'Since we cannot do any Business to-day, I may as well go to the meeting too,' and I went with him. There stood up a Man in Black, and began to talk to the People very angrily. I did not understand what he said; but, perceiving that he look'd much at me and at Hanson, I imagin'd he was angry at seeing me there; so I went out, sat down near the House, struck Fire, and lit my Pipe, waiting till the Meeting should break up. I thought too, that the Man had mention'd something of Beaver, and I suspected it might be the Subject of their Meeting. So, when they came out, I accosted my Merchant. 'Well, Hans,' says I, 'I hope you have agreed to give more than four Shillings a Pound.' 'No,' says he, 'I cannot give so much; I cannot give more than three shillings and sixpence.' I then spoke to several other Dealers, but they all sung the same song,— Three and sixpence,—Three and sixpence. This made it clear to me, that my Suspicion was right; and, that whatever they pretended of meeting to learn *good Things,* the real purpose was to consult how to cheat Indians in the Price of Beaver. Consider but a little, Conrad, and you must be of my Opinion. If they met so often to learn *good Things,* they would certainly have learnt some before this time. But they are still ignorant. You know our Practice. If a White Man, in travelling thro' our Country, enters one of our Cabins, we all treat him as I treat you; we dry him if he is wet, we warm him if he is cold, we give him Meat and Drink, that he may allay his Thirst and Hunger; and we spread soft Furs for him to rest and sleep on; we demand nothing in return. But, if I go into a white Man's House at Albany, and ask for Victuals and Drink, they say, 'Where is your Money?' and if I have none, they say, 'Get out, you Indian Dog.' You see they have not yet learned those little *Good Things,* that we need no Meetings to be instructed in, because our Mothers taught them to us when we were Children; and therefore it is impossible their Meetings should be, as they say, for any such purpose, or have any such Effect; they are only to contrive *the Cheating of Indians in the Price of Beaver."*

—*Remarks Concerning the Savages of North America*

Franklin's piece was published in 1784, and my radio sermon was heard in 1947, so it seems the style of preaching sermons in black has not essentially changed, although literary styles have. My point is, if a sermon sounds bad when you don't understand a word of it, it can't improve when you do.

Why is it so mournful, I mean the "glad tidings"? Thoreau also noted in his *Journals,* when he was quite young, about "Divine Service in the Academy Hall": "In dark places and dungeons those words might perhaps strike root and grow, but utter them in the daylight and their husky hues are apparent. From this window I can compare the written with the preached word: within is weeping and wailing and gnashing of teeth; without, grain fields and grasshoppers, which give those the lie direct." [3]

The "wickedness" of it all was apparent. It must have been the same feeling of closeness, of hothouse and artificial cultivation that made Oliver Wendell Holmes say parenthentically, "I am not a church-man—I don't believe in planting oaks in flower-pots. . . . Talk about it as much as you like,—one's breeding shows itself nowhere more than in religion." [4] And listen to Mrs. Lincoln. The implied contrast between being religious and going to church is pathetic. Mary Todd herself went to church; her social instinct was strong. She said of her husband, "Mr. Lincoln had no faith and no hope in the usual accepta-tion of those words. He never joined a church; but still, as I believe, he was a religious man by nature. He first seemed to think about the subject when our boy Willie died, and then more than ever about the time he went to Gettysburg; but it was a kind of poetry in his nature, and he was never a technical Christian." [5] It seems no longer possible today to determine whether this age is religious or irreligious by counting the noses of the persons who go to church. To decide that this is an irreligious age by counting churchgoers does not indicate anything to me; I do not go to church on Sundays, and many of my religious friends, men and women who live truly by a religious and reverent view of life and God and their fellow men do not go to church.

But artistically the best picture of the position of the church is drawn by David Grayson in *The Friendly Road*. I say artistically because the Black Spectre in a black cloak, black hat, black tie, black trousers, and black shoes, carrying black books, comes with such a powerful shock, on that beautiful, matchless, triumphant spring day. It is at the same time a picture and a comment, and I include it here because it gives the typically charming world of Grayson.

[3] Quoted in Odell Shepard (Ed.), *The Heart of Thoreau's Journals*, pp. 8–9. Houghton Mifflin Company.
[4] *The Autocrat of the Breakfast Table*, XII.
[5] Quoted in Herndon's *Lincoln*, 1890 ed., p. 445.

A Sunday in Spring

BY DAVID GRAYSON

It is one of the prime joys of the long road that no two days are ever remotely alike—no two hours even; and sometimes a day that begins calmly will end with the most stirring events.

It was thus, indeed, with that perfect spring Sunday when I left my friends, the Vedders, and turned my face again to the open country. It began as quietly as any Sabbath morning of my life, but what an end it had! I would have traveled a thousand miles for the adventures which a bounteous road that day spilled carelessly into my willing hands.

I can give no adequate reason why it should be so, but there are Sunday mornings in the spring—at least in our country—which seem to put on, like a Sabbath garment, an atmosphere of divine quietude. Warm, soft, clear, but, above all, immeasurably serene.

Such was that Sunday morning; and I was no sooner well afoot than I yielded to the ingratiating mood of the day. Usually I am an active walker, loving the sense of quick motion and the stir it imparts to both body and mind, but that morning I found myself loitering, looking widely about me, and enjoying the lesser and quieter aspects of nature. It was a fine wooded country in which I found myself, and I soon struck off the beaten road and took to the forest and the fields. In places the ground was almost covered with meadow-rue, like green shadows on the hillsides, not yet in seed, but richly umbrageous. In the long green grass of the meadows shone the yellow star-flowers, and the sweet-flags were blooming along the marshy edges of the ponds. The violets had disappeared, but they were succeeded by wild geraniums and rank-growing vetches. . . .

Well, I loitered through the fields and woods for a long time that Sunday forenoon, not knowing in the least that Chance held me close by the hand and was leading me onward to great events. I knew, of course, that I had yet to find a place for the night, and that this might be difficult on Sunday, and yet I spent that forenoon as a man spends his immortal youth—with a glorious disregard for the future.

Some time after noon—for the sun was high and the day was growing much warmer—I turned from the road, climbed an inviting little hill, and chose a spot in an old meadow in the shade of an apple tree, and there I lay down on the grass and looked up into the dusky shadows of the branches above me. I could feel the soft airs on my face; I could hear the buzzing of bees in the meadow flowers, and by turning my head just a little I could see the slow fleecy clouds, high up, drifting across the perfect blue of the sky. And the scent of the fields in spring!—he who has known it, even once, may indeed die happy.

Men worship God in various ways: it seemed to me that Sabbath morning, as I lay quietly there in the warm silence of midday, that I was truly worshipping God. That Sunday morning everything about me seemed somehow to be a miracle—a miracle gratefully accepted and explainable only by the presence of God. There was another strange, deep feeling which I had that morning, which I have had a few other times in my life at the rare heights of experience—I hesitate always when I try to put down the deep, deep things of the human heart—a feeling immeasurably real, that if I should turn my head quickly, I should indeed *see* that Immanent Presence. . . .

One of the few birds I know that sings through the long midday is the vireo. The vireo sings when otherwise the woods are still. You do not see him; you cannot find him; but you know he is there. And his singing is wild, and shy, and mystical. Often it haunts you like the memory of some former happiness. That day I heard the vireo singing. . . .

I don't know how long I lay there under the tree in the meadow, but presently I heard, from no great distance, the sound of a church-bell. It was ringing for the afternoon service which among the farmers of this part of the country often takes the place, in summer, of both morning and evening services.

"I believe I'll go," I said, thinking first of all, I confess, of the interesting people I might meet there.

But when I sat up and looked about me the desire faded, and rummaging in my bag I came across my tin whistle. Immediately I began practising a tune called "Sweet Afton," which I had learned when a boy; and, as I played, my mood changed swiftly, and I began to smile at myself as a tragically serious person, and to think of pat phrases with

which to characterize the execrableness of my attempts upon the tin
whistle. I should have liked some one near to joke with.

Long ago I made a motto about boys: Look for a boy anywhere.
Never be surprised when you shake a cherry tree if a boy drops out
of it; never be disturbed when you think yourself in complete solitude
if you discover a boy peering out at you from a fence corner.

I had not been playing long before I saw two boys looking at me
from out of a thicket by the roadside; and a moment later two others
appeared.

Instantly I switched into "Marching Through Georgia," and began
to nod my head and tap my toe in the liveliest fashion. Presently one
boy climbed up on the fence, then another, then a third. I continued to
play. The fourth boy, a little chap, ventured to climb up on the fence.

They were bright-faced, tow-headed lads, all in Sunday clothes.

"It's hard luck," said I, taking my whistle from my lips, "to have to
wear shoes and stockings on a warm Sunday like this."

"You bet it is!" said the bold leader.

"In that case," said I, "I will play 'Yankee Doodle.' "

I played. All the boys, including the little chap, came up around me,
and two of them sat down quite familiarly on the grass. I never had
a more devoted audience. I don't know what interesting event might
have happened next, for the bold leader, who stood nearest, was becoming dangerously inflated with questions—I don't know what might
have happened had we not been interrupted by the appearance of a
Spectre in Black. It appeared before us there in the broad daylight in
the middle of a sunny afternoon while we were playing "Yankee
Doodle." First I saw the top of a black hat rising over the rim of the
hill. This was followed quickly by a black tie, a long black coat, black
trousers, and, finally, black shoes. I admit I was shaken, but being a
person of iron nerve in facing such phenomena I continued to play
"Yankee Doodle." In spite of this counter-attraction, toward which all
four boys turned uneasy glances, I held my audience. The Black
Spectre, with a black book under its arm, drew nearer. Still I continued to play and nod my head and tap my toe. I felt like some
modern Pied Piper piping away the children of these modern hills—
piping them away from older people who could not understand them.

I could see an accusing look on the Spectre's face. I don't know

what put it into my head, and I had no sooner said it than I was sorry
for my levity, but the figure with the sad garments there in the matchless and triumphant spring day affected me with a curious sharp
impatience. Had any one the right to look out so dolefully upon such
a day and such a scene of simple happiness as this? So I took my
whistle from my lips and asked:

"Is God dead?"

I shall never forget the indescribable look of horror and astonishment that swept over the young man's face.

"What do you mean, sir?" he asked with an air of stern authority
which surprised me. His calling for the moment lifted him above
himself: it was the Church which spoke.

I was on my feet in an instant, regretting the pain I had given
him; and yet it seemed worth while now, having made my inadvertent
remark, to show him frankly what lay in my mind. Such things
sometimes help men.

"I meant no offense, sir," I said, "and I apologize for my flummery,
but when I saw you coming up the hill, looking so gloomy and disconsolate on this bright day, as though you disapproved of God's
world, the question slipped out before I knew it."

My words evidently struck deep down into some disturbed inner
consciousness, for he asked—and his words seemed to slip out before
he thought:

"Is *that* the way I impressed you?"

I found my heart going out strongly toward him. "Here," I thought
to myself, "is a man in trouble."

I took a good long look at him. He was still a young man, though
worn-looking—and sad, as I now saw it, rather than gloomy—with
the sensitive lips and the unworldly look one sees sometimes in the
faces of saints. His black coat was immaculately neat, but the worn
button-covers and the shiny lapels told their own eloquent story.
Oh, it seemed to me I knew him as well as if every incident of his life
were written plainly upon his high, pale forehead! I have lived long
in a country neighborhood, and I knew him—poor flagellant of the
rural church—I knew how he groaned under the sins of a community
too comfortably willing to cast all its burdens on the Lord, or on the
Lord's accredited local representative. I inferred also the usual large

family and the low salary (scandalously unpaid) and the frequent
moves from place to place.

Unconsciously heaving a sigh the young man turned partly aside
and said to me in a low, gentle voice:

"You are detaining my boys from church."

"I am very sorry," I said, "and I will detain them no longer," and
with that I put aside my whistle, took up my bag and moved down
the hill with them.

"The fact is," I said, "when I heard your bell I thought of going to
church myself."

"Did you?" he asked eagerly. "Did you?"

I could see that my proposal of going to church had instantly
affected his spirits. Then he hesitated abruptly with a sidelong glance
at my bag and rusty clothing. I could see exactly what was passing
in his mind.

"No," I said, smiling, as though answering a spoken question, "I
am not exactly what you would call a tramp."

He flushed.

"I didn't mean—I *want* you to come. That's what a church is for.
If I thought—"

But he did not tell me what he thought; and, though he walked
quietly at my side, he was evidently deeply disturbed. Something of
his discouragement I sensed even then, and I don't think I was ever
sorrier for a man in my life than I was for him at that moment. Talk
about the sufferings of sinners! I wonder if they are to be compared
with the trials of the saints?

So we approached the little white church, and caused, I am certain,
a tremendous sensation. Nowhere does the unpredictable, the unusual,
excite such confusion as in that settled institution—the church.

I left my bag in the vestibule, where I have no doubt it was the
object of much inquiring and suspicious scrutiny, and took my place
in a convenient pew. It was a small church with an odd air of domes-
ticity, and the proportion of old ladies and children in the audience
was pathetically large. As a ruddy, vigorous, out-of-door person, with
the dust of life upon him, I felt distinctly out of place.

I could pick out easily the Deacon, the Old Lady Who Brought
Flowers, the President of the Sewing Circle, and, above all, the Chief

Pharisee, sitting in his high place. The Chief Pharisee—his name I learned was Nash, Mr. J. H. Nash (I did not know then that I was soon to make his acquaintance)—the Chief Pharisee looked as hard as nails, a middle-aged man with stiff white chin-whiskers, small, round, sharp eyes, and a pugnacious jaw.

"That man," said I to myself, "runs this church," and instantly I found myself looking upon him as a sort of personification of the troubles I had seen in the minister's eyes.

I shall not attempt to describe the service in detail. There was a discouraging droop and quaver in the singing, and the mournful-looking deacon who passed the collection-plate seemed inured to disappointment. The prayer had in it a note of despairing appeal which fell like a cold hand upon one's living soul. It gave one the impression that this was indeed a miserable, dark, despairing world, which deserved to be wrathfully destroyed, and that this miserable world was full of equally miserable, broken, sinful, sickly people.

The sermon was a little better, for somewhere hidden within him this pale young man had a spark of the divine fire, but it was so dampened by the atmosphere of the church that it never rose above a pale luminosity.

I found the service indescribably depressing. I had an impulse to rise up and cry out—almost anything to shock these people into opening their eyes upon real life. Indeed, though I hesitate about setting it down here, I was filled for some time with the liveliest imaginings of the following serio-comic enterprise:

I would step up the aisle, take my place in front of the Chief Pharisee, wag my finger under his nose, and tell him a thing or two about the condition of the church.

"The only live thing here," I would tell him, "is the spark in that pale minister's soul; and you're doing your best to smother that."

And I fully made up my mind that when he answered back in his chief-pharisaical way I would gently but firmly remove him from his seat, shake him vigorously two or three times (men's souls have often been saved with less!), deposit him flat in the aisle, and—yes—stand on him while I elucidated the situation to the audience at large. While I confined this amusing and interesting project to the humors of the imagination I am still convinced that something of the sort would have helped enormously in clearing up the religious and moral atmosphere of the place.

I had a wonderful sensation of relief when at last I stepped out again into the clear afternoon sunshine and got a reviving glimpse of the smiling green hills and the quiet fields and the sincere trees— and felt the welcome of the friendly road.

—*The Friendly Road* (IV)

It turned out that the young minister sought him out after church and invited him to his house, where he saw the minister's wife, a faded-looking woman who had once possessed a delicate sort of prettiness, waiting for her husband on the steps with a fine chubby baby on her arm—number five. There Grayson, aided and abetted by Mrs. Minister, stirred up a mighty battle in which Christian met Apollyon, that is, the Minister met and vanquished the Pharisee, by telling his wife to get the ginger jar in the kitchen containing money that she had saved up to buy a sewing machine. He counted out the coins—twenty-four dollars and sixteen cents—and adding one dollar and eighty-four cents out of his pocket handed Mr. Nash twenty-six dollars, the latter's contribution to the church during the past year and practically told him to go to the place where Pharisees belong in afterlife. He was going to run his church his own way! "Oh, I knew exactly what was the trouble with his religion which, under the pressure of that church, he felt obliged to preach! It was the old groaning, denying, resisting religion. It was the sort of religion which sets a man apart and assures him that the entire universe in the guise of the Powers of Darkness is leagued against him. What he needed was a reviving draught of the new faith which affirms, accepts, rejoices, which feels the universe triumphantly behind it."

4. THREE GREAT RELIGIOUS NATURES

I have been interested in studying the private religious faiths of certain great Americans, and of how they had to keep these beliefs to themselves. I refer to the author of the famous "Second Inaugural Address," probably the most devoutly religious document in all American political history; the writer of the Declaration of Independence;

and the man who corrected it, the charmer of lightnings and ladies. I
refer, of course, to Lincoln, Jefferson, and Franklin. They differ from
Mary Todd Lincoln, but I don't think they differ much from Lidian
Emerson, our average man and woman, in their attitude toward the
church.

I regard Lincoln's "Second Inaugural" as the most beautiful and
magnificent blossom of all American literature, religious or nonreligious, and as expressing the best in Christian sentiments. Who can read
unmoved even for the tenth time these lines: "With malice toward
none; with charity for all; with firmness in the right as God gives us
the light to see the right, let us strive on to finish the work we are
in; to bind up the nation's wounds; to care for him who shall have
borne the battle, and for his widow, and his orphan—to do all which
may achieve and cherish a just and lasting peace among ourselves,
and with all nations." Charles Francis Adams, Jr., brother of Henry
Adams, wrote to his father about the address. "What think you of
the inaugural? That rail-splitting lawyer is one of the wonders of the
day. . . . The inaugural strikes me in its grand simplicity and directness as being for all time the historical keynote of this war; in it a
people seemed to speak in the sublimely simple utterance of ruder
times. What will Europe think of this utterance of the rude ruler, of
whom they have nourished so lofty a contempt? Not a prince or
minister in all Europe could have risen to such an equality with the
occasion." The expression of such sublimely simple sentiments echoing
"ruder times" must have its strong roots in the faith of a man of God.
One might say, "There, that is the best of Christianity—faith in Providence, humility and a sense of human limitations, firmness in the
right and compassion." Yet to analyze the sentiments is futile; the
whole comes inevitably from the man Lincoln. Beside that, the best
of Jeremiah and Isaiah seem to pale; only some of the best of the
psalms might match it in its breathless beauty of spirit, yet without
its tragic grandeur. "Fondly do we hope—fervently do we pray—that
this mighty scourge of war may speedily pass away. Yet if God wills
that it continue until all the wealth piled by the bondman's two
hundred and fifty years of unrequited toil shall be sunk, and until
every drop of blood drawn with the lash shall be paid by another
drawn with the sword, as was said three thousand years ago, so still

it must be said, 'The judgments of the Lord are true and righteous altogether.'"

Abraham Lincoln was not what we would call an intellectual. He read no foreign language, and when his law partner, William H. Herndon, had subscribed for and kept on their office table the *Westminster* and *Edinburgh Review,* he had little success in inducing Lincoln to read them. There were Spencer and Darwin, too, and the works of other English scientists. "Occasionally he would snatch one up and peruse it for a little while, but he soon threw it down with the suggestion that it was entirely too heavy for an ordinary mind to digest." [6]

The facts of Lincoln's religious beliefs are curious and indicate how the articles of belief and dogmas struck a profoundly religious nature like his and operated upon it without destroying it, so that a gentleman's agreement of silence was concluded. There are altogether too many testimonials to the contrary to make it possible for any fair reader to make him out as an orthodox or "technical Christian," as Mrs. Lincoln put it. At least in his New Salem days, in the exuberance of youth, he loved to shock people with his infidelity. He was strongly under the influence of Tom Paine's *Age of Reason* (I must say that Tom Paine was given the cold shoulder by the American nation which owed to him so much). Lincoln thought for himself; he kept his belief in the divine Providence of God, the Fatherhood of God, the brotherhood of men, and some kind of immortal life, but he had thrown out of the window the innate depravity of man, the atonement, the infallibility of the written revelation, the miracles, and future rewards and punishments, which, as J. W. Fell (to whom Lincoln first confided the details of this biography) says, would definitely place him "outside the Christian pale." "Yet," Fell continues, "to my mind, such was not the true position, since his principles and practices and the spirit of his whole life were of the very kind we universally agree to call Christian." If we are to believe Herndon, as I think we must, Lincoln prepared an extended essay in his New Salem days, striving to prove that the Bible was not inspired and Jesus Christ was not the son of God, carried it to the store where it was read and freely discussed, and intended to have it published. That was in 1834. "His friend and em-

[6] Herndon's *Lincoln,* pp. 436–7.

ployer, Samuel Hill, was among the listeners, and, seriously questioning the propriety of a promising young man like Lincoln fathering
such unpopular notions, he snatched the manuscript from his hands
and thrust it into the stove. The book went up in flames, and Lincoln's
political future was secure." [7] One must go back to what Clarence
Day says about the rarity of spiritual visions, the inevitability of the
incrustation of creeds, and the mass of "secondhand believers." In
all history of human religions, whenever there was a man who perceived a spiritual truth, the masses of simiankind first killed him
bodily and then grew a sort of incrustation around him spiritually.
Lincoln was a good enough rail-splitter to arrange a truce between
his private beliefs and the public's beliefs; he kept his own and
tolerated that of others, and as far as I know, during the presidential
campaign no epithet of atheist was thrown at him. That was because
of his deep honesty to see the light as God gave him to see the light;
he knew that God was with him. There has to be a truce always; the
sanctity of private beliefs and the right to those beliefs were the very
motive force of the Dissenters who came to found the colonies, and
of Protestantism itself. That is why it is all the more mysterious that
when Emerson preached that God builds his temple in the hearts of
men, he could be so badly misunderstood, or not understood, by a
so-called Protestant nation. But while Lincoln kept silent on religious
questions in his later years, there was no evidence that he had revised
his opinion and accepted the dogmas. I must essay the opinion that
the "Second Inaugural" was written without the benefit of the creeds;
it came so near to the core of the Christian spirit itself. Lincoln's religious position was on the whole near that of Theodore Parker, the
Unitarian. His belief was much more direct. "When I do good I feel
good, when I do bad, I feel bad, and that's my religion." [8] What was
good enough for Lincoln is good enough for me.

Benjamin Franklin and Thomas Jefferson lived in the eighteenth
century and might be broadly described as believers in "natural reli-

[7] For the material of this paragraph, see Herndon's *Lincoln,* pp. 439–446, which
included the testimonies of Lincoln's early associates, like John T. Stuart, David Davis,
William H. Hannah, I. W. Keys, and J. W. Fell, besides that of Mrs. Lincoln. Samuel
Hill was a good politician; as postmaster of New Salem he neglected the distribution
of mail and sold liquor in his store.

[8] Quoting "an old man named Glenn, in Indiana." Herndon's *Lincoln,* p. 439.

gion." It was an age that believed in reason, and the man of the Enlightenment had much more faith and hope that reason was going
to set everything right; modern man believes in reason too, but has
no hope that it will. Those were broad minds, very broad minds, both
of them. Franklin was more of a natural scientist, but he had read
Locke, Shaftesbury, Cotton Mather, and Anthony Collins (who declared war against the authoritarianism of the priests) between the
ages of twelve and eighteen, which is more than many a youth can
accomplish nowadays. Both were inventors. Franklin identified lightning (twice he escaped being electrocuted), invented the lightning rod
and the Franklin stove and discovered the Gulf Stream. He initiated
the fire company of Philadelphia, the postal service, the American
Philosophical Society at a very young age, and even thought of starting a swimming school in London. Thomas Jefferson, his junior
assistant at Paris, was more of a classical scholar than Franklin; he
read Greek, Latin, French, Italian, Spanish, and not only founded the
University of Virginia, but planned the curriculum himself. He loved
Epictetus but had no patience with Plato. At Nîmes, he stood before
the Maison Carrée, transfixed in his admiration of classic architecture,
until passers in the street thought him crazy. But he was a connois-
seur of figs and olives, wines and cheese, as well as of Greek architecture, and started a nail factory as well as a university. Scholar, botanist,
zoologist, architect, self-appointed general observer plenipotentiary of
human affairs, he invented a swivel chair that matched Franklin's
weathervane. He invented the Monroe doctrine and the "dumb-
waiter." [9] He was almost everything, including being a gentleman, all
except being a born writer. He invented also faith in the common man;
he did not invent the Declaration of Independence, no, he merely
wrote down for the American nation what it thought and felt. His
whole life was a quest for liberty, intellectual, political and religious
liberty. He compiled the Jefferson Bible, purged it of all the miracles
and controversial issues, as Franklin revised the Lord's Prayer. What
minds! How people could think without the benefit of *New York*
Times, the motor car, and the radio!

Suppose we begin with Franklin, who had the audacity to revise

[9] See his letter to President Monroe, October 24, 1823, and his letter to William
Short, August 4, 1820.

the Lord's Prayer, as illustrating the kind of eighteenth-century reason at work. Franklin took issue, not indeed with the question of what Jesus actually said, but with the appropriateness of the phraseology of the old version, and he placed the old version against the version of "B.F." In the case of the line, "Forgive us our debts as we forgive our debtors," he noticed that our liturgy uses neither the "Debtors" of Matthew, nor the "indebtedness" of Luke, but instead speaks of "those that trespass against us." Franklin dryly commented, "Perhaps the Considering it a Christian Duty to forgive Debtors was by the Compilers thought an inconvenient Idea in a trading Nation." But B.F. didn't like the whole presentation of the idea itself. It "has the Air of proposing ourselves as an Example of Goodness for God to imitate. *We hope you will be as good as we are;* you see we forgive one another, and therefore we pray that you would forgive us." [10] The critical mind was at work cheerfully, hopefully, serenely. Franklin was a much better writer than Jefferson; he was a born writer; the light touch and gentle play of humor and occasional flashes of venom revealed it. But the lucidity of his style was only a reflection of the serenity and clarity and pleasing warmth of his inner world. Franklin was enjoying himself; I don't think he was ever brought to distraction by anything political, intellectual, or religious; when he disagreed, he merely let forth some wholesome anger by telling the English and teaching them some "Rules by Which a Great Empire May be Reduced to a Small One," etc., etc. After he was good and angry and wrote this piece, or some similar piece of satire, he recovered his Franklinian equanimity. The outstanding quality of his mind was good sense.

That being the case, Franklin conceived for himself a warm adoration of the greatness of God and a sense of the smallness of man, with an overwhelming emphasis on practical morality rather than on theoretical dogmas. There is the Franklin we know in *The Way to Wealth* and also in his whole theological system. From his boyhood he was so much influenced by Cotton Mather's *Bonifacius* that the first things he wrote appeared under the pen name of "Silence Dogood." There was then a kind of wholesome ethical stability in the simple belief that God wants us to be happy, and since there can be

---

[10] "The Lord's Prayer" can be found in *Franklin,* American Writers Series, pp. 414–7.

no happiness without virtue, He also delights to see us virtuous.[11]
Nothing more complicated than that. God delights to see man happy
and enjoy himself. What a cheerful, comforting philosophy! As for the
other things, Franklin believed with the scientists of his times that
there was a plurality of gods for the plurality of universes, that there
were different "degrees of being" differing in perfection, that our God
created our solar system and looks in a general way after our welfare,
that it is all right to praise and adore him by singing and prayer, which
is a good thing to do on our part as showing gratitude for this gift of
life and this magnificent universe, but that we are really so small in
God's eyes that one "cannot conceive otherwise than that he the
Infinite Father expects or requires no Worship or Praise from us, but
that he is even infinitely above it." [12] As a matter of fact, Franklin
doubted, with Clarence Day today, that God would look after our
laundry, as it were. I have heard a laundrywoman praise God for
letting the sun shine on Monday, her washing day—what a terrific
affront to God, what a combination of brute stupidity, heathen bad
manners, and impudence and impertinence to the Almighty! With his
good sense Franklin struck a pleasant balance. In 1768, when English
troops had been sent to Boston, Franklin wrote to his English friend,
Rev. George Whitefield, "I *see* with you that our affairs are not well
managed by our rulers here below; I wish I could *believe* with you that
they are well attended to by those above; I rather suspect, from certain
circumstances, that though the general government of the universe is
well administered, our particular little affairs are perhaps below notice,
and left to take the chance of human prudence or imprudence, as either
may happen to be uppermost. It is, however, an uncomfortable thought,
and I leave it."

Even so, Franklin was one who didn't like to "disturb others in

[11] "Next to the Praise resulting from and due to his Wisdom, I believe he is pleased
and delights in the Happiness of those he has created; and since without Virtue Man
can have no Happiness in this World, I firmly believe he delights to see me Virtuous,
because He is pleased when He sees Me Happy. And since he has created many Things
which seem purely design'd for the Delight of Man, I believe he is not offended when
he sees his Children solace themselves in any manner of pleasant exercises and Innocent
Delights; and I think no Pleasure innocent, that is to Man hurtful." Benjamin Franklin's
"Articles of Belief and Acts of Religion," reprinted in *Franklin,* American Writers
Series, p. 132.
[12] *Franklin,* American Writers Series, p. 131.

334 ON THE WISDOM OF AMERICA

their belief." When he was eighty-four, Ezra Stiles, President of Yale, asked Franklin for a portrait to hang in the same room with Governor Yale and inquired of him about his religious belief. In his often quoted reply to Stiles, he stated his creed briefly in about a page: He believed in one God (whether this was a change from his position, mentioned above, is not clear from the context), in Providence, in immortality and justice in another life, and "that the most acceptable Service we render to him is doing good to his other Children." These Franklin took to be the fundamentals of all religions. As to Jesus of Nazareth, he had "with most of the present Dissenters in England some Doubts as to his Divinity," but he saw no harm, however, in its being believed, "if that Belief has the good Consequence" (almost in pragmatic phraseology). Then follows the significant postscript: he wanted to raise no questions in the public, he wanted peace in his old age. "I confide that you will not expose me to Criticism and censure by publishing any part of this Communication to you. I have ever let others enjoy their religious Sentiments, without reflecting on them for those that appeared to me unsupportable and even absurd. All Sects here, and we have a great Variety, have experienced my good will in assisting them with Subscriptions for building their new Places of Worship; and, as I have never opposed any of their Doctrines, I hope to go out of the World in Peace with them all."

Jefferson revealed more of the rationalist temper of his age than Franklin. His letter to his nephew and protégé, Peter Carr, for whose education he was responsible and who later became his secretary, shows best this characteristic temper of absolute faith in man's rational faculty, in his unquestioned right to question everything. On the whole, the advice was not so very different from what a modern liberal scholar would give to his son on the subject of religion. It may be called an experimental attitude in so far as he did not demand that Peter Carr arrive at one conclusion or another, but he did ask him to "lay aside all prejudice on both sides, and neither believe nor reject anything, because any other persons or descriptions of persons, have rejected or believed it."

"Your own reason is the only oracle given you by heaven."

DEAR PETER,

. . . Your reason is now mature enough to examine this object. In the first place, divest yourself of all bias in favor of novelty and singularity of opinion. Indulge them in any other subject rather than that of religion. It is too important, and the consequences of error may be too serious. On the other hand, shake off all the fears and servile prejudices, under which weak minds are servilely crouched. Fix reason firmly in her seat, and call to her tribunal every fact, every opinion. Question with boldness even the existence of a God; because, if there be one, he must more approve of the homage of reason, than that of blindfolded fear. . . .

Do not be frightened from this inquiry by any fear of its consequences. If it ends in a belief that there is no God, you will find incitements to virtue in the comfort and pleasantness you feel in its exercise, and the love of others which it will procure you. If you find reason to believe there is a God, a consciousness that you are acting under his eyes, and that he approves you, will be a vast additional incitement; if that there be a future state, the hope of a happy existence in that increases the appetite to deserve it; if that Jesus was also a God, you will be comforted by a belief of his aid and love. In fine, I repeat, you must lay aside all prejudice on both sides, and neither believe nor reject anything, because any other persons, or description of persons, have rejected or believed it. Your own reason is the only oracle given you by heaven, and you are answerable, not for the rightness, but uprightness of the decision.

—Thomas Jefferson, letter to Peter Carr, Paris, August 10, 1787.

Jefferson was a theist, that is, a believer in God, of whom the natural world is sufficient evidence, without the necessity of a special revelation. This is made clear in his letter to John Adams in 1823 (they had been reconciled again after both had retired from the political arena, and had started a long correspondence with each other).[13] He showed why

[13] There is an interesting small volume *Correspondence of John Adams and Thomas Jefferson,* selected by Paul Wilstach, Bobbs-Merrill, 1925. However, the material is very much abridged.

he believed in the pre-existence of a First Cause, rather than an atheistic "pre-existence of the world" without it, and he outlined to Adams the prevalent argument of believers in natural religion, that we see "proofs of the necessity of a superintending power." He rejected therefore the belief of many materialists of the nineteenth and twentieth centuries that the world merely evolved out of itself, working by "blind laws." When it came to Calvinism, his intellectual temper flashed forth. "I can never join Calvin in addressing *his* God. He was indeed an atheist, which I can never be; or rather his religion was daemonism. If ever man worshiped a false God, he did. The Being described in his five points, is not the God whom you and I acknowledge and adore, the Creator and benevolent Governor of the world; but a daemon of malignant spirit. It would be more pardonable to believe in no God at all than to blaspheme him by the atrocious attributes of Calvin. Indeed, I think that every Christian sect gives a great handle to atheism by their general dogma, that, without a revelation, there would not be sufficient proof of the being of a God. Now one-sixth of mankind only are supposed to be Christians; the other five-sixths then, who do not believe in the Jewish and Christian revelation are without a knowledge of the existence of God." [14]

The last line of the above suggests that Jefferson was a religious liberal of the broadest type. In his *Autobiography* he made it plain that the bill to establish religious freedom was to cover all religions, and not the Christian religion only. "The bill for establishing religious freedom, the principles of which had, to a certain degree, been enacted before, I had drawn in all the latitude of reason and right. It still met with opposition; but, with some mutilations in the preamble, it was finally passed; and a singular proposition proved that its protection of opinion was meant to be universal. Where the preamble declares, that coercion is a departure from the plan of the holy author of our religion, an amendment was proposed by inserting the word 'Jesus Christ,' so that it should read, 'a departure from the plan of Jesus Christ, the holy author of our religion'; the insertion was rejected by a great majority, in proof that they meant to comprehend, within the

[14] In the letter to John Adams referred to, April 11, 1823.

mantle of its protection, the Jew and the Gentile, the Christian and
Mahometan, the Hindoo, and Infidel of every denomination."

To non-Christians such as the Chinese the Jefferson Bible is often
the best introduction to the teachings of Jesus. He had worked on this
for years after he retired as President. In his preface he said he had
left out all "controversial issues"; what he left out were all the miracles
and the miraculous birth of Jesus, so that the reader after a few pages
devoted to his childhood is plunged straight into his moral sayings.
Naturally the epithet of atheist was thrown at him in the bitter
election year. He won; he had gained the respect and confidence of
the common people.

Yet, like Franklin in his old age, he too wanted "tranquillity." In
his letter to James Smith, a theological writer of Ohio, who had sent
him his pamphlet on Unitarianism, he gave his approval to Unitarianism. He was for the doctrine of one God, not three gods. "Nor was
the unity of the Supreme Being ousted from the Christian creed by the
force of reason, but by the sword of civil government, wielded at the
will of the fanatic Athanasius. . . . In fact, the Athanasian paradox that
one is three, and three but one, is so incomprehensible to the human
mind, that no candid man can say he has any idea of it, and how can
one believe what presents no idea? He who thinks he does, only
deceives himself." Thus the truce is established. "I write with freedom,
because while I claim a right to believe in God, if so my reason tells
me, I yield as freely to others that of believing in three. Both religions,
I find, make honest men, and that is the only point society has any
right to look to. Although this mutual freedom should produce mutual
indulgence, yet I wish not to be brought in question before the public
on this or any other subject, and I pray you to consider me as writing
under that trust. I take no part in controversies, religious or political.
At the age of eighty, tranquillity is the greatest good of life, and the
strongest of our desires that of dying in the good will of all mankind.
And with the assurance of all my good will to Unitarian and Trinitar-
ian, to Whig and Tory, accept for yourself that of my entire respect."

I have told the story of three great Americans, three of the greatest
in wisdom, intellect, and character, to show the dilemma that the
church is in. Perhaps, the thing to do is to let the dilemma continue;
I don't know. Heated controversies never produce anything satisfac-

tory. On the other hand, by that thinking which raised man from the slime of animal existence, conflicts of belief and profession, or enforced silence, always produce a feeling of inner discomfort, and to me at least there seems no considerable advantage in keeping such stumbling blocks to belief as the "resurrection of the flesh" (not of the spirit), based on the belief of St. Paul's generation of men that they were going to rise bodily from their graves on Christ's second coming, which was expected anywhere between A.D. 70 and 90. The antithesis between modern religious consciousness and established institutional religion is there and must be recognized as a force weakening the hold of the church.

We presume too much. Because the women of Asia Minor two thousand years ago thought themselves inferior and believed they would please God by wearing one particular costume, by putting on a veil during worship, we assume that modern New York and Ohio women think the same, not out of tolerance but out of conviction. St. Paul defied the authority of the law and the prophets by returning to common sense on the subject of circumcision, but when he established another kind of rite, no one thought fit to defy him on such subjects concerning purely local costume. And so institutional religion inevitably gathers a collection of impedimenta, which have nothing to do with religion, and turns us into idolaters all.

5. THE SPIRIT OF INQUIRY

I am not against any particular dogma, but rather against a more basic evil, the spirit of dogmatism itself. What any church practically says is that dogmas are the very bases of religion and that without them the church might as well not exist. If this has any meaning at all, it means that the church resents and is opposed to the spirit of free inquiry, that it sacredly holds that truth is all there, neatly packaged and delivered, and need not be explored again by the individual soul. If theologians should consent to teach religion by the same method and in the same spirit as professors of science teach their subjects, that is, by demanding personal observation and coming to personal conclusions rather than accepting *a priori* conclusions handed out by the professor beforehand, the result would be an explosion which might blacken the faces of some professionals, but after the smoke lifted, God would be seen on his throne, serene, intact, and untouchable. But at present, the church stands pat both on its dogmas and its dogmatism. It would rather perish with its dogmas than prosper without them. So we call a truce. I have a feeling something is being overprotected, being embalmed.

I have read discussions on the subject of science and religion by great contemporary scientists and philosophers, Julian Huxley, Alfred North Whitehead, John Dewey, Robert Andrews Millikan, and Albert Einstein, and have been struck by the similarity of their conclusions, and even in their phrasing: (1) that the unnecessary conflict between science and religion is due to the fixity and certitude (what I call dogmatism) of religion, (2) that this fixity "loads" organized religion with the nonreligious elements of the past, (3) that science constantly revises itself, but religion doesn't, and (4) that religion should do so in order to become always fresh and vital. Perhaps we might regard Professor Whitehead as an American, but I don't know. Anyway, he makes the point very clear. He reminds us that change is of the very essence of progress in scientific ideas. He points out that science constantly revises itself without any loss of face. "No man of science could subscribe without qualification to Galileo's beliefs or Newton's beliefs, or to all his own beliefs of ten years ago."

"Religion will not regain its old power until it can face change in the same spirit as science."

BY ALFRED NORTH WHITEHEAD

The present state of religion among the European races illustrates the statements which I have been making. The phenomena are mixed. There have been reactions and revivals. But on the whole, during many generations, there has been a gradual decay of religious influence in European civilization. Each revival touches a lower peak than its predecessor, and each period of slackness a lower depth. The average curve marks a steady fall in religious tone. In some countries the interest in religion is higher than in others. But in those countries where the interest is relatively high, it still falls as the generations pass. Religion is tending to degenerate into a decent formula wherewith to embellish a comfortable life. . . .

. . . Consider this contrast: when Darwin or Einstein proclaims theories which modify our ideas, it is a triumph for science. We do not go about saying that there is another defeat for science, because its old ideas have been abandoned. We know that another step of scientific insight has been gained.

Religion will not regain its old power until it can face change in the same spirit as does science. Its principles may be eternal, but the expression of those principles requires continual development. This evolution of religion is in the main a disengagement of its own proper ideas from the adventitious notions which have crept into it by reason of the expression of its own ideas in terms of the imaginative picture of the world entertained in previous ages. Such a release of religion from the bonds of imperfect science is all to the good. It stresses its own genuine message. The great point to be kept in mind is that normally an advance in science will show that statements of various religious beliefs require some sort of modification. It may be that they have to be expanded or explained, or indeed entirely restated. If the religion is a sound expression of truth, this modification will only exhibit more adequately the exact point which is of importance. This process is a gain. In so far, therefore, as any religion has any contact with physical facts, it is to be expected that the point of view of those facts must be continually modified as scientific knowledge advances. In this way, the exact relevance of these facts for religious thought will grow more and more clear. The progress of science must result in the unceasing codification of religious thought to the great advantage of religion.

—Science and the Modern World

What Professor Whitehead means is perfectly clear: religion, in order to be a living religion, requires constant reformulation, if for no other reason than the constant change of concepts through the centuries and the accidents of language itself. So long as religion remains a high perception of the Great Spirit and reverence for sentient life, it is eternal: the moment it comes into contact with facts, those facts and the concepts about facts are likely to be changed. Concepts of the spirit are eternal; concepts about facts are temporal. Such concepts about facts are, for instance, those that lie behind the doctrines of crime and punishment, mercy and justice, and those about sexual equality, local costumes, the shape of the earth, the body and the flesh (their essential sinfulness), the act of birth (whether a mother after childbirth requires a purification ceremony), the actual location and meaning of heaven and hell, etc. The ancient men liked to leave justice to the future life because, I suspect, the judicial system was pretty bad in those days; modern men would prefer to rely upon the FBI to have the maker of counterfeit bills tracked and punished here and now. Hell decreases its importance as the FBI increases its efficiency. And even the notion of God itself changes with our changing attributions to Him of constant wrathfulness, His desire for vengeance, and love of roast meat. As long as St. Paul talked about the natural man and the spiritual man, he was on fairly stable grounds. When he borrowed the image of the sacrificial lamb, he was making his idea of justice square with that of his generation, predicated upon the savage God's love to see blood drawn and drink it, even as the cannibal drank it himself. To say that God created man is a valid spiritual conception always; to say that He created man out of clay is immediately to put that "adventitious" element into the belief, which is due to the fact that early man was incapable of conceiving the infinitely more fascinating process of creation by evolution. The fundamentalist would have it that it was literal, fundamentalist clay, and nothing else. These are what Professor Whitehead calls the adventitious elements with which a religion formulated one or two thousand years ago was accidentally colored.

John Dewey expresses the same idea against fixity and arrives at the same conclusion. "In science and in industry the fact of constant change is generally accepted. Moral, religious, and articulate philosophic creeds are based upon the idea of fixity." [15] "Yet it is conceivable that the present depression in religion is closely connected with the fact that religions now prevent, because of their weight of historical encumbrances, the religious quality of experience from coming to consciousness," he said in that important book *A Common Faith*. "I pointed out that religion—or religions—is charged with beliefs, prac-

[15] *Living Philosophies,* Simon and Schuster, p. 25.

tices and modes of organization that have accrued to and been loaded upon the religious element in experience by the state of culture in which religions have developed." [16]

Millikan is one of the most religious men living. He believes in the need for participating in organized religion, and has belonged to a Union church and a Congregational church. He, too, distinguishes between the essentials of religion and the excrescences. Discussing the unnecessary conflict of science and religion, he says, "Whence, then, arises this strange idea, so often heard in popular discussions, of an incompatibility between science and religion? Here again I think the answer is clear. There is obviously no incompatibility between science and *the essentials of religion* as I have defined them. But individual religions, or branches of a religion, often contain more than these essentials"—such as Jesus' teachings. ". . . there has grown up, as I think, another excrescence upon the essentials of religion which intro-duces us into the very heart of the alleged conflict between science and religion. . . . But throughout the past two thousand years, his [Jesus'] followers, unlike him, have in many instances *loaded* their various branches of his religion with creedal statements which are full of their own woefully human frailties. The difference is so enormous as to justify calling his statements Godlike in comparison. For what are these man-made creeds? Admittedly they have been written by men, or groups of men, called together for the purpose—men so uninspired that very few of them have ever left any lasting memory of themselves. How many people now know of any name that was ever associated with any of them? In their creeds these men have often reflected in detail the state of knowledge, or the state of ignorance, of the universe, or of God—whichever term you prefer—characteristic of their times." [17]

Einstein sums up his religious beliefs in two paragraphs which come as close to a true religious feeling, of reverence in its pure form, as any I have read.

[16] John Dewey, *A Common Faith,* pp. 9 and 84. Copyright, 1934, by Yale University Press. Reprinted by permission. What John Dewey is most against is of course the ele-ment of supernaturalism in religion, which is a denial of faith in present experience.

[17] *Living Philosophies.* Copyright, 1930, Forum Publishing Company. Copyright, 1931, Simon and Schuster. Reprinted by permission. See also Millikan's strong con-demnation of the dogmatic spirit in *Evolution in Science and Religion,* pp. 86–7.

"The most beautiful thing we can experience is the mysterious. It is the source of all true art and science. He to whom this emotion is a stranger, who can no longer pause to wonder and stand rapt in awe, is as good as dead: his eyes are closed. This insight into the mystery of life, coupled though it be with fear, has also given rise to religion. To know that what is impenetrable to us really exists, manifesting itself as the highest wisdom and the most radiant beauty which our dull faculties can comprehend only in their most primitive forms— this knowledge, this feeling, is at the center of true religiousness. In this sense, and in this sense only, I belong in the ranks of devoutly religious men.

"I cannot imagine a God who rewards and punishes the objects of his creation, whose purposes are modeled after our own—a God, in short, who is but a reflection of human frailty. Neither can I believe that the individual survives the death of his body, although feeble souls harbor such thoughts through fear or ridiculous egotism. It is enough for me to contemplate the mystery of conscious life perpetuating itself through all eternity, to reflect upon the marvelous structure of the universe which we can dimly perceive, and to try humbly to comprehend even an infinitesimal part of the intelligence manifested in nature." [18]

The confusion between beliefs in spiritual truths and those regarding the laws of the factual world produces a condition wherein, according to Whitehead, religion "is tending to degenerate into a decent formula wherewith to embellish a comfortable life," instead of a vital source of power by which the spirit of man finds his highest fulfillment. Religious people today support the church not because they believe or ever think much about its dogmas, but rather because they tolerate them and are willing to leave them alone. Clarence Day left its dogmas, but Day's father also did, which is more significant. Day's father who paid five thousand dollars for his family pew was willing to leave the dogmas alone, if the church left him alone. Unbelievers cannot do the church any harm; it is the so-called "believers" who do. That is the dilemma of the church today.

Science stands for humility, for open-mindedness, for the spirit of in-

[18] *Living Philosophies*. Copyright, 1931, Forum Publishing Company. Copyright, 1931, Simon and Schuster. Reprinted by permission.

quiry; today the church stands for its antithesis, for fixity and certitude, for dogmatism and possession of all truth, often on matters temporal as well as on matters spiritual. Science tells men to inquire, the church tells men to stop inquiring. But what is the worth of the freedom of belief if we haven't the freedom to inquire? In the realm spiritual as well as in the realm temporal, anything which refuses and denies the spirit of inquiry dies.

I wish to close with the fine words of Robert Millikan: "Personally, I believe that essential religion is one of the world's supremest needs, and I believe that one of the greatest contributions that the United States ever can, or ever will, make to world progress—greater by far than any contribution which we ever have made, or can make, to the science of government—will consist in *furnishing an example to the world of how the religious life of a nation can evolve intelligently, inspiringly, reverently, completely divorced from all unreason, all superstition, and all unwholesome emotionalism.*" [19] If John Dewey's philosophy prevails and takes root, and if the American faith in present experience, in the experimental method of inquiry, is true to itself, this may really come to pass some centuries from now.

[19] *Living Philosophies,* p. 53. Copyright, 1930, Forum Publishing Company. Copyright, 1931, Simon and Schuster. Reprinted by permission.

Chapter XIII

LOVE

I. MARRIAGE

THERE is nothing so intimate in a man's life, or in a woman's, as marriage, nothing that goes so far toward leaving an imprint on the texture of life and on man's soul itself. Not even the love of a parent for his child, which certainly is the motive force of a good part of our lives and activities, goes quite so far in influencing one's character and the flavor and tone of living. It colors one's evenings at home, gives a personal atmosphere to one's garden, leaves an aroma in one's kitchen, cheers or depresses, soothes or wrecks one's nerves, and makes all the difference in the tremendous trifles of daily life—whether the jug of milk is warm, whether the coffee is hot at breakfast when the president of a corporation is going to meet his board of directors at ten that morning. "You are wrong there," I hear my reader say. "The president's wife has nothing to do with his breakfast nowadays." *"Tant pis,"* would be my reply. "Do you mean to say that the president of a corporation is no longer able to have the privilege which the farmer has, the knowledge that the scrambled egg is done not by a stranger, but by one he loves, even as his scrambled egg was prepared by his mother in his childhood?" If you take such a small daily disadvantage and add up all the small disadvantages of daily living that come from the loss of the intimate joy of association of two persons of different sex, life is hardly worth living.

No, you don't escape these things. You either have got them or you haven't. In times of peace and in times of crisis a wife counts for man and a husband counts for woman. That is because of the natural solitariness of the egg from which we were born. Once an egg is vitalized by the junction of the two sexes, it becomes an individual and through its journey from life to death, the egg's soul is shut up in solitary confinement, no matter how sociable its surroundings, and only

345

from another junction with the opposite sex can it ever forget its own loneliness. Now this love, which is one of the most uplifting feelings a man or woman can experience on this earth, and at the same time extends all the way down to a union of the flesh, is, as everyone should recognize, one of the most complicated subjects. Love, sexual love, is a thousand things. At its lowest form it is simply animal "heat," which is what St. Paul meant when he said it is better to marry than to burn. It is also the rustle of the angel's wing in heaven when a man is in love. It is the light that glows in a humble cottage across the railroad track. It is the chimney fire that keeps the hearth warm when outside is bleakness and desolation. It is the quilt that kept Edgar Allan Poe's young, fragile wife's heart warm, beating to its last second, in an unheated room—besides Poe's greatcoat and the cat and Poe's hands and his mother-in-law's hands. Sometimes I wonder. Was she happy? Was she *not* happy, so poor but so surrounded by love? What did she feel, what would any woman have felt when she read the letter her husband sent her, the only one preserved?

JUNE 12, 1846

MY DEAR HEART—MY DEAR VIRGINIA,—Our mother will explain to you why I stay away from you this night. I trust the interview I am promised will result in some *substantial good* for me—for your dear sake and hers—keep up your heart in all hopefulness, and trust yet a little longer. On my last great disappointment I should have lost my courage *but for you*—my little darling wife. You are my *greatest* and *only* stimulus now, to battle with this uncongenial, unsatisfactory, and ungrateful life.

I shall be with you to-morrow . . . P. M., and be assured until I see you I will keep in *loving remembrance* your *last words,* and your fervent prayer!

Sleep well, and may God grant you a peaceful summer with your devoted

EDGAR

I am speaking of sex and marriage of course, not sex alone in its raw animal state, but as part of a man's life. Human life differs so much already from animal existence. Instead of a colt trotting on its own feet the moment it is born and forgetting entirely its mother after

weaning, and the mother cow forgetting her calf, we have the prolonged human childhood, from which come the long years of association and knowing each other well. There is the same difference in sex
between animals and men. When I speak of sex, I mean the home, and
the home is woman. You either have got a home, or you haven't, no
matter how married you are. Nor can woman escape it either, no matter how intellectual she is. Even high-thoughted woman finds herself
thought of as a snare, says the American sage. There is a truth for the
centuries.[1]

I think of Abigail Adams. People sometimes think that women
nowadays are smarter than their grandmothers. It simply isn't so. To
be sure, the American Revolution took place at a time when there was
a conjunction of men of great character, wisdom, courage, and intellect, but I imagine the colonial wives were back of them, with the
same fire, same grit, same undaunted spirit. The fire of hatred of
the injustices and wrongs perpetrated by the English king must have
smoldered in those colonial homes in the bleak winter evenings before
it broke out and spread over the land. Something of that is seen in
Abigail Adam's letter to her husband the day after the Bunker Hill
battle began.

Abigail Adams to her husband on the Bunker Hill battle

SUNDAY, 18TH OF JUNE, 1775

DEAREST FRIEND:—

The day, perhaps the decisive day, is come, on which the fate of
America depends. My bursting heart must find vent at my pen. I have
just heard that our friend, Dr. Warren, is no more, but fell gloriously
fighting for his country; saying, "better to die honorably in the field,
than ignominiously hang upon the gallows." Great is our loss. He has
distinguished himself in every engagement, by his courage and fortitude, by animating the soldiers, and leading them on by his example.

---

[1] "Love is necessary to the righting of the estate of woman in this world. Otherwise
nature itself seems to be in conspiracy against her dignity and welfare; for the cultivated,
high-thoughted, beauty-loving, saintly woman finds herself unconsciously desired for her
sex, and even enhancing the appetite of her savage pursuers by these fine ornaments she
has piously laid on herself. She finds with indignation that she is herself a snare, and was
made such. I do not wonder at her occasional protest, violent protest against nature, in
fleeing to nunneries, and taking black veils. Love rights all this deep wrong." Thus wrote
Emerson.

A particular account of these dreadful, but I hope glorious, days, will be transmitted you, no doubt, in the exactest manner.

"The call is not to the swift, nor the battle to the strong; but the God of Israel is he that giveth strength and power unto his people. Trust in him at all times, ye people, pour out your hearts before him; God is a refuge for us." Charlestown is laid in ashes. The battle began upon our entrenchments, upon Bunker Hill, Saturday morning about three o'clock, and has not ceased yet, and it is now three o'clock Sabbath afternoon.

It is expected they will come out over the Neck to-night, and a dreadful battle must ensue. Almighty God, cover the heads of our countrymen, and be a shield to our dear friends! How many have fallen, we know not. The constant roaring of the cannon is so distressing, that we cannot eat, drink, or sleep. May we be supported and sustained in the dreadful conflict! I shall tarry here until it is thought unsafe by my friends, and then I have secured myself a retreat at your brother's, who has kindly offered me part of his house. I cannot compose myself to write any further at present. I will add more as I hear further.

—Abigail Adams

John Adams wrote to her, a year later, on a still greater day when the Declaration of Independence was about to be published.

John Adams to his wife on the birth of the new nation

Yesterday the greatest question was decided, which ever was debated in America, and a greater, perhaps, never was nor will be decided among men. A resolution was passed without one dissenting colony, "that these United Colonies are, and of right ought to be, free and independent States, and as such they have, and of right ought to have, full power to make war, conclude peace, establish commerce, and to do all other acts and things which other States may rightfully do." You will see in a few days a Declaration setting forth the causes which have impelled us to this mighty revolution, and the reasons which will justify it in the sight of God and man. A plan of confederation will be taken up in a few days.

You will think me transported with enthusiasm, but I am not.

I am well aware of the toil, and blood, and treasure, that it will cost us to maintain this declaration, and support and defend these States. Yet, through all the gloom, I can see the rays of ravishing light and glory. I can see that the end is more than worth all the means, and that posterity will triumph in that day's transaction, even although we should rue it, which I trust in God we shall not.

PHILADELPHIA, 3 JULY, 1776.

—John Adams

Of all the crudities of modern thinking by modern writers, that about love is often the shallowest. The so-called "realists" would rather take castor oil than write about a happy marriage. Others, equally unable to see life whole, take a certain pride in explaining away mother love by certain secretions and sexual love by the action of hormones, and conclude that that is all there is to it. Human experience has shown that a successful marriage, that is, a successful interweaving of two personalities and a common sharing of struggles, has always meant something more than what these "realists" would have us believe, and is at the same time as fascinating and as full of pathos and humor as material for fiction. Read, for instance, Hawthorne's letter to his wife Sophia Peabody, sister of the famous transcendentalist and bookshop keeper, Elizabeth Peabody. The letter is intrinsically valuable, not only because it expresses very well the essence of what love means, but because the author speaks there of his chamber where he sat and worked and brooded for so many years, and out of the dreams that flitted in that chamber came the *Twice-Told Tales* and other notable fiction. Elizabeth herself probably had designs upon Hawthorne, but he fell in love with the younger invalid sister. At the time of the writing they were secretly engaged, although Hawthorne speaks here of himself as her husband.

"Indeed, we are but shadows—till the heart is touched."

SALEM, OCTOBER 4TH, 1840.—½ past 10 A.M.

MINE OWNEST,

Here sits thy husband in his old accustomed chamber, where he used to sit in years gone by, before his soul became acquainted with thine. Here I have written many tales—many that have been burned to ashes—many that doubtless deserved the same fate. This deserves to be called a haunted chamber; for thousands upon thousands of visions have appeared to me in it; and some few of them have become visible to the world. If ever I should have a biographer, he ought to make great mention of this chamber in my memoirs, because so much of my lonely youth was wasted here, and here my mind and character were formed; and here I have been glad and hopeful, and here I have been despondent; and here I sat a long, long time, waiting patiently for the world to know me, and sometimes wondering why it did not know me sooner, or whether it would ever know me at all—at least, till I were in my grave. And sometimes (for I had no wife then to keep my heart warm) it seemed as if I were already in the grave, with only life enough to be chilled and benumbed. But oftener I was happy—at least, as happy as I then knew how to be, or was aware of the possibility of being. By and by, the world found me out in my lonely chamber, and called me forth—not, indeed, with a loud roar of acclamation, but rather with a still, small voice; and forth I went, but found nothing in the world that I thought preferable to my old solitude, till at length a certain Dove was revealed to me, in the shadow of a seclusion as deep as my own had been. And I drew nearer and nearer to the Dove, and opened my bosom to her, and she flitted into it, and closed her wings there—and there she nestles now and forever, keeping my heart warm, and renewing my life with her own. So now I begin to understand why I was imprisoned so many years in this lonely chamber, and why I could never break through the viewless bolts and bars; for if I had sooner made my escape into the world, I should have grown hard and rough, and been covered with earthly dust, and my heart would have become callous by rude encounters with the multitude; so that I should have been all unfit to shelter a heavenly Dove in my arms. But living in solitude till the fullness of time was come, I still kept the dew of my youth and the freshness of my heart, and had these to offer to my Dove.

Well, dearest, I had no notion what I was going to write, when I began; and indeed I doubted whether I should write anything at all; for after such intimate communion as that of our last blissful evening, it seems as if a sheet of paper could only be a veil betwixt us. Ownest, in the times that I have been speaking of, I used to think that I could imagine all passions, all feelings, all states of the heart and mind; but how little did I know what it is to be mingled with another's being! Thou only hast taught me that I have a heart—thou only hast thrown a deep light downward, and upward, into my soul. Thou only hast revealed me to myself; for without thy aid, my best knowledge of myself would have been merely to know my own shadow—to watch it flickering on the wall, and mistake its fantasies for my own real actions. Indeed, we are but shadows—we are not endowed with real life, and all that seems most real about us is but the thinnest substance of a dream—till the heart is touched. That touch creates us—then we begin to be—thereby we are beings of reality, and inheritors of eternity. Now, dearest, dost thou comprehend what thou hast done for me? And is it not a somewhat fearful thought, that a few slight circumstances might have prevented us from meeting, and then I should have returned to my solitude, sooner or later (probably now, when I have thrown down my burthen of coal and salt) and never should have been created at all! But this is an idle speculation. If the whole world had stood between us, we must have met—if we had been born in different ages, we could not have been sundered.

Belovedest, how dost thou do? If I mistake not, it was a southern rain yesterday, and, next to the sunshine of Paradise, *that* seems to be thy element.

—Nathaniel Hawthorne [2]

Another great love letter is one written by John Jay Chapman to his first wife, Minna Timmins Chapman, who died during confinement after childbirth. She was of Italian descent and called this *"La miraculosa littera d'amore,"* the miraculous love letter. Chapman was temperamentally impulsive. During his courtship of Minna there was an incident he could not live down for years. After beating up a man who he believed had intruded himself upon Minna's attention, he went back to his solitary room, thrust his left hand cold-bloodedly into a glowing coal fire and then walked to the Massachusetts General

[2] Mrs. Hawthorne had the habit of scissoring or inking out certain lines from her husband's letters. Some experts in the Huntington Library restored the inked-out passages and found they contained only such phrases as "your warm kisses"—to our great astonishment and disappointment!

Hospital to have it amputated. No wonder that, in his letter, his spirit took wings and circled the universe in its inspired passage.

"Is love a hand or a foot?"

[Littleton, Colo. Sept. 21, 1892]

I have sealed up each one of these letters thinking I had done—and then a wave of happiness has come over me—remembering you—only you, my Minna—and the joy of life. Where were you, since the beginning of the world? But now you are here, about me in every space, room, sunlight, with your heart and arms and the light of your soul—and the strong vigor your presence. It was not a waste desert in Colorado. It is not a waste time, for you are here and many lives packed into one life, and the green shoot out of the heart of the plant, springing up blossoms in the night, and many old things have put on immortality and lost things have come back knocking within, from before the time I was conceived in the womb, there were you also. And what shall we say of the pain! it was false—and the rending, it was unnecessary. It was the breaking down of the dams that ought not to have been put up—but being up it was the sweeping away of them that the waters might flow together.

This is a love letter, is it not? How long is it since I have written you a love letter, my love, my Minna? Was the spring hidden that now comes bubbling up overflowing curb and coping-stone, washing my feet and my knees and my whole self? How are the waters of the world sweet—if we should die, we have drunk them. If we should sin —or separate—if we should fail or secede—we have tasted of happiness —we must be written in the book of the blessed. We have had what life could give, we have eaten of the tree of knowledge, we have known —we have been the mystery of the universe.

Is love a hand or a foot—is it a picture or a poem or a fireside—is it a compact or a permission or eagles that meet in the clouds—No, no, no, no. It is light and heat and hand and foot and ego. If I take the wings of the morning and remain in the uttermost parts of the sea, there art thou also—He descended into Hell and on the third day rose

again—and there art thou also—in the lust or business—in the stum-
blings and dry places, in sickness and health—every sort of sickness
there also—what matter is it what else the world contains—if you only
are in it in every part of it? I can find no corner of it without you—
my eyes would not see it. It is empty—I have seen all that is there and
it is nothing, and over creation are your wings. Have we not lived
three years now together—and daily nearer—grafted till the very sap
of existence flows and circulates between us—till I know as I write this
—your thoughts—till I know as a feeling, a hope, a thought, passes
through me—it is yours? Why the agony of those old expressions and
attempts to come by diligent, nervous, steady, fixing of the eye on
the graver's tool, as if the prize depended on drawing it straight, those
pounds of paper and nights of passionate composition—did they indeed so well do their work that the goal was carried—or was it the
silent communion—of the night—even after days of littleness or quarrel
that knitted us together? It does not matter, love, which it was. It put
your soul so into my body that I don't speak to you to convey meaning. I write only for joy and happiness. How diligently have we set
fact to fact and consideration against consideration during the past
years—as if we were playing dominoes for our life. How cloudy I have
been—dragging you down, often nailing useless nails, cutting up and
dissecting, labeling, crucifying small things—and there was our great
love over us, growing, spreading—I wonder we do not shine—or
speak with every gesture and accent giving messages from the infinite
—like a Sibyl of Michael Angelo. I wonder people do not look after us
in the street as if they had seen an angel.

—Tuo Giovanni

2. GREAT MEN IN TROUBLE: FRANKLIN

The fact that great men are sometimes in trouble, which here means
in love, brings them closer to us. For only in death and love do we
recognize their equality with us, their consanguine kinship with all
of mankind. Some men have made fools of themselves, like Mark
Antony, although he would hotly deny it, would maintain that only
in the company of Cleopatra did he really come to life, really live.
Life is so relative that we would not dare to pass dogmatic judgments.

ON THE WISDOM OF AMERICA

Every man must judge for himself. But even if Mark Antony or Julius Caesar had thrown away his power and a possible empire for his mistress, the world merely pretends that in acting thus he had acted like a fool. By the very curiosity and warmth with which we love to read such a story, we recognize that we might have done the same, or at least that we could easily understand it and, moreover, we pay inward homage to it.

It is because the great men are so like ourselves when they are in love that we like to know how they felt and acted. We have, of course, to read their love letters, if there is no objection on the reader's part. We will take again Franklin, Jefferson, and Lincoln, whose religious views we have just studied. In the case of Benjamin Franklin, he was seventy-two when he met Madame Brillon in Paris and began the light, playful, gallant courtship, which was like the game of chess they used to play together every Wednesday and Saturday evening; the sage always tried to make a move, and Madame Brillon always countered, and Franklin never really won his objective. She neither rejected nor forbade his advances, and they came back to the game again and again. With Franklin's wit, these letters make delightful and often amusing reading.[3] Of course Mrs. Franklin had died, but Monsieur Brillon, a French Treasury official, was still living. Madame Brillon (her full name was d'Hardancourt Brillon de Jouy) was witty, charming, sociable and gifted. She directly inspired Franklin's "Dialogue between the Gout and M. Franklin"; it was in her company that "The Ephemera" was conceived, and the famous "The Whistle" ("paying too much for the whistle") was in the form of a letter to her. Madame Brillon was forty years his junior, the mother of several children, and that was a strong link in the established French family system. Unquestionably she was fond of the American sage, as he was of her. Typical of the sort of gallantry that went on between them

[3] There are altogether seven from Franklin. The manuscripts are preserved in the American Philosophical Society. Franklin sometimes wrote in French, and various versions in French and English are published in Smyth's *The Writings of Benjamin Franklin,* the *Proceedings* of the American Philosophical Society, and *Putnam's Monthly,* for October-December, 1906 (which gives the English translations). They are best edited and sometimes given complete for the first time in Carl van Doren's *Benjamin Franklin's Autobiographical Writings,* beginning pp. 436, 469, 476, 489, 511, 584 and 586, with complete introductory notes by Carl van Doren. The letters cover the period between 1778 and 1782. This volume is published by the Viking Press.

was the exchange of correspondence between them on "The Gout." Madame Brillon had composed and sent him "Le sage et la goutte," a fable in verse, in which she accused the sage of eating too much, coveting wives and devoting his time to chess and ladies. Franklin composed in return the "Dialogue." He defends himself by admitting that he loves, has loved, and will always love; by insisting that it is true wisdom to enjoy the good things that heaven sends—such as a little punch, a pretty mistress, or two or three or four mistresses; and by pointing out that he does not always win at chess.[4] "One of the personages of your fable, viz., Gout," wrote Franklin to her, "seems to me to reason rather well except in supposing mistresses have had a part in causing this painful malady. I myself believe very much the contrary, and this is my argument. When I was a young man and enjoyed more of the favors of the sex than I do at present, I had no gout at all. So, if the ladies of Passy had more of that kind of Christian charity which I have so often vainly recommended to you, I should not be having the gout now. This seems to me good logic."[5] Franklin knew what he was about. It was written in the same delightful vein in which in the "Dialogue"[6] he made fun of his own horrible, unsanitary way of eating and living, and castigated his own bad habits— his inordinate breakfast consisting of four dishes of tea with cream, one or two slices of buttered toast and slices of hung beef, immediately sitting down after breakfast to write at his desk, sitting again engaged at chess for two or three hours after dinner, and his aversion to walking and relying on his carriage.

Madame Brillon promised to be his wife in heaven, provided he would be more faithful than she seemed to believe he could. Franklin heartily accepted the idea, not, however, without a misgiving. "Probably more than forty years will elapse after my arrival there before

[4] See Carl van Doren's note, *Benjamin Franklin's Autobiographical Writings,* p. 484.
[5] Ibid., pp. 489–90.
[6] This "Dialogue on Gout," and many of Franklin's best essays, hoaxes, bagatelles, like his "Advice to a Young Man (on taking an old mistress)," "The Ephemera," "The Whistle," "The Speech of Polly Baker," "The Sale of the Hessians," and his other political satires are available now in the cheap Pocket Book edition, *Benjamin Franklin: The Autobiography, with sayings of Poor Richard, Hoaxes, Bagatelles, Essays and Letters,* edited by Carl van Doren, who knows and understands this great man better than any other American living.

you follow me—I have therefore thought of proposing that you give me your word of honor not to renew there your contract with Mr. B. . . . But that gentleman is so good, so generous towards us, he loves you so much and we love him, that I cannot think of this proposal without some scruples of conscience. And yet the idea of an eternity in which I shall be favored with no more than permission to kiss your hands, or sometimes your cheeks, and to pass two or three hours in your sweet society on Wednesdays and Saturdays is frightful. . . . Decide as you will, I feel that I shall love you for all eternity. . . ." And he concluded his plan for Paradise, "We shall eat apples of Paradise roasted with butter and nutmeg. And we shall pity those who are not dead."

Franklin never pretended that his love was platonic. He felt that it would be incomplete if it were. He constantly played upon the biblical Commandment not to covet thy neighbor's wife, which he thought good enough for the Jews but too uncomfortable for good Christians. In fact, the suggestion of both the inadequacy and the undesirability of the Ten Commandments was given in the very first letter, written on March 10, 1778.

To Madame Brillon

PASSY, MARCH 10 [1778].

I am charmed with the goodness of my spiritual guide, and resign myself implicitly to her conduct, as she promises to lead me to heaven in so delicious a road when I could be content to travel thither even in the roughest of all ways with the pleasure of her company.

How kindly partial to her penitent in finding him, on examining his conscience, guilty of only one capital sin, and to call that by the gentle name of foible!

I lay fast hold of your promise to absolve me of all sins past, present, and future on the easy and pleasing condition of loving God, America, and my guide above all things. I am in rapture when I think of being absolved of the future.

People commonly speak of Ten Commandments. I have been taught that there are twelve. The first was: Increase and multiply and re-plenish the earth. The twelfth is: A new Commandment I give unto you, that you love one another. It seems to me that they are a little misplaced, and that the last should have been the first. However, I never made any difficulty about that, but was always willing to obey them both whenever I had an opportunity. Pray tell me, my dear Casuist, whether my keeping religiously these two Commandments, though not in the Decalogue, may not be accepted in compensation for my breaking so often one of the ten? I mean that which forbids coveting my neighbour's wife, and which I confess I break constantly (God forgive me), as often as I see or think of my lovely confessor; and I am afraid I should never be able to repent of the sin even if I had the full possession of her.

And now I am consulting you upon a case of conscience, I will mention the opinion of a certain Father of the Church which I find myself willing to adopt, though I am not sure it is orthodox. It is this: that the most effectual way to get rid of a certain temptation is, as often as it returns, to comply with and satisfy it. Pray instruct me how far I may venture to practice upon this principle?

But why should I be so scrupulous, when you have promised to absolve me of the future?

Adieu, my charming Conductress, and believe me ever with the sincerest esteem and affection, your most obedient humble servant. . . .

—Benjamin Franklin

Three years later, during the winter of 1780–1, Madame Brillon was staying in the South of France and Franklin still carried on the theme of the Ninth Commandment. "I often pass before your house," he wrote. "It appears desolate to me. Formerly I often broke the Commandment by coveting it along with my neighbor's wife. Now I do not covet it any more, so I am less a sinner. But as to his wife I always find these Commandments inconvenient and I am sorry that they were ever made. If in your travels you happen to see the Holy Father, ask him to repeal them, as things given only to the Jews and too uncomfortable for good Christians." And so the love game was carried on until Madame Brillon, unreasonably or humorously, complained that in her absence Franklin had neglected writing her but had had time for other ladies of her country, and she drew up a treaty, in elaborate legal form, which, if signed, would assign all of Franklin's love to one person,

Madame Brillon herself. Franklin, in the midst of preparing other weightier political treaties, showed his diplomatic skill by proposing his own draft, in the form of a "Treaty Letter" [7] which substantially reserved and protected his own right to love any other ladies he liked.

The most witty as well as gallant letter of Franklin's, however, was addressed to Madame Helvétius, widow of a French philosopher. It was so irresistibly good that Franklin printed it twice at his own private press at Passy. He composed the letter one morning after he had spent an evening with her in "extravagant nonsense," in the course of which Franklin had proposed and been rejected. As Carl van Doren says Franklin was not a tragic lover. He could not be, and besides, he was courting Madame Brillon at the same time.

To Madame Helvétius

Mortified at the barbarous resolution pronounced by you so positively yesterday evening, that you would remain single the rest of your life as a compliment due to the memory of your husband, I retired to my chamber. Throwing myself upon my bed, I dreamt that I was dead and was transported to the Elysian Fields.

I was asked whether I wished to see any persons in particular to which I replied that I wished to see the philosophers. "There are two who live here at hand in this garden; they are good neighbours, and very friendly towards one another." "Who are they?" "Socrates and Helvétius." "I esteem them both highly; but let me see Helvétius first, because I understand a little French, but not a word of Greek." I was conducted to him. He received me with much courtesy, having known me, he said, by character, some time past. He asked me a thousand questions relative to the war, the present state of religion, of liberty, of the government in France. "You do not inquire, then," said I, "after your dear friend, Madame Helvétius; yet she loves you exceedingly. I was in her company not more than an hour ago." "Ah," said he, "you make me recur to my past happiness, which ought to be forgotten in order to be happy here. For many years I could think of nothing but her, though at length I am consoled. I have taken another wife, the most like her that I could find; she is not indeed altogether so

[7] *Benjamin Franklin's Autobiographical Writings*, pp. 584-6. Viking Press.

handsome, but she has a great fund of wit and good sense, and her whole study is to please me. She is at this moment gone to fetch the best nectar and ambrosia to regale me; stay here awhile and you will see her." "I perceive," said I, "that your former friend is more faithful to you than you are to her; she has had several good offers, but has refused them all. I will confess to you that I loved her extremely; but she was cruel to me, and rejected me peremptorily for your sake." "I pity you sincerely," said he, "for she is an excellent woman, handsome and amiable. But do not the Abbé de La Roche and the Abbé Morellet visit her?" "Certainly they do; not one of your friends has dropped her acquaintance." "If you had gained the Abbé Morellet with a bribe of good coffee and cream, perhaps you would have succeeded; for he is as deep a reasoner as Duns Scotus or St. Thomas; he arranges and methodizes his arguments in such a manner that they are almost irresistible. Or if by a fine edition of some old classic you had gained the Abbé de La Roche to speak *against* you, that would have been still better, as I always observed that when he recommended anything to her, she had a great inclination to do directly the contrary." As he finished these words the new Madame Helvétius entered with the nectar, and I recognized her immediately as my former American friend, Mrs. Franklin! I reclaimed her, but she answered me coldly: "I was a good wife to you for forty-nine years and four months, nearly half a century; let that content you. I have formed a new connection here, which will last to eternity."

Indignant at this refusal of my Eurydice, I immediately resolved to quit those ungrateful shades, and return to this good world again, to behold the sun and you; here I am; let us *avenge ourselves.*

—Benjamin Franklin

It is so hard to describe Franklin. I can best summarize by saying that Franklin was always at ease, that he was morally and intellectually happy. It won't do to say merely that he was a man of the world. Because he was a man, he loved.[8] He was about as moral as Goethe, though he spoke more like a good newspaper editor who

---

[8] Franklin had an illegitimate son; so did his son; so did his son's son. Confucius divorced his wife; so did his son; so did his son's son. What is it? I am curious. Franklin was so like Confucius anyway. Confucius, too, was completely happy always.

knows how to display his ideas in clear, sensible language than like a poet from Mount Parnassus. Above all, he had a clear mind, and it was from that clear, equitable temper of mind that the warm glow of humor and serenity flowed through his writings. It seems to me that he always knew what he wanted and was happy about it. How few of us can say that about ourselves! Above all, his was always a searching mind. If anything, he was original. He had said many good and sensible things about marriage and love in his "Reflections on Courtship and Marriage." He had claimed marriage as "the original fountain from whence the greatest and most extensive governments have derived their beings." (Confucius again!) But he saw also the case for mothers of illegitimate children, thus somewhat antedating modern Swedish laws. He made such a spirited defense of these mothers in "The Speech of Polly Baker" that it still strikes the modern reader as a forceful and convincing argument. This is a vexed question, and we do not propose to go into it, but if there is any inalienable right a human being may be said to possess, it is woman's right to motherhood. The conclusion of this piece of fiction is satisfying; the judge married the woman himself, as, I believe, any modern judge today would.

The Speech of Polly Baker

BY BENJAMIN FRANKLIN

The Speech of Miss Polly Baker before a Court of Judicature, at Connecticut near Boston in New England; where she was prosecuted the fifth time, for having a Bastard Child: Which influenced the Court to dispense with her Punishment, and which induced one of her Judges to marry her the next Day—by whom she had fifteen Children.

"May it please the honourable bench to indulge me in a few words: I am a poor, unhappy woman, who have no money to fee lawyers to plead for me, being hard put to it to get a living. I shall not trouble your honours with long speeches; for I have not the presumption to expect that you may, by any means, be prevailed on to deviate in your Sentence from the law, in my favour. All I humbly hope is, that your honours would charitably move the governor's goodness on my behalf, that my fine may be remitted. This is the fifth time, gentlemen, that

I have been dragg'd before your court on the same account; twice I
have paid heavy fines, and twice have been brought to publick punishment, for want of money to pay those fines. This may have been agreeable to the laws, and I don't dispute it; but since laws are sometimes
unreasonable in themselves, and therefore repealed; and others bear
too hard on the subject in particular circumstances, and therefore there
is left a power somewhere to dispense with the execution of them; I
take the liberty to say, that I think this law, by which I am punished,
both unreasonable in itself, and particularly severe with regard to me,
who have always lived an inoffensive life in the neighbourhood where I
was born, and defy my enemies (if I have any) to say I ever wrong'd
any man, woman, or child. Abstracted from the law, I cannot conceive
(may it please your honours) what the nature of my offense is. I have
brought five fine children into the world, at the risque of my life; I
have maintain'd them well by my own industry, without burthening
the township, and would have done it better, if it had not been for the
heavy charges and fines I have paid. Can it be a crime (in the nature
of things, I mean) to add to the king's subjects, in a new country, that
really wants people? I own it, I should think it rather a praiseworthy
than a punishable action. I have debauched no other woman's husband,
nor enticed any other youth; these things I never was charg'd with;
nor has any one the least cause of complaint against me, unless, perhaps, the ministers of justice, because I have had children without
being married, by which they have missed a wedding fee. But can this
be a fault of mine? I appeal to your honours. You are pleased to allow
I don't want sense; but I must be stupified to the last degree, not to
prefer the honourable state of wedlock to the condition I have lived
in. I always was, and still am willing to enter into it; and doubt not
my behaving well in it, having all the industry, frugality, fertility, and
skill in economy appertaining to a good wife's character. I defy any
one to say I ever refused an offer of that sort: on the contrary, I readily
consented to the only proposal of marriage that ever was made me,
which was when I was a virgin, but too easily confiding in the person's
sincerity that made it, I unhappily lost my honour by trusting to his;
for he got me with child, and then forsook me.

"That very person, you all know, he is now become a magistrate of
this country; and I had hopes he would have appeared this day on the

bench, and have endeavoured to moderate the Court in my favour; then I should have scorn'd to have mentioned it; but I must now complain of it, as unjust and unequal, that my betrayer and undoer, the first cause of all my faults and miscarriages (if they must be deemed such), should be advanced to honour and power in this government that punishes my misfortunes with stripes and infamy. I should be told, 'tis like, that were there no act of Assembly in the case, the precepts of religion are violated by my transgressions. If mine is a religious offense, leave it to religious punishments. You have already excluded me from the comforts of your church communion. Is not that sufficient? You believe I have offended heaven, and must suffer eternal fire: Will not that be sufficient? What need is there then of your additional fines and whipping? I own I do not think as you do, for, if I thought what you call a sin was really such, I could not presumptuously commit it. But, how can it be believed that heaven is angry at my having children, when to the little done by me towards it, God has been pleased to add his divine skill and admirable workmanship in the formation of their bodies, and crowned the whole by furnishing them with rational and immortal souls?

"Forgive me, gentlemen, if I talk a little extravagantly on these matters; I am no divine, but if you, gentlemen, must be making laws, do not turn natural and useful actions into crimes by your prohibitions. But take into your wise consideration the great and growing number of batchelors in the country, many of whom, from the mean fear of the expenses of a family, have never sincerely and honourably courted a woman in their lives; and by their manner of living leave unproduced (which is little better than murder) hundreds of their posterity to the thousandth generation. Is not this a greater offense against the publick good than mine? Compel them, then, by law, either to marriage, or to pay double the fine of fornication every year. What must poor young women do, whom customs and nature forbid to solicit the men, and who cannot force themselves upon husbands, when the laws take no care to provide them any, and yet severely punish them if they do their duty without them; the duty of the first and great command of nature and nature's God, *encrease and multiply;* a duty, from the steady performance of which nothing has been able to deter me, but for its sake I have hazarded the loss of the publick esteem, and have frequently endured publick disgrace and punishment; and therefore ought, in my humble opinion, instead of a whipping, to have a statue erected to my memory."

—*Gentleman's Magazine*, April, 1794

3. JEFFERSON IN TROUBLE

How different is the story of Jefferson in love! Jefferson's was a perfect marriage. His brunette wife was a finely educated person, warm, graceful, vivacious, a graceful dancer and musician, and born of a very rich family. She was a fine flower of the Virginian aristocracy of those days. After giving birth to five children in ten years, her health broke down, and when the sixth came she succumbed after lingering four months in bed. Jefferson's grief was such that he fell into a long faint, and afterward paced up and down his room, lost and frightened to live without her. Classical scholar that he was, he had her epitaph inscribed in Greek, to guard the sanctity of his private emotions. It was indeed a long time before the wound healed. The story was that Mrs. Jefferson on her deathbed had made him promise never to give their children (of whom three had died) a stepmother, and this promise he kept for forty-four years until his death. When four years later, he met Mrs. Cosway and her husband in Paris, he had a mighty battle between his head and his heart. None of the placidity and gallantry of Franklin was his. Perhaps because he loved fewer women, he was bitten harder. His head won, as we can well guess, but not without some anguish.

Mrs. Cosway (Maria Cecilia Cosway) was a miniature painter, as was her husband, and they were traveling in Europe. In Paris they visited with Jefferson St. Germain, St. Cloud, and the art galleries. At their departure Jefferson sat down to write a fourteen-page letter to pour out his grief to the wife. He wrote this long epistle with his left hand because his right wrist had been hurt.

According to Jefferson, her charms were her music, modesty, beauty, and "that softness of disposition which is the ornament of her sex," qualities revealing the feminine ideal of Jefferson's days. Jefferson, we know, was an intellectual. But he felt, as well as thought—it made him a fuller man. I like him for speaking about "the solid pleasure of one generous spasm of the heart."

Thomas Jefferson to Mrs. Cosway: Dialogue of the Head and the Heart

PARIS, OCTOBER 12, 1786

MY DEAR MADAM,—Having performed the last sad office of handing you into your carriage, at the pavilion de St. Denis, and seen the wheels get actually into motion, I turned on my heel and walked, more dead than alive, to the opposite door, where my own was awaiting me. . . . I was carried home. Seated by my fireside, solitary and sad, the following dialogue took place between my Head and my Heart.

Head. Well, friend, you seem to be in a pretty trim.

Heart. I am indeed the most wretched of all earthly beings. Overwhelmed with grief, every fibre of my frame distended beyond its natural powers to bear, I would willingly meet whatever catastrophe should leave me no more to feel, or to fear.

Head. These are the eternal consequences of your warmth and precipitation. This is one of the scrapes into which you are ever leading us. You confess your follies, indeed; but still you hug and cherish them; and no reformation can be hoped where there is no repentance.

Heart. Oh, my friend! this is no moment to upbraid my foibles. I am rent into fragments by the force of my grief! If you have any balm, pour it into my wounds; if none, do not harrow them by new torments. Spare me in this awful moment! At any other, I will attend with patience to your admonitions.

[Jefferson went on in this manner, suggesting that of Franklin's "Dialogue between the Gout and Franklin," which he must have read and admired, but in this case the Head was chiding the Heart for its folly. He reviewed the days they had spent together. The Heart blamed the Head for being occupied with diagrams and crochets, and the Head defended itself by saying that it was thinking how to build a market place at Richmond and put on it the noble dome of the Halle aux Bleds, how the Heart had really betrayed him, making him send lying messages to break an engagement in order to get into a scrape with the charming Mrs. Cosway, and how, after the first day, he retraced the journey with fond recollections and urged him on to a second meeting!

*Then the Head reminded him that he should have known that the visit
of Mrs. Cosway was to be short, and they would probably never meet
again.*]

Heart. But they told me they would come back again, the next year.

Head. But, in the meantime, see what you suffer; and their return,
too, depends on so many circumstances, that if you had a grain of
prudence, you would not count upon it. Upon the whole, it is im-
probable, and therefore you should abandon the idea of ever seeing
them again.

Heart. May heaven abandon me if I do!

Head. Very well. Suppose, then, they come back. They are to stay
two months, and, when these are expired, what is to follow? Perhaps
you flatter yourself they may come to America?

Heart. God only knows what is to happen.

[*Jefferson went on to write of the beauties of America. But the Head
speaks again, and the reader has a feeling already that the Head is
going to win. There follows a beautiful passage on the art of happiness.*]

Head. Remember the last night. You knew your friends were to leave
Paris to-day. This was enough to throw you into agonies. All night you
tossed us from one side of the bed to the other; no sleep, no rest. The
poor crippled wrist, too, never left one moment in the same position;
now up, now down, now here, now there; was it to be wondered at,
if its pains returned? The surgeon then was to be called, and to be
rated as an ignoramus, because he could not divine the cause of this
extraordinary change. In fine, my friend, you must mend your manners.
This is not a world to live at random in, as you do. To avoid those
eternal distresses, to which you are forever exposing us, you must learn
to look forward, before you take a step which may interest our peace.
Everything in this world is a matter of calculation. Advance then with
caution, the balance in your hand. Put into one scale the pleasures
which any object may offer; but put fairly into the other, the pains
which are to follow, and see which preponderates. . . . Do not bite at
the bait of pleasure, till you know there is no hook beneath it. The art
of life is the art of avoiding pain; and he is the best pilot, who steers
clearest of the rocks and shoals with which it is beset. Pleasure is always

before us; but misfortune is at our side: while running after that, this arrests us.

[*A digression on Friendship follows, and then the Heart has the final say, on the subject of the division of office between the Heart and the Head.*]

Let the gloomy monk, sequestered from the world, seek unsocial pleasures in the bottom of his cell! Let the sublimated philosopher grasp visionary happiness, while pursuing phantoms dressed in the garb of truth! Their supreme wisdom is supreme folly; and they mistake for happiness the mere absence of pain. Had they ever felt the solid pleasure of one generous spasm of the heart, they would exchange for it all the frigid speculations of their lives, which you have been vaunting in such elevated terms. Believe me, then, my friend, that that is a miserable arithmetic which could estimate friendship at nothing, or at less than nothing. Respect for you has induced me to enter into this discussion, and to hear principles uttered which I detest and abjure. Respect for myself now obliges me to recall you into the proper limits of your office. When nature assigned us the same habitation, she gave us over it a divided empire. To you, she allotted the field of science; to me, that of morals. When the circle is to be squared, or the orbit of a comet to be traced; when the arch of greatest strength, or the solid of least resistance, is to be investigated, take up the problem; it is yours; nature has given me no cognizance of it. In like manner, in denying to you the feelings of sympathy, of benevolence, of gratitude, of justice, of love, of friendship, she has excluded you from their control. To these, she had adapted the mechanism of the heart. Morals were too essential to the happiness of man, to be risked on the uncertain combinations of the head. She laid their foundation, therefore, in sentiment, not in science. . . . A few facts, however . . . will suffice to prove to you, that nature has not organized you for our moral direction. . . . If our country, when pressed with wrongs at the point of the bayonet, had been governed by its heads instead of its hearts, where should we have been now? Hanging on a gallows as high as Haman's. You began to calculate, and to compare wealth and numbers: we threw up a few pulsations of our blood; we supplied enthusiasm against wealth and numbers; we put our existence to the hazard, when the hazard seemed against us, and we saved our country: justifying, at the same time, the ways of Providence, whose precept is, to do always what is right, and leave the issue to Him. In short, my friend, as far as my recollection serves me, I do not know that I ever did a good thing on your suggestion, or a dirty one without it. . . .

I thought this a favorable proposition whereon to rest the issue of the dialogue. So I put an end to it by calling for my nightcap. Methinks, I hear you wish to heaven I had called a little sooner, and so spared you the ennui of such a sermon. . . . I will promise you, on my honor, that my future letters shall be of reasonable length. I will agree to express but half my esteem for you, for fear of cloying you with too full a dose. But, on your part, no curtailing. If your letters are as long as the Bible, they will appear short to me. Only let them be brimful of affection. I shall read them with the dispositions with which Arlequin, in *Les deux billets,* spelt the words *"je t'aime,"* and wished that the whole alphabet had entered into their composition.

—Thomas Jefferson

4. LINCOLN IN TROUBLE

Lincoln's trouble was that he was *not* in love, not with his wife. Such a bald statement may be sufficiently justified by the sentence which he wrote a week after his marriage: "Nothing new here, except my marrying, which to me is a matter of profound wonder." [9] His attitude was rather that, as his father said to him, when he was a little boy, "When you make a bad bargain, hug it all the tighter." He was in love only with one woman, the beautiful Ann Rutledge, the blonde, blue-eyed girl of New Salem who alone could have made his home life happy for him. Unfortunately Ann Rutledge died suddenly of malaria, and thereafter Lincoln could never be sure of any woman because he could never be sure of himself. His is a case in point proving that women can make great men nervous, surely a tribute to the power of woman! Not that we need any proof that great men, no matter how great, will look twice at a chorus girl if she is really beautiful. How some women can contrive to ignore this essential fact is the real mystery.

[9] Letter to Samuel D. Marshall, November 11, 1842.

The stories of Lincoln and Mary Todd are well known, including the stories how once Mrs. Lincoln chased her husband to the door with a broomstick and once poured down a bucket of water from the second story when he was knocking at the door to be let in—stories in their nature unconfirmable, therefore neither true nor false. It is agreed, however, that it was a pretty dreary home for Lincoln; that flowers which his sister-in-law, Mrs. Edwards, had tried to plant in front of their house on Eighth Street were uncared for and withered and died, that Lincoln was seen once by his neighbor chopping wood at one o'clock after midnight "to cook his supper," that the budding political figure could be seen going to market on some mornings, with a basket on his arm, and an old gray shawl, rolled into a coil, wrapped like a rope around his neck, that Mrs. Lincoln with her other good qualities nevertheless was subject to periodic tantrums and terrified housemaids, icemen and delivery boys. According to their neighbors, the Gourleys, when one of her fits of temper came, Mr. Lincoln at first seemed to pay no attention. "Frequently he would laugh at her, which is a risky thing to do in the face of an infuriated wife; but generally, if her impatience continued, he would pick up one of the children and deliberately leave home as if to take a walk." However, the picture of Lincoln lying on the floor as his favorite position for reading, is a charming one, as told by Harriet Chapman, daughter of Dennis Hanks, who once lived in the Springfield household for over a year. "I fancy I see him now lying at full length in the hall of his old home. He would turn a chair down on the floor with a pillow on it. He was very fond of reading poetry and would often, when he appeared to be in a brown study, commence reading aloud 'The Burial of Sir John Moore!" [10] Yes, we can understand: Lincoln with his brown studies and his general melancholy, his awkwardness with ladies, his deep and persistent introspection and his constant abstracted air of being lost in some profound meditations; and Mrs. Lincoln with her fits of uncontrollable temper, fit for psychiatric analysis. Herndon told the story, doubted by some historians, of the "fatal First of January" (1841), when Mary Todd stood in her bridal robe in the Edwards mansion, the feast prepared and the guests gathered, and the bridegroom

---

[10] This material is conveniently brought together and treated in a spirit of fairness in Paul M. Angle's *Lincoln Reader*, Chap. IX.

deliberately failed to appear,—then the untouched dinner, the quietly withdrawing guests, and the unmarried bride returning to her solitary room! When Lincoln did marry her, twenty-three months later, she knew he had married to save his honor and redeem a promise. It was said that while dressing for the wedding in his room at Butler's house, the latter's little boy, Speed, seeing Lincoln so handsomely attired, in boyish innocence asked him where he was going. "To hell, I suppose," was Lincoln's reply.[11]

Various biographers of Lincoln have touched upon the domestic life of this sad and melancholy figure, chiseled in granite by God himself. It is best, however, to go direct to the original source of these books, William H. Herndon, for twenty years his law partner and friend. In reading Herndon, one must allow for the fact that the writer and Mrs. Lincoln never liked each other, and that Herndon's sympathies lay entirely with the husband, as our own often do when we regard the married life of our friends. Still, what went on inside the house on Eighth Street and at the White House is sufficiently known to turn my sympathy to Abraham Lincoln and make me give him credit for the fact that their marriage did not fail. How Lincoln made a bad bargain and hugged it all the tighter is well described in Herndon's *Lincoln,* which makes very smooth reading. Could it be true, as Herndon suggests at the end, that what Lincoln got out of hugging tightly the bargain was a Presidency? If so, the ways of the Lord are truly inscrutable!

Lincoln's Home Life

BY WILLIAM H. HERNDON

In dealing with Mr. Lincoln's home life perhaps I am revealing an element of his character that has heretofore been kept from the world; but in doing so I feel sure I am treading on no person's toes, for all the actors in this domestic drama are dead, and the world seems ready to hear the facts. As his married life, in the opinion of all his friends, exerted a peculiar influence over Mr. Lincoln's political career there can be no impropriety, I apprehend, in throwing the light on it now. Mrs. Lincoln's disposition and nature have been dwelt upon in another

[11] See Herndon's *Lincoln,* pp. 214 and 229.

chapter, and enough has been told to show that one of her greatest misfortunes was her inability to control her temper. Admit that, and everything can be explained. However cold and abstracted her husband may have appeared to others, however impressive, when aroused, may have seemed his indignation in public, he never gave vent to his feelings at home. He always meekly accepted as final the authority of his wife in all matters of domestic concern.* This may explain somewhat the statement of Judge Davis that, "as a general rule, when all the lawyers of a Saturday evening would go home and see their families and friends, Lincoln would find some excuse and refuse to go. We said nothing, but it seemed to us all he was not domestically happy." He exercised no government of any kind over his household. His children did much as they pleased. Many of their antics he approved, and he restrained them in nothing. He never reproved them or gave them a fatherly frown. He was the most indulgent parent I have ever known. He was in the habit, when at home on Sunday, of bringing his two boys, Willie and Thomas—or "Tad"—down to the office to remain while his wife attended church. He seldom accompanied her there. The boys were absolutely unrestrained in their amusement. If they pulled down all the books from the shelves, bent the points of all the pens, overturned inkstands, scattered law-papers over the floor, or threw the pencils into the spittoon, it never disturbed the serenity of their father's good-nature. Frequently absorbed in thought, he never observed their mischievious but destructive pranks—as his unfortunate partner did, who thought much, but said nothing—and, even if brought to his attention, he virtually encouraged their repetition by declining to show any substantial evidence of parental disapproval. After church was over the boys and their father, climbing down the office stairs, ruefully turned their steps homeward. They mingled with the throngs of well-dressed people returning from church, the majority of whom might well have wondered if the trio they passed were going to a fireside where love and white-winged peace reigned supreme. A near relative of Mrs. Lincoln, in explanation of the unhappy condition

---

* One day a man making some improvements in Lincoln's yard suggested to Mrs. Lincoln the propriety of cutting down one of the trees, to which she willingly assented. Before doing so, however, the man came down to our office and consulted Lincoln himself about it. "What did Mrs. Lincoln say?" enquired the latter. "She consented to have it taken away." "Then, in God's name," exclaimed Lincoln, "cut it down to the roots!"—*Herndon's note.*

of things in that lady's household, offered this suggestion: "Mrs. Lincoln came of the best stock, and was raised like a lady. Her husband was her opposite, in origin, in education, in breeding, in everything; and it is therefore quite natural that she should complain if he answered the door-bell himself instead of sending the servant to do so; neither is she to be condemned if, as you say, she raised 'merry war' because he persisted in using his own knife in the butter, instead of the silver-handled one intended for that purpose." * Such want of social polish on the part of her husband of course gave Mrs. Lincoln great offense, and therefore in commenting on it she cared neither for time nor place. Her frequent outbursts of temper precipitated many an embarrassment from which Lincoln with great difficulty extricated himself.

Mrs. Lincoln, on account of her peculiar nature, could not long retain a servant in her employ. The sea was never so placid but that a breeze would ruffle its waters. She loved show and attention, and if, when she glorified her family descent or indulged in one of her strange outbreaks, the servant could simulate absolute obsequiousness or had tact enough to encourage her social pretensions, Mrs. Lincoln was for the time her firmest friend. One servant, who adjusted herself to suit the lady's capricious ways, lived with the family for several years. She told me that at the time of the debate between Douglas and Lincoln she often heard the latter's wife boast that she would yet be mistress of the White House. The secret of her ability to endure the eccentricities of her mistress came out in the admission that Mr. Lincoln gave her an extra dollar each week on condition that she would brave whatever storms might arise, and suffer whatever might befall her, without complaint. It was a rather severe condition, but she lived rigidly up to her part of the contract. The money was paid secretly and without

* A lady relative who lived for two years with the Lincolns told me that Mr. Lincoln was in the habit of lying on the floor with the back of a chair for a pillow when he read. One evening, when in this position in the hall, a knock was heard at the front door and although in his shirt-sleeves he answered the call. Two ladies were at the door whom he invited into the parlor, notifying them in his open familiar way, that he would "trot the women folks out." Mrs. Lincoln from an adjoining room witnessed the ladies' entrance and overheard her husband's jocose expression. Her indignation was so instantaneous she made the situation exceedingly interesting for him, and he was glad to retreat from the mansion. He did not return till very late at night and then slipped quietly in at a rear door.—*Herndon's note.*

the knowledge of Mrs. Lincoln. Frequently, after tempestuous scenes between the mistress and her servant, Lincoln at the first opportunity would place his hand encouragingly on the latter's shoulder with the admonition, "Mary, keep up your courage." It may not be without interest to add that the servant afterwards married a man who enlisted in the army. In the spring of 1865 his wife managed to reach Washington to secure her husband's release from the service. After some effort she succeeded in obtaining an interview with the President. He was glad to see her, gave her a basket of fruit, and directed her to call the next day and obtain a pass through the lines and money to buy clothes for herself and children. That night he was assassinated. . . .

A man once called at the house to learn why Mrs. Lincoln had so unceremoniously discharged his niece from her employ. Mrs. Lincoln met him at the door, and being somewhat wrought up, gave vent to her feelings, resorting to such violent gestures and emphatic language that the man was glad to beat a hasty retreat. He at once started out to find Lincoln, determined to exact from him proper satisfaction for his wife's action. Lincoln was entertaining a crowd in a store at the time. The man, still laboring under some agitation, called him to the door and made the demand. Lincoln listened for a moment to his story. "My friend," he interrupted, "I regret to hear this, but let me ask you in all candor, can't you endure for a few moments what I have had as my daily portion for the last fifteen years?" These words were spoken so mournfully and with such a look of distress that the man was completely disarmed. It was a case that appealed to his feelings. Grasping the unfortunate husband's hand, he expressed in no uncertain terms his sympathy, and even apologized for having approached him. He said no more about the infuriated wife, and Lincoln afterward had no better friend in Springfield.

Mr. Lincoln never had a confidant, and therefore never unbosomed himself to others. He never spoke of his trials to me or, so far as I knew, to any of his friends. It was a great burden to carry, but he bore it sadly enough and without a murmur. I could always realize when he was in distress, without being told. He was not exactly an early riser, that is, he never usually appeared at the office till about nine o'clock in the morning. I usually preceded him an hour. Sometimes, however, he would come down as early as seven o'clock—in fact, on one occasion I remember he came down before daylight. If, on arriving at the office, I found him in, I knew instantly that a breeze had sprung up over the domestic sea, and that the waters were troubled. He would either be lying on the lounge looking skyward, or doubled up in a chair with his feet resting on the sill of a back window. He would not look up on my entering, and only answered my "Good morning" with a grunt. I at once busied myself with pen and paper, or ran through the leaves of some book; but the evidence of his melancholy and distress was so plain, and his silence so significant, that I would grow restless myself, and finding some excuse to go to the court-house or elsewhere, would leave the room.

The door of the office opening into a narrow hallway was half glass, with a curtain on it working on brass rings strung on wire. As I passed out on these occasions I would draw the curtain across the glass, and before I reached the bottom of the stairs I could hear the key turn in the lock, and Lincoln was alone in his gloom. An hour in the clerk's office at the court-house, an hour longer in a neighboring store having passed, I would return. By that time either a client had dropped in and Lincoln was propounding the law, or else the cloud of despondency had passed away, and he was busy in the recital of an Indiana story to whistle off the recollections of the morning's gloom. Noon having arrived I would depart homeward for my dinner. Returning within an hour, I would find him still in the office,—although his house stood but a few squares away,—lunching on a slice of cheese and a handful of crackers which, in my absence, he had brought up from a store below. Separating for the day at five or six o'clock in the evening, I would still leave him behind, either sitting on a box at the foot of the stairway, entertaining a few loungers, or killing time in the same way on the court-house steps. A light in the office after dark attested his presence there till late along in the night, when, after all the world had gone to sleep, the tall form of the man destined to be the nation's President could have been seen strolling along in the shadows of trees and buildings, and quietly slipping in through the door of a modest frame house, which it pleased the world, in a conventional way, to call his home.

Some persons may insist that this picture is too highly colored. If so, I can only answer, they do not know the facts. The majority of those who have a personal knowledge of them are persistent in their silence. If their lips could be opened and all could be known, my conclusions and statements, to say the least of them, would be found to be fair, reasonable, and true. A few words more as to Lincoln's domestic history, and I pass to a different phase of his life. One of his warmest and closest friends, who still survives, maintains the theory that, after all, Lincoln's political ascendency and final elevation to the Presidency were due more to the influence of his wife than to any other person or cause. "The fact," insists this friend, "that Mary Todd, by her turbulent nature and unfortunate manner, prevented her husband from becoming a domestic man, operated largely in his favor; for he was thereby kept out in the world of business and politics. Instead of spending his evenings at home, reading the papers and warming his toes at his own fireside, he was constantly out with the common people, was mingling with the politicians, discussing public questions with the farmers who thronged the offices in the court-house and state house, and exchanging views with the loungers who surrounded the stove of winter evenings in the village store. The result of this continuous contact with the world was, that he was more thoroughly known than any other man in his community. His wife, therefore, was one of the unintentional means of his promotion. If, on the other hand, he had married some less ambitious but more domestic woman, some honest farmer's quiet daughter,—one who would have looked up to and worshipped him because he uplifted her,—the result might have been different. For, although it doubtless would have been her pride to see that he had clean clothes whenever he needed them; that his slippers were always in their place; that he was warmly clad and had plenty to eat; and, although the privilege of ministering to his every wish and whim might have been to her a pleasure rather than a duty; yet I fear he would have been buried in the pleasures of a loving home, and the country would never have had Abraham Lincoln for its President."

—The Life of Lincoln

The great fact remains that Lincoln and his wife got adjusted to each other, as the years went by. Mrs. Lincoln felt sorry for her periodic outbursts, and Lincoln himself was a Socrates. More important than

Herndon's conjecture that Lincoln's married life might have helped
him toward the Presidency was the fact that two temperamentally in-
compatible human beings did make a go of it. I like immensely Carl
Sandburg's summing up.

"The marriage contract is complex."

BY CARL SANDBURG AND PAUL M. ANGLE

Mrs. Lincoln knew that her husband understood her faults. She
believed she knew his failings and instructed him. Across their twenty-
two years of married life there were times when she was a help. Often
too she knew she presumed on his patience and good nature, knowing
that when calm settled down on the household he would regard it as
"a little explosion" that had done her good. In the matter of faults
she may have heard him tell of meeting a farmer who wanted Lincoln
to bring suit against a next door neighbor. And Lincoln suggested
that the farmer should forget it; neighbors are like horses; they all
have faults and there is a way of accommodating yourself to the faults
you know and expect; trading a horse whose faults you are used to
for one who has a new and a different set of faults may be a mistake.
Undoubtedly Lincoln had a theory that a turbulent woman and an
unruly horse must be met with a patience much the same for either
the woman or the horse. . . .

The marriage contract is complex. "Live and let live," is one of its
terms. It travels on a series of readjustments to the changes of life
recurring in the party of the first part and the party of the second part.
Geared to incessant ecstasy of passion, the arrangement goes smash.
Mutual ambitions, a round of simple and necessary duties, occasional
or frequent separations as the case may be, relieved by interludes of
warm affection—these are the conditions on which many a longtime
marriage has been negotiated. The mood and color of this normal
married life permeates the letters that passed between Lincoln and his
wife when he was in Congress. Their household talk across the twenty-
two years must have run along many a day and hour in the mood
of these letters; exchanges of news, little anxieties about the children

From *Mary Lincoln: Wife and Widow,* by Carl Sandburg and Paul M. Angle. Copyright, 1932, by Harcourt, Brace & Company.

and the home, the journeyings of each reported to the other. When he hurried home from the law office during a thunderstorm, knowing that she was a terror-struck and sick woman during a thunderstorm, it was an act of accommodation by one partner for another. . . .

All romance is interrupted by the practical. The most passionate of lovers must either go to a hotel or set up housekeeping. And either is a humdrum piece of business in a sheer romance. Many a woman has said, "I love you, but the roast is burning and we must leave our kisses till after dinner." Managing a family and household is the work and care of a husband and wife as distinguished from two lovers. . . .

We can be sure, too, that for much of the time Lincoln and his wife went about their concerns peacefully and with quiet affection for each other. Domestic flareups, nerve-snappings, come to all couples; perhaps to these two they simply came more frequently and more violently. Authentic records—letters written without any thought of future readers—contain many glimpses of placid relations. One can read nothing but calm contentment into Lincoln's sentence about a novel he had received from a friend: "My wife got hold of the volume I took home, read it half through last night, and is greatly interested in it." Only the comradeship that comes to those who understand each other can be inferred from Mrs. Lincoln's comment on a trip east: "When I saw the large steamers at the New York landings I felt in my heart inclined to sigh that poverty was my portion. How I long to go to Europe. I often laugh and tell Mr. Lincoln that I am determined my next husband shall be rich."

—*Mary Lincoln: Wife and Widow*

5. SEX AND MODESTY

I am afraid I am not a Freudian. It would be enough to concede that sex is an important and powerful factor of the human mind. What prudery in the century immediately preceding ours, though not in the sixteenth and seventeenth, I am sure! From this prudery to the repeal of reticence in the twentieth is quite a leap for the modern western mind and it can't do it gracefully. "Come to bed with me," the persistent entreaty of the soldier to the nurse in *Farewell to Arms,* sounds like a sophomore preoccupied with sex and his first discovery of manhood. It was in line with the glorification of the dark, primitive instincts of the post-Versailles "lost generation," when all values had ceased to exist. But this affectation of primitivism, whether in art or in literature, is obviously a trait of adolescence, of immaturity. The modern man simply is not primitive; in nervous constitution he is pronouncedly self-conscious and altogether complex. You just can't say, I am going to paint like a six-year-old child or sculp like an African savage, because you aren't that simple person. So when modern artists go primitive, we are well aware of the fact that they are studiously trying to be spontaneous, methodically trying to be naïve, sophisticatedly trying to be innocent, circumspectly trying to be abandoned, and sentimentally trying to be rude. Back of primitivism is the severe criticism of modern culture and profound emotional distrust of modern intellectual civilization. Primitivism, literary or artistic, is culture distrusting itself. So the simplicity that is presented to us is not the sweet and simple delight of man at the dawn of civilization, healthy and strong like a chanticleer's song, but is indicative of a dark despair, of jagged nerves and distraught minds. Always the defense is that Dali and Picasso are masters in the old technique, so revealing a confession! It is said that Picasso could paint a beautiful woman if he wanted to. Why he did not want to is the crucial question, cutting deep into the woes and agonies of the modern self-conscious mind. Why did he choose to paint the pregnant woman like a pig? Why have modernist statues always the eyes of an idiot, and why is idiocy written over the entire structure of their shoulders and limbs? The answer to this question is the key to all primitivism in art and literature.

We have forgotten to take things in their natural proportions, because we have lost the sense of harmony and balance. We want to laugh at all this mess of civilization. By all means laugh, for mirth and self-criticism are good, but contortions and affectations of bellyaches do not always impress me. The true spirit of comedy is a different thing and of another order altogether. It merely sees life as it is and finds it mirthful and expresses it with a quiet, wry smile, as Dorothy Parker does. Absent from such spirit of true comedy is the hatred of man for himself. But we are desperate; we take the soul to pieces; we are anxious to lay it on the vivisection table and anatomize its workings, the better to understand why we are such rotten creatures—and all this done in the name of naturalism. The existence of this state of things explains why there was prudery in the first place.

Europeans cannot treat natural things naturally, says Santayana, writing on the treatment of sensuality in art and literature. "Perhaps the emancipated plebeians of the future will expect their comic poets to play upon sensuality as upon something altogether innocent and amiable: comic, too, because all reality is comic, and especially a phase of it where illusion, jollity, conceit, mishap, and chagrin follow one another in such quick alternation. If this subject could be passed by the Censor,[12] and treated judiciously, it would enrich the arts and at the same time disinfect the mind in one of its most troubled and sullen moods, by giving it a merry expression. In the *Arabian Nights* I find something of this kind; but erotic art in Europe, even in antiquity, seems to have been almost always constrained and vicious. A man who is moralized politically, as Europeans are, rather than religiously or poetically like Orientals, cannot treat natural things naturally. He respects the uttered feelings of others more than his own feelings un-uttered, and suppresses every manifestation of himself which a spectator might frown upon, even if behind the Censor's back everybody would rejoice in it. So long as this social complication lasts public art and the inner life have to flow separately, the one remains conventional the other clouded and incoherent. If poets under these circumstances tried to tell the whole truth, they would not only offend the public but do a grave injustice to their theme, and fail to make it explicit, for want of discipline and grace of expression. It is as well that the Censor, by imposing silence, keeps them from attempting the impossible."

The problem of treating sensuality in literature clearly, truthfully, and naturally is a well-nigh hopeless task for a modern writer. As Clarence Day says well, "as to modesty and decency, if we are simians we have done well, considering; but if we are something else—fallen angels—we have indeed fallen far. Not being modest by instinct we invent artificial ideals, which are doubtless well-meaning but are inherently of course second-rate, so that even at our best we smell

---

[12] The "Censor" here is "an important official of the inner man." His old name "was not Reason, but Vanity or Self-love," *i.e.*, conventional respect for society, "the father of all shams." The selection is from Santayana's essay, "The Censor and the Poet," *Soliloquies in England.*

prudish. And as for our worst, when we say let ourselves go, we dirty the life-force unspeakably, with chuckles and leers. But a race so indecent by nature as the simians are would naturally have a hard time behaving as though they were not: and the strain of pretending that their thoughts were all pretty and sweet, would naturally send them to smutty extremes for relief." [13]

I have heard Cornelia Otis Skinner deliver a clever monologue on sex education by the modern scientific, emancipated parent. Of course the child is truthful, and the parent tries hard to be, but cannot. As I remember, the parent started with reproduction among the fish and at the crucial point quickly switched the topic and went on to bees. Again at the point that the child really wanted to know, the parent hemmed and hawed and went on, perhaps, to chickens. The child wasn't better informed than before. Now the egg is a pretty simple story. Why couldn't the parent simply tell it? The hen is the mother, and the cock is the father. The hen has got the egg inside her, but the egg wouldn't hatch without the father. So the cock comes and sits on top of the hen and ejects a life-giving fluid into the hen's body through the back. Then the egg has life, and the mother hen sits over it, giving its warmth, and in three weeks, there comes the little chick! Why can't the modern parent do it?

Of course, that does not answer all the questions of the child, and the conversation, if it was begun, would continue something like this:

The Child: Is that all?
The Parent: Yes, that's all.
(The Child lingers around.)
The Parent: Are there any other questions on your mind, darling?
The Child: Yes, do you and Father do it?
The Parent: Yes, we do. That was how Father and I gave birth to you. It is a secret.
The Child: Why?
The Parent: Because it is a secret.
The Child: Why?
The Parent: Because—because we are human beings, not like cocks

[13] Reprinted from *This Simian World*, by Clarence Day, by permission of Alfred A. Knopf, Inc. Copyright, 1920, 1948, Katherine B. Day and Clarence Day.

and hens. We don't do it in public.

The Child: Why can't you do it in public?

The Parent: Because it would not be nice.

The Child: Why would it not be nice?

The Parent: I am glad you ask that question. I just said we are human beings. You see, darling, cocks and hens have no family life, no father and mother and brothers and sisters, or if they have, they don't know it. They have no family, and we human beings have. The cock just goes about and takes any girl he likes; he has no responsibility, and the chick never knows who his father is. Of course you would be sorry if you didn't know who was your father. But if I went and took any man that came along, that is, if we were not married and had a home, you would not know who your father is, would you? The result is, the cock goes about and sits on any young, pretty chicken, and he is not ashamed of it. Your father can't do that, and I can't do that, and that's how we have a home, and how we can always stay together and take care of each other and you. So you never see your mother take off her clothes and panties and walk naked on Fifth Avenue, do you? It would not be nice, not decent. It would mean I would be willing to go and sleep with any man who desires me.

The Child: I understand. What was that word you used? You said it would not be nice or what?

The Parent: It would not be *decent.* That is the word. That is the word I would use if you sloshed your milk all over the table or slobbered over your soup. It would not be decent. Remember it, for it is a good word. Remember that your mother taught you this word today.

(The Child is silent for a moment.)

The Parent: Is there anything else?

The Child: Yes, Mother, why do my playmates always smile when they talk about kissing and having babies. Is it a lot of fun?

The wise Parent: Yes, it is a lot of fun when your father and I kiss each other and love each other, like my kissing you and loving you and holding your hands and pinching your cheeks.

The Child: Does Father pinch your cheeks, mother?

The Mother: (blushing now) Yes, he does . . . well, that is enough, darling, now toddle along!

Any child, I think, should be satisfied with that. And I believe the basic facts, the real facts, are not more complicated than that. I do not understand why American parents do not explain the simple facts in this simple manner.

No, the problem of sex cannot be solved unless and until the problem of modesty and decency is solved first. Without a proper sense of modesty and decency, you cannot approach the problem of sex, or it soon slobbers all over the place and smuts all human life like dirty linen.

6. WHITMAN'S SEX DEMOCRACY

Walt Whitman is the best case in point. When Walt Whitman decided to let it all out, as he loudly proclaimed, "Walt, you contain enough, why don't you let it all out, then?"[14] the result was a remarkable exhibition of pruriency. Walt would deny it, of course, as he indignantly denied the charge of homosexuality. But the fact remains that he had a prurient mind. His open glorification of sexuality and animality did not, for that reason, make it less prurient. It is exactly because Whitman claimed to have a clean view of sex that we must subject his views to a careful analysis. Franklin's view of sex was clean, as Whitman's was not, and Franklin was as clear and brilliant as Whitman was confused and mediocre in his intellectual equipment.

When I was in college in China and first read Whitman, I was struck by the fundamental soundness of his instinct about the sacredness of the flesh. The revolt against prudery was sound enough. His ebullient amativeness merely amused me, and I said to myself, Here is a man who is truly unashamed of his body and of himself, which is well. But on second reading, he could not hold up; his view of sex is decidedly warped; the all-round view isn't there. It is just bad erotic poetry. Proclaiming that he is erotic does not make him less fundamentally and grossly erotic.

Walt Whitman am I, a Kosmos, of mighty Manhattan the son,
Turbulent, fleshy and sensual, eating, drinking and breeding.[15]

Fine, I say, but what of it? What happiness, what satisfaction comes of it, I would like to be told. He dared not tell it; in fact, he could not

[14] "Song of Myself," section 25.
[15] "Song of Myself," section 24.

tell it; he failed in giving the true satisfaction and exultation of sex, as all truly good erotic poetry gives it, as *This is My Beloved* by Walter Benton gives it. He fumbled and failed abominably; his New England conscience would not leave him alone, and he had to moralize. He seemed to justify his sex act by the curiously forced note that he was by the act of impregnating great mothers founding a republic of bards and heroes and orators. It just doesn't go.

Why can't we admire sex and woman's nudity in all their glory without this tomfoolery? There is a story of a Greek courtesan of Athens who was accused of wrecking many homes and being a danger to public morals. The Athenians wanted to try her, and her only request was that she be tried on the seashore, with the citizens seated on the beach, and she standing in water. There standing nude, with the water up to her neck, she listened quietly to all the accusations of the Athenian wives, who demanded death. Then she walked up slowly and sedately from the water, revealing more and more the dignity and grace of her divine form. The entire beach was silent. "Well, do you want me to die?" she asked simply. An emphatic *"no!"* rose thunderously from the Athenian public, and the courtesan was acquitted. That was the true worship of nudity; it was true naturalism. No one of the Athenians thought of founding a republic of bards and heroes with her as the "great mother." She was just good, because she was beautiful to perfection, and that was its own justification.

But we must come back to the pruriency of Whitman's mind. Whitman was nowhere more subtle and more representative of the Boston mind than in his description of the twenty-eight bathers with the twenty-ninth, a lady, peeping from behind the blinds of her window, taking part in her imagination with the twenty-eight men, letting them souse her with their spray, nowhere more obscene than when she saw their bulging bellies. In its extreme subtlety and pruriency of imagination, this is one of the best Whitman ever wrote:

Twenty-eight young men by the shore;
Twenty-eight young men, and all so friendly;
Twenty-eight years of womanly life, and all so lonesome.

She owns the fine house by the rise of the bank;
She hides, handsome and richly drest, aft the blinds of the
  window.

Which of the young men does she like the best?
Ah, the homeliest of them is beautiful to her.
Where are you off to, lady? for I see you:
You splash in the water there, yet stay stock still in your room.

Dancing and laughing along the beach came the twenty-ninth
  bather.
The rest did not see her, but she saw them and loved them.

The beards of the young men glisten'd with wet, it ran from
  their long hair,
Little streams pass'd all over their bodies.

An unseen hand also pass'd over their bodies,
It descended tremblingly from their temples and ribs.

The young men float on their backs, their white bellies bulge
  to the sun, they do not ask who seizes fast to them,
They do not know who puffs and declines with pendant and
  bending arch,
They do not think whom they souse with spray.[16]

Whitman was certainly not prudish, but his mind was prurient. We
can well take for granted that no one in the present generation, or
only very few, are prudish; the trend is rather to the contrary. But
the vast majority of men and women still have modesty, which cannot
be simply talked away. We may therefore take it for granted that the
question is not one of prudery, but simply of a frank, sane, and
healthy view of sex, which Whitman said he was going to preach,
but in which he failed. Whitman gave, and still gives, a sense of
fundamental indecency, not of innocence. For Whitman not only

[16] "Song of Myself," section 11.

peeped from the blinds of windows, he saw nudity "through the broadcloth and gingham whether or no," [17] and the form of a man struck him as it would strike a neurotic woman, "The strong sweet quality he has, strikes through the cotton and broadcloth, To see him pass conveys as much as the best poem, perhaps more, You linger to see his back, and the back of his neck and shoulder-side." [18]

Whitman said he was "no more modest than immodest," and, "what is this blurt about virtue and about vice?" which sound awfully like *Thus Spake Zarathustra*. The funny thing about modesty or immodesty is that no one should be consciously so. Modesty is instinctive. Try as he might, Whitman could not succeed. And so when he desired to celebrate "the act divine" with his man companion, when he was about to provide the metaphysical basis for the new democracy of the future, cemented by the "new friendship," the manly love of comrades, it was: "Or else by stealth in some wood for trial, Or back of a rock in the open air. . . . But just possibly with you on a high hill, first watching lest any person for miles around approach unawares. Or possibly with you sailing at sea, or on the beach of the sea or some quiet island, Here to put your lips upon mine I permit you, With the comrade's long-dwelling kiss or the new husband's kiss, For I am the new husband and I am the comrade." [19] This sort of comradeship is, of course, a little frightening and repulsive to the American masses, to which he addressed himself. And so though he made himself out as "candidate for the future," the poet of the proletariat, the American masses have not accepted him.

If then love was to be practiced by going up a hill and looking around circumspectly for miles around to see that no one would see them unaware, our impression of love cannot be very clean. Modesty, if you will have it that way, was still there, and Whitman had not escaped.

Perhaps we can understand Whitman's mind better by noting the background, on which he threw some light in his own editorials in the *Brooklyn Daily Times*. What a difference between the attitude toward public bathing in Whitman's times and our own! On July

---

[17] "Song of Myself," section 7.
[18] "I Sing the Body Electric," section 2.
[19] "Whoever You Are Holding Me Now in Hand."

20, 1857, two years after his publication of the *Leaves of Grass,* he complained in an editorial that public bathers on Brooklyn's shores, men and boys, were arrested by the police and brought to the station. He defended the bathers by saying that invariably they had selected some corner where there was no frequented thoroughfare, and he suggested that perhaps some ordinance might be issued prohibiting bathing in certain spots, specially named—"close to ferries, for example." Those were the times, according to these editorials, when girls still fainted, were sickly and feeble, indeed drank little of anything but tea; headache or nausea was a familiar sight at balls; they had never seen the sun rise, and if it were not for the almanacs, would hardly know that the luminary in question shone at all. Even Emerson thought that seeing a ballet at Boston and returning to their academic cells with visions of the tripping satin slippers was not the safest thing for Harvard students.[20]

The trouble with peeping into the editorials of Walt Whitman is that they[21] reveal more a portrait of Whitman the man himself, than of the times. He had written the *Leaves of Grass,* had prepared the second edition of 1856, which included the "Children of Adam" and "Calamus" poems. His first edition did not sell, in spite of Emerson's endorsement, and he was something more than what we call a showman when he told Emerson that it "sold readily." Nor did the second edition, to which had been added another twenty poems, more fleshy, more openly gross and carnal, and less inspired. He thought he could live by these *Leaves,* but he couldn't, and he accepted the job at the *Brooklyn Daily Times* as the defender of public morality. You want to tear your hair out when you compare the *Leaves of Grass* and the entirely pharisaical mouthings of the editorial writer. On the one hand, if we don't misread Whitman's "Democracy" (and Whitman makes it impossible for us to misread him), here is "an American bard at last!" he announces in an anonymous review of his own book, who "right and left flings his arms, drawing men and women with undeniable love to his close embrace," and according

---

[20] *Journals,* October, undated, 1841.
[21] *I Sit and Look Out, Editorials from the Brooklyn Daily Times,* by Walt Whitman, selected and edited by Emory Holloway and Vernolian Schwartz, Columbia University Press, 1932. See especially pp. 103 and 111–122.

to whom (in the "Calamus" poems) this somewhat promiscuous kissing was to be "the salute of American comrades land and sea," in fact the metaphysical basis of his democracy. "Yet comes one a Manhattanese and ever at parting parting kisses me lightly on the lips with robust love, and I on the crossing of the street or on the ship's deck give a kiss in return." On the other—he wrote this editorial in 1857!—"perhaps some of our readers have noticed the alarming increase in late years, in the custom of kissing among ladies," which is a "profanation." We should "use it wisely, with a noble chariness," if we would, as Mary Forster said, "preserve this gift a sweet and holy token, beautiful and sanctified to the beloved." On the one hand, "I will go stay with her who waits for me, and with those women that are warm-blooded and sufficient for me, I see that they understand me and do not deny me, I will be the robust husband of those women." On the other, the editorial "we [which is Whitman] *tremble* at the number of sins [he was writing on the subject of conjugal infidelity] that do come to exposure while we *shudder* at the amount of secret wickedness that boils and bubbles." (Italics are mine.) On the one hand, "From my voice resonant—singing the phallus, Singing the song of procreation . . . Singing what, to the soul, entirely redeem'd her, the faithful one, even the prostitute, who detain'd me when I went to the city; Singing the Song of prostitutes." On the other, he denounced prostitution like a mayor who has seven mistresses, as "the vice most general, most costly, and most ruinous to health and morals, of all vices." (The line about singing "the Song of prostitutes" and the long line immediately preceding it were dropped from his deathbed edition by the Good Gray Poet, who, in old age, was careful to wrap up, as far as he could, the less noble and respectable qualities of that poet personality.) As we might say, there are so many aspects to a great man's personality, and we can never exhaust our knowledge of a great poet, can we? [22]

---

[22] On the subject of attaining a healthy and sane view of sex, which Whitman said he wanted to bring about in "A Memorandum at a Venture," note the tortuous sex imagery, which is essentially the prurient mind speaking, in the following: "The treacherous tip of me," the "prurient provokers," the "red marauder," the "root of wash'd sweet jag [which is the calamus]! timorous pond-snipe! nest of guarded duplicated eggs! . . . mix'd tussled hay of head, beard, brawn . . . trickling sap of maple! fibre of manly wheat!" and the token of the male sexual organ, the calamus root which has the hardiest blades! I am not sure but the opening of the "Song of the Broad Axe" contains rather

If Whitman would say, "I am a sensualist" and leave it at that, it would not be so amusing. There are many avowed sensualists, and we wouldn't be surprised. But his New England conscience was moralizing incoherently, pathetically—he had to moralize. Sex could not be just sex, just enjoyment. It must have a moral purpose. It was then that Whitman became really entertaining, when he tried to connect democracy with sex. Whitman had a vision that he was the poet of America, not the sordid America of his days [23] but the America of the future, and that he was the poet of this Americanism and the new democracy. You might, if you have a good instinct, fear that America, or American democracy, was falling into bad hands. Somewhere his vision of this new American democracy became terribly mixed up with procreativeness and flinging around of arms right and left and drawing men in close and ardent embrace. It was not when Whitman's New England conscience was dormant, but when it was wide awake that America should be alarmed. In a mental daze, as it were, he thought of the words "love" and "friendship" and "brotherhood," which should be the strong bond of a democracy. America was to throw off the yoke of the old literature; she was to have strong, brave men and great mothers, to have poets and heroes and orators. How are these poets, heroes, and orators to come into this world? Evidently by being born. Who are to give them birth? Evidently the mothers, who must be great. And how are they to be great? By being firm of flesh and tanned and athletic. And after these bards and athletes are born, how can you have a republic? It must be cemented with friendship, with the manly love of comrades. Here the words "love" and "friendship" became confused, or rather fused with the "fierce affection" of sex. He was quite serious about this point. He insisted in his preface to the Centennial Edition (published in 1876) that the significance of the "Calamus" poems was *political,* and since every prophet must have a message and a mission, his was, "I will establish in the Manhattana and in every city of these States inland

---

definite sex imagery: "Weapon shapely, naked, wan, Head from the mother's bowels drawn! . . . Resting the grass amid and upon, To be lean'd, and to lean on." It was really extraordinary: "Winds whose soft-tickling genitals rub against me," and "Something I cannot see puts upward libidinous prongs; Seas of bright juice suffuse heaven"—this in a song about winds and the sea!
[23] See the terrible lashing at his contemporary America in the *Democratic Vistas.*

and seaboard . . . the institution of the dear love of comrades." [24] It was both consistent and logical to go further and maintain that this friendship, to be the strong bond of democracy, must not be confined to one's own acquaintances, but must be universal. It must be extended to strangers, to "whoever you are, holding me now in hand," coupled with a fair warning to "the new person drawn toward me" that it was not going to be easy "to have me become your lover." Unless democracy was to decay into an aristocracy of the few, this love and friendship must necessarily be broad and extended and therefore somewhat promiscuous! "Passing stranger, you do not know how longingly I look upon you, You must be he I was seeking, or [Whitman added cautiously] she I was seeking." The American salute of kissing must be given on decks and in the streets, "whoever you are."

> To cotton-field drudge or cleaner of privies I lean;
> On his right cheek I put the family kiss,
> And in my soul I swear, I never will deny him. [25]

He was there defending the sanctity and the identity of the average plebeian individuals, the "powerful, uneducated persons"; he was not fooling. One would think that such a democracy might be excruciating to live in. But every man must learn to mix in the crowds and sit in a ferry or a railroad room and touch the warm waist and sense the smell of his neighbor and be content, as Whitman said he did. "I do not thank you for liking me as I am, and liking the touch of me—I know it is good for you to do so."

As a result, we have a loving American city, where, "My lovers suffocate me! Crowding my lips, thick in the pores of my skin, Jostling me through streets and public halls—coming naked to me at night, Crying by day *Ahoy!* from the rocks of the river. . . . Bussing my body with soft balsamic busses. . . ." If you extend this picture from city to city, from land to land, you have a loving, invulnerable republic, for in this republic everyone loves everyone else, consumed by their fierce affection for mankind. It can very well happen, of course, that some brother in this republic may not like the soft press of the stranger's arm around his waist or the bussing with soft balsamic busses, may in

---

[24] "I Hear It Was Charged against Me."
[25] "Song of Myself," section 40.

fact resent it; he may not relish "the scent of these arm-pits, aroma finer than prayer" or be not quite able to endure Whitman's "scented herbage of the breast" and inhale the "faint odor," but Whitman "believe[s] a few will." We should not disturb the poet there; he is perfectly serious: after staring at their "pink-tinged roots" and bidding them, "Do not remain down there so ashamed, herbage of my breast," he exclaims, "Come, I am determined to unbare this broad breast of mine . . . I will give an example to lovers, to make permanent shape and will through the States." A few will, I agree. Be serious, very serious now, and read very carefully the next selection, "For You O Democracy," which directly follows "Scented Herbage of My Breast" and "Whoever You Are Holding Me Now in Hand," according to Whitman's own sequence in the "death-bed edition":

Come, I will make the continent indissoluble,
I will make the most splendid race the sun shone upon,
I will make divine magnetic lands,
    With the love of comrades,
        With the life-long love of comrades.

I will plant companionship thick as trees along the rivers
    of America, and along the shores of the great
        lakes and all over the prairies,
I will make inseparable cities with their arms about each other's necks,
    By the love of comrades,
        By the manly love of comrades.

Of course, we do not know whose arms and whose necks they are; if they belong to the cities, the figure is a little far-fetched, and in any case the love of comrades cannot produce a race at all. Whitman could not have meant it literally.

But we are skipping slightly ahead. Whitman has not forgotten that man and man don't produce babies, no matter how ardent. Where are the bards and heroes to come from? They have to be born first. Somebody has to "jet the stuff of far more arrogant republics," and "start bigger and nimbler babes" "on women fit for conception." And so sex for Whitman became virility in man and procreativeness in woman, and in the transmogrification that occurred in the poet's mind, women became the "great mothers." That became definitely their duty. But you can run through the twenty-four thousand words of *Democratic Vistas* and find no clue as to how American women are to become great mothers, except by the common quality we celebrate in the Easter rabbit, namely, procreativeness. Naturally the inadequacy of Whitman's view on sex extends to his inadequate view of womanhood. Woman was to be the "teeming mother of mothers." They are to be supple; "Their flesh has the old divine suppleness and strength, They know how to swim, row, ride, wrestle, shoot, run, strike, retreat, advance, resist, defend themselves." But of course women don't produce alone, either. So here comes the virile poet!

> I am for you, and you are for me, not only for our own sake,
>   But for others' sake;
> Envelop'd in you sleep greater heroes and bards,
> They refuse to awake at the touch of any man but me.
> On you I graft the grafts of the best-beloved of America.
> The drops I distil upon you shall grow fierce and athletic
>   girls, new artists, musicians, singers,
> The babes I beget you are to beget babes in their turn,
> I shall demand perfect men and women out of our love-spendings.
> I shall expect them to interpenetrate with others, as
>   I and you interpenetrate now.

And so the song of love became merely the glorification of procreativeness.

> Urge, urge and urge;
> Always the procreant urge of the world.

We can understand therefore why the failure to produce offspring, little Whitman babes, was such a bitter humiliation to the poet—and why he had to declare to John Addington Symonds that he had six illegitimate children (doubted very much by literary historians) none of whom had come forward to claim the Good Gray Poet as his father.

And so Whitman "exhaled" his love (even to the ashes of dead soldiers) and he moistened, he effused, he jetted, he distilled drops, he pushed, he pressed, he kissed the brotherly kiss, and thought it was all wonderful. Democracy in the meanwhile became something limp and sticky and a little uncomfortable and suffocating to live in. The fact is, democracy cannot be brought about by every man flinging his arms around everybody else and putting a family kiss on him. I would hate to live in such a state.

We must unwillingly come to the conclusion that Whitman was deficient in intellect.[26] He had no ability to elaborate a thesis. As he says, while others debated he just went to bathe and admire himself. His *Democratic Vistas,* his longest and most ambitious exposition of his doctrines of democracy, is incoherent and, we must say, bad prose. He wrote brilliantly and with inspiration in the 1855 preface to the *Leaves of Grass;* [27] he said many true and beautiful things there on poetry, naturally and without effort, and his voice was truly fresh. In the "Backward Glance" he wrote what seems to me the most coherent and well-ordered prose exposition of his life, when he was old and at long last mature, when his thoughts about the world, about Old World literature, and about his "wonderful" self had clarified, when for the first time he showed a humility of spirit. But it took him so long to learn it.

It may be said, therefore, that Whitman's treatment of love is a complete failure. I am inclined to agree with Mark van Doren that he had no normal experience in love. Critics all feel Whitman's experience of "amativeness" (in the terms of the then prevailing pseudo-science of phrenology) [28] of love between man and woman, was cold, forced, brutal, while his experience of "adhesiveness" (of love between man and man) was tender and real. Only in his homosexual songs, "Of the Terrible Doubt of Appearances" and "When I Heard at the Close of the Day," did he actually speak of happiness, whereas his description of the normal sex act with woman, ending in "you villain touch," sounds really like the barbaric yawp of a bitch over the roofs of the world.

[26] Whitman's reading of Homer, Aeschylus, etc., I think was all bunk. There is no evidence of his understanding any of the Old World authors except perhaps George Sand. Probably he quite liked Shakespeare, for he could never stop berating Shakespeare, and yet he does not show anywhere his real understanding of Shakespeare's qualities as a poet.
[27] Mark van Doren and Christopher Morley are both enthusiasts for this piece by Whitman and regret that it is not more often read by students of English.
[28] Whitman had his lumps read.

The whole point about Whitman is that he tried to shock people on sex, but was himself childish in the understanding of it, and that his *Leaves of Grass,* the one book of his life, worked over and over again in about ten revisions up to the time of his death, still left enormous gaps in that one main subject of which he claimed to be the prophet. It may have occurred to his readers that *Leaves of Grass* has next to nothing to say about woman's love or love of woman, as we understand the word usually. He could not tell us about love, for all the research of critics and scholars could not reveal that he ever loved one woman among the many he boasted of having slept with. As a book, *Leaves of Grass* is unique in containing the maximum of sexual embrace and the minimum of romantic passion. Had he loved three, seven, ten, twelve women passionately, he might be a more satisfactory poet of love. His philandering took place in such milieu that nobody has been able to reveal the name of one woman—a Suzette, a Phyllis, or a Delilah—whom he loved or even thought of as an individual. So many great mothers, fit for conception, so few with whom he could form an abiding friendship! This is certainly curious in the life of a poet of "love." We do hear of Pete Doyle, the streetcar conductor.

The pity and humor of the situation was that Whitman took himself so seriously; he was conscious that he was preaching a new doctrine (the sacredness of the body is about as old as the Renaissance), and he wanted to set the tone for future American men of letters to imitate and follow. "Voices of sexes and lusts—voices veil'd, and I remove the veil; Voices indecent, by me clarified and transfigured." He did not clarify and transfigure them, but as Clarence Day says, when he decided to let himself go, he dirtied the life force unspeakably. In "A Memorandum at a Venture" [29] he made a serious effort to defend his views, by distinguishing three points of view on sex, the furtive and morbid, the open and natural (of Rabelais and Shakespeare), and the scientific view of "the sanity of birth, nature and humanity," which was his own. "*That* is what I felt in my inmost brain and heart, when I only answer'd Emerson's vehement arguments with silence, under the old elms of Boston Common." But his failure remains complete. If there was beauty in woman's love, as Solomon saw it, he did not see it because he did not have the experience. If sex was a soothing and ennobling as well as an animal act, if it was something wholesome and healthy and good and enjoyable, as Franklin saw it, he did not see it, or failed to make the point. So this sensuality remained on the level of a bull riding a cow.

As for his honesty, why did he deny to John Addington Symonds the facts of his young life in words reminiscent of his *Brooklyn Daily Times* editorials? Denying homosexuality as evidenced by the "Calamus" poems, he wrote pompously, "That the Calamus part has ever allowed the possibility of such construction as mentioned is terrible. I am fain to hope that the pages themselves are not even to be mentioned for such gratuitous and quite at the same time undreamed and unwished possibility of morbid inference—which are disavowed by me and seem damnable." [30] The only possible inference is that Walt Whitman never saw the "Calamus" poems about which he was talking to Symonds.[31] So you have modesty come back to New England in a new guise in words of untruth.

As regards modesty, Thoreau expressed it best. Thoreau's reaction is essentially that of the modern reader. We must start out with the plain, unglamourized fact that the sex act is always slightly ridiculous in its animal aspects and can become beautiful only by the evocation of the spiritual emotions of love, and he who is going to preach about the sacredness of the body, which we all accept without question, will have a hard time making sex seem glorious if he proceeds the way

[30] Quoted in *The Complete Poetry and Prose of Walt Whitman*, I, 15.
[31] See the entire "Calamus" group. *The Complete Poetry and Prose of Walt Whitman*, I, pp. 131–148; but the homosexuality is especially clear on pp. 137–139. Canby thinks that Whitman was autosexual. I think he was autosexual, homosexual, heterosexual, and just plain sexual. How would Walt Whitman have Symonds interpret the following passage: "For the one I love most lay sleeping by me under the same cover in the cool night, In the stillness in the autumn moonbeams his face was inclined toward me, And his arm lay lightly around my breast—and that night I was happy," and "Who knew too well the sick, sick dread lest the one he lov'd might secretly be indifferent to him," etc.? And this about the symbol of the male organ, the calamus root: "O here I last saw him that tenderly loves me, and returns again never to separate from me, And this, O this shall henceforth be the token of comrades, this calamus-root shall, Interchange it youths with each other! . . . I will give of it, but only to them that love as I myself am capable of loving" ("These I Singing in Spring"). Whom was he fooling? The construction the old Whitman now wished to be put upon it would be then that this was "friendship," perhaps ardent friendship, but nonsexual—oh, no, that would be horrible for the sanctimonious Whitman!

Whitman did. "Copulation," says Whitman, "is no more rank to me than death is."

True, but the copulation of human beings is no more beautiful or less ridiculous than that of dogs and bitches in the streets. You just cannot afford to step over the boundary under penalty of descending from the sublime to the ridiculous. Modesty is merely a flight from the ridiculousness of it, and in this sense modesty is natural for men and women, though it is not for dogs and bitches. Therefore Thoreau is right. "He does not celebrate love at all. It is as if the beasts spoke. I think that men have not been ashamed of themselves without reason. . . . I have found his poem exhilarating, encouraging. As for its sensuality . . . I do not so much wish that those parts were not written as that men and women were so pure that they could read them without harm, that is, without understanding them. One woman told me that no woman could read it,—as if a man could read what a woman could not. Of course Walt Whitman can communicate to us no experience, and if we are shocked, whose experience is it that we are reminded of?" [32]

The question may be asked, Why did Emerson endorse *Leaves of Grass*, and why did he hail it with extravagant praise two weeks after it was out—Emerson, the symbol of American idealism and intellectual and moral probity? The answer was of course in the vitality, genuineness, intensity, and courage of the first edition, principally the long "Song of Myself." It must be remembered Emerson was exactly looking for an American genius with courage, with nerve and force, and there was much of Emerson's own child in it, that sound core of every man believing in himself and declaring himself good, which Whitman had imbibed from Emerson himself. (Though Whitman tried to deny having read his essays before he wrote *Leaves of Grass,* the evidence is clear in the eyes of all critics.) Emerson had been looking for greatness. We are all so near greatness. Why can't we take that leap? It seemed to Emerson, on reading *Leaves of Grass,* that Whitman had taken it. Emerson had seen no evidence of greatness among his contemporaries that met his high demands. "I extend the remark to all the American geniuses. Irving, Bryant, Greenough, Everett, Chan-

[32] Thoreau's letter to H. G. Blake, quoted in Henry Seidel Canby, *Walt Whitman, an American*, p. 152. Houghton Mifflin Company.

ning, even Webster in his recorded eloquence, all lack nerve and
dagger." "In sculpture Greenough is picturesque; in painting, Allston;
in poetry, Bryant; in eloquence, Channing; in architecture ———; in
fiction, Irving, Cooper; in all, feminine, no character." "Everyone an
imperfect specimen; respectable, not valid. Irving thin, and Channing
thin, and Bryant and Dana; Prescott and Bancroft. There is Webster,
but he cannot do what he would; he cannot do Webster." Everett,
who was followed like an Apollo from church to church, had neither
intellectual nor moral principles to teach. "He had no thoughts." Such
entries ran through Emerson's *Journals* from 1836 to 1844. Now here at
last came the American bard who seemed to meet Emerson's requirements, for Whitman had announced himself as virile, turbulent, imperious, robust, manly, sensual, stout as a horse, affectionate, haughty,
electrical, hankering, gross, mystical, rude, and all that. And after all,
here was a new voice, and Emerson was too good a critic to miss a
genuine voice when he heard it. So he rubbed his eyes a little to see
if this sunbeam was no illusion, but the solid sense of the book was
before him, a sober certainty. And so encouraged by the greatest man
of letters of his times, Whitman went on with his "Children of Adam"
and "Calamus" poems, which disappointed Emerson, who found them
too fleshy in their natural frankness. "Tell Walt I am not satisfied, not
satisfied," he said to a friend of his, Mr. Marvin. "I expect—him—to
make—the songs of the Nation—but he seems—to be contented to—
make inventories." [33]

Whitman knew perfectly well what he was about. Canby wouldn't
blame him for plugging his own book to increase its sales, even by
writing unsigned reviews of it himself. Well—but Whitman should
not have told Emerson that the first edition "sold readily," which
wasn't true. Whitman himself knew that the book was "an incon-
gruous hash of mud and gold." Charles Eliot Norton, who was yet
young, gave a characterization that was exact: these were lawless
poems in a sort of excited prose, and Whitman was a compound of
the New England transcendentalist and a New York rowdy. Emerson
tersely remarked to his friend that Whitman had real inspiration but
was choked by "titanic abdomen." Thoreau said that the poet put him

[33] *The Heart of Burroughs's Journals*, p. 56. Entry of 1871.

in a suitable frame of mind to see wonders, set him upon a hill, as it were, stirred him up and then threw in a thousand of brick.[34] To this day, most readers must have the same impression.

This is not intended as a complete study of Whitman. I have left out of the discussion the reasons for Whitman's success as a poet—some of his great poems, some immortal, perfectly fashioned lines, his poems on the Civil War scene, and above all, the fact that he brought the natural rhythm and phraseology of American speech into American poetry—in fact, had created a new medium of expression. Nevertheless, I am dealing with the central problem of Whitman, the uplifting and glorifying of sex and the recognition of our fleshly existence. It is here that he wishes to be judged, and must be judged with modern tolerance but without levity. If he fails by the most modern standard and understanding of sex, then he fails surely, completely. No Chinese can be accused of prudery (witness sex in Chinese literature and in street talks), but the reader of any country or nationality must be repelled by mere animality. And because Whitman is a world author, he must be judged by a universal as well as an American standard.

[34] For all these contemporary opinions, see Henry Seidel Canby's interesting and sharp portrait of the poet in *Walt Whitman, an American*, pp. 120–4 and 148–157.

Chapter XIV

LAUGHTER

I. HUMOR

FRANK MOORE COLBY tells us that all discussions of humor are apt to be strenuous and accompanied by the sound of heavy blows. I have never read a dissertation on humor, the psychology and anatomy of it, without getting furious. So we will not discuss humor. (I suspect my discussion of Walt Whitman's sexual democracy has already been accompanied by the sound of heavy blows, with which some reader or other had already felled me without my knowledge.) So we will not discuss humor. We will not discuss what kind of jokes the Americans laugh at, whether they are highbrow, lowbrow, refined or coarse, wholesome or bawdy, or even whether there are six or seven varieties of humor, or whether a horse laugh is or is not better than an intellectual chuckle. The great thing about laughter is laughter itself. Let's not try to explain it. We Chinese say there is a "laughing spleen" in a person, apparently somewhere below the ribs, and when it is poked neatly and exactly at the right place, you laugh. And when one is poked properly and at exactly the right place, one feels very good. That is about all I know about humor. President Wilson liked to attend, not serious drama, but vaudeville shows in the evening, and I know why. Any American President after writing notes to Germany and Austria during the day needs it. Will Rogers will tell us:

Wilson Could Laugh at a Joke on Himself
BY WILL ROGERS

Owing to the style of Act I used, my stuff depended a great deal on what had happened that particular day or week. It just seemed by an odd chance for me every time I played before President Wilson that on that particular day there had been something of great importance

From *The Illiterate Digest*. Copyright, 1924, Albert and Charles Boni. Reprinted by permission.

that he had just been dealing with. For you must remember that each day was a day of great stress with him. He had no easy days. So when I could go into a Theatre and get laughs out of our President by poking fun at some turn in our National affairs, I don't mind telling you it was the happiest moments of my entire career on the stage.

The first time I shall never forget, for it was the most impressive and for me the most nervous one of them all. The Friars Club of New York one of the biggest Theatrical Social Clubs in New York had decided to make a whirlwind Tour of the principal Cities of the East all in one week. . . . We were billed for Baltimore but not for Washington. President Wilson came over from Washington to see the performance. It was the first time in Theatrical History that the President of the United States came over to Baltimore just to see a Comedy.

It was just at the time we were having our little Set Too, with Mexico, and when we were at the height of our Note Exchanging career with Germany and Austria. The house was packed with the Elite of Baltimore. . . .

I was on late, and as the show went along I would walk out of the Stage door and out on the Street and try to kill the time and nervousness until it was time to dress and go on. I had never told Jokes even to a President, much less about one, especially to his face. Well, I am not kidding you when I tell you that I was scared to death. I am always nervous. I never saw an Audience that I ever faced with any confidence. For no man can ever tell how a given Audience will ever take anything.

But here I was, nothing but a very ordinary Oklahoma Cowpuncher who had learned to spin a Rope a little and who had learned to read the Daily Papers a little, going out before the Aristocracy of Baltimore, and the President of the United States, and kid about some of the Policies with which he was shaping the Destinies of Nations. . . .

At the time of his entrance into the House, everybody stood up, and there were Plain Clothes men all over the place, back stage and behind his Box. How was I to know but what one of them might not take a shot at me if I said anything about him personally?

Finally a Warden knocked at my dressing room door and said, "You die in 5 more minutes for kidding your Country." They just literally shoved me out on the Stage.

Now, by a stroke of what I call good fortune, (for I will keep them always) I have a copy of the entire Acts that I did for President Wilson on the Five times I worked for him. My first remark in Baltimore was, "I am kinder nervous here tonight." Now that is not an especially bright remark, and I don't hope to go down in History on the strength of it, but it was so apparent to the audience that I was speaking the truth that they laughed heartily at it. After all, we all love honesty.

Then I said, "I shouldn't be nervous, for this is really my second Presidential appearance. The first time was when Bryan spoke in our town once, and I was to follow his speech and do my little Roping Act." Well, I heard them laughing, so I took a sly glance at the President's Box and sure enough he was laughing just as big as any one. So I went on, "As I say, I was to follow him, but he spoke so long that it was so dark when he finished, they couldn't see my Roping." That went over great, so I said "I wonder what ever become of him." That was all right, it got over, but still I had made no direct reference to the President.

Now Pershing was in Mexico at the time, and there was a lot in the Papers for and against the invasion. I said "I see where they have captured Villa. Yes, they got him in the morning Editions and the Afternoon ones let him get away." Now everybody in the house before they would laugh looked at the President, to see how he was going to take it. Well, he started laughing and they all followed suit.

"Villa raided Columbus New Mexico. We had a man on guard that night at the Post. But to show you how crooked this Villa is, he sneaked up on the opposite side." "We chased him over the line 5 miles, but run into a lot of Government Red Tape and had to come back." "There is some talk of getting a Machine Gun if we can borrow one. The one we have now they are using to train our Army with in Plattsburg. If we go to war we will just about have to go to the trouble of getting another Gun."

Now, mind you, he was being criticized on all sides for lack of preparedness, yet he sat there and led that entire audience in laughing at the ones on himself.

At that time there was talk of forming an Army of 2 hundred thousand men, so I said, "we are going to have an Army of 2 hundred thousand men. Mr. Ford makes 3 hundred thousand Cars every year.

I think, Mr. President, we ought to at least have a Man to every Car."
"See where they got Villa hemmed in between the Atlantic and
Pacific. Now all we got to do is to stop up both ends." "Pershing
located him at a Town called, Los Quas Ka Jasbo. Now all we have to
do is to locate Los Quas Ka Jasbo." "I see by a headline that Villa
escapes Net and Flees. We will never catch him then. Any Mexican
that can escape Fleas is beyond catching." "But we are doing better
toward preparedness now, as one of my Senators from Oklahoma has
sent home a double portion of Garden Seed."

After various other ones on Mexico I started in on European affairs
which at that time was long before we entered the war. "We are
facing another Crisis tonight, but our President here has had so many
of them lately that he can just lay right down and sleep beside one of
those things."

Then I first pulled the one which I am proud to say he afterwards
repeated to various friends as the best one told on him during the War.
I said, "President Wilson is getting along fine now to what he was
a few months ago. Do you realize, People, that at one time in our
negotiations with Germany that he was 5 Notes behind?"

How he did laugh at that! Well, due to him being a good fellow and
setting a real example, I had the proudest and most successful night
I ever had on the stage.

—*Illiterate Digest*

Clarence Day's humor is unique and inimitable. The following are
passages from a book which is enjoyable from beginning to end.

God and My Father

BY CLARENCE DAY

My father's ideas of religion seemed straightforward and simple.
He had noticed when he was a boy that there were buildings called
churches; he had accepted them as a natural part of the surroundings
in which he had been born. He would never have invented such things
himself. Nevertheless they were here. As he grew up he regarded

Reprinted from *God and My Father,* by Clarence Day, by permission of Alfred A.
Knopf, Inc. Copyright, 1931, 1932, Clarence Day.

them as unquestioningly as he did banks. They were substantial old structures, they were respectable, decent, and venerable. They were frequented by the right sort of people. Well, that was enough. . . .

As to living a spiritual life, he never tackled that problem. Some men who accept spiritual beliefs try to live up to them daily: other men, who reject such beliefs, try sometimes to smash them. My father would have disagreed with both kinds entirely. He took a more distant attitude. It disgusted him when atheists attacked religion: he thought they were vulgar. But he also objected to have religion make demands upon him—he felt that religion too was vulgar, when it tried to stir up men's feelings. It had its own proper field of activity, and it was all right there, of course; but there was one place religion should let alone, and that was a man's soul. He especially loathed any talk of walking hand in hand with his Saviour. And if he had ever found the Holy Ghost trying to soften his heart, he would have regarded Its behavior as distinctly uncalled for; even ungentlemanly.

The only religious leader or prophet I can think of who might have suited my father was Confucius—though even Confucius would have struck him as addled. . . . There was one saying of Confucius', however, with which he would have agreed: "Respect spiritual beings—if there are any—but keep aloof from them." My father would have regarded that principle as thoroughly sound.

When Confucius was asked about the rule to return good for evil, he said: "What then will you return for good? No: return good for good; for evil, return justice." If my father had been asked to return good for evil he would have been even more pithy—his response would have consisted of a hearty and full-throated "Bah!". . .

When Father went to church and sat in his pew, he felt he was doing enough. Any further spiritual work ought to be done by the clergy.

When hymns were sung he sometimes joined in mechanically, for the mere sake of singing; but usually he stood as silent as an eagle among canaries and doves, leaving others to abase themselves in sentiments that he didn't share. . . .

How did Father think God felt towards my mother? Why, about the way he did. God probably knew she had faults, but He saw she was lovely and good; and—in spite of some mistaken ideas that she had about money—He doubtless looked on her most affectionately. Father didn't expect God to regard *him* affectionately—they stood up man to man—but naturally God loved my mother, as everyone must. At the gate of Heaven, if there was any misunderstanding about his own ticket, Father counted on Mother to get him in. That was her affair.

This idea runs far back, or down, into old human thoughts. "The unbelieving husband is sanctified by the wife." (First Corinthians, vii, 14.) Medical missionaries report that today, in some primitive tribes, a healthy woman will propose to swallow medicine in behalf of her sick husband. This plan seems to her husband quite reasonable. It seemed so—in religion—to Father. . . .

I never saw Father kneel in supplication . . . On the contrary he usually talked with God lying in bed. My room was just above Father's, and he could easily be heard through the floor. On those rare nights when he failed to sleep well, the sound of damns would float up—at first deep and tragic and low, then more loud and exasperated. Fragments of thoughts and strong feelings came next, or meditations on current bothers. At the peak of these, God would be summoned. I would hear him call "Oh God?" over and over, with a rising inflection, as though he were demanding that God should present himself instantly, and sit in the fat green chair in the corner, and be duly admonished. Then when Father seemed to feel that God was listening, he would begin to expostulate. He would moan in a discouraged but strong voice: "Oh God, it's too much. Amen. . . I say it's too damned much. . . No, no, I can't stand it. Amen." After a pause, if he didn't feel better, he would seem to suspect that God might be trying to sneak back to Heaven without doing anything, and I would hear him shout warningly: "Oh God! I *won't* stand it! Amen. Oh damnation! A-a-men.". . .

The very next Sunday after an outburst he would be back in church. Not perhaps as a worshiper or a devotee, but at least as a patron. . . .

The Episcopal service in general he didn't criticize; it was stately and quiet; but the sermon, being different every Sunday, was a very bad gamble. And once in awhile there would be an impromptu prayer that he would take great offense at. Sometimes he disliked its subject or sentiments—if he chanced to be listening. Sometimes he decided it was too long, or its tone too lugubrious. I remember seeing him so restive during a prayer of that kind, that—although the entire congregation was kneeling in reverence—he suddenly gave a loud snort, sat up straight in his pew, and glared at the minister's back as though planning to kick it.

I glanced over at Mother. She had been sailing along devoutly, as best she could, in the full tide of prayer, with the lovely rapt look that would come at such times on her face; but she had also begun to watch Father out of one eye—for whenever a prayer was longer than usual she feared its effect on him—and now here he was sitting up and she had to stop praying and turn away from God to this obstinate, obstinate man. "Put your head down," she whispered fiercely; and then, when he wouldn't, she felt so furious at him, and so impotent, and so guilty for having such feelings, and so torn between her yearning to sink back again into the sweet peace of prayer and her hot determination to make the bad boy in Father behave, that she sent him a look like a flash of lightning, shooting out through quick tears; indignant to the very roots of her red hair, and as hurt as a child. This sank into him. He never would at any time kneel in church—she had given up struggling for that—but at last with a deep angry growl he once more bent stiffly down. . . .

Dr. Garden had come over to New York from England, but by descent he was Welsh. He had a broad red face, thick black hair, and a square blue-black beard. His robes were red, black and white. His strong English accent was a point in his favor, in an Episcopal church; it seemed to go well with the service. But owing we understood to his Welsh descent he was very emotional, and he used to plead with us at times in his sermons, in a sort of high mellow howl. My father disliked this. In the first place he heartily detested having anyone plead with him; in the second place Dr. Garden seldom could plead without crying. It wasn't put on at all; he was deeply moved by his own words. The atmosphere became tense and still when he leaned from his pulpit, and stretched out his arms yearningly to us, and sobbed, "Oh, my people." The whole church was hushed. At such moments Father would testily stir in his seat. "The damned Welshman, there he goes sniveling again," he would mutter.

This would horrify Mother. From her end of the pew she would signal him that he must stop. If he didn't notice, she would tell my small brothers to pass word along to me that I must make Father keep still. It was like expecting a boy to make the jungle behave. The most I felt up to was to get him to see Mother's signals, and that meant that I had to pull myself together and poke him. This was nervous work. He was a muscular, full-barreled man; there was nothing soft in him to poke; and he had a fiery way even of sitting still. It was like poking a stallion. When he became aware that he was being prodded, by my small, timid finger, he would turn fiercely upon me and I would hastily gesture toward Mother. Mother would whisper, "Clare! You mustn't!" and he would reply, "Bah!"

"Oh, Clare!"

"I know, Vinnie; but I can't stand that damned—"

"Sh—sh! Oh, hush!". . .

[*Father always put in a dollar when the plate came round, no more, no less.*] But after awhile Mother found a counter-argument which actually beat both of his: she made him feel that it was beneath his own dignity not to put in more, sometimes. Even then he didn't surrender; he compromised instead on this method: before starting for church, he put his usual dollar in his right-hand waist-coat pocket, but in the left-hand pocket he put a new five dollar bill; and he stated that from now on he would make a handsome offer to Garden: let him preach a decent sermon for once and he would give him the five.

This made every sermon a sporting event, in our pew. When Dr. Garden entered the pulpit we boys watched with a thrill, as though he were a race-horse at the barrier, jockeying for a good start. He looked rather fat for a race-horse, but he was impressive and confident, and it was kind of awe-inspiring to see him go down every time to defeat. He always either robbed himself of the prize in the very first lap by getting off on the wrong foot—a wrong key of some sort—or else in spite of a blameless beginning he would fail later on: he would as it were run clear off the course that Father had in silence marked out for him, and gallop away steadily and unconsciously in some other direction. It gave a boy a sobering sense of the grimness of fate.

"I don't see what the matter was today," Mother would declare, going home. "You should have given more than a dollar today, Clare.

It was a very nice sermon." But Father would merely say with a twinkle that Garden ought to get a new barrelful.

The only time I saw Father tested was one Sunday in Lent. It was remarkable enough that he should have been present that Sunday, for the one thing he always gave up in Lent was going to church. Dr. Garden's flow of grief in that season was more than he could stomach. But on this particular morning, to our surprise. Father went without question. It turned out afterward he didn't know it was Lent—he had "thought the damn thing was over." And as luck would have it, Dr. Garden was absent, ill in bed with a cold; and the substitute clergyman who took his place won Father's approval. He was a man who showed no emotions, he was plain and matter of fact, and his subject was the needs of some lumber country in the northwest. He had worked there, he knew the men, knew the business, and he described it in detail. I listened awhile, but there were no bears in it or cowboys; it was mostly business statistics; and I was studying a picture on the wall of an angel who looked like Mr. Gregg—a large, droopy angel with wrinkled garments, only he had no mustache—when my brother George secretly nudged me and pointed at Father. Father was listening closely. We glued our eyes on him. His face was keen and set; he had his arms folded; he was taking in every word. But we couldn't tell whether he liked it. The sermon went on a few minutes; and then, before we thought the man was half-through, he stopped. He had finished.

The organist began playing the offertory. There was a rustling of skirts; a stray cough. Imagine our excitement as we waited for the plate to come round. It seemed to take Mr. Gregg hours to get up the aisle, he stood so long, stooping and bulgy, at the end of each pew. "He wouldn't even hurry to see a fire-engine," George whispered indignantly. At last he got to the Hamiltons' pew in front of us—and then he stood at ours. We were all watching Father. But he hardly noticed Mr. Gregg, he was thinking about something else, and his thumb and finger slid automatically into his one-dollar pocket.

We let out our breaths and relaxed from the strain, disappointed. But just as we were slumping dejectedly down, Father paused; he put the one-dollar bill back, and decisively took out the five.

We could barely help cheering aloud at that substitute clergyman's triumph. And yet he himself never realized what he had done—he stepped quietly out of the pulpit and went back to obscurity. This man had won a victory that none of his profession had gained but nobody knew it except the Recording Angel and the four little Day boys.

—God and My Father

After the appearance of *The Education of H*y*m*a*n K*a*p*l*a*n* by Leonard Q. Ross (Leo C. Rosten), any collection of American humor would be incomplete without something from it. I include it here, however, because I got more laughs out of it than from any of the other selections. I think it is positively hilarious. The English language stands a great deal of chance to improve in effectiveness if it will follow K*a*p*l*a*n's system of conjugation and comparison: "fail, failed, bankropt"; "good, better, high-cless"; "bad, voice, rotten"; "cold, colder, below zero."

Mr. K*a*p*l*a*n and English Grammar

by Leonard Q. Ross

[*Kaplan was in the American Night Preparatory School for Adults.*]
For a long time Mr. Parkhill had believed that the incredible things which Mr. Hyman Kaplan did to the English language were the products of a sublime and transcendental ignorance. That was the only way, for example, that he could account for Mr. Kaplan's version of the name of the fourth President of the United States: "James Medicine." Then Mr. Parkhill began to feel that it wasn't ignorance which governed Mr. Kaplan so much as *impulsiveness*. That would explain the sentence Mr. Kaplan had given in vocabulary drill, using the word "orchard": "Each day he is giving her a dozen orchards." But then came Mr. Kaplan's impetuous answer to the question: "And what is the opposite of 'rich'?"

"Skinny!" Mr. Kaplan had cried.

Now a less conscientious teacher might have dismissed that as a fantastic guess. But Mr. Parkhill thought it over with great care. (Mr. Parkhill stopped at nothing in his pedagogical labors.) And he realized

From *The Education of H*y*m*a*n K*a*p*l*a*n*, by Leonard Q. Ross. Copyright, 1937, Harcourt Brace and Company, Inc.

that to Mr. Kaplan wealth and avoirdupois were inseparable aspects of one natural whole: rich people were fat. Grant this major premise and the opposite of "rich" *must* be—it was all too clear—"skinny."

The more Mr. Parkhill thought this over the more was he convinced that it was neither ignorance nor caprice which guided Mr. Kaplan's life and language. It was Logic. A secret kind of logic, perhaps. A private logic. A dark and baffling logic. But Logic. And when Mr. Kaplan fell into grammatical error it was simply because his logic and the logic of the world did not happen to coincide. Mr. Parkhill came to suspect that on such occasions there was only one defensible position to take: *de gustibus non est disputandum.*

Any final doubts Mr. Parkhill might have felt on the whole matter were resolved once and for all when Mr. Kaplan conjugated "to die" as "die, dead, funeral."

It was on a Monday night, several weeks after Mr. Kaplan's incomparable analysis of "to die," that Mr. Parkhill was given a fresh glimpse of the dialectical genius of his most remarkable student. The class was making three-minute addresses. Miss Rochell Goldberg was reciting. She was describing her experience with a ferocious dog. The dog's name, according to Miss Goldberg, was Spots. He was a "Scotch terror."

"Was he a beeg, wild dug!" Miss Goldberg said, her eyes moving in recollective fear. "Honist, you would all be afraid somthing tarrible! I had good rizzon for being all scared. I was trying to pat Spots, nize, on the had, and saying, 'Here, Spots, Spots, Spots!'—and Spots bite me so hod on the——"

" 'Bite' is the *present* tense, Miss Goldberg."

A look of dismay wandered into Miss Goldberg's eyes.

"You want the—er—*past* tense." Mr. Parkhill spoke as gently as he could: Miss Goldberg had a collapsible nervous system. "What *is* the past tense of 'to bite'?"

Miss Goldberg hung her head.

"The past tense of 'to bite'—anyone?"

Mr. Kaplan's Samaritan impulses surged to the fore. "Isn't 'bited,' uf cawss," he ventured archly.

"No, it isn't—er—'bited'!" Mr. Parkhill couldn't tell whether Mr. Kaplan had uttered a confident negation or an oblique question.

Miss Mitnick raised her hand, just high enough to be recognized. " 'Bit,' " she volunteered quietly.

"Good, Miss Mitnick! 'Bite, *bit,* bitten.' "

At once Mr. Kaplan closed his eyes, cocked his head to one side, and began whispering to himself. "Mitnick gives 'bit.' . . . *'Bit'* Mitnick gives. . . . My!"

This dramaturgic process indicated that Mr. Kaplan was subjecting Miss Mitnick's contribution to his most rigorous analysis. Considering the ancient and acrid feud between these two, to allow one of Miss Mitnick's offerings to go unchallenged would constitute a psychological defeat of no mean proportions to Mr. Kaplan. It would be a blow to his self-respect. It would bring anguish to his soul.

" 'Bite, *bit,* bitten?' . . . Hmmmm. . . . Dat sonds awful fonny!"

It was no use for Mr. Parkhill to pretend that he had not heard: the whole class had heard.

"Er—isn't that clear, Mr. Kaplan?"

Mr. Kaplan did not open his eyes. *"Clear,* Mr. Pockheel? Foistcless clear! Clear like gold! Only I don' see vy should be dat 'bit.' . . . It don' makink *sanse!"*

"Oh, it doesn't make *sense,"* Mr. Parkhill repeated lamely. Suddenly he glimpsed a golden opportunity. "You mean it isn't—er—*logical?"*

"Exactel!" cried Mr. Kaplan happily. "Dat 'bit' isn't logical."

"Well, Mr. Kaplan. Surely you remember our verb drills. The verb 'to bite' is much like, say, the verb 'to hide.' 'To hide' is conjugated 'hide, hid, hidden.' Why, then, isn't it—er—logical that the principal parts of 'to bite' be 'bite, bit, bitten'?"

Mr. Kaplan considered this semisyllogism in silence. Then he spoke. *"I* t'ought de pest time 'bite' should be —'bote.' "

Miss Mitnick gave a little gasp.

" 'Bote?' " Mr. Parkhill asked in amazement. " 'Bote?' "

" 'Bote!' " said Mr. Kaplan.

Mr. Parkhill shook his head. "I don't see your point."

"Vell," sighed Mr. Kaplan with a modest shrug, "if is 'write, wrote, written,' so vy isn't 'bite, bote, bitten'?"

Psychic cymbals crashed in Mr. Parkhill's ears.

"There is not such a word 'bote,' " protested Miss Mitnick, who took this all as a personal affront. Her voice was small but desperate.

"'Not-soch-a-void!'" Mr. Kaplan repeated ironically. "Mine dear Mitnick, don' *I* know is not soch a void? Did I said *is* soch a void? All I'm eskink is, isn't logical *should be* soch a void!"

The silence was staggering.

"Mr. Kaplan, there is *no such word,* as Miss Mitnick just said." (Miss Mitnick was in agony, biting her lips, twisting her handkerchief, gazing with bewilderment at her shoes. Her plight was that of common humanity's, faced by genius.) "Nor is it—er—logical that there *should* be such a word." Mr. Parkhill recapitulated the exercise on regular and irregular verbs. He gave the principal parts of a dozen samples. He analyzed the whole system of verb conjugation. Mr. Parkhill spoke with earnestness and rare feeling. He spoke as if a good deal depended on it.

By the time Mr. Parkhill had finished his little lecture Mr. Kaplan had seen the light and submitted, with many a sigh, to the tyranny of the irregular verb; Miss Mitnick's normal pallor had returned; Mrs. Moskowitz was fast asleep; and Miss Goldberg, completely forgotten in the clash between two systems of thought, had taken her seat with the air of one washing her hands of the whole business.

Recitation and Speech went on.

Mr. Sam Pinsky delivered a short address on the mysteries of his craft, baking. (It came out that Mr. Pinsky had produced literally thousands of "loafers" of "brat" in his career.) Miss Valuskas described a wedding she had recently attended. Mrs. Moskowitz, refreshed by her slumbers, indulged in a moving idyll about a trip she was hoping to make to a metropolis called "Spittsburgh." Then the recess bell rang.

The second student to recite after the recess was Hyman Kaplan. He hurried to the front of the room, glowing with joy at the opportunity to recite. He almost seemed to give off a radiance.

"Ladies an' gantleman, Mr. Pockheel," Mr. Kaplan began, with customary éclat. "Tonight I'll gonna talkink abot noosepeppers, dose movvelous——"

"Pardon me." Mr. Parkhill knew it would be nothing short of fatal to give Mr. Kaplan free rein. "It's 'Tonight I *am going* . . . to *talk.*' And the word is '*news*papers,' not "noose-peppers.'" Mr. Parkhill went to the board and printed "NOOSE," "PEPPER," and "NEWSPAPER." He explained the meaning of each word. When he pointed out that "pepper"

was a strong condiment ("Salt . . . pepper, Mr. Kaplan. Do you see?"),
everyone smiled. Miss Mitnick rejoiced. Mr. Kaplan beamed. Mr.
Kaplan was amazed by the ingenious combination ("noose-pepper")
which he had brought into being.

"Vell," Mr. Kaplan took up his tale after Mr. Parkhill was done,
"de *news*papers is to me de finest kind t'ing ve have in tsivilization.
Vat *is* a newspaper? Ha! It's a show! It's a comedy! It's aducation! It's
movvelous!" Rhapsodically Mr. Kaplan painted the glory and the
miracle of journalism. "From newspapers de messes gat——"

" 'M*a*sses,' Mr. Kaplan, 'm*a*sses'!" Mr. Parkhill felt that "messes"
might have consequences too dreadful to contemplate.

"—de m*a*sses loin abot de voild. Even de edvoitismants in de paper
is a kind lasson. An' uf cawss de odder pots a newspaper: de hatlininks,
de auditorials, de cottoons, de fine pages pictchiss on Sonday, dat ve
callink rotogravy sactions."

" 'Rotogr*avure!*' "

"An' in newspapers ve find ot all dat's heppenink all hover de voild!
Abot politic, crimes, all kinds difference *scendels* pipple makink, abot
if is goink to be snow or rainink, an' uf cawss—'spacially in U. S.—all
abot sax!"

Mr. Parkhill closed his eyes.

"Mitout newspapers vat vould ve humans be?" Mr. Kaplan paused
dramatically. "Ha! *Sawages* ve vould be, dat's vat! *Ignorance* ve vould
fill, dat's all. No fects! No knolledge! No aducation!" A shudder
passed through the body scholastic at the mere thought of such a barbaric state.

"Vell, dis mornink I vas readink a noos—a *news*paper. English newspaper!" Mr. Kaplan paused, awaiting the acclaim of his colleagues.
They were inert. *"English* newspaper I vas readink!" Mr. Kaplan
repeated delicately. Mr. Bloom snickered, ever the skeptic. Mr. Kaplan
shot him a look composed of indignation, pain, and ice. "I vas readink
abot how vill maybe be annodder Voild Var. So vat de paper said?
Vell, he said dat——"

"Mr. Kaplan," Mr. Parkhill *had* to interpolate. "It's '*it* said,' not '*he*
said'!"

Mr. Kaplan was stunned. "Not 'he'?"

"No, not 'he.' 'It'! Er—you know the rules for pronouns, Mr. Kaplan. 'He' is masculine, 'she' is feminine. Sometimes, of course, we say 'she' for certain objects which have no sex—a country, for example, or a ship. But for newspapers we use the neuter pronoun." Mr. Parkhill had an inspiration. "Surely *that's* logical!"

Mr. Kaplan sank into mighty thought, shaking his head at regular intervals. He whispered to himself: "Not mascoolin. . . . Not faminine. . . . But in de *meedle!*"

Mr. Parkhill waited with the patience of his calling.

"Aha!" Some cosmic verity had groped its way into Mr. Kaplan's universe. "Plizz, Mr. Pockheel. I unnistand *fine* abot mascoolin, faminine, an' neutral; but——"

" 'Neu*ter*,' Mr. Kaplan!"

"—an' neu*ter*. But is maybe all right ve should say 'he' abot *som* papers! Ven dey havink mascoolin *names?*"

Mr. Parkhill frowned. "I don't see what the name of the paper has to do with it. We say of the New York *Times,* for instance, 'it said.' Or of the New York *Post*——"

"*Dose* papers, yassir!" Mr. Kaplan cried. "But ven a paper got a real *mascoolin* name?"

Mr. Parkhill spoke with calculated deliberation. "I don't understand, Mr. Kaplan. Which newspaper would you say has a—er—*masculine* name?"

Mr. Kaplan's face was drenched with modesty. "*Harold Tribune,*" he said.

—*The Education of H*y*m*a*n K*a*p*l*a*n*

Mark Twain is immortal, and even a few selections show us why.

From "Pudd'nhead Wilson's Calendar"

BY MARK TWAIN

Tell the truth or trump—but get the trick.

Adam was but human—this explains it all. He did not want the apple for the apple's sake, he wanted it only because it was forbidden. The mistake was in not forbidding the serpent; then he would have eaten the serpent.

Adam and Eve had many advantages, but the principal one was that they escaped teething.

Training is everything. The peach was once a bitter almond; cauliflower is nothing but cabbage with a college education.

Let us endeavor so to live that when we come to die even the undertaker will be sorry.

Habit is habit and not to be flung out of the window by any man but coaxed down-stairs a step at a time.

The holy passion of Friendship is of so sweet and steady and loyal and enduring a nature that it will last through a whole lifetime, if not asked to lend money.

Why is it that we rejoice at a birth and grieve at a funeral? It is because we are not the person involved.

When angry, count four; when very angry, swear.

When I reflect upon the number of disagreeable people who I know have gone to a better world, I am moved to lead a different life.

Nothing so needs reforming as other people's habits.

If you pick up a starving dog and make him prosperous, he will not bite you. This is the principal difference between a dog and a man.

July 4. Statistics show that we lose more fools on this day than in all the other days of the year put together. This proves, by the number left in stock, that one Fourth of July per year is now inadequate, the country has grown so.

Few things are harder to put up with than the annoyance of a good example.

It were not best that we should all think alike; it is difference of opinion that makes horse-races.

He is useless on top of the ground; he ought to be under it, inspiring the cabbages.

April 1. This is the day upon which we are reminded of what we are on the other three hundred and sixty-four.

From "Following the Equator"

BY MARK TWAIN

Noise proves nothing. Often a hen who has merely laid an egg cackles as if she had laid an asteroid.

He was as shy as a newspaper is when referring to its own merits.

It could probably be shown by facts and figures that there is no distinctly native American criminal class except Congress.

Everything human is pathetic. The secret source of Humor itself is not joy but sorrow. There is no humor in heaven.

There are those who scoff at the school-boy, calling him frivolous and shallow. Yet it was the school-boy who said, "Faith is believing what you know ain't so."

We can secure other people's approval if we do right and try hard, but our own is worth a hundred of it and no way has been found out of securing that.

Truth is stranger than Fiction, but it is because Fiction is obliged to stick to possibilities; Truth isn't.

There is a Moral Sense and there is an Immoral Sense. History shows us that the Moral Sense enables us to perceive morality and how to avoid it, and that the Immoral Sense enables us to perceive immorality and how to enjoy it.

Pity is for the living, envy is for the dead.

It is by the goodness of God that in our country we have those three unspeakably precious things: freedom of speech, freedom of conscience, and the prudence never to practise either of them.

Be careless in your dress if you must but keep a tidy soul.

There is no such thing as "the Queen's English." The property has gone into the hands of a joint stock company and we own the bulk of the shares.

There are people who can do all fine and heroic things but one: keep from telling their happinesses to the unhappy.

Man is the Only Animal that blushes. Or needs to.

Let us be thankful for the fools. But for them the rest of us could not succeed.

The man with a new idea is a Crank until the idea succeeds.

Let us be grateful to Adam our benefactor. He cut us out of the "blessing" of idleness and won for us the "curse" of labor.

The Autocrat of Russia possesses more power than any other man in the earth, but he cannot stop a sneeze.

There are several good protections against temptations but the surest is cowardice.

To succeed in the other trades, capacity must be shown; in the law, concealment of it will do.

It takes your enemy and your friend, working together, to hurt you to the heart, the one to slander you and the other to get the news to you.

Simple rules for saving money: To save half, when you are fired by an eager impulse to contribute to a charity, wait and count forty. To save three-quarters, count sixty. To save it all, count sixty-five.

He had had much experience of physicians, and said "the only way to keep your health is to eat what you don't want, drink what you don't like, and do what you'd druther not."

The man who is ostentatious of his modesty is twin to the statue that wears a fig-leaf.

Let me make the superstitions of a nation and I care not who makes its laws or its songs either.

Do not undervalue the headache. While it is at its sharpest it seems a bad investment, but when relief begins the unexpired remainder is worth four dollars a minute.

There are two times in a man's life when he should not speculate: when he can't afford it and when he can.

Don't part with your illusions. When they are gone you may still exist but you have ceased to live.

In the first place God made idiots. This was for practice. Then He made School Boards.

In statesmanship get the formalities right, never mind about the moralities.

Every one is a moon and has a dark side which he never shows to anybody.

The very ink with which all history is written is merely fluid prejudice.

2. SATIRE

Benjamin Franklin was one of the great natural humorists of the United States. This was partly because his was an original mind, of which very few exist in this world. He wrote several parables, fairly good, rewrote a good number of proverbs and made some of his own, and composed several humorous reflective essays, several gallant love letters, being in love gallantly but not desperately, and a good number of political satires. The best-known of these satires is perhaps "The Sale of the Hessians," but there were others just as good: "An Edict by the King of Prussia," "Rules by Which a Great Empire May Be Reduced to a Small One," "Dialogue between Britain, France, Spain, Holland, Saxony and America"—all of which are rather hard on the British, especially the last [1]—and a satire "on the Slave-Trade," where he satirized the defenders of Negro slavery by defending the Arabs holding Christian slaves. In spite of the hot feelings against the British in those days, the characteristic of Franklin's humor was that it was never bitter.

The Sale of the Hessians

BY BENJAMIN FRANKLIN

From the Count de Schaumbergh to the Baron Hohendorf, Commanding the Hessian Troops in America

Rome, February 18, 1777.

MONSIEUR LE BARON:—

On my return from Naples, I received at Rome your letter of the 27th December of last year. I have learned with unspeakable pleasure the courage our troops exhibited at Trenton, and you cannot imagine my joy on being told that of the 1,950 Hessians engaged in the fight, but 345 escaped. There were just 1,605 men killed, and I cannot sufficiently commend your prudence in sending an exact list of the dead to my minister in London. This precaution was the more necessary,

---

[1] *"America.* I shall not surrender my Liberty and Property, but with my Life. . . . *Britain.* You impudent b——h! Am not I your Mother Country? Is that not a sufficient Title to your Respect and Obedience? *Saxony. Mother country!* Hah, hah, he! What Respect have *you* the front to claim as a Mother Country? You know that *I* am *your* Mother Country, and yet you pay me none. Nay, it is but the other day, that you hired Ruffians to rob me on the Highway, and burn my House! For shame! Hide your Face and hold your Tongue. If you continue this Conduct, you will make yourself the Contempt of Europe! *Britain.* O Lord! Where are my friends? *France, Spain, Holland, and Saxony, all together.* Friends! Believe us, you have none, nor ever will have any, 'till you mend your Manners. How can we, who are your Neighbours, have any regard for you, or expect any Equity from you, should your Power increase, when we see how basely and unjustly you have us'd both your *own Mother and your own Children?"*

as the report sent to the English ministry does not give but 1,455 dead. This would make 483,450 florins instead of 643,500 which I am entitled to demand under our convention. You will comprehend the prejudice which such an error would work in my finances, and I do not doubt you will take the necessary pains to prove that Lord North's list is false and yours correct.

The court of London objects that there were a hundred wounded who ought not to be included in the list, nor paid for as dead; but I trust you will not overlook my instructions to you on quitting Cassel, and that you will not have tried by human succor to recall the life of the unfortunates whose days could not be lengthened but by the loss of a leg or an arm. That would be making them a pernicious present, and I am sure they would rather die than live in a condition no longer fit for my service. I do not mean by this that you should assassinate them; we should be humane, my dear Baron, but you may insinuate to the surgeons with entire propriety that a crippled man is a reproach to their profession, and that there is no wiser course than to let every one of them die when he ceases to be fit to fight.

I am about to send to you some new recruits. Don't economize them. Remember glory before all things. Glory is true wealth. There is nothing degrades the soldier like the love of money. He must care only for honour and reputation, but this reputation must be acquired in the midst of dangers. A battle gained without costing the conqueror any blood is an inglorious success, while the conquered cover themselves with glory by perishing with their arms in their hands. Do you remember that of the 300 Lacedæmonians who defended the defile of Thermopylæ, not one returned? How happy should I be could I say the same of my brave Hessians!

It is true that their king, Leonidas, perished with them: but things have changed, and it is no longer the custom for princes of the empire to go and fight in America for a cause with which they have no concern. And besides, to whom should they pay the thirty guineas per man if I did not stay in Europe to receive them? Then, it is necessary also that I be ready to send recruits to replace the men you lose. For this purpose I must return to Hesse. It is true, grown men are becoming scarce there, but I will send you boys. Besides, the scarcer the commodity the higher the price. I am assured that the women and little girls have begun to till our lands, and they get on not badly. You did right to send back to Europe that Dr. Crumerus who was so successful in curing dysentery. Don't bother with a man who is subject to looseness of the bowels. That disease makes bad soldiers. One coward will do more mischief in an engagement than ten brave men will do good. Better that they burst in their barracks than fly in a battle, and tarnish the glory of our arms. Besides, you know that they pay me as killed for all who die from disease, and I don't get a farthing for runaways. My trip to Italy, which has cost me enormously, makes it desirable that there should be a great mortality among them. You will therefore promise promotion to all who expose themselves; you will exhort them to seek glory in the midst of dangers; you will say to Major Maundorff that I am not at all content with his saving the 345 men who escaped the massacre of Trenton. Through the whole campaign he has not had ten men killed in consequence of his orders. Finally, let it be your principal object to prolong the war and avoid a decisive engagement on either side, for I have made arrangements for a grand Italian opera, and I do not wish to be obliged to give it up. Meantime I pray God, my dear Baron de Hohendorf, to have you in his holy and gracious keeping.

There are two good satires on the press, James Russell Lowell's "The Pious Editor's Creed" and Mark Twain's "Journalism in Tennessee," written from entirely different angles. Now that the Mexican War is over, we can enjoy Lowell's piece for the fun of it.

"The Pious Editor's Creed"

BY JAMES RUSSELL LOWELL

> I du believe in Freedom's cause,
>   Ez fur away ez Payris is;
> I love to see her stick her claws
>   In them infarnal Phayrisees;
> It's wal enough agin a king
>   To dror resolves an' triggers,—

But libbaty 's a kind o' thing
  Thet don't agree with niggers.

I du believe the people want
  A tax on teas an' coffees,
Thet nothin' aint extravygunt,—
  Purvidin' I'm in office;
Fer I hev loved my country sence
  My eye-teeth filled their sockets,
An' Uncle Sam I reverence,
  Partic'larly his pockets. . . .

I du believe in prayer an' praise
  To him thet hez the grantin'
O' jobs,—in every thin' thet pays,
  But most of all in Cantin';
This doth my cup with marcies fill,
  This lays all thought o' sin to rest,—
I *don't* believe in princerple,
  But oh, I *du* in interest.

I du believe in bein' this
  Or thet, ez it may happen
One way or t' other hendiest is
  To ketch the people nappin';
It aint by princerples nor men
  My preudunt course is steadied,—
I scent wich pays the best, an' then
  Go into it baldheaded.

I du believe thet holdin' slaves
  Comes nat'ral to a Presidunt,
Let 'lone the rowdedow it saves
  To hev a wal-broke precedunt;
Fer any office, small or gret,
  I could n't ax with no face,

'uthout I 'd ben, thru dry an' wet,
Th' unrizzest kind o' doughface.

I du believe wutever trash
　'll keep the people in blindness,—
Thet we the Mexicuns can thrash
　Right inter brotherly kindness,
Thet bombshells, grape, an' powder 'n' ball
　Air good-will's strongest magnets,
Thet peace, to make it stick at all,
　Must be druv in with bagnets.

In short, I firmly du believe
　In Humbug generally,
Fer it 's a thing thet I perceive
　To hev a solid vally;
This heth my faithful shepherd ben,
　In pasturs sweet heth led me,
An' this 'll keep the people green
　To feed ez they hev fed me.

May 4, 1848

—*Biglow Papers*

It takes somewhat more than ordinary literary ability to write good fables, and James Thurber has done it. Many there are who can write novels; only the chosen few can write fables and stories for children like the tales of Andersen. Consequently, one good fable is worth ten novels and is more likely to survive the ages. I am including here two selections from Thurber's *Fables for Our Time* as well as a selection from "University Days" (in *My Life and Hard Times*).

The Owl Who Was God

BY JAMES THURBER

Once upon a starless midnight there was an owl who sat on the branch of an oak tree. Two ground moles tried to slip quietly by, unnoticed. "You!" said the owl. "Who?" they quavered, in fear and astonishment, for they could not believe it was possible for anyone to see them in that thick darkness. "You two!" said the owl. The moles hurried away and told the other creatures of the field and forest that the owl was the greatest and wisest of all animals because he could see in the dark and because he could answer any question. "I'll see about that," said a secretary bird, and he called on the owl one night when it was again very dark. "How many claws am I holding up?" said the secretary bird. "Two," said the owl, and that was right. "Can you give me another expression for 'that is to say' or 'namely'?" asked the secretary bird. "To wit," said the owl. "Why does a lover call on his love?" asked the secretary bird. "To woo," said the owl.

The secretary bird hastened back to the other creatures and reported that the owl was indeed the greatest and wisest animal in the world because he could see in the dark and because he could answer any question. "Can he see in the daytime, too?" asked a red fox. "Yes," echoed a dormouse and a French poodle. "Can he see in the daytime, too?" All the other creatures laughed loudly at this silly question, and they set upon the red fox and his friends and drove them out of the region. Then they sent a messenger to the owl and asked him to be their leader.

When the owl appeared among the animals it was high noon and the sun was shining brightly. He walked very slowly, which gave him an appearance of great dignity, and he peered about him with large, staring eyes, which gave him an air of tremendous importance. "He's God!" screamed a Plymouth Rock hen. And the others took up the cry "He's God!" So they followed him wherever he went and when he began to bump into things they began to bump into things, too. Finally he came to a concrete highway and he started up the middle of it and all the other creatures followed him. Presently a hawk, who was acting as outrider, observed a truck coming toward them at fifty miles an hour, and he reported to the secretary bird and the secretary bird reported to the owl. "There's danger ahead," said the secretary bird. "To wit?" said the owl. The secretary bird told him. "Aren't you afraid?" he asked. "Who?" said the owl calmly, for he could not see the truck. "He's God!" cried all the creatures again, and they were still crying "He's God!" when the truck hit them and ran them down. Some of the animals were merely injured, but most of them, including the owl, were killed.

Moral: You can fool too many of the people too much of the time.

The Shrike and the Chipmunk

BY JAMES THURBER

Once upon a time there were two chipmunks, a male and a female. The male chipmunk thought that arranging nuts in artistic patterns was more fun than just piling them up to see how many you could pile up. The female was all for piling up as many as you could. She told her husband that if he gave up making designs with the nuts there would be room in their large cave for a great many more and he would soon become the wealthiest chipmunk in the woods. But he would not let her interfere with his designs, so she flew into a rage and left him. "The shrike will get you," she said, "because you are helpless and cannot look after yourself." To be sure, the female chipmunk had not been gone three nights before the male had to dress for a banquet and could not find his studs or shirt or suspenders. So he couldn't go to the banquet, but that was just as well, because all the chipmunks who did go were attacked and killed by a weasel.

The next day the shrike began hanging around outside the chipmunk's cave, waiting to catch him. The shrike couldn't get in because the doorway was clogged up with soiled laundry and dirty dishes. "He will come out for a walk after breakfast and I will get him then," thought the shrike. But the chipmunk slept all day and did not get up and have breakfast until after dark. Then he came out for a breath of air before beginning work on a new design. The shrike swooped down to snatch up the chipmunk, but could not see very well on account of the dark, so he batted his head against an alder branch and was killed.

A few days later the female chipmunk returned and saw the awful mess the house was in. She went to the bed and shook her husband. "What would you do without me?" she demanded. "Just go on living, I guess," he said. "You wouldn't last five days," she told him. She swept the house and did the dishes and sent out the laundry, and then she made the chipmunk get up and wash and dress. "You can't be healthy if you lie in bed all day and never get any exercise," she told him. So she took him for a walk in the bright sunlight and they were both caught and killed by the shrike's brother, a shrike named Stoop.

Moral: Early to rise and early to bed makes a male healthy and wealthy and dead.

—*Fables for Our Time*

The Football Tackle and the Class in Economics

BY JAMES THURBER

One of the courses at college that I didn't like, but somehow managed to pass, was economics. I went to that class straight from the botany class, which didn't help me any in understanding either subject. I used to get them mixed up. But not as mixed up as another student in my economics class who came there direct from a physics laboratory. He was a tackle on the football team, named Bolenciecwcz. At that time Ohio State University had one of the best football teams in the country, and Bolenciecwcz was one of its outstanding stars. In order to be eligible to play it was necessary for him to keep up in his studies, a very difficult matter, for while he was not dumber than an ox he was not any smarter. Most of his professors were lenient and helped him along. None gave him more hints, in answering questions, or asked him simpler ones than the economics professor, a thin, timid man named Bassum. One day when we were on the subject of transportation and distribution, it came Bolenciecwcz's turn to answer a question. "Name one means of transportation," the professor said to him. No light came into the big tackle's eyes. "Just any means of transportation,"

said the professor. Bolenciecwcz sat staring at him. "That is," pursued the professor, "any medium, agency, or method of going from one place to another." Bolenciecwcz had the look of a man who is being led into a trap. "You may choose among steam, horse-drawn, or electrically propelled vehicles," said the instructor. "I might suggest the one which we commonly take in making long journeys across land." There was a profound silence in which everybody stirred uneasily, including Bolenciecwcz and Mr. Bassum. Mr. Bassum abruptly broke this silence in an amazing manner. "Choo-choo-choo," he said, in a low voice, and turned instantly scarlet. He glanced appealingly around the room. All of us, of course, shared Mr. Bassum's desire that Bolenciecwcz should stay abreast of the class in economics, for the Illinois game, one of the hardest and most important of the season, was only a week off. "Toot, toot, too-toooooooot!" some student with a deep voice moaned, and we all looked encouragingly at Bolenciecwcz. Somebody else gave a fine imitation of a locomotive letting off steam. Mr. Bassum himself rounded off the little show. "Ding, dong, ding, dong," he said, hopefully. Bolenciecwcz was staring at the floor now, trying to think, his great brow furrowed, his huge hands rubbing together, his face red.

"How did you come to college this year, Mr. Bolenciecwcz?" asked the professor. "*Chuf*fa chuffa, *chuf*fa chuffa."

"M'father sent me," said the football player.

"What on?" asked Bassum.

"I git an 'lowance," said the tackle, in a low, husky voice, obviously embarrassed.

"No, no," said Bassum. "Name a means of transportation. What did you *ride* here on?"

"Train," said Bolenciecwcz.

"Quite right," said the professor. "Now, Mr. Nugent, will you tell us——"

—"University Days"

Chapter XV

WAR AND PEACE

I. WORLD GOVERNMENT

EVERYBODY is agreed now that the United Nations as it is not functioning today can stop everything except war. No one can be suspected of being captious on the subject of peace today. We are all in the same boat.

All my life, in China and abroad, I have been an enemy of the experts and a friend of simplification. I shall not try to write here a treatise on how peace can be surely secured but rather to present in a short space what some serious minds have said on the subject. Yet the question, as far as I can see it, can be very simply stated in one paragraph. When two states quarrel, there are two, and only two ways of settling it, by a fight or by the due process of law and order. But in order that a question may be peaceably settled, there must exist an organization standing for law and order above all its individual members which enjoys the confidence of the peoples, with the power to enforce its decisions against recalcitrants. This truth is so axiomatic that it is clear to everybody. The public must be so used to the idea that it regards with contempt anyone who would think of defying the law and order thus represented. If such an organization exists, acquiescence in its decisions is easy for all, as in any civilized human community. If no such organization exists, or if it does not enjoy the confidence of the public, then every state, in obedience to the law of self-preservation, is in duty bound to look out for itself by preparations to meet force with force. Unless such an organization is developed, any armed service of a nation would be guilty of criminal negligence in its duty to the state and to its citizens, if it did not prepare the nation for war in all emergencies, or even further, if it did not take measures to place itself in the best strategical advantage lest war should come. The simple principle of law and order, which has proved efficacious in settling private quarrels inside a state, and no other, can settle quarrels among the states. World federalism is therefore in my opinion the only solution.

Such an organization does not exist today; therefore there will be war. The cause of this lies squarely with the so-called "big powers." They are not ready to try the regular democratic process in a world organization. They have not pledged, and will not pledge, themselves to abide by its majority decisions. Each of the Big Five wants to have the power of the despot to veto the will of the majority. They believe they cannot afford to have a democratic machinery for peace such as exists inside the civilized nations. In other words, the big nations are not educated enough to want the normal, civilized democratic setup in this organization. What they wish is to keep control of the world's fate in their own hands. Consequently, they do not want the General Assembly to have power. Moreover, they do not want the United Nations to have power; they do not give it the authority to write treaties with Germany or Japan. They want to settle all the important, all the strategic and crucial problems, all the problems of balance of power and spheres of influence from which wars arise, at their "foreign ministers' conferences," outside the United Nations. The latter is thought of only as the shopfront for an abstract idea of world unity, which they firmly believe will remain an ideal only, which it would be unrealistic to strive for now. In an atomic age, they believe it is realistic now still to follow Metternich, Talleyrand, and Clemenceau. In other words, the Big Five are not ready to change the pattern of power politics. They will talk about educating and feeding the less advanced nations, but God knows it is the nations that today have education and good food and sanitation that will start the next war, not the Eskimos or the Javanese. The big powers, which have started two world wars for us, are not yet ashamed of themselves.

And yet, if put that way, the big nations will deny it. They will take shelter under the wing of the experts, saying the thing is enormously complicated, it can't be done. The world federalists are the dreamers; they are the realists. I am still for simplification. The crux of the problem is not whether it can or cannot be done, but whether the big powers of today are ready for such an organization. The truth behind it is that there is no real effort made toward such an organization because there is no will behind it. Hence the third and the most important point: we have to settle first, whether we want to stop war by all means even if it means giving up something, or whether, if the organization is so imperfect as to threaten or even make certain another war, we are willing to stand passively by, and try to meet another war. The choice is between democracy and peace on the one hand, and privilege, power, and war on the other. If war and world federalism are the only two alternatives—and the big powers cannot demonstrate that a third alternative exists—it simply means that the big powers choose war rather than world federalism. Who are the realists and who are the confused?

Human intelligence always should mean a capacity to see and meet a new situation, while there is something doggish in mere stubbornness and love of old tricks. Human realism is properly scared by the atom bomb; dog realism says it is not afraid, that we have time, that we can afford to dillydally a while yet. Human realism tells us that the road of power politics and alliances and spheres of power has led to two disastrous world wars and inevitably will lead to a third; dog realism says, "Power feels good in my hands. Let me keep it a while; let me try again and see if I can't juggle with alliances and spheres a little better than Clemenceau and Lloyd George did; perhaps I am cleverer." Human realism says the world has shrunk; dog realism asks, hesitantly, "Is that so?" Human realism says the modern weapons have abolished all national frontiers and no nation is safe; dog realism asks, "Do you really think so?" Human realism says a guided missile can cross the English Channel and even the Atlantic; dog realism asks innocently, "Can it?" Human realism reminds us there was a time when we all agreed there would be no use of international law without international police enforcement; dog realism says, "The experts say it is too complicated anyway." Human realism reminds us that there was a time in the nineteen tens, when a great American President became the voice of the world's conscience, when the whole mass of mankind thought we were going to have self-determination and that there was to be no more "distinction between the strong and the weak," and that "the small nations shall not be handed over from sovereignty to sovereignty" like pawns in their game; but in the nineteen forties the dog realism has forgotten about all that, in only thirty years, and is playing that game right now. Wilson touched the heart of the world when he announced the objective of World War I, as "peace without victory"; foul dog realism announced its objective in World War II as victory without peace, victory in full measure without discount, victory unconditional—a victory which has as little to do with Beethoven's Fifth Symphony as Hannibal or Genghis Khan had to do with the brotherhood of mankind. The world today is in the grip, not of war and the threat of war, but of this dog realism made manifest. Unless every man can drive this out from his inner soul, he must expect war. He does not deserve better.

What do some of the best American minds of today say? The following quotations are from E. B. White's *The Wild Flag*, considered by many as the best recent writing (along with Emery Reves' *Anatomy of Peace*) on the most crucial topic in the world. It did seem for a time that the *New Yorker* was the only serious magazine in the United States—taking the Hiroshima story seriously, besides editorializing on world government. That I ascribe to the simplicity of humorists, who refuse to be confused or frightened or cajoled by prevaricating experts in political science and international affairs. I hope the reader will not miss the message written by E. B. White himself just before Christmas, 1945, which I have put in the almanac along with his own selections. May posterity remember that this was written only six months after the conclusion of World War II. What a Christmas piece for man only shortly relieved from the six-year war!

A World Government Almanac

BY E. B. WHITE

December 8, 1945

Almanac to be hung by the wood box in the kitchen:

APRIL 26—Doctor T. V. Soong addressing the United Nations Conference in San Francisco: 'If there is any message that my country . . . wishes to give to this Conference, it is that we are prepared . . . to yield if necessary a part of our sovereignty to the new international organization in the interest of collective security.'

JUNE 13—Emery Reves in *The Anatomy of Peace*: 'As the twentieth-century crisis is a worldwide clash between the social units of sovereign nation-states, the problem of peace in our time is the establishment of a legal order to regulate relations among men, beyond and above the nation-states.'

AUGUST 12—Robert Maynard Hutchins, Chancellor of the University of Chicago, in a broadcast: 'Up to last Monday, I must confess, I didn't have much hope for a world state. I believed that no moral basis for it existed, that we had no world conscience and no sense of world community sufficient to keep a world state together. But the alternatives now seem clear.' ...

AUGUST 18—Norman Cousins in the *Saturday Review of Literature:* 'Already he [Man] has become a world warrior; it is but one additional step—though a long one—for him to develop a world conscience. . . . He shall have to recognize the flat truth that the greatest obsolescence of all in the Atomic Age is national sovereignty.' ...

SEPTEMBER 1—Cord Meyer, Jr., in the *Atlantic Monthly:* 'In international society there is no final authority to which the national states must refer their disputes for settlement. . . . We should frankly recognize this lawless condition as anarchy, where brute force is the price of survival. As long as it continues to exist, war is not only possible but inevitable.' ...

OCTOBER 20—Editorial in the *Saturday Evening Post:* 'We have come to the point where nothing less than world government will suffice to tailor international politics to hitherto-undreamed-of resources of power.'

OCTOBER 22—Ralph Barton Perry in *One World in the Making:* 'The one world of which we fondly dream is not designed to satisfy the exclusive interest of any man or any group. It contains no masters' or servants' quarters. It serves each interest only by serving all interests. It rests on this widest and all-inclusive base, and on nothing else. It is not an idle dream. It is not a mere playful exercise of the imagination but a project to which men are driven by practical necessity.'

NOVEMBER 1—Professor Albert Einstein in the *Atlantic Monthly:* 'Do I fear the tyranny of a World Government? Of course I do. But I fear still more the coming of another war or wars. Any government is certain to be evil to some extent. But a World Government is preferable to the far greater evil of wars, particularly with their intensified destructiveness.'

NOVEMBER 23—Mr. Bevin in the House of Commons: 'I feel we are driven relentlessly along this road; we need a new study for the purpose of creating a world assembly elected directly from the people of the world, as a whole. . . . I am willing to sit with anybody, of any party, of any nation, to try to devise a franchise or a constitution— just as other great countries have done—for a world assembly . . .'

NOVEMBER 24—Doctor J. Robert Oppenheimer in the *Saturday Review of Literature:* 'It is a practical thing to recognize as a common responsibility, wholly incapable of unilateral solution, the completely common peril that atomic weapons constitute for the world, to recognize that only by a community of responsibility is there any hope of meeting that peril.'

DECEMBER 22—[*Mr. E. B. White himself now—in* The New Yorker] 'We walked home in the cold afternoon past Franklin Simon's windows, where the children of all nations revolved steadily in the light. Most of the stores were concentrating on the gift aspect of the Nativity, displaying frankincense, myrrh, and bath salts, but Franklin Simon advertised the Child Himself, along with a processional of other children of assorted races, lovely to behold. We stood and watched passers-by take in this international and interracial scene, done in terms of childhood, and we observed the gleam in the eyes of colored people as they spotted the little colored child in with the others.

'There hasn't been a Christmas like this one since the first Christmas —the fear, the suffering, the awe, the strange new light that nobody understands yet. All the traditional characteristics of Christmas are this year in reverse: instead of the warm grate and the happy child, in most parts of the world the cold room and the starveling. The soldiers of the triumphant armies return to their homes to find a hearty welcome but an unfamiliar air of uneasiness.' [1]

---

[1] The above passages appeared in *The Wild Flag,* published by Houghton Mifflin Company, originally published in *The New Yorker.* Emery Reves' *The Anatomy of Peace* was published by Harper & Brothers, New York. The quotation from Cord Meyer is from his article, "A Serviceman Looks at the Peace," *Atlantic Monthly,* September, 1945. *One World in the Making,* by Ralph Barton Perry, is copyright, 1945, Ralph Barton Perry and the quotation is used by permission of Current Books, Inc., A. A. Wyn, Publisher, New York.

I like E. B. White's instructions to the American delegates to the
United Nations. Those are truly fine words from a wise man. Put
in a simple way, these instructions reach the heart of the matter and
represent the spirit that must eventually make a democratic United
Nations possible. Of course, the whole trouble with the UN is that
there are no great and simple minds in it, minds like those of Abraham Lincoln and of Albert Einstein.

"Blow your nose frequently and listen to the universal sound."

BY E. B. WHITE

January 12, 1946

Make an original and four copies, Miss Eberhard, one for each delegate. A delegate, on his way to assembly, carries two sets of instructions: one dictated by his own conscience (but not read) and one
handed him by his constituents. Herewith we hand to each delegate
to the first assembly of the United Nations Organization his instructions:

When you sit down, sit down as an American if it makes you feel
comfortable, but when you rise to speak, get up like a man anywhere.

Do not bring home any bacon; it will have turned rancid on the
journey. Bring home instead a silken thread, by which you may find
your way back.

Bear in mind always that foreign policy is domestic policy with its
hat on. The purpose of the meeting, although not so stated anywhere,
is to replace policy with law, and to make common cause.

Make common cause.

Think not to represent us by safeguarding our interests. Represent
us by perceiving that our interests are other people's, and theirs ours.

When you think with longing of the place where you were born,
remember that the sun leaves it daily to go somewhere else. When you
think with love of America, think of the impurity of its bloodlines
and of how no American ever won a prize in a dog show.

Carry good men with you in your portfolio, along with the order
of the day. Read the men with the short first names: Walt Whitman,

John Donne, Manny Kant, Abe Lincoln, Tom Paine, Al Einstein. Read them and weep. Then read them again, without tears.

If you would speak up for us, do not speak up for America, speak up for people, for the free man. We are not dispatching you to build national greatness. Unless you understand this, and believe it, you might better be at the race track, where you can have a good time simply by guessing wrong.

Never forget that the nature of peace is commonly misstated. Peace is not to be had by preventing aggression, for it is always too late for that. Peace is to be had when people's antagonisms and antipathies are subject to the discipline of law and the decency of government.

Do not try to save the world by loving thy neighbor; it will only make him nervous. Save the world by respecting thy neighbor's rights under law and insisting that he respects yours (under the same law). In short, save the world.

Observe that Chapter IV, Article II, Paragraph 3 of the Charter asks the General Assembly to 'call the attention of the Security Council to situations which are likely to endanger international peace and security.' We instruct you, accordingly, to call the Council's attention to the one situation which most consistently endangers peace: absolute national sovereignty. Remind the Council of the frailty, the insubstantiality, of your own Organization, in which members are not people but states.

Do not be confused by the noise of the atomic bomb. The bomb is the pea shooter come home to roost. But when you dream, dream of essential matters, of mass-energy relationships, of man-man relationships. The scientists have outdreamed you, little delegate, so dream well.

Be concerned with principles, not with results. We do not ask for results, merely for a soil-building program. You are not at a chess game, even though it has the appearance of one; you are at a carnival of hope. . . .

As talisman, do not carry a colored flag for the special occasion; carry a white handkerchief for the common cold. Blow your nose frequently and listen to the universal sound.

Finally, now that the Emperor has disclaimed divinity, we charge you to believe in yourself and to love truth. Build the great republic.

The foundation is inescapable. The foundation is unity. It is what your initials suggest: UNO.

—*The Wild Flag* [2]

2. WOODROW WILSON

The logic of war, without the existence of an alternative to it, is inescapable. The only question now is how soon, how ruinous, and who will win? I could not believe that civilization, apart from its material aspects, had progressed when I saw a photograph of Himmler hanging three Poles, or read the report of the subtle, scientific and refined torture of Cardinal Mindszenty to prepare him for his trial. These things are done in our times by our fellow men while we boast of progress. Our hearts cry, and we can only repeat the words of Abraham Lincoln silently like a prayer. "Fondly do we hope—fervently do we pray—that this mighty scourge of war may speedily pass away. Yet, if God wills that it continue until every drop of blood drawn with the lash shall be paid by another drawn with the sword, as was said three thousand years ago, so still it must be said, 'The judgments of the Lord are true and righteous altogether.'" The logic of another war was clear to President Wilson when he said with the last beatings of his heart at St. Louis, September 5, 1919, three weeks before he collapsed at Pueblo on his uncompleted journey:

"And the glory of the Armies and Navies of the United States is gone like a dream in the night, and there ensues upon it, in the suitable darkness of the night, the nightmare of dread which lay upon the nation before this war came; and there will come sometime, in the vengeful Providence of God, another struggle in which, not a few hundred thousand fine men from America will have to die, but as many millions as are necessary to accomplish the final freedom of the peoples of the world."

Reading President Wilson is a curious experience. Things said thirty years ago seem as if they were said not in 1918 but in A.D. 2018, not because Wilson moved too fast ahead, but because we ourselves have moved backward. Wilson's logic was clear; without a rational substitute

[2] Originally published in *The New Yorker*. *The Wild Flag* was published by Houghton Mifflin Company.

for war, only war would remain, and we didn't want that. I am an old Wilsonian. I remember my emotion when I was a young teacher at Peking on reading his conditions of peace in the winter of 1916–17; it was an emotion shared by all the people in remote Asia. We out there saw a light and a world leader. The phrase "peace without victory" has remained always in my mind. There was to be no victory but the "victory of mankind." Only by reading again that speech made on January 22, 1917, before America entered the war, can I recapture those moments when the world believed. I respect America, not because there were many Wilsons, but because there was at least one Wilson who *believed*. In all my life I have been moved only by two political speeches, Lincoln's "Second Inaugural" and this one. But reading it now, the words seem incredible—incredible that the world had advanced that far then, before foul dog realists settled upon our minds and the world's minds. With clear logic and unmistakable meaning Wilson enunciated certain principles that we have totally forgotten, principles whose every antithesis our statesmen are practicing today. "Is the present war a struggle for a just and secure peace, or only for a new balance of power? If it be only a struggle for a new balance of power, who can guarantee the stable equilibrium of the new arrangement? . . . There must be, not a balance of power, but a community of power; not organized rivalries, but an organized common peace." But what does the dog realist of today say? "First of all, it must be a peace without victory." But today we have preferred victory without peace. "The guarantees must neither recognize, nor imply a difference between big nations and small, between those that are powerful and those that are weak." What have our dog realists done about the distinction of big and small? "No right anywhere exists to hand peoples about from sovereignty to sovereignty as if they were property." Have not millions of people been so handled by the big powers? Where is the right of the people in Lithuania, Rumania, Outer Mongolia, and South Manchuria? As for "open covenants openly arrived at," that phrase is forgotten long ago; in fact, the authors of secret treaties are rather pleased with themselves. And so we go on, but it cannot be said that we progress. President Wilson was correct then when he said that in speaking thus he spoke "for the silent mass of mankind everywhere who have as yet no place or opportunity to speak their real hearts out concerning the death and ruin they see to have come already upon the persons and the homes they hold most dear." That seems to be no longer true now, that era of hope and faith has gone. The foul dog sits there, fouling the waters of our belief. Our inner faith trembles, for every time we speak for a new order realistically based on new world conditions, this dog realism raises its forefinger and says, "You are a dreamer!" There was a time when things were different, when an American President was a thinker and not a good and successful politician who thought that he was going to live forever and that peace was only a matter of cordiality between three magnetic personalities. For this reason President Wilson's speech on "The Idea of a League of Nations" must be reread, lest we forget, and if only to show the chasm that has separated us from the man of thirty years ago. A few paragraphs have been omitted for considerations of space.

The Idea of a League of Nations (September 27, 1918)

BY WOODROW WILSON

At every turn of the war we gain a fresh consciousness of what we mean to accomplish by it. When our hope and expectation are most excited we think more definitely than before of the issues that hang upon it and of the purposes which must be realized by means of it. For it has positive and well-defined purposes which we did not determine and which we cannot alter. No statesman or assembly created them; no statesman or assembly can alter them. They have arisen out of the very nature and circumstances of the war. The most that statesmen or assemblies can do is to carry them out or be false to them. They were perhaps not clear at the outset; but they are clear now.

The war has lasted more than four years and the whole world has been drawn into it. The common will of mankind has been substituted for the particular purposes of individual states. Individual statesmen may have started the conflict, but neither they nor their opponents can stop it as they please. It has become a peoples' war, and peoples of all sorts and races, of every degree of power and variety of fortune, are involved in its sweeping processes of change and settlement. We came into it when its character had become fully defined and it was plain that no nation could stand apart or be indifferent to its outcome. Its challenge drove to the heart of everything we cared for and lived for. The voice of the war had become clear and gripped our hearts. Our brothers from many lands, as well as our own murdered dead under the seas, were calling to us, and we responded, fiercely and of course.

The air was clear about us. We saw things in their full, convincing proportions as they were; and we have seen them with steady eyes and unchanging comprehension ever since. We accepted the issues of the war as facts, not as any group of men either here or elsewhere had defined them, and we can accept no outcome which does not squarely meet and settle them. Those issues are these:

Shall the military power of any nation or group of nations be suffered to determine the fortunes of peoples over whom they have no right to rule except the right of force?

Shall strong nations be free to wrong weak nations and make them subject to their purpose and interest?

Shall peoples be ruled and dominated, even in their own internal affairs, by arbitrary and irresponsible force or by their own will and choice?

Shall there be a common standard of right and privilege for all peoples and nations or shall the strong do as they will and the weak suffer without redress?

Shall the assertion of right be haphazard and by casual alliance or shall there be a common concert to oblige the observance of common rights?

No man, no group of men, chose these to be the issues of the struggle. They *are* the issues of it; and they must be settled—by no arrangement or compromise or adjustment of interests, but definitely and once for all and with a full and unequivocal acceptance of the principle that the interest of the weakest is as sacred as the interest of the strongest.

This is what we mean when we speak of a permanent peace, if we speak sincerely, intelligently, and with a real knowledge and comprehension of the matter we deal with. . . .

It is of capital importance that we should also be explicitly agreed that no peace shall be obtained by any kind of compromise or abatement of the principles we have avowed as the principles for which we are fighting. There should exist no doubt about that. I am, therefore, going to take the liberty of speaking with the utmost frankness about the practical implications that are involved in it.

If it be in deed and in truth the common object of the Governments associated against Germany and of the nations whom they govern, as I believe it to be, to achieve by the coming settlements a secure and lasting peace, it will be necessary that all who sit down at the peace table shall come ready and willing to pay the price, the only price, that will procure it; and ready and willing, also, to create in some virile fashion the only instrumentality by which it can be made certain that the agreements of the peace will be honored and fulfilled.

That price is impartial justice in every item of the settlement, no matter whose interest is crossed; and not only impartial justice, but also the satisfaction of the several peoples whose fortunes are dealt with. That indispensable instrumentality is a League of Nations formed under covenants that will be efficacious. Without such an instrumentality, by which the peace of the world can be guaranteed, peace will rest in part upon the word of outlaws and only upon that word. For Germany will have to redeem her character, not by what happens at the peace table, but by what follows.

And, as I see it, the constitution of that League of Nations and the clear definition of its objects must be a part, is in a sense the most essential part, of the peace settlement itself. It cannot be formed now. If formed now, it would be merely a new alliance confined to the nations associated against a common enemy. It is not likely that it could be formed after the settlement. It is necessary to guarantee the peace; and the peace cannot be guaranteed as an afterthought. The reason, to speak in plain terms again, why it must be guaranteed is that there will be parties to the peace whose promises have proved untrustworthy, and means must be found in connection with the peace settlement itself to remove that source of insecurity. It would be folly to leave the guarantee to the subsequent voluntary action of the Governments we have seen destroy Russia and deceive Rumania.

But these general terms do not disclose the whole matter. Some details are needed to make them sound less like a thesis and more like a practical program. These, then, are some of the particulars, and I state them with the greater confidence because I can state them authoritatively as representing this Government's interpretation of its own duty with regard to peace:

First, the impartial justice meted out must involve no discrimination between those to whom we wish to be just and those to whom we do not wish to be just. It must be a justice that plays no favorites and knows no standard but the equal rights of the several peoples concerned;

Second, no special or separate interest of any single nation or any group of nations can be made the basis of any part of the settlement which is not consistent with the common interest of all;

Third, there can be no leagues or alliances or special covenants and understandings within the general and common family of the League of Nations;

Fourth, and more specifically, there can be no special, selfish economic combinations within the League and no employment of any form of economic boycott or exclusion except as the power of economic penalty by exclusion from the markets of the world may be vested in the League of Nations itself as a means of discipline and control;

Fifth, all international agreements and treaties of every kind must be made known in their entirety to the rest of the world.

Special alliances and economic rivalries and hostilities have been the prolific source in the modern world of the plans and passions that produce war. It would be an insincere as well as insecure peace that did not exclude them in definite and binding terms. . . .

And the forces that fight for them draw into closer and closer array, organize their millions into more and more unconquerable might, as they become more and more distinct to the thought and purpose of the peoples engaged. It is the peculiarity of this great war that while statesmen have seemed to cast about for definitions of their purpose and have sometimes seemed to shift their ground and their point of view, the thought of the mass of men, whom statesmen are supposed to instruct and lead, has grown more and more unclouded, more and more certain of what it is that they are fighting for. National purposes have fallen more and more into the background and the common purpose of enlightened mankind has taken their place. The counsels of plain men have become on all hands more simple and straightforward and more unified than the counsels of sophisticated men of affairs, who still retain the impression that they are playing a game of power and playing for high stakes. That is why I have said that this is a peoples' war, not a statesmen's. Statesmen must follow the clarified common thought or be broken.

I take that to be the significance of the fact that assemblies and associations of many kinds made up of plain workaday people have demanded, almost every time they came together, and are still demanding, that the leaders of their Governments declare to them plainly what it is, exactly what it is, that they were seeking in this war, and what they think the items of the final settlement should be. They are not yet satisfied with what they have been told. They still seem to fear that they are getting what they ask for only in statesmen's terms—only in the terms of territorial arrangements and divisions of power, and not in terms of broad-visioned justice and mercy and peace and the satisfaction of those deep-seated longings of oppressed and distracted men and women and enslaved peoples that seem to them the only things worth fighting a war for that engulfs the world. Perhaps statesmen have not always recognized this changed aspect of the whole world of policy and action. Perhaps they have not always spoken in direct reply to the questions asked because they did not know how searching those questions were and what sort of answers they demanded.

But I, for one, am glad to attempt the answer again and again, in the hope that I may make it clearer and clearer that my one thought is to satisfy those who struggle in the ranks and are, perhaps above all others, entitled to a reply whose meaning no one can have any excuse for misunderstanding, if he understands the language in which it is spoken or can get someone to translate it correctly into his own. . . . Germany is constantly intimating the "terms" she will accept; and always finds that the world does not want terms. It wishes the final triumph of justice and fair dealing.

—Address at the Metropolitan Opera
House, New York, September 27, 1918

I do think that there will certainly come a time when the spirit and the letter of these words will sound clear and convincing again, when mankind will pick up again where Woodrow Wilson left off. I do not think such clear thinking and prophetic words can be forgotten.

3. WAR AND PEACE

George Santayana was quite prophetic also, but from a different point of view. His "Tipperary," written in 1918, is one of the saddest and most beautiful things ever written by this author. He has perhaps too deep knowledge of mankind's folly to believe that men will ever be ready for peace and has rather counseled acceptance of struggle with a philosophical, even a cheerful, spirit. There is a certain animal faith about it; if the reading of it is small comfort, yet one gets a strange feeling of being at peace when his philosophy has won an insight into the "eternity of everything."

*"Be sad if you will ... but be brave....
Your heart and mine may remain there, but it's a long, long
way that the world has to go."*

BY GEORGE SANTAYANA

The bells that announced the Armistice brought me no news; a week sooner or a week later they had to ring. Certainly if the purpose of the war had been conquest or victory, nobody had achieved it; but the purposes of things, and especially of wars, are imputed to them rhetorically, the impulses at work being too complicated and change-ful to be easily surveyed; and in this case, for the French and the English, the moving impulse had been defense; they had been sus-tained through incredible trials by the awful necessity of not yielding. That strain had now been relaxed; and as the conduct of men is deter-mined by present forces and not by future advantages, they could have no heart to fight on. It seemed enough to them that the wanton blow had been parried, that the bully had begged for mercy. It was amusing to hear him now. He said that further bloodshed this time would be horrible; his tender soul longed to get home safely, to call it quits, and to take a long breath and plan a new combination before the next bout. His collapse had been evident for days and months; yet these bells that confirmed the fact were pleasant to hear. Those mean little flags, hung out here and there by private initiative in the streets of Oxford, had almost put on a look of triumph; the very sunlight and brisk autumnal air seemed to have heard the tidings, and to invite the world to begin to live again at ease. Certainly many a sad figure and many a broken soul must slink henceforth on crutches, a mere survival; but they, too, will die off gradually. The grass soon grows over a grave.

So musing, I suddenly heard a once familiar strain, now long despised and out of favor, the old tune of *Tipperary*. In a coffee-house frequented at that hour some wounded officers from the hospital at Somerville were singing it, standing near the bar; they were breaking all rules, both of surgeons and of epicures, and were having champagne in the morning. And good reason they had for it. They were reprieved, they should never have to go back to the front, their friends—such as were left—would all come home alive. Instinctively the old grumbling, good-natured, sentimental song, which they used to sing when they first joined, came again into their minds. It had been indeed a long, long way to Tipperary. But they had trudged on and had come round full circle; they were in Tipperary at last.

I wonder what they think *Tipperary* means—for this is a mystical song. Probably they are willing to leave it vague, as they do their notions of honor or happiness or heaven. Their soldiering is over; they remember, with a strange proud grief, their comrades who died to make this day possible, hardly believing that it ever would come; they are overjoyed, yet half ashamed, to be safe themselves; they forget their wounds; they see a green vista before them, a jolly, busy, sporting, loving life in the old familiar places. Everything will go on, they fancy, as if nothing had happened.

Good honest unguided creatures!—They are hardly out of the fog of war when they are lost in the fog of peace. . . . They think that the war—perhaps the last of all wars—is over!

Only the dead are safe; only the dead have seen the end of war. . . . Free life has the spirit of comedy. It rejoices in the seasonable beauty of each new thing, and laughs at its decay, covets no possessions, demands no agreement, and strives to sustain nothing in being except a gallant spirit of courage and truth, as each fresh adventure may renew it.

This gallant spirit of courage and truth, you young men had it in those early days when you first sang *Tipperary;* have you it still, I wonder, when you repeat the song? Some of you, no doubt. I have seen in some of you the smile that makes light of pain, the sturdy humility that accepts mutilation and faces disability without repining or shame; armless and legless men are still God's creatures, and even if you cannot see the sun you can bask in it, and there is joy on earth— perhaps the deepest and most primitive joy—even in that. But others of you, though you were driven to the war by contagious example, or by force, are natural cowards; you are perhaps superior persons, intellectual snobs, and are indignant at having been interrupted in your important studies and made to do useless work. You are disgusted at the stupidity of all the generals, and whatever the Government does is an outrage to your moral sense. You were made sick at the thought of the war before you went to it, and you are sicker of it now. You are pacifists, and you suspect that the Germans, who were not pacifists, were right after all. I notice you are not singing *Tipperary* this morning; you are too angry to be glad, and you wish it to be understood that you can't endure such a vulgar air. You are willing, however, to sip your champagne with the rest; in hospital you seem to have come forward a little socially; but you find the wine too dry or too sweet, and you are making a wry face at it.

Ah, my delicate friends, if the soul of a philosopher may venture to address you, let me whisper this counsel in your ears: Reserve a part of your wrath; you have not seen the worst yet. You suppose that this war has been a criminal blunder and an exceptional horror; you imagine that before long reason will prevail, and all these inferior people that govern the world will be swept aside, and your own party will reform everything and remain always in office. You are mistaken. This war has given you your first glimpse of the ancient, fundamental, normal state of the world, your first taste of reality. It should teach you to dismiss all your philosophies of progress or of a governing reason as the babble of dreamers who walk through one world mentally beholding another. . . . War is but resisted change; and change must needs be resisted so long as the organism it would destroy retains any vitality. Peace itself means discipline at home and invulnerability abroad—two forms of permanent virtual war; peace requires so vigorous an internal regimen that every germ of dissolution or infection shall be repelled before it reaches the public soul. This war has been a short one, and its ravages slight in comparison with what remains standing: a severe war is one in which the entire manhood of a nation is destroyed, its cities razed, and its women and children driven into slavery. In this instance the slaughter has been greater, perhaps, only because modern populations are so enormous; the disturbance has been acute only because the modern industrial system is so dangerously complex and unstable; and the expense seems prodigious because we were so extravagantly rich. Our society was a sleepy glutton who thought himself immortal and squealed inexpressibly, like a stuck pig, at the first prick of the sword. An ancient city would have thought this war, or one relatively as costly, only a normal incident; and certainly the Germans will not regard it otherwise. . . .

Certainly war is hell, as you, my fair friends, are fond of repeating; but so is rebellion against war. To live well you must be victorious. It is with war as with the passion of love, which is a war of another kind: war at first against the beloved for favor and possession; war afterward against the rest of the world for the beloved's sake. Often love, too, is a torment and shameful; but it has its laughing triumphs, and the attempt to eliminate it is a worse torture, and more degrading. When was a coward at peace? . . .

Be sad if you will, there is always reason for sadness, since the good which the world brings forth is so fugitive and bought at so great a price; but be brave. If you think happiness worth enjoying, think it worth defending. Nothing you can lose by dying is half so precious as the readiness to die, which is man's charter of nobility; life would not be worth having without the freedom of soul and the friendship with nature which that readiness brings. The things we know and love on earth are, and should be, transitory; they are, as were the things celebrated by Homer, at best the song or oracle by which heaven is revealed in our time. We must pass with them into eternity, not in the end only but continually, as a phrase passes into its meaning; and since they are part of us and we of them, we should accompany them with a good grace: it would be desolation to survive. The eternal is always present, as the flux of time in one sense never is, since it is all either past or future; but this elusive existence in passing sets before the spirit essences in which spirit rests, and which can never vary; as a dramatic poet creates a character which many an actor afterward on many a night may try to enact. Of course the flux of matter carries the poets away too; they become old-fashioned, and nobody wishes any longer to play their characters; but each age has its own gods. Time is like an enterprising manager always bent on staging some new and surprising production, without knowing very well what it will be. Our good mother Psyche, who is a convolution of this material flux, breeds us accordingly to mindlessness and anxiety, out of which it is hard for our youthful intellect to wean itself to peace, by escaping into the essential eternity of everything it sees and loves. So long as the world goes round we shall see Tipperary only, as it were, out of the window of our troop-train. Your heart and mine may remain there, but it's a long, long way that the world has to go.

—"Tipperary," *Soliloquies in England*

Chapter XVI

THE SUMMING UP

I. TO EVERY MAN HIS OWN PHILOSOPHY

THE grand tour of America is completed. I am glad that I have taken it. Of course, every tourist misses some important points which every one said he must see, but the schedule did not fit. Once on arriving at Sorrento I missed the boat for Capri. All one could do was to throw up one's hands and say, "Oh, well, one can't see everything," and be satisfied. Every writer trying to survey a field must be conscious of a guilty feeling, not about what he has included, but about what he has left out. I have limited my field to American writing relevant to the wisdom of living, to the proper appreciations of the gifts of life which we have, without yearning after the perfectionist heaven which we have not. I have also excluded fiction. But the limitation is also personal. There is such a thing as personal affinity of authors; the mind is attracted toward certain authors and shuts itself up against others. I have no room for the professional pessimists, misanthropes, misogynists, "realists," and all those people who wish they had not been born upon this earth, but somewhere else.

On the other hand, I have tried to see how some American writers have looked at life at the common level and at the problems of living and the arts of living, for the individual—in other words, how they like having been born into this world.

Almost seven generations have passed since the founding of the American Republic. Great ones have walked upon the earth, looked at life, lived their allotted span and gone. Each generation was occupied with its particular problems, perhaps the political issues of the times, but in the stuff that makes up life, in their more personal lives, they faced the same *human* problems as ourselves. Maybe they were not wiser than we, but we are not wiser than they, either. Who knows more about life today than Franklin and Jefferson knew of yore?

445

The cavalcade passes. Franklin, Jefferson, Adams, Emerson, Hawthorne, Lincoln marched past in succession. They all made their guesses at life and went away. And the human problems are still with us.

It has been a pleasure for me to read Jefferson's letter to his child, to see Franklin playing chess with Madame Brillon, to listen to the awesome loquaciousness of Oliver Wendell Holmes at the breakfast table, to observe Emerson going off at night with Margaret Fuller, watching the moon over the water "interrogating, interrogating," to overhear Lincoln's remark to a boy when dressed for the wedding, to read the private letters and journals of so many distinguished Americans. Each of us falls in love, too, gets married, perhaps has a growing child, looks at the moon—and it is still the same moon. What you make of all these tremendous trifles is the burden of the wisdom of living.

It is extraordinary what one can do with some of these things. Thoreau once thought the moon was larger over the United States than over the Old World, the sky bluer, the stars brighter, the thunder louder, the rivers longer, the mountains higher, the prairies vaster, and he mystically concluded that the spirit of man in America should be larger and more expansive—"else why was America discovered?" Thoreau was wrong, and Thoreau was right. There is no value in life except what you choose to place upon it, and no happiness in any place except what you bring to it yourself.

Why argue? Never, never shall we come nearer to the truths of life than did man two thousand years ago. There is nothing new under the sun and too much study is a weariness of the flesh. The wisest of philosophers have knocked at the door of the universe in vain. The history of philosophy is a rehash of old truths. We nod and wake up and nod again. Homer sometimes nods, Plato nods, Lucian nods, Schopenhauer nods. We all nod. And we all romanticize life and history according to our favorite individual points of view. No one is objective; he who thinks he is only deceives himself. A philosophy is merely a bias, a chosen or preferred vantage point from which to look at life. The history of philosophy is a story of the shifting of biases, like a housewife who sweeps the dust of the sitting room into the dining room and sweeps it again from the dining room into the sitting room, depending on where she wants to live. We rehash Plato or Plotinus or St. Thomas Aquinas while the universe goes about its way with the silence and imperturbability of a God. Meanwhile we make blind jabs at the dark with our feeble fingers. We adore the soul with Plato in the morning, get enthusiastic about matter with Haeckel at lunch, and agree with Montaigne when we turn off the light in bed and say, "What do we know?"

What sadness! And yet that sadness, that refusal to yield to illusion, is the beginning of a wise philosophy of living. Wisdom begins with the elimination of uncertainties. Uncertainty is bad because it makes a man nervous. If one is stranded on an island and knows for certain that no boat will pass for a whole year, one has at least the comfort of certainty. One composes oneself and directs one's energies to making the island a comfortable place to live in. Human life is such an island. Knowing what we cannot do, we can do what we can, and arrange ourselves accordingly. Brushing aside all idle, uncertain speculations, we know that we live. We know this life; this I affirm, because I know how it affects my happiness. We know only as we live, and we shall know life as we make it. Within the limits of mortal existence, we can work, we can exercise our powers, we can arrange ourselves to labor happily, rest quietly and live peaceably. What more should one ask? One need not argue whether God created the stars for man to look at. We shall never know. But if it is good to look at the stars, look at them.

This attitude of acceptance of life and all its sensory beauties and limitations—the poetic "naturalism" of Santayana—can be a great source of peace and inner content, for in belief in the earth there is tremendous strength. So we shall live without illusion and yet without disillusion, and while planting our feet firmly on the ground and trying to keep the furrow straight, we shall not forget, as David Grayson advises us, to pause now and then and look up at the sky.

The "acceptance of finitude" (the phrase is Santayana's), coupled with a lurking idler's suspicion that God created man to play as well as to work, that man is spirit also and this spirit is free—these two things, common sense and wistfulness about living, are, as I said at the beginning, the ingredients of human wisdom.

What, then, is the human ideal? Can there be a universal human ideal? The answer is probably no. Every man must find his own philosophy. Every man has, in fact, his own philosophy, his attitude toward life. At least, every taxicab driver I know is a philosopher. I have found the most loving taxicab drivers in New York, and I have found hard-boiled, cynical Schopenhauers among them. Atheists, communists, Platonists, Jeffersonian democrats, and just plain observers who enjoy looking at life and think everybody in this world is crazy —they are all there. Each one has found life as he makes it. If the taxicab driver chucks his job and buries himself in the public library for ten or twenty years and comes out with a *magnum opus* in philosophy, the article is still the same. The only difference is that what was a philosophic feeling before has become a philosophic concept. It is possible that if he is born again into another life, with another type of temperament, he will write another book of philosophy to contradict his own.

2. JUSTICE HOLMES'S CREDO

Many great Americans have found their own ideals of life, and some have summed them up in less than a thousand words. These summings-up interest us because they are beliefs which are based on life-long experience, and which have actuated the lives of these great men. Perhaps I am more interested in the type of personality which American thought and culture have produced than in American thought itself. The thought is to me a means to an end, the man. It does one's heart good to see broadly cultured types of humanity as actually living persons in one's generation, more than to read about this or that type as a theoretic ideal. There are always in every generation such persons who embody or typify the best of culture of that nation. So strange is life that people living in the same age and in the same town may be actuated by totally different motives, so that they seem to belong to different worlds. Some are devoted to pleasures, some to secret ambitions of their own, some never rise above the slime of existence and some become Bowery saints. Some are wonderful, great personalities, an honor to a living culture. We sometimes have doubts about the contemporary culture, but then one remembers that that culture has also produced great men, Justice Holmes, Thomas Edison, Luther Burbank, for example, in our generation. They are subject to the same environment as ourselves, but it is what they make of themselves that counts.

What I like about Justice Holmes is that he was really wise, that his soul was under discipline but not without those flashes of quaking joys at the gift of life, that the divine fire in him did not go out or go wild, but was nourished and tended for the service of his fellow men, so that it shone both with warmth and light. I respect him as I respect Jefferson for his discipline, his industry and his indefatigable scholarship. Somehow, I say to myself, that is the kind of ideal a man should have, not a gushing ecstatic genius like Thomas Wolfe or Edgar Allan Poe, nor the humdrum, unimaginative run of common men! Let that genius be yoked with hard work and a sense of responsibility, and yet under the gray surface of daily events, the divine fire is never quenched, but is banked and emits a long, lasting radiance.

Reading Justice Holmes's summing up of his life beliefs, one finds perhaps nothing very exciting or sensational. Human wisdom always has a familiar ring about it, because what is very true always finds a familiar echo in our hearts. That is what Chinese scholars have always admired in Confucius. I do not think Confucius was ever characterized by surface brilliance. He never said he was. He denied being a "sage" and described himself merely as one who "had never stopped learning and never tired of teaching others." Holmes's wisdom has the same familiar quality of plain and solid sustenance.

"Life is action, the use of one's powers."

BY JUSTICE OLIVER WENDELL HOLMES

We cannot live our dreams. We are lucky enough if we can give a sample of our best, and if in our hearts we can feel that it has been nobly done.

Some changes come about in the process, changes not necessarily so much in the nature as in the emphasis of our interest. I do not mean in our wish to make a living and to succeed—of course, we all want those things—but I mean in our ulterior intellectual or spiritual interest, in the ideal part, without which we are but snails or tigers.

Reprinted from *Speeches*, by Oliver Wendell Holmes, by permission of Little, Brown & Company.

One begins with a search for a general point of view. After a time he finds one, and then for a while he is absorbed in testing it, in trying to satisfy himself whether it is true. But after many experiments or investigations all have come out one way, and his theory is confirmed and settled in his mind, he knows in advance that the next case will be but another verification, and the stimulus of anxious curiosity is gone. He realizes that his branch of knowledge only presents more illustrations of the universal principle; he sees it all as another case of the same old *ennui,* or the same sublime mystery—for it does not matter what epithets you apply to the whole of things, they are merely judgments of yourself. At this stage the pleasure is no less, perhaps, but it is the pure pleasure of doing the work, irrespective of further aims, and when you reach that stage you reach, as it seems to me, the triune formula of the joy, the duty, and the end of life.

It was of this that Malebranche was thinking when he said that, if God held in one hand truth, and in the other the pursuit of truth, he would say: "Lord, the truth is for thee alone; give me the pursuit." The joy of life is to put out one's power in some natural and useful or harmless way. There is no other. And the real misery is not to do this. The hell of the old world's literature is to be taxed beyond one's powers. This country has expressed in story—I suppose because it has experienced it in life—a deeper abyss, of intellectual asphyxia or vital *ennui,* when powers conscious of themselves are denied their chance.

The rule of joy and the law of duty seem to me all one. I confess that altruistic and cynically selfish talk seem to me about equally unreal. With all humility, I think "Whatsoever thy hand findeth to do, do it with thy might" infinitely more important than the vain attempt to love one's neighbor as one's self. If you want to hit a bird on the wing, you must have all your will in a focus, you must not be thinking about yourself, and, equally, you must not be thinking about your neighbor; you must be living in your eye on that bird. Every achievement is a bird on the wing.

The joy, the duty, and, I venture to add, the end of life. I speak only of this world, of course, and of the teachings of this world. I do not seek to trench upon the province of spiritual guides. But from the point of view of the world the end of life is life. Life is action, the use of one's powers. As to use them to their height is our joy and duty, so it is the one end that justifies itself. Until lately the best thing that I was able to think of in favor of civilization, apart from blind acceptance of the order of the universe, was that it made possible the artist, the poet, the philosopher, and the man of science. But I think that is not the greatest thing. Now I believe that the greatest thing is a matter that comes directly home to us all. When it is said that we are too much occupied with the means of living to live, I answer that the chief worth of civilization is just that it makes the means of living more complex; that it calls for great and combined intellectual efforts, instead of simple, uncoördinated ones, in order that the crowd may be fed and clothed and housed and moved from place to place. Because more complex and intense intellectual efforts mean a fuller and richer life. They mean more life. Life is an end in itself, and the only question as to whether it is worth living is whether you have enough of it.

I will add but a word. We all are very near despair. The sheathing that floats us over its waves is compounded of hope, faith in the unexplainable worth and sure issue of effort, and the deep, sub-conscious content which comes from the exercise of our powers. In the words of a touching negro song—

> Sometimes I's up, sometimes I's down,
> Sometimes I's almost to the groun';

but these thoughts have carried me, as I hope they will carry the young men who hear me, through long years of doubt, self-distrust, and solitude. They do now, for, although it might seem that the day of trial was over, in fact it is renewed each day. The kindness which you have shown me makes me bold in happy moments to believe that the long and passionate struggle has not been quite in vain.

—Speech at the Boston Bar Association, March 7, 1900

There, a great and wise American has spoken.

3. EINSTEIN'S INTIMATE CREDO

In 1930 Albert Einstein, asked to sum up his beliefs in the form of an "intimate credo," wrote a short piece that has remained in my mind as one of the best summings up I have read. In 1939, when he was asked to confirm, restate, or modify it, his new statement reflected a sharp change, as if in the interval of a trying decade a whole world of beliefs had collapsed and the things he had written ten years before had seemed "curiously remote and changed." "In these ten years," he wrote, "confidence in the stability, yes, even the very basis for existence of human society has largely vanished. One senses not only a threat to man's cultural heritage, but also that a lower value is placed upon all that one would like to see defended at all costs." It was not only the collapse of the League of Nations, or Hitlerism and all that it stood for, or World War II. It was not just dangers that have always beset human society and human life. It was a reversal of values and a collapse of values. I should call it the confusion in the minds of men. "Awareness of this state of affairs overshadows every hour of my present existence, while ten years ago it did not yet occupy my thoughts." So it was with a curious feeling that he reread his own words, which seemed to him both remote and yet "essentially as true as ever." [1] The sense of insecurity still hangs over us today, but I think these words are still true and beautifully expressed. This is a personal philosophy, and we are grateful for the brief and concise expression of his belief by one of the greatest men living with us. The statement of the things he does not care for seems to me even more interesting than that of the things he believes in.

A Personal Credo—"A simple and unassuming manner is best for everyone."

BY ALBERT EINSTEIN

Strange is our situation here upon earth. Each of us comes for a short visit, not knowing why, yet sometimes seeming to divine a purpose.

From the standpoint of daily life, however, there is one thing we do know: that man is here for the sake of other men—above all for those upon whose smile and well-being our own happiness depends, and also for the countless unknown souls with whose fate we are con-

From *Living Philosophies.* Copyright, 1930, Forum Publishing Company. Copyright, 1931, Simon and Schuster. Reprinted by permission.

[1] The quotations are from *I Believe.* Simon and Schuster.

nected by a bond of sympathy. Many times a day I realize how much my own outer and inner life is built upon the labors of my fellow-men, both living and dead, and how earnestly I must exert myself in order to give in return as much as I have received. My peace of mind is often troubled by the depressing sense that I have borrowed too heavily from the work of other men.

I do not believe we can have any freedom at all in the philosophical sense, for we act not only under external compulsion but also by inner necessity. Schopenhauer's saying—"A man can surely do what he wills to do, but he cannot determine what he wills"—impressed itself upon me in youth and has always consoled me when I have witnessed or suffered life's hardships. This conviction is a perpetual breeder of tolerance, for it does not allow us to take ourselves or others too seriously; it makes rather for a sense of humor.

To ponder interminably over the reason for one's own existence or the meaning of life in general seems to me, from an objective point of view, to be sheer folly. And yet everyone holds certain ideals by which he guides his aspiration and his judgment. The ideals which have always shone before me and filled me with the joy of living are goodness, beauty, and truth. To make a goal of comfort or happiness has never appealed to me; a system of ethics built on this basis would be sufficient only for a herd of cattle.

Without the sense of collaborating with like-minded beings in the pursuit of the ever unattainable in art and scientific research, my life would have been empty. Ever since childhood I have scorned the commonplace limits so often set upon human ambition. Possessions, outward success, publicity, luxury—to me these have always been contemptible. I believe that a simple and unassuming manner of life is best for everyone, best both for the body and the mind.

My passionate interest in social justice and social responsibility has always stood in curious contrast to a marked lack of desire for direct association with men and women. I am a horse for single harness, not cut out for tandem or team work. I have never belonged wholeheartedly to country or state, to my circle of friends, or even to my own family. These ties have always been accompanied by a vague aloofness, and the wish to withdraw into myself increases with the years.

Such isolation is sometimes bitter, but I do not regret being cut off from the understanding and sympathy of other men. I lose something by it, to be sure, but I am compensated for it in being rendered independent of the customs, opinions, and prejudices of others, and am not tempted to rest my peace of mind upon such shifting foundations.

My political ideal is democracy. Everyone should be respected as an individual, but no one idolized. It is an irony of fate that I should have been showered with so much uncalled-for and unmerited admiration and esteem. Perhaps this adulation springs from the unfulfilled wish of the multitude to comprehend the few ideas which I, with my weak powers, have advanced.

Full well do I know that in order to attain any definite goal it is imperative that *one* person should do the thinking and commanding and carry most of the responsibility. But those who are led should not be driven, and they should be allowed to choose their leader. It seems to me that the distinctions separating the social classes are false; in the last analysis they rest on force. I am convinced that degeneracy follows every autocratic system of violence, for violence inevitably attracts moral inferiors. Time has proved that illustrious tyrants are succeeded by scoundrels.

For this reason I have always been passionately opposed to such regimes as exist in Russia and Italy today. The thing which has discredited the European forms of democracy is not the basic theory of democracy itself, which some say is at fault, but the instability of our political leadership, as well as the impersonal character of party alignments.

I believe that those in the United States have hit upon the right idea. A President is chosen for a reasonable length of time and enough power is given him to acquit himself properly of his responsibilities. In the German government, on the other hand, I like the state's more extensive care of the individual when he is ill or unemployed. What is truly valuable in our bustle of life is not the nation, I should say, but the creative and impressionable individuality, the personality—he who produces the noble and sublime while the common herd remains dull in thought and insensible in feeling.

This subject brings me to that vilest offspring of the herd mind— the odious militia. The man who enjoys marching in line and file to the strains of music falls below my contempt; he received his great brain by mistake—the spinal cord would have been amply sufficient. This heroism at command, this senseless violence, this accursed bombast of patriotism—how intensely I despise them! War is low and despicable, and I had rather be smitten to shreds than participate in such doings.

Such a stain on humanity should be erased without delay. I think well enough of human nature to believe that it would have been wiped out long ago had not the common sense of nations been systematically corrupted through school and press for business and political reasons.

—*Living Philosophies*

Albert Einstein has repeatedly stated his belief in the organization of the world for peace by some kind of world government; specifically he has supported the World Federalist movement. Anyone who feels inclined to criticize the World Federalists as visionaries or bad thinkers should at least feel a compulsion to revise his own thinking. Einstein gave us the formula that predicted the tremendous atomic power realized some forty years after his formula was completed. Visionary it was forty years ago, but bad thinking it was decidedly not. I have the strongest hope that the new type of world organization that his piercing mind sees so clearly as a new vision may be realized before another forty years have passed, when it might be too late. His second vision may save the world, which his first vision, in the hands of bat-eyed politicians, could be exploited to destroy.

4. A TOAST TO MODERATION

I have said that I am interested in the human ideal, not as talked about, but as lived by a real person. I believe that there are such men who in their respective, perhaps even undistinguished, walks of life have found a stable equilibrium, a satisfactory and comfortable philosophy of living.

I do not know which American gentleman David Grayson was referring to in the following—could it be President Wilson? But he is, or was, a real American, and I believe there are many Americans like this one, not by any means famous, who in their personal lives have achieved a sense of proportion, a sense of poise, and an inner harmony with the order of things. It is these unknown Americans who are the mainstay of the American democracy.

"A fine, up-standing hearty old gentleman"
BY DAVID GRAYSON

And this reminds me inevitably of a mellow-spirited old friend who lives not a thousand miles from here—I must not tell his name—whose greatest word is "proportion." At this moment, as I write, I can hear the roll of his resonant old voice on the syllable p-o-r—prop-o-rtion. He is the kind of man good to know and to trust.

If ever I bring him a hard problem, as, indeed, I delight to do, it is a fine thing to see him square himself to meet it. A light comes in his eye, he draws back his chin a little and exclaims occasionally: "Well—well!"

He will have all the facts and circumstances fully mobilized, standing up side by side before him like an awkward squad, and there's nothing more awkward than some facts that have to stand out squarely in daylight! And he inquires into their ancestry, makes them run out their tongues, and pokes them once or twice in the ribs, to make sure that they are lively and robust facts capable of making a good fight for their lives. He never likes to see any one thing too large, as a church, a party, a reform, a new book, or a new fashion, lest he see something else too small; but will have everything, as he says, in true proportion. If he occasionally favors a little that which is old, solid, well-placed, it is scarcely to be measured to him as a fault in an age so overwhelmed with the shiny new.

He is a fine, up-standing, hearty old gentleman with white hair and rosy cheeks, and the bright eyes of one who has lived all his life with temperance. One incident I cannot resist telling, though it has nothing directly to do with this story, but it will let you know what kind of a man my old friend is, and when all is said, it would be a fine thing to know about any man. Not long ago he was afflicted with a serious loss, a loss that would have crushed some men, but when I met him not long afterward, though the lines around his eyes were

grown deeper, he greeted me in his old serene, courtly manner. When
I would have comforted him with my sympathy, for I felt myself near
enough to speak of his loss, he replied calmly:

"How can we know whether a thing is evil until we reach the end
of it? It may be good!"

One of the events I esteem among the finest of the whole year is
my old friend's birthday party. Every winter, on the twenty-sixth of
February, a party of his friends drop in to see him. Some of us go out
of habit, drawn by our affection for the old gentleman; others, I think,
he invites, for he knows to perfection the delicate shadings of companionship which divide those who come unbidden from those, not less
loved but shyer, who must be summoned.

Now this birthday gathering has one historic ceremony which none
of us would miss, because it expresses so completely the essence of our
friend's generous and tolerant, but just, nature. He is, as I have said,
a temperate man, and dislikes as much as any one I know the whole
alcohol business; but living in a community where the struggle for
temperance has often been waged intemperately, and where there is a
lurking belief that cudgeling laws can make men virtuous, he publishes
abroad once a year his declaration of independence.

After we have been with our friend for an hour or so, and are
well warmed and happy with the occasion, he rises solemnly and goes
to the toby-closet at the end of his generous fireplace, where the apple-
log specially cut for the occasion is burning merrily, and as we all fall
silent, knowing well what is coming, he unlocks the door and takes
from the shelf a bottle of old peach brandy which, having uncorked,
he gravely smells of and possibly lets his nearest neighbor smell of too.
Then he brings from the sideboard a server set with diminutive glasses
that have been polished until they shine for the great occasion, and,
having filled them all with the ripe liquor, he passes them around to
each of us. We have all risen and are becomingly solemn as he now
proposes the toast of the year—and it is always the same toast:

"Here's to moderation—in all things!"

He takes a sip or two, and continues:

"Here's to temperance—the queen of the virtues."

So we all drink off our glasses. Our mellow old friend smacks his lips, corks the tall bottle, and returns it to his toby-closet, where it reposes undisturbed for another year.

"And now, gentlemen," he says, heartily, "let us go in to dinner.". . .

—Great Possessions

THE END

INDEX